# California Water

Arthur L. Littleworth
and Eric L. Garner

Solano Press Books
Point Arena, California

# California Water

**Solano Press Books**
Post Office Box 773
Point Arena, California 95468
Phone (707) 884-4508
Fax (707) 884-4109


Cover design by Judy Hicks, Oakland, California
Cover photograph of the San Pablo Dam Reservoir
    copyright Armand Wright, 1990; courtesy of the East
    Bay Municipal Utilities District, Oakland, California
Book design by Canterbury Press, Berkeley, California
Index by Paul Kish, Mendocino, California
Printed by West Coast Print Center, Berkeley, California

ISBN 0-923956-25-5


Trees are one of nature's renewable resources.
To preserve this invaluable resource for future
generations, Solano Press Books makes annual
contributions to the *American Forests Global
ReLeaf Program. American Forests* is the nation's
oldest nonprofit citizens' conservation organization.

✪ Printed on partially recycled paper

NOTICE
This book is designed to assist you in understanding
California water regulations. It is necessarily general
in nature and does not discuss all exceptions and
variations to general rules. Also, it may not reflect
the latest changes in the law. It is not intended as
legal advice and should not be relied on to address
legal problems. You should always consult an attorney
for advice regarding your specific factual situation.

This book is dedicated
to the memory of

JAMES H. KRIEGER
(1913-1975)

An innovative and charismatic leader in western water rights
and water resources, as well as an able and respected lawyer,
Jim Krieger founded and led our firm's water practice for
a generation. We still feel his tragic loss in a mid-air plane
collision some twenty years ago.

*I think that, as life is action and passion, it is required of a
man that he should share the passion and action of his time
at peril of being judged not to have lived.*

Oliver Wendell Holmes, Jr.
1884 Memorial Day Address

# Preface

The idea for this book emerged gradually over thirty-five years of practice in the charged arena of water politics, water litigation and water development. Countless times I have been asked if there were not something on water that people could read to give them a general background. Sometimes the inquiries have come from legislators, newly thrust into the sectional battles over water. Sometimes from a local water district manager, board member, or city official. Sometimes from an engineer or planner, or a lawyer whose practice has never before touched the field of water. Sometimes from a developer who was just beginning to appreciate its water problems. Occasionally even judges have asked for help.

Unfortunately the answer always had to be the same—that no handy, comprehensive book was available. Wells Hutchins' "bible" that we all used at one time has long been out of date.[1] A two-volume textbook exists, but that is not usually what people have in mind; nor is it current.[2] Even less appealing and accessible are the chapters on California water law included in still larger multi-volume national or state sets.

Of course, there is no shortage of excellent current material on water issues in law reviews and other periodicals and services. But these writings generally focus on narrow subjects, and often are crafted for use principally by lawyers. More general and basic questions about water still receive little comprehensive attention. Where does our water come from? How much water does California have? Are we

[1] *The California Law of Water Rights* by Wells A. Hutchins, published in 1956.
[2] *Water for California,* Rogers & Nichols, published in 1967.

really a water-short State? How is our water used? How much do we need? What is the future role of the great aqueduct systems that have sustained California by moving water from the mountain snowpacks and rivers to major urban and agricultural areas: San Francisco's Hetch-Hetchy Project that takes water from the Tuolumne River near Yosemite; Los Angeles' Owens Valley system; the Mokelumne River aqueduct of the East Bay Municipal Utility District; the Colorado River aqueduct of The Metropolitan Water District of Southern California; the Federal Government's enormous Central Valley Project, supplying water primarily for agriculture; and finally, the State Water Project that stores Feather River water in Oroville Reservoir, releases it into the Sacramento River, and then diverts it from the San Francisco Bay-Delta to supply some 21,000,000 Californians.

Anyone writing about water today must also consider the dramatic changes in law that have occurred in the last decade or more. Venerable court decisions that historically defined the rules governing riparian, appropriative and overlying water rights are now less relevant to California water issues than the Federal Endangered Species Act, the Clean Water Act, the public trust doctrine, "fixing" the Delta, the thicket of state and local regulations affecting water transfers, and the newly developing programs to manage local supplies. Moreover, the distinction between water rights and water quality has become increasingly blurred.

It is the aim of this book, therefore, to meet a wide array of needs: to deal with current issues as well as the traditional concepts of water law; to provide at the same time some history and general background information concerning our water supplies, their use and their development; and finally to produce a readable document that will be of value to more than just those in the legal profession. It is essentially a handbook on California water, and while there is a strong overview of water law, the book is not intended to provide a comprehensive legal analysis of any specific aspect of water law.

There is always danger that a book treating current problems will soon be out of date. However, much of the historical and background information in this book should enjoy a happier fate. For it is against these circumstances, at least as a starting point, that continuing developments need to be analyzed. Water law, and the principles guiding the allocation of our water supplies, are undergoing rapid changes. We used to think of a water "right" as an absolutely secure property right as long as the water was reasonably used. The Governor's Commission to Review California Water Rights Law in its 1978 Report confirmed the traditional rule that "Water rights are property rights."[3] But the "vested" nature of such rights is being steadily eroded, and with it, the reliability of California's water supply.

Regulation through the courts and administrative agencies applying the federal Endangered Species Act, provisions of the California Fish and Game Code, and the federal Clean Water Act, to say nothing of the public trust doctrine, have greatly reduced the amounts of water available to supply cities and farms. By regulation, the "rights" to such water supplies are being reallocated for environmental purposes. While certainly there is widespread support in the State for the protection of our fish and wildlife resources, the full impact of these newer statutes on water supply is not generally understood. The public has yet to realize that restricting diversions to provide water for instream uses has cut deeply into the supplies developed by earlier generations to carry the State through drought periods, and to meet future growth needs.

The reconciliation of environmental water demands with the water needs of farms and cities now stands as the great issue for the future. No single approach to this dilemma is likely to be successful. However, perhaps establishing a secure funding source that would provide for the acquisition of water rights for environmental purposes, through voluntary water transfers or participation in water supply projects, would begin to take us off the present path of destructive conflict. The new federal Central Valley Improvement Act (PL 102-575; 106 Stat. 4600 § 3401) makes a start at providing money for environmental improvements, establishing a restoration fund of up to $50 million per year to be financed in part by charges against water users.[4]

California's rich history has always been tied to its water supply. It is that supply which has led to the State's growth and prosperity, and to how and where urbanization has taken place—maybe more so in California than anywhere else in North America. Water will be no less vital in the future. We hope that this book will help to

---

[3]  Final Report, page 16. The Commission was chaired by the then recently retired Chief Justice of the California Supreme Court, the Honorable Donald R. Wright. I served as one of the two practicing lawyers on the Commission.

[4]  In draft Water Right Decision 1630, December 1992, the California State Water Resources Control Board also established a fund to mitigate the impacts of water use from the Delta watershed on public trust resources. All major diverters from the Delta and upstream tributaries were made subject to a charge of $5 or $10 an acre foot, including DWR for the State Water Project, the City of San Francisco, and the East Bay Municipal Utility District. This draft Decision, however, was withdrawn.

increase understanding of the vital water issues that impact California and the law that governs them.

Now, on a personal note, it is difficult to write about California water issues without viewing them from one perspective or another, or at least being perceived to have done so. Nonetheless, our effort has been to keep the book impartial and useful to a broad readership. But in this Preface I do want to express some of my own opinions. We are not short of water in this State, although our supplies generally come at the wrong time and not where they are most needed. Storage, at least in part, remains a key to meeting future needs. This does not have to mean more dams across more rivers. Storage can be off-stream, and in groundwater basins.[5] Reclaimed water use can be expanded, and more coordinated use of surface and groundwater supplies is also essential. And because any additional construction of significance will require at least a decade, some reallocation among present uses, at least for an interim period, must play a role. Some water can be transferred from agriculture on a voluntary basis without grave injury to that vital industry or to the rural communities which agriculture supports. But we should recognize that agriculture too is short of water, and meets its present needs partially from groundwater overdraft. A wise long term policy must also provide a reliable water supply for agriculture, as well as for urban and environmental needs.

By far the most difficult problem, however, is to find a solution for the present Delta diversions. This is not a question of biological science, or hydrology, or economics, or engineering, but rather a matter of political trust. For more than a decade this issue has kept us stuck in conflict. Perhaps the new standards now under consideration for the Delta will provide the necessary foundation to resolve the issue, and to assure California's future water supply for urban communities, agricultural interests and the environment.

In any event, it is time to come together and take charge of our own future. We have been living too long off works constructed by previous generations, and relying too much on policies of the past.

Arthur L. Littleworth

March 1995

---

[5] Los Banos Grande in the San Joaquin Valley south of the Delta, and Domenigoni near Hemet in Southern California, are both examples of off-stream reservoirs fed from the aqueduct systems of the State Water Project and the Metropolitan Water District of Southern California, rather than by direct river flow. DWR's Kern Water Bank represents a large groundwater storage project. These projects are in the planning or construction stages.

# Acknowledgments

The preparation of this book would have been impossible without the help of many people. There is not sufficient space here to thank all of them, but I would like to single out a few for their extraordinary contributions in helping with the publication of this volume. Two of our fellow partners, Anne T. Thomas and Gregory K. Wilkinson served as an editorial board for the book. Ms. Thomas has been a partner with Best, Best & Krieger for nearly 20 years and is an expert in all aspects of water law. Her review of several of the chapters, particularly the water rights chapter, was invaluable. Mr. Wilkinson has over 20 years of experience in California and international water law. For much of that time he has been a key participant in the Bay-Delta process. His contributions to the book give it depth and insight that could not be have been obtained simply by relying on secondary sources.

Janice L. Weis was the primary author of the chapters on endangered species and water transfers. She was an associate with Best, Best & Krieger for six years and is currently on the staff at Lewis and Clark School of Law in Portland, Oregon. Michelle Ouellette was the primary author of the water rights chapter. She is a sixth year associate with Best, Best & Krieger. I also must thank the firm's management and policy board for its continued support in allowing Art and me to work on this book. Without their faith that this volume would be completed, it would never have been published.

Many summer associates, paralegals, and staff helped with the researching, proofreading, and cite checking of this volume. One in particular, Kevin Clark, must be singled out for the extraordinary amount of time and effort he put into reviewing the text. Others who were particularly helpful were Deborah Bogen, Theresa Lamboy, and Sandy Simmons.

Finally, I would be remiss if I did not extend a special thanks to my wonderful wife Joan, and to Chelsea and Ananda, who graciously tolerated my seemingly interminable absences on nights and weekends over the past four years.

Eric L. Garner
March 1995

# Chapters at a Glance

# Contents

## Appendices

## Tables

## Maps

**CHAPTER ONE**

# A Brief History of California's Water Supply and Development

## Introduction

In the 19th century, some argued that the settlement of the western United States was a futile enterprise. One of the influential opponents to westward expansion was Daniel Webster, the prominent senator from New Hampshire. Addressing Congress, he said—

> What do you want of that vast and worthless area, that region of savages and wild beasts, of deserts, of shifting sands and whirling wind, of dust, of cactus and prairie dogs? To what use could we ever hope to put those great deserts and those endless mountain ranges, impenetrable and covered to their very base with eternal snow? What can we ever do with the Western coast, a coast of 3,000 miles, rockbound, cheerless, and uninviting?[1]

While today this limited vision seems surprising, even difficult to understand, a century and a half ago these were legitimate questions. Indeed, without the development of technology to transport vast quantities of water, California might have remained much as Webster described. This book begins with a discussion of California's water supply and the history of its development. This background is an essential element in understanding California water law and policy.

*Without the development of technology to transport vast quantities of water, California might have remained much as Daniel Webster described.*

[1]  Kinney, *Irrigation and Water Rights,* second edition, San Francisco, California, Bender-Moss Company, 1912, page 216.

## California's Water Supply

California's surface water comes from an average annual statewide precipitation of almost two feet. This precipitation ranges from almost nothing in desert areas to more than 100 inches in the mountainous regions along the northern coast.

Sixty percent of this precipitation is evaporated or transpired by trees and other natural vegetation. The other forty percent is equal to about 71 million acre-feet of stream flow. (An acre-foot is the amount of water needed to cover an acre of land to the depth of one foot. It is also usually considered to be the approximate amount of water used over two years by a household of four people.) Flows from the Colorado River currently supply another 4.8 million acre-feet, and inflow from streams in Oregon adds an additional 1.4 million acre-feet to this supply. In an average year, California has available slightly more than 78 million acre-feet.

California as a whole is not short on water, but the supply is difficult to utilize fully because of its distribution and variability. Almost 29 million acre-feet, approximately 40 percent of the average statewide runoff, occurs in the north coast region, the least populated part of the state. Annual runoff has also varied between a low of 15 million acre-feet in 1977 and a high of more than 135 million in 1983. In 1986, nearly 8 million acre-feet flowed past the City of Sacramento in the Sacramento River and the Yolo Bypass in just ten consecutive days. This is more water than is used by all the cities in the state in a year. Water developers in California have focused on compensating for this variability by storing high winter and spring flows for later use in the summer and early fall.[2]

Many of the reservoirs that have been built in California in the last 50 years were designed to maintain deliveries through a repeat of a 7-year dry period equivalent to that of 1928 to 1934. However, various constraints on the use of facilities, and the failure to complete planned projects, saw California suffer severe shortages during the 6 dry years from 1987 to 1992.

California has some 450 groundwater basins that store approximately 850 million acre-feet of water. By comparison, California's surface reservoirs hold 43 million acre-feet of water. However, the total amount of groundwater storage is deceptive because much less than 50 percent of California's groundwater is close enough to the surface to be economically pumped. Another constraint is that a

*On average, California has an available water supply of about 77 million acre-feet per year.*

*California as a whole is not short of water, but to meet the state's demands water must be stored and transported large distances.*

---

[2] "California Water Plan Update," *State Department of Water Resource,* Bulletin No. 160-93, volume 1, pages 49-51.

reliable supply cannot be based on removing stored groundwater that will not be replenished.

An average of 15 million acre-feet of groundwater is pumped each year in California, which meets about 20 percent of the state's water requirements for municipal, industrial and agricultural uses. This water is "recharged" (put back into groundwater storage) from three sources. Natural recharge through rainfall, snowmelt and stream seepage recharges 7.0 million acre-feet of water annually. Water that seeps back into the ground after municipal, industrial, and agricultural usage adds another 6.65 million acre-feet of recharge. Also, additional water is added annually as part of groundwater recharge programs. Despite this recharge, each year Californians use about 1.3 million acre-feet of groundwater that is not replenished. This excess withdrawal is referred to as "overdraft," defined generally as the deficit between the water pumped from a groundwater basin and the long-term recharge.[3]

*California has major groundwater supplies which meet about 20 percent of the state's water requirements.*

*However, the state's groundwater supplies are being overdrafted by about 1.3 million acre-feet a year.*

Overdraft has played a crucial role in the development of California's water supply and the state economy. Declining local groundwater tables forced the City of Los Angeles to look to the Owens Valley and the Colorado River for additional supplies. Falling groundwater tables were also a primary factor in the development of the Central Valley Project.

## California's Water Use

The history of developed water use in California began with the Spanish missions in the late 1700s. Initially, most irrigation water came directly from streams or small ditches that diverted streams. There were no storage facilities, and, since summertime flows were very low, the amount of acreage that could be irrigated was extremely small. However, the need for storage began to be remedied with the construction of dams in the late 1800s.

In the northern and central parts of California, water was diverted from streams or artesian flows, while in the Sierra Nevada mountains, water was taken from mining ditches. Irrigation was driven by the population expansion that accompanied and followed the gold rush. Most early irrigation was done by individuals, but as early as 1856 a "commercial" company constructed canals to irrigate wheat in Yolo County. At the same time, groups of irrigators began to join together to build ditches up and down the state.[4]

---

[3] *California Water Plan Update,* volume 1, pages 5-6, 80-82.
[4] "Water Utilization and Requirements of California," volume I, *State of California Bulletin,* No. 2, June 1955, page 22.

**Water Project Facilities in California**

Clair Engle Lake

Shasta Lake

• Redding

Tehama-Colusa Canal

Lake Oroville

Folsom Lake

Folsom South Canal

North Bay Aqueduct

**Sacramento**

Mokelumne Aqueduct

Hetch Hetchy Aqueduct

**San Francisco** •

South Bay Aqueduct

Delta-Mendota Canal

Madera Canal

San Felipe Unit

Millerton Lake

**Monterey**

San Luis Reservoir

**Fresno**

Coalinga Canal

Friant-Kern Canal

Coastal Branch

California

Cross Valley Canal

Los Angeles Aqueduct

**San Luis Obispo**

Kern Water Bank

**Bakersfield**

East Branch

Aqueduct

Colorado River Aqueduct

West Branch

**Santa Barbara**

**Los Angeles**

Coachella Canal

San Diego Aqueducts

All American Canal

**San Diego**

——— State Water Project Facilites

——— Federal Water Project Facilities

- - - Local Water Project Facilities

*The 20th century has been marked by the development of major public water projects in all parts of the state.*

In the 20th century, water use has been marked by the development of major public projects and the formation of hundreds of public agencies to supply water. The Central Valley and State Water Projects and the Hetch-Hetchy, Los Angeles, Mokelumne, and Colorado River Aqueducts have altered the state's landscape in a manner unimaginable to Daniel Webster and to the irrigators of the

19th century. How water is used and distributed in California is at the heart of the ongoing conflicts in California's water law and policy.

The major water projects discussed later in this chapter provide much of California's water supply. Dependable supplies from the State Water Project were estimated under Decision 1485 at 2.3 million acre-feet per year. However, future State Board or federal standards and the requirements for endangered species will likely reduce this firm yield. Almost half of this water comes from Lake Oroville in Butte County, and the rest is developed from surplus flows in the Sacramento-San Joaquin Delta. Some of these flows are re-regulated in the San Luis Reservoir. The State Water Project has contracted to deliver 4.2 million acre-feet. The facilities originally planned to meet these requirements have not been completed, and completion is now uncertain. The Central Valley Project has contracted to deliver 9.3 million acre-feet of water to over 250 contractors of the federal Central Valley Project. Average year deliveries have been about 7.3 million acre-feet of water per year.

California is apportioned 4.4 million acre-feet of Colorado River water per year, although in wet years it is possible for California to receive more water. California has generally received more than its entitlement because of a number of consecutive wet years and Arizona's failure to fully develop its Colorado River use. However, as Arizona takes more water, California cannot depend on receiving more than 4.4 million acre-feet per year without changes in the laws and regulations governing the Colorado River.[5]

The largest user of California's water is agriculture. In an average year, agriculture uses about 31.1 million acre-feet of water or approximately 80 percent of the state's developed water supply. Agriculture's share of California's total water supply, as opposed to the amount "developed" for use, is approximately 40 percent. Agriculture boomed in California from the World War I era to the 1980s. The approximately 5 million acres under irrigation in the 1930s grew to 9.7 million acres by 1981, although acreage in agricultural use has declined somewhat since 1981 to about 9.2 million acres in 1990.[6] With the increasing prevalence of water transfers from agricultural to urban use, this trend is likely to continue.

It is important to note that a significant percentage of the water used by agriculture percolates back into the ground or flows into streams, where it can be used again for other uses. Thus,

*Agriculture is the largest user of California's water supply.*

[5] *California Water Plan Update,* volume 1, pages 43, 63-64, 69.
[6] *California Water Plan Update,* volume 1, page 8.

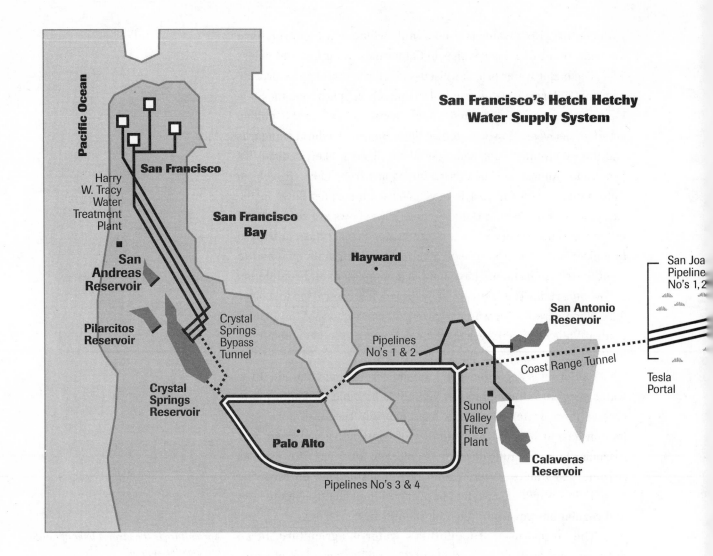

San Francisco's Hetch Hetchy
Water Supply System

Pacific Ocean

San Francisco

Harry
W. Tracy
Water
Treatment
Plant

San
Andreas
Reservoir

Pilarcitos
Reservoir

San Francisco
Bay

Hayward

San Antonio
Reservoir

San Joa
Pipeline
No's 1, 2

Crystal
Springs
Bypass
Tunnel

Pipelines
No's 1 & 2

Coast Range Tunnel

Tesla
Portal

Crystal
Springs
Reservoir

Palo Alto

Sunol
Valley
Filter
Plant

Calaveras
Reservoir

Pipelines No's 3 & 4

*Urban use totals about 7.8 million acre-feet a year.*

agriculture's net use is about 26.8 million acre-feet annually. A significant portion of this water is used for water-intensive crops such as alfalfa, cotton, and irrigated pasture, which comprise over three million acres of California's agriculture.[7]

Urban use in California is about 7.8 million acre-feet per year, but not nearly as much urban water can be reused as agricultural water, and therefore the net urban water usage is 6.7 million acre-feet. Environmental water uses also take a significant amount of water. The average annual outflow from California's wild and scenic river system is 17.8 million acre-feet, and 7.9 million acre-feet in drought years. This water cannot be stored and diverted for consumptive use. In addition, the minimum outflow standards for the Sacramento-San Joaquin Delta (as set forth in

[7] *California Water Plan Update,* volume 1, page 179.

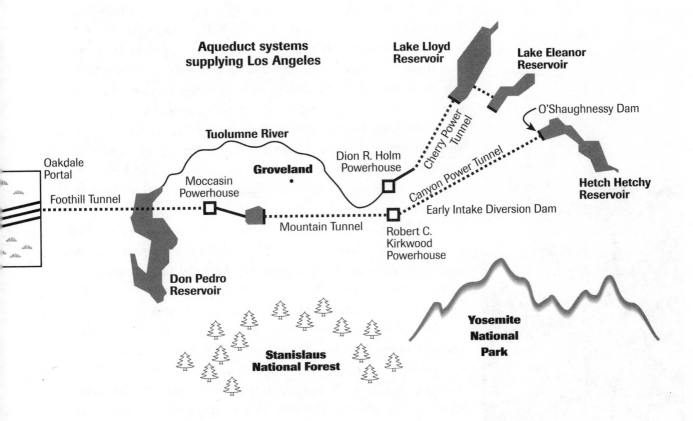

**Aqueduct systems supplying Los Angeles**

Lake Lloyd Reservoir

Lake Eleanor Reservoir

O'Shaughnessy Dam

Tuolumne River

Cherry Power Tunnel

Canyon Power Tunnel

Dion R. Holm Powerhouse

Groveland

Hetch Hetchy Reservoir

Oakdale Portal

Foothill Tunnel

Moccasin Powerhouse

Mountain Tunnel

Early Intake Diversion Dam

Robert C. Kirkwood Powerhouse

Don Pedro Reservoir

Stanislaus National Forest

Yosemite National Park

State Water Resources Control Board Decision 1485) and other instream environmental needs require approximately 9.56 million acre-feet of water annually in average years, and 7.6 million acre-feet in drought years.[8]

These relative usages can also be seen in regional water use statistics. Most of the water used in California is used in the Central Valley, where over 19 million acre-feet of water is applied each year, mostly to agricultural lands. The Sacramento River region uses 11.7 million acre-feet of water annually, followed by the South Coast region at 4.6 million and the Colorado River region at just over 4 million.[9]

*On the order of 26 million acre-feet annually are dedicated to wild and scenic rivers and to environmental protection.*

[8] *California Water Plan Update,* volume 1, pages 338, 217.
[9] *California Water Plan Update,* volume 2, pages 130, 119.

## The San Francisco Bay Area

### The City of San Francisco

Before the gold rush of 1849, the San Francisco Bay Area obtained its water supplies from nearby springs and streams. During the rapid population growth of the gold rush days, San Francisco suffered its first water shortage, and water was brought by barge across San Francisco Bay from Sausalito and distributed from wagons. Imported water was first brought to San Francisco through a series of flumes and tunnels that were constructed by the San Francisco Water Works Company between the City and Lobos Creek. This system was completed in 1857. Local water supplies were fully developed by 1890, by which time four reservoirs had been constructed on the peninsula. San Francisco then turned to Alameda Creek for further supplies.[10]

San Francisco residents eventually became dissatisfied with the service of the San Francisco Water Works Company, and, in the charter of 1901, an authorization was included for a municipally owned water system. Pursuant to this authorization, available sources of supply outside the San Francisco Bay Area were investigated. The Tuolumne River, which flowed through the Hetch Hetchy Valley in Yosemite National Park, was chosen as the best source.

The first plan for the Hetch Hetchy project, drawn in 1882, showed a canal from the mountains to San Francisco, and the United States Geological Survey recommended using Hetch Hetchy as a water source in 1891. Although chosen for the purity of its water and its freedom from contamination, as well as its proximity to San Francisco, because Hetch Hetchy was located within Yosemite National Park, federal government approval was required for its use.

In 1901, the city filed for a reservoir and right-of-way within Yosemite, but this application was denied by the Secretary of the Interior in 1903. These papers were refiled in 1908, and the permit for reservoir construction was granted the same year. In 1912, after San Francisco hired M. M. O'Shaughnessey to construct Hetch Hetchy, the project drew significant opposition. Some opposition came from downstream farmers in the Turlock and Modesto areas who saw San Francisco as a threat to the water they claimed, and some was stimulated by the Spring Valley Water Company, which did not want to lose its monopoly as the city's only water supplier. The most vehement opposition came from John Muir and other naturalists who fought bitterly to save the Tuolumne River from being

John Muir with hiking stick overlooking Merced River in Yosemite

*San Francisco filed for the Hetch Hetchy project in Yosemite in 1901.*

*John Muir fought bitterly, but unsuccessfully, to save the Tuolumne River from being dammed.*

[10] *State of California Bulletin,* No. 2, page 81.

dammed and the beautiful Hetch Hetchy Valley from being flooded.[11]

In the fall of 1912, the city presented a 400-page report on the project to every member of the United States Congress. The Spring Valley Water Company's vigorous opposition continued as it presented a rebuttal report to Congress. However, Congress was persuaded by the city and in 1913 passed the Raker Act authorizing the construction of Hetch Hetchy. President Wilson signed it into law on December 19, 1913. The Hetch Hetchy project became functional in 1934 with the completion of a 150-mile-long aqueduct extending from Hetch Hetchy Reservoir to Crystal Springs Reservoir in San Mateo County.[12] It was one of the first projects to take water that otherwise would have flowed into the Delta, and to transport the water around the Delta. Today the project supplies about 157,000 acre-feet of water per year, not only to San Francisco but also to other cities on the San Francisco Peninsula.

San Francisco's O'Shaughnessy Dam and Hetch Hetchy Reservoir

*San Francisco's Hetch Hetchy aqueduct (150 miles long) was completed in 1934 and was one of the first projects to take water that otherwise would have flowed into the Delta.*

## East Bay Municipal Utility District

The principal water service agency in the East Bay area is the East Bay Municipal Utility District (EBMUD). From the 1840s until the early 1900s the East Bay was completely reliant on local sources, nearly depleting each source before it could develop a new one. The area suffered from both water quality problems and unreliable water deliveries. In 1906, the Peoples Water Company was incorporated. Although its goal was to solve the water problems of the East Bay, dramatic population increases in the area made this goal unreachable. Peoples Water Company encountered financial difficulties, and in 1916 the East Bay Water Company was incorporated to bail it out. Soaring costs and the continued unreliability of service prompted an election to determine whether the area should be served by a municipal utility district.

EBMUD was established by the voters of the East Bay on May 8, 1923. EBMUD immediately began searching for a supply of water that it could import to meet the burgeoning needs of its service area. The nearest adequate water source was the Mokelumne River. An election in 1924 authorized the bonds for this project, and construction began in 1926. In June 1929, Mokelumne River water from the Pardee Reservoir reached the East Bay for the first time.

**EBMUD = East Bay Municipal Utility District**

[11] M. M. O'Shaughnessey, *Hetch Hetchy—Its Origin and History*, 1934, The Recorder Printing and Publishing Company, page 20, 24, 33-36.
[12] *Hetch Hetchy,* pages 130-131.

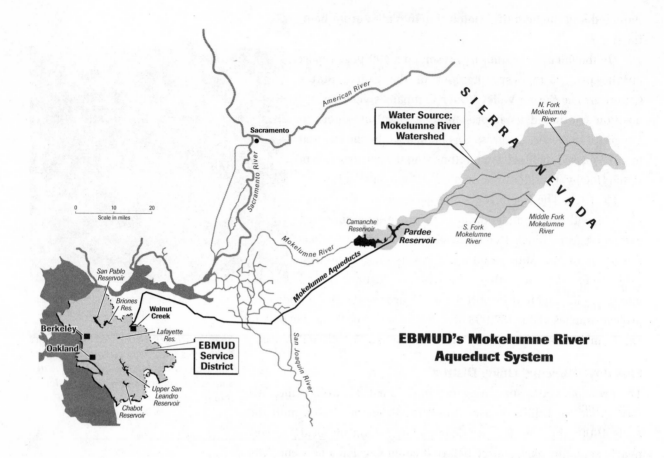

**EBMUD's Mokelumne River Aqueduct System**

*EBMUD completed Pardee Reservoir and its first aqueduct system to deliver Mokelumne River water to the Bay area in 1929.*

This aqueduct system also reduced the inflow into the Delta. As seems to be inevitable in California, the supply was sufficient for only a relatively short period of time.[13]

The original planners of the Mokelumne system could never have foreseen the tremendous growth that the area experienced during and after World War II. In 1946, a bond issue was approved for the construction of a second barrel of the Mokelumne Aqueduct, which was completed in 1949. A third Mokelumne Aqueduct was completed in 1963, the district having had the foresight, or luck, to acquire sufficient rights-of-way for three pipelines. In 1964, EBMUD completed a second dam on the Mokelumne, Camanche Dam, which created a ten-mile lake for additional water storage. EBMUD also has a contractual right with the Bureau of Reclamation for 150,000 acre-feet of water from the American River.[14] Although no water has yet been taken under this contract, it has survived a major legal challenge. *See* discussion in chapter 3.

San Francisco's San Andreas Water Filtration Plant

[13] John Noble, *Its Name Was M.U.D.* (1970), pages 7-8, 12, 16, 26.
[14] *M.U.D.,* pages 66, 152, 165.

## The Los Angeles and Southern California Area

### City of Los Angeles

The City of Los Angeles, which was founded on September 4, 1781, began its history as a Spanish pueblo. Dramatic population increases are nothing new to Los Angeles. In 1790, the population of Los Angeles was 139. It grew to 315 by 1800, to 365 by 1810, and to 1,610 by 1850. By 1877, the Los Angeles population was 9,000, and its domestic water supply was taken from an open ditch in which laundry was beaten against rocks and children swam.

Early development in Los Angeles took place near reliable water supplies, and the plaza and old town of Los Angeles were located in such areas. Throughout the 19th century, the Los Angeles River was a reliable source of water. During the period of Mexican rule, ranchos were located on every perennial spring or stream throughout the basin. Because these spring-fed streams provided the only dependable water supply, irrigation in the area was very limited. As of 1879, only 8,400 acres were under irrigation, and the area suffered seriously from a lack of water.

*The original pueblo of Los Angeles was located where the Los Angeles River rose to the surface to provide a dependable water supply.*

Until 1870, most of Southern California was still included in huge ranchos, and grazing was virtually the sole economic activity. However, by the mid-1870s, the vagaries of the region's water supply had virtually eliminated the ranchos. In 1856-57, 100,000 head of cattle were lost in Los Angeles County because of drought, and between 1862 and 1864 even larger numbers of cattle were lost. Sheep used to replace cattle were also depleted by drought. Rancho Centinella alone lost 22,000 sheep in 1877.[15]

Citrus cultivation began in Southern California around 1854, and by 1862 the state had 25,000 orange trees. Large-scale citrus development began in Southern California after the navel orange was introduced from Brazil in 1873. In fact, the parent navel orange tree is located and still alive in Riverside. Huge financial returns from citrus growing provided the impetus for developing the region's water supply. But, because the region's surface supply was rapidly overappropriated, residents had to turn to groundwater. Although artesian wells were initially available, after water tables began to drop, pumped wells were used. The dramatic drop in the water table is illustrated by U.S. Geological Survey statistics, which indicate that Southern California had 2,500 artesian wells in 1900, but only 22 by 1930.

[15] The Metropolitan Water District, History and First Annual Report, 1939, pages 10-11, 12-13, 17-18.

William Mulholland, Architect of LADWP's Owens Valley Aqueduct System

*Local supplies having been fully used, Los Angeles approved a $23 million bond issued in 1907 to import water from the Owens Valley.*

1913—First water arriving from Owens Valley

The year 1877 was pivotal in the history of Southern California's water supply. In that year, William Mullholland arrived in the City of Los Angeles and became superintendent of the system. He rapidly upgraded the open ditch system, first with wooden flumes and then with steel mains. In 1902, the city purchased the water system and named Mullholland chief engineer. By 1905, the City of Los Angeles was diverting the full normal runoff of the Los Angeles River. To augment that supply, it had built underground galleries across the narrows of the river to collect subterranean flow. Since the supply was still insufficient, a study of potential new water sources was undertaken.

Among the rivers studied was the Mojave, but it appeared that obtaining water from this river would have entailed costly litigation. An investigation in 1904 determined that the best source of water was the Owens River, and, in 1905, a bond issue of $1.5 million was approved for preliminary engineering and the purchase of water rights and rights-of-way. In 1907, a $23 million bond issue was approved to cover construction of the project, and, in 1913, the Owens River Aqueduct was completed.[16]

Only ten years after the completion of the Owens River Aqueduct, the demands of increasing population and industry and a dry cycle in the Sierra Nevada made this supply inadequate to fill the aqueduct. Once again, Los Angeles was forced to search for a new supply—

> With present sources being overdrawn continually, it was clear that new importation to meet the needs not only of Los Angeles but of the entire Southern California metropolitan area must be made. The only new source found available was the Colorado River.[17]

In October 1923, Mullholland recommended to the City of Los Angeles that a survey be conducted to investigate the feasibility of importing the Colorado River water into Southern California. His recommendation was accepted, the feasibility of an aqueduct from the Colorado River established, and, on June 28, 1924, the City of Los Angeles filed with the State of California for 1,500 cubic feet per second (cfs) of water from the Colorado River.[18] Thus, the Colorado River Aqueduct was planned, not only as a Los Angeles project, but as a Southern California enterprise.

[16] First Annual Report, pages 12-14, 18-19.
[17] First Annual Report, page 20.
[18] First Annual Report, page 36.

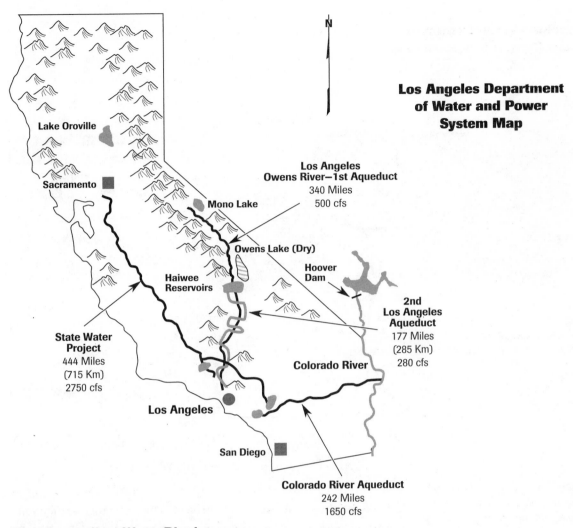

**Los Angeles Department
of Water and Power
System Map**

N

**Lake Oroville**

**Sacramento**

**Mono Lake**

**Los Angeles
Owens River—1st Aqueduct**
340 Miles
500 cfs

**Owens Lake (Dry)**

**Haiwee
Reservoirs**

**Hoover
Dam**

**2nd
Los Angeles
Aqueduct**
177 Miles
(285 Km)
280 cfs

**State Water
Project**
444 Miles
(715 Km)
2750 cfs

**Colorado River**

**Los Angeles**

**San Diego**

**Colorado River Aqueduct**
242 Miles
1650 cfs

## The Metropolitan Water District

The need for the Colorado River Aqueduct was described in the
following terms—

> The extreme aridity of the Southern California climate is not imme-
> diately evident to the recently arrived resident or tourist, with only
> the luxuriant subtropical vegetation of the cultivated areas as a
> basis for judgment. The sharp contrast with the Sahara-like deserts
> that must be crossed by everyone approaching Los Angeles over-
> land increases the impressions of abundant rainfall, until the fact is
> finally realized that all this vegetation is continuously dependent
> upon frequent irrigation. The region constitutes in reality a great
> oasis, sharply bounded in every landward direction by deserts of
> utter sterility. It derives a limited and extremely variable water
> supply from the 1,000 square miles of rocky, steeply sloping
> mountain watersheds which drain into the basin from the north
> and east. On these mountain slopes the rainfall averages about 30

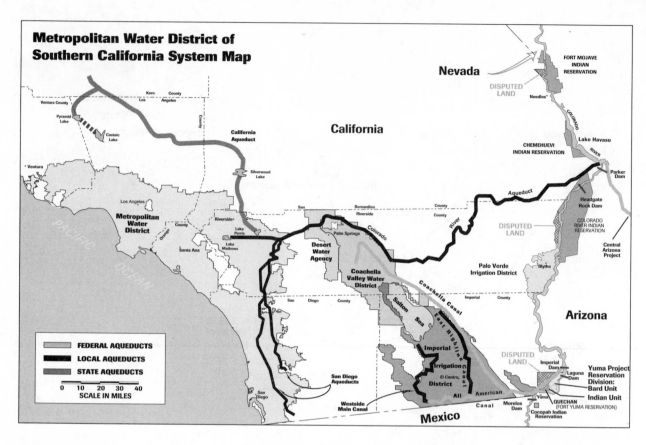

**Metropolitan Water District of Southern California System Map**

FEDERAL AQUEDUCTS
LOCAL AQUEDUCTS
STATE AQUEDUCTS

0   10   20   30   40
SCALE IN MILES

inches annually, but this rate decreases toward the ocean to only 15 inches at Los Angeles and about 10 inches at the beaches.[19]

Three legislative enactments and three contracts were required to implement the Colorado River project. The legislative enactments were the Colorado River Compact, the Metropolitan Water District Act, and the Boulder Canyon Project Act. Secondly, there were contracts between The Metropolitan Water District and the United States for power and water, and finally the Seven Party Agreement between the members of the "agricultural group" and those of the "city group" for the allocation of California's rights to Colorado River water.

The Metropolitan Water District of Southern California (MWD) was organized as a public corporation on December 6, 1928, pursuant to the Metropolitan Water District Act, which is found in the California Water Code Appendix, page 109-1. The Act provided a means for cities and other governmental subdivisions to join together to develop a water supply. As of 1938, the members were the cities of Anaheim, Beverly Hills, Burbank, Compton, Fullerton, Glendale, Long Beach, Los Angeles, Pasadena, San Marino, Santa Ana, Santa Monica, and Torrance. MWD has since grown to include San

*As population continued to grow and more water was needed, Southern California turned to the Colorado River.*

**MWD = Metropolitan Water District of Southern California**

[19] First Annual Report, page 7.

Fernando, Calleguas Municipal Water District, Central Basin Municipal Water District, Chino Basin Municipal Water District, Coastal Municipal Water District, Eastern Municipal Water District, Foothill Municipal Water District, Las Virgenes Municipal Water District, Municipal Water District of Orange County, San Diego County Water Authority, Three Valleys Municipal Water District, Upper San Gabriel Valley Municipal Water District, West Basin Municipal Water District, and Western Municipal Water District of Riverside County.[20]

Lining Metropolitan Water District canal to San Diego

The purpose of the district was to supply the area within its original boundaries with supplemental water and to provide a means of supplying water to surrounding areas that might later choose to join MWD. The first major activity of MWD was to construct the Colorado River Aqueduct. The 242-mile-long aqueduct was completed in 1939, and water deliveries began in 1941. The aqueduct extends from the Colorado River near Parker, Arizona, to Lake Matthews near Riverside.

At the time the aqueduct was built, MWD could barely give the water away.[21] Each of MWD's member agencies was offered free use of the water for 60 days. Ten agencies tried, and after the trial period five canceled their orders. Today, however, MWD is the most important water supplier in Southern California. About one-third of Southern California's water needs are still met by local sources, but it has been the imported supplies from the Owens Valley, the Delta, and the Colorado River that have helped to generate an economy and metropolitan population that are among the largest in the world.

*Today, about one-third of Southern California's water needs are still met from local sources, the balance coming from the Owens Valley, the Colorado River, and the Delta through the State Water Project.*

### The Colorado Desert Area

In 1860, Dr. O. M. Wozencraft and Ebenezer Hadley, the county surveyor for San Diego County, designed a project to irrigate and colonize three million acres in the Imperial Valley, a project involving diversion of water from the Colorado River through the Alamo River and Mexico. Although the California legislature approved the project, Congress rejected it.[22] The Colorado River Irrigation Company was formed in 1892 but failed to secure financing, and, in 1896, the California Development Company was formed. Using the method of Wozencraft and Hadley, the California Development Company made

---

[20] First Annual Report, pages 1-2, 26.
[21] Aqueduct, No. 2, 1991, Metropolitan Water District Publication, page 15.
[22] First Annual Report, page 27.

possible the delivery of water to the Imperial Valley in 1901. However, the company soon encountered its own difficulties. In 1905, the Mexican Government made two dredger cuts in the banks of the Colorado River below the international boundary, but control gates were not installed at the cuts. In that winter, the Colorado River reached flood stage and breached the lower cut, the uncontrolled flow reaching the Salton Sea. It took three years to close the break and confine the Colorado River to its channel. Judgments for damages resulting from the flow of Colorado River water through the dredger cut forced the company into receivership from 1909 until 1916, during which time major development of the Imperial Valley occurred.

In 1911, the Imperial Irrigation District was organized and, five years later, purchased the California Development Company properties from the Southern Pacific Company for $3 million. The earlier canal breach spurred an attempt to build a canal wholly in the United States, which led to the construction of the "All-American Canal" as part of the Boulder Canyon Project Act (BCPA). The BCPA is discussed in greater detail in chapter 10.

Development in the Coachella Valley has occurred primarily in the 20th century. Agriculture first began around 1894, when the Southern Pacific Company drilled a well in Mecca and developed a supply of high-quality artesian water, but increased dramatically after 1900 when improved methods of drilling became economical. By 1907, more than 400 wells existed between Indio and the Salton Sea, and, incredible as it may seem today, 300 of them were artesian. In 1918, the Coachella Valley County Water District was organized, primarily to protect the existing water supply in the area and, because agriculture in the area was being limited by an insufficient water supply, to obtain water from the Colorado River. In 1934, Coachella Valley entered into a contract with the United States Bureau of Reclamation to construct facilities to import Colorado River water to the Coachella Valley. This resulted in the construction of the Coachella branch of the All-American Canal, which carries Colorado River water along the east side of the Coachella Valley, crosses the valley just north of the City of Indio, and then turns south along the west side of the valley.[23]

## The Central Valley Project

The evolution of water use in California is again evident in the history of water development in the vast Central Valley, the rich agricultural area supplied by the Sacramento and San Joaquin Rivers.

[23] Bulletin No. 2, pages 185, 205-207.

Before California became a state, there was little activity in the Central Valley, and the most highly developed ranch in the area was John Sutter's New Helvetia, which is now Sacramento. The mining boom in 1849 and 1850 dramatically increased the need for agricultural produce and livestock and prompted the first attempts to grow wheat. Dry farming was initially used for many of the necessary grains and hay, although irrigation was utilized for truck crops.[24] Dry farming was accomplished by deep plowing after rains. The runoff entered the subsoil, and a dust blanket created by a machine that pulverized the surface prevented evaporation.[25] The first water developments in the Central Valley were earth ditches conveying the summer flows of local streams and later abandoned mining ditches.

*The gold rush and consequent population growth was the stimulus for commercial agriculture in the Central Valley.*

The population growth caused by the gold rush brought about the first attempts at farming in the Central Valley, and wheat was the first major crop. Not only did California produce more wheat than any state in the nation in 1874 and 1875, but during those years irrigation became a commercial enterprise in the Central Valley. Throughout the 1870s, extensive irrigation of tens of thousands of acres occurred. In 1877, the legislature adopted the Wright Act, which allowed the formation of public irrigation districts. Its constitutionality was litigated for nine years, primarily by riparian interests which did not want to see water distributed throughout the valley. Once the Act's legality was established, irrigation districts were at the forefront of great agricultural expansion, and from 1900 to 1920 the irrigated land in the Central Valley almost tripled.

*The Wright Act, adopted in 1877, opened the way for the formation of public irrigation districts and extensive agricultural expansion.*

The development of the centrifugal pump allowed deep wells to be drilled, and thousands of Central Valley farmers took advantage of the new technology. By the mid-1920s, California had surpassed Iowa as the richest agricultural state in the country.[26] It has been estimated that when groundwater pumping began almost 750 million acre-feet of water was present in the aquifers under the Central Valley. Over the past 70 years groundwater pumping has dramatically decreased this amount, and the current overdraft (the deficit between the water pumped from a groundwater basin and the long-term recharge) in the Central Valley is estimated to be slightly under one million acre-feet per year. By the 1930s, the negative effects of groundwater overdraft

---

[24] Bulletin No. 2, page 149.
[25] Hundley Jr., Norris, *The Great Thirst*, 1992, page 88.
[26] Lloyd J. Mercer and W. Douglas Morgan, "Irrigation, Drainage, and Agricultural Developments in the San Joaquin Valley" in *The Economics and Management of Water and Drainage in Agriculture,* 1991, page 11, 15, 18, 20, 22.

*By the 1930s, it was clear that additional water was needed for Central Valley agriculture.*

**CVP = Central Valley Project**

*The Central Valley Project Act was adopted in 1933 as the initial part of the State Water Plan.*

*Because of the depression, the state was unable to market bonds for the project, and it was turned over to the federal government.*

were being felt in the Central Valley, leading to searches for new sources of water to supply the still-growing agricultural industry.

The result of this search was the federal Central Valley Project (CVP), now California's largest water supplier. The Central Valley Project was originally proposed by Colonel Robert Bradford Marshall of the United States Geological Survey in 1920—

> The people of California, indifferent to the bountiful gifts that Nature has given them, sit idly by waiting for rain, indefinitely postponing irrigation, and allowing every year millions and millions of dollars in water to pour unused into the sea, when there are hungry thousands in this and in other countries pleading for food and when San Francisco and the Bay Cities, the metropolitan district of California, are begging for water.... My solution of the whole problem is to turn the Sacramento River into the San Joaquin Valley, a feat which is now shown to be practicable as an engineering enterprise that is possible of execution within ten years and that would justify a cost, if necessary, of $750,000,000, be safe for the investor, present no legal obstructions, and provide for the present as well as the prospective land owner the most attractive proposition ever offered in the State. Remember, however, that the plan is a big, State-wide plan and also remember that success, as California measures success, is assured only when the enterprise is planned and carried out in its entirety.[27]

The initial part of the State Water Plan, the CVP, was adopted as the Central Valley Project Act of 1933. Cal. Wat. Code § 11100 *et seq.* Voters passed a 1933 referendum approving the Central Valley Project Act and included the authorization for $170 million of revenue bonds. Because of the Depression, the state was not able to market the bonds to finance the CVP and had to abandon the project. The state then asked the federal government to undertake the project.

A federal Central Valley Project was first authorized by the Rivers and Harbors Act of August 30, 1935. Re-authorized for construction by the Department of Interior, the project was made subject to reclamation laws by the Rivers and Harbors Act of August 26, 1937.[28] The 1937 Act provided that the dams and reservoirs should be used for (1) river regulation, improvement of navigation, and flood

---

[27] Marshall, "Irrigation of Twelve Million Acres of Land in California," 1920, pages 6-7, cited in Graham, "The Central Valley Project: Resource Development of a Natural Basin," 38 *California Law Review,* pages 588, 590.

[28] Interim Central Valley Project Operations Criteria and Plan (CVP-OCAP), February 1992, page 2.

control; (2) irrigation and domestic uses, and (3) power. Water for environmental purposes was not included among the original stated purposes of the project.

The Central Valley extends 500 miles, from the convergence of the Coast Range and the Sierra Nevada at Mount Shasta in the north to the Tehachapi Mountains in the south. It has an average width of 120 miles and includes more than one-third of the area of California.

As the court wrote in *Ivanhoe Irrigation District v. McCracken* (1958) 357 U.S. 275, the CVP made possible the full development of the Central Valley—

> Rainfall on the valley floor comes during the winter months—85% from November to April—and summers are quite dry.... The climate is ideal with a frost-free period of over seven months and a mild winter permitting production of some citrus as well as deciduous fruits and other specialized crops. The absence of rain, however, makes irrigation essential, particularly in the southern region.
>
> In the mountain ranges precipitation is greater, and the winters more severe. The Northern Sierras average 80 inches of rainfall and the Southern 35 inches.... In the higher recesses of the mountains precipitation is largely snow which, when it melts, joins the other runoff of the mountain areas to make up an annual average of 33,000,000 acre-feet of water coming from the mountain regions. Nature has not regulated the timing of the runoff water, however, and it is estimated that half of the Sierra runoff occurs during the three months of April, May, and June. Resulting floods cause great damage, and waste this phenomenal accumulation of water so vital to the valley's rich alluvial soil. The object of the [CVP] plan is to arrest this flow and regulate its seasonal and year-to-year variations, thereby creating salinity control to avoid the gradual encroachment of ocean water, providing an adequate supply of water for municipal and irrigation purposes, facilitating navigation, and generating power. *Ivanhoe,* pages 280-282.

The operating scheme of the Central Valley Project is fairly simple. Shasta Reservoir, which has a capacity of 4,552,000 acre-feet, stores the surplus winter runoff of the Sacramento River. This water, in addition to repelling salinity intrusion and providing water for domestic irrigation and industrial uses in the Delta and Bay areas, is transferred through the Delta Cross-Channel and lifted by the Tracy Pumping Plant into the Delta-Mendota Canal. This canal carries water south by gravity flow to the Mendota Pool. The water is used in the San Joaquin Valley to replace the San Joaquin River water that is stored behind Friant Dam near Fresno. Thus, Sacramento River water is brought down to replace the San Joaquin River water held in Millerton Lake and diverted farther south through the Friant-Kern and Madera Canals. Trinity River water is used in part to augment the Sacramento River diverted at Shasta.

The Central Valley Project is divided into nine divisions: (1) Trinity River, (2) Shasta, (3) Sacramento River, (4) American River, (5) Delta, (6) West San Joaquin, (7) Friant, (8) East Side, and (9) San Felipe.[29]

The Trinity River Division was constructed to increase the supply of water available for irrigation in the Central Valley. The dominant feature of the Trinity River division is Claire Engle Lake, which is formed by Trinity Dam and stores a maximum of 2,448,000 acre-feet of Trinity River water. This water is combined with water from the Sacramento River to provide irrigation service to lands in the Sacramento Valley and other areas of the Central Valley Project.

The Shasta Division includes Shasta Dam and Lake, located on the Sacramento River, with its storage capacity of 4.5 million acre-feet. In many ways it is the hub of the Central Valley Project, and its uses include irrigation in the Sacramento Valley, navigation flows, conservation of fish life in the Sacramento River, protection of the Sacramento-San Joaquin Delta from intrusion of saline ocean water, transfer of water to the Mendota Pool via the Delta-Mendota Canal in exchange for San Joaquin River water diverted by Friant Dam, and provision of water for municipal, industrial and irrigation use in Contra Costa County and other areas.

The Sacramento River division consists primarily of the Sacramento Canal unit. This includes the Red Bluff diversion dam, which diverts water from the Sacramento River to the Corning Canal and Tehama-Colusa Canal service areas.

The primary feature of the American River Division is Folsom Dam and Lake, which has a storage capacity of 1,010,000 acre-feet. The Delta Division consists of four major facilities: (1) the Delta Cross Channel, (2) the Contra Costa Canal, (3) the Tracy Pumping Plant, and (4) the Delta-Mendota Canal. The Delta Cross Channel moves water through the Delta to the Tracy Pumping Plant and the Contra Costa Canal.

The Tracy Pumping Plant was constructed to lift surplus Sacramento River water into the Delta-Mendota Canal for transmission

Trinity River in Northern California

[29] CVP-OCAP, pages iii-iv, 6-8.

to the Mendota Pool. The Delta-Mendota Canal carries water southeast from the Tracy Pumping Plant to the San Luis Unit and replaces San Joaquin River water stored by Friant Dam and used in the Friant-Kern and Madera systems. The Delta-Mendota Canal is about 117 miles long and terminates in the Mendota Pool, which is located about 30 miles west of Fresno. By bringing Sacramento River water to the lands which could no longer receive San Joaquin River water after the construction of Friant Dam, the canal is the facility that made the Central Valley Project possible.

The West San Joaquin Division's primary feature is the San Luis Unit. It is a joint Central Valley Project and California State Water Project facility, authorized, built, and operated jointly by the federal government and the state of California. The storage capacity of San Luis is about 4 million acre-feet, of which 55 percent is federal storage and 45 percent is state storage. The San Luis Unit greatly increased flexibility in operating the southern portion of the CVP and increased the amount of water that can be served to irrigation districts in the San Joaquin Valley.

The Friant Division consists of: (1) Friant Dam and Millerton Lake, (2) Madera Canal, and (3) Friant-Kern Canal. It has a capacity of 520,500 acre-feet and controls San Joaquin River flows. It provides downstream releases to meet requirements above the Mendota Pool, and provides conservation storage and diversion into Madera and Friant-Kern Canals. The Madera Canal carries water from Millerton Lake northward to lands in Madera County. The Madera Canal is 36 miles long and terminates at the Chowchilla River. The Friant-Kern Canal carries water southward from Millerton Lake to lands in Fresno, Tulare, and Kern counties. It is about 152 miles long and terminates at the Kern River about 4 miles west of Bakersfield.

Census figures demonstrate the success of the CVP. Between 1940 and 1969, irrigated acreage in the seven Central Valley counties increased from 1,706,137 acres to 3,736,014 acres.[30]

## State Water Project

The Feather River is the most important tributary of the Sacramento River. Its drainage area, located above Oroville, is approximately 3600 square miles. Runoff from the Feather River varies between 1.2 million acre-feet and 9 million acre-feet, with a mean of about 4.5 million acre-feet. In 1931 the state engineer recommended the construction of a dam at Oroville that would impound approximately

*The State Water Project stores Feather River water behind Oroville Dam and then releases that water to augment flows of the Sacramento River into the Delta.*

[30] Mercer and Morgan, page 24.

**Major State Water Project Facilities**

Antelope Lake

Lake Davis

Frenchman Lake

Thermalito Forebay

Thermalito Afterbay

Lake Oroville

Redding

North Bay Aqueduct

Sacramento

Clifton Court Forebay

San Francisco

Lake Del Valle

San Luis Reservoir

O'Neill Forebay

Monterey

Fresno

Coastal Branch

California

Kern Water Bank

San Luis Obispo

Bakersfield

Aqueduct

East Branch

Pyramid Lake

Silverwood Lake

West Branch

Castaic Lake

Santa Barbara

Los Angeles

Lake Perris

San Diego

**SWP = State Water Project**

*Diversions of water supplied by the SWP are made from the Delta.*

1.7 million acre-feet of water. This plan was adopted by the legislature in 1941.

The Report on Feasibility for this plan concluded that the most logical and practical point of diversion for importing water from areas of surplus and transferring it to areas of deficient supply was the Sacramento-San Joaquin Delta. The report set forth the many practical advantages of using the Delta as the source of supply and point of diversion: (1) it was below all riparian owners and users of water in the basins above the Delta and thus not dependent on the flows of a single stream, (2) any water developed in the Sacramento or San Joaquin River basins could be transported by gravity to the Delta, and (3) the same was true of surplus water transferred from the northern coastal area. None of the disadvantages to fish and wildlife were discussed, if indeed they were then known. It was determined that Oroville Reservoir could be operated so as to make approximately 2.8 million acre-feet of water available each year for export from the Sacramento-San Joaquin Delta.[31]

Plans for the development of the Feather River were postponed because of World War II. In 1947, the state legislature authorized the Division of Water Resources (now the Department of Water Resources) to begin a Statewide Water Resources Investigation. There were three phases to the Investigation: (1) the identification of the water resources of California, (2) the determination of present and potential "ultimate" water requirements, and (3) planning for the orderly development of the state's water resources to meet its potential ultimate requirements. These phases resulted in three publications: (1) Water Resources of California, Bulletin 1; (2) Water Utilization and Requirements of California, Bulletin 2; and (3) The California Water Plan, Bulletin 3. The latter document provided a comprehensive master plan to control, distribute, and utilize the waters of California.

The Feather River Project was the first unit of the California Water Plan, and, in May 1951, State Engineer A.D. Edmonston presented the first complete report on the Feather River Project. This report proposed a multipurpose dam and reservoir on the Feather River near Oroville, a Delta cross-channel, an aqueduct to transport water from the Delta to Santa Clara and Alameda counties, and an aqueduct to transport water from the Delta to the San Joaquin Valley and Southern California. The proposed project was authorized by the legislature in 1951 for further study. It was revised in 1955 to add new facilities.

In 1959, the legislature enacted the California Water Resources Development Bond Act, or the Burns-Porter Act, named after its authors Senator Hugh Burns of Fresno and Assemblyman Carley V. Porter of Compton. The Act authorized the issuance of $1.75 billion

*The SWP was authorized by the Burns-Porter Act in 1959 and approved by a statewide vote in 1960.*

[31] Report on Feasibility of Feather River Project and Sacramento-San Joaquin Delta Diversion Projects Proposed as Features of the California Water Plan, State Water Resources Control Board, May 1951, pages 2-3, 81-83.

in general obligation bonds to assist in financing the construction of the state water facilities. In 1960, the voters of California approved the project and the method of financing. The facilities to be constructed by this authorization were set forth in Water Code Section 12934(d).

The State Water Project now supplies water to some 30 public agencies. The Metropolitan Water District of Southern California signed the first contract with the Department of Water Resources on November 4, 1960. This contract became the prototype for all of the State Water Project water supply contracts. The contracting agencies and their contractual entitlements are set forth in Table 1-1.

Although there are contracts for more than 4.2 million acre-feet, the dependable yield of the project under the 1978 decision of the State Water Resources Control Board (D-1485) is about 2.3 million acre-feet. More recent applications of the Endangered Species Act have reduced this yield further.[32] *See* discussion in chapter 5.

The State Water Project was constructed with financing from general obligation bonds, revenue bonds, and capital resources. The general obligation bonds are repaid by revenues from the water supply contractors. The contractors pay all capital, operating, and maintenance costs, whether or not they actually take water. Over the life of the contracts, until 2035, the contractors will pay $21.4 billion in fixed amounts.[33] The water purchased is in addition to this cost.

The State Water Project facilities function together in the following manner. Water released from the main storage facility, Lake Oroville, flows down the Feather River into the Sacramento River and then into the networked channels of the Sacramento-San Joaquin Delta. Near the northern edge of the Delta, water is diverted into the North Bay Aqueduct, delivering water to Napa and Solano counties. The water is transferred through the Delta in natural sloughs and channels. A cross-Delta transfer facility was originally planned but has not yet been built. At the southern edge of the Delta, 15 miles southwest of Stockton and 10 miles northwest of Tracy, are the Clifton Court Forebay and the Delta Pumping Plant. This plant is named for Harvey O. Banks, the distinguished State Engineer during much of the planning and construction of the State Water Project. The Clifton Court Forebay, which serves as a water regulating reservoir for the Delta pumping plant, ensures the reliability and flexibility of

[32] Bulletin 160-83, page 16; Bulletin 3, pages xxv, 4; Bulletin 132-63, pages 9, 17, 21, 156; Bulletin 132-88, page 4; Bulletin 160-87, page 43.
[33] Bulletin 132-99, page 159; Bulletin 132-93, Appendix B.

## Table 1-1
## State Water Project Contracting Agencies
## and Their Entitlements

| Contracting Agency | First Year of Service | Maximum Annual Entitlement *acre-feet* |
|---|---|---|
| *Upper Feather Area* | | |
| City of Yuba City | 1968 | 9,600 |
| County of Butte | 1968 | 27,500 |
| Plumas County Flood Control and Water Conservation District | 1968 | 2,700 |
| *North Bay Area* | | |
| Napa County Flood Control and Water Conservation District | 1968 | 25,000 |
| Solano County Flood Control and Water Conservation District | 1988 | 42,000 |
| *South Bay Area* | | |
| Alameda County Flood Control and Water Conservation District, Zone 7 | 1962 | 46,000 |
| Alameda County Water District | 1962 | 42,000 |
| Santa Clara Valley Water District | 1965 | 100,000 |
| *San Joaquin Valley Area* | | |
| County of Kings | 1968 | 4,000 |
| Devil's Den Water District* | 1968 | 12,700 |
| Dudley Ridge Water District | 1968 | 57,700 |
| Empire West Side Irrigation District | 1968 | 3,000 |
| Kern County Water Agency | 1968 | 1,153,400 |
| Oak Flat Water District | 1968 | 5,700 |
| Tulare Lake Basin Water Storage District | 1968 | 118,500 |
| *Central Coastal Area* | | |
| San Luis Obispo County Flood Control and Water Conservation District | N/A | 25,000 |
| Santa Barbara County Flood Control and Water Conservation District | 1990 | 45,486 |
| *Southern California Area* | | |
| Antelope Valley-East Kern Water Agency | 1972 | 138,400 |
| Castaic Lake Water Agency | 1979 | 41,500 |
| Coachella Valley Water District | 1973 | 23,100 |
| Crestline-Lake Arrowhead Water Agency | 1972 | 5,800 |
| Desert Water Agency | 1973 | 38,100 |
| Littlerock Creek Irrigation District | 1972 | 2,300 |
| Mojave Water Agency | 1972 | 50,800 |
| Palmdale Water District | 1985 | 17,300 |
| San Bernardino Valley Municipal Water District | 1972 | 102,600 |
| San Gabriel Valley Municipal Water District | 1974 | 28,800 |
| San Gorgonio Pass Water Agency | N/A | 17,300 |
| The Metropolitan Water District of Southern California | 1972 | 2,011,500 |
| Ventura County Flood Control District | N/A | 29,000 |
| **TOTAL STATE WATER PROJECT** | | 4,217,786 |

* The entitlement of Devil's Den Water District has been transferred to Castaic Lake Water Agency.

*Information condensed from Department
of Water Resources Bulletin 132-90, page 5.*

pumping project water at the Delta pumping plant. It also allows a substantial portion of the pumping requirement of the California Aqueduct system to be accomplished at night and other times when the cost for power is less expensive and allows diversions from the Delta to be adjusted to coincide with favorable tide conditions.[34]

The Delta Fish Protective Facility, whose main purpose is to prevent floating debris and fish from being carried into the pumps, is built directly across the intake channel from the Delta pumping plant. The entire intake flow to the pumps passes through the primary channel of the Fish Protective Facility. The Delta pumping plant lifts water nearly 250 feet into the California Aqueduct. The South Bay Aqueduct branches away at this point and delivers water to Santa Clara. The remaining water is then carried south 444 miles in the California Aqueduct and delivered to contractors in the Central Valley and southern California.

*Construction of the State Water Project has never been completed.*

*The Peripheral Canal is still seen by many as a solution to fish problems in the Delta.*

For many years, an isolated facility commonly known as the "peripheral canal" has been proposed as a method of diverting water north of the Delta and transporting it around the eastern side of the Delta to facilities south of the Delta. Although the proposal for a peripheral canal was badly defeated in a referendum in 1982, the concept is still under consideration.[35] A primary reason that an isolated Delta facility is still "alive," if not healthy, is because many water interests, including the Department of Fish and Game, believe that it is environmentally better to transfer water around the Delta than to pull it through the Delta with large pumps. Opposition to a peripheral canal has come mainly from those who believe that an isolated facility could dramatically decrease the amount of water flowing through the Delta and from those who are concerned about maintaining its ecology. This is discussed in greater detail in chapter 4.

[34] Delta Water Facilities Bulletin 76, July 1978, page 25.
[35] Department of Water Resources Bulletin 160-87, page 77.

## CHAPTER TWO
# Water Rights in California[1]

## Introduction to Water Rights

### General

Water law in California is complex, incorporating aspects of century old mining customs, English common law, judicial and administrative decisions, statutes, and local ordinances. California recognizes several categories of water rights, each relating to various characteristics of the water. Water rights in surface waters are generally classified as riparian, appropriative, or prescriptive, while water rights for underground waters are classified according to water type (percolating, underflow, or underground stream) and use (overlying, appropriative or riparian, or prescriptive). Water rights are usufructuary, a right to the use of water, not a right to own it.

*California water "law" is a complex mixture of court decisions, statutes, State Board rulings, and local controls.*

The type of right that attaches to a water source is important, particularly in light of the existing demands for agriculture, the growing demands from urban users, and environmental needs, coupled with a limited developed supply. The following chapter provides an overview of California water rights law for both surface and underground water.

### Water Rights as Real Property Rights

Water rights traditionally have been considered as rights in real property. *San Bernardino v. Riverside* (1921) 186 Cal. 7, 13; *San Francisco v. Alameda County* (1936) 5 Cal.2d 243, 245-247. A riparian

*Water rights have traditionally been treated as real property rights.*

---

[1]  The principal author of this chapter was Michelle Ouellette.

right is "part and parcel" of riparian land, and the right to the flow is real property. *Title Ins. & Trust Co. v. Miller & Lux* (1920) 183 Cal. 71, 81. Real property remedies are therefore available for riparian rights. *Miller & Lux v. Enterprise Canal & Land Co.* (1915) 169 Cal. 415, 444. An appropriative right is also an interest in real property. *Wright v. Best* (1942) 19 Cal.2d 368, 382. Thus, appropriative rights may be, but are not necessarily, appurtenant to the land. If they are appurtenant, the right is incidental to the land. *Wright,* pages 377-378. Percolating water rights are also real property rights. *Stanislaus Water Co. v. Bachman* (1908) 152 Cal. 716, 725. The right to use percolating waters is part and parcel of the land. *Pasadena v. Alhambra* (1949) 33 Cal.2d 908, 925; *Rank v. Krug* (S.D. Cal. 1950) 90 F.Supp. 773, 787.

## Reasonable, Beneficial Use of All Water in California

*The reasonable use requirements of the Constitution apply to all uses of water, including water for instream or environmental purposes.*

Article X, Section 2, of the California Constitution, which applies to all water rights and prohibits waste of water, requires reasonableness of use, method of use, and method of diversion for all uses of water. Cal. Const. art. X, § 2. This includes the use of water for instream or environmental purposes. Wat. Code § 1243; *National Audubon Society v. Superior Court* (1983) 33 Cal.3d 419, 443. To the extent the use is wasteful or otherwise unreasonable, it is not part of a water right. *Joslin v. Marin Municipal Water Dist.* (1967) 67 Cal.2d 132, 141-145. Each riparian is limited to reasonable, beneficial use pursuant to Article X, Section 2, subject to reasonable uses made by the upstream riparians.[2] Cal. Const. art. X, § 2. The reasonableness of a riparian use can only be ascertained after determining the water needs of other riparians along the same watercourse. *Pabst v. Finmand* (1922) 190 Cal. 124, 129.

Water obtained pursuant to an appropriative right must also be put to reasonable, beneficial use, or the right may be forfeited. *Erickson v. Queen Valley Ranch* (1971) 22 Cal.App.3d 578; Cal. Const. art. X, § 2; Water Code § 1240 and § 1241. The State Water Resources Control Board ("State Board") is directed to take all appropriate action to prevent the waste or misuse of water in the state. Water Code § 275; Cal. Code Regs., tit. 23, §§ 4000-4007. Beneficial uses include mining, irrigation of cropped and uncropped land, agricultural, power, industrial, and municipal uses. Water Code §§ 1262-65; *Antioch v. Williams* (1922) 188 Cal. 451, 467-468; For a complete list of codified, beneficial uses, *see* Cal. Code Regs., tit. 23, § 659 *et seq.*

**State Board = State Water Resources Control Board**

---

[2]  Hutchins, *The California Law of Water Rights,* 1956, page 81; Anderson, *Riparian Water Rights in California,* Governor's Commission to Review California Water Rights, Staff Paper No. 4, 1977, page 30.

The correlative rights doctrine discussed below, together with Article X, Section 2, gives an owner of land overlying a groundwater basin a right to the reasonable, beneficial use of a share of the basin's supply for use on or in connection with the overlying land. *Lodi v. East Bay Municipal Utility Dist.* (1936) 7 Cal.2d 316, 338; *Tulare Irrigation Dist. v. Lindsay-Strathmore Irr. Dist.* (1935) 3 Cal.2d 489, 524-526.

## Types of Water Rights

### Riparian Water Rights

***Introduction.*** In California, most surface water rights are governed by two doctrines: (1) the riparian doctrine and (2) the doctrine of prior appropriation. *United States v. State Water Resources Control Bd.* (1986) 182 Cal.App.3d 82, 101. Riparian water rights have been an important part of state water rights since the mid-1800s. A riparian right is the right to the use of water as a result of the ownership of property that abuts a natural watercourse. *Lux v. Haggin* (1886) 69 Cal. 255, 390-391. This water right gives the owner of a parcel of land contiguous to a watercourse the right to divert water for reasonable, beneficial use on that property. *People v. Shirokow* (1980) 26 Cal.3d 301, 307. A riparian right is not gained by use, nor generally lost by disuse, but is part and parcel of the land.

*A riparian right results from the ownership of land that abuts a natural stream.*

Unlike an appropriative right, a riparian right is not quantified, but is instead a right to use a portion of the natural flow of the water in common with other riparian users. *Pabst,* page 129. This is called a "correlative right." Each riparian may apply as much water to the riparian land as is necessary to make a reasonable, beneficial use of the land, as long as other riparians are not injured. *Gin S. Chow v. Santa Barbara* (1933) 217 Cal. 673, 695. The amount reasonably needed by an owner is a question of fact to be determined after an analysis of the circumstances of each particular case. *Deetz v. Carter* (1965) 232 Cal.App.2d 851, 856. In times of water shortage, all riparians must decrease their water use and share the available water. *United States v. State Water Resources Control Board* (1986) 182 Cal.App.3d 82, 104.

*A riparian right is not quantified; rather, it is the right held in common with other riparians to take the amount necessary for reasonable use on the land.*

### Development of the Riparian Right in California

*Early history of riparian rights.* The origin of riparian water rights is found in English common law. The riparian doctrine developed from the concept that legal access to water was generally limited to those who owned property contiguous to a watercourse.[3]

---

[3] Shaw, *Development of the Law of Waters in the West,* 1922, 189 Cal. 779, 783.

*The doctrine of riparian rights originated in England and was adopted in California as part of the English common law.*

*Appropriative rights arise from mining customs in early California.*

*The dual system of riparian and appropriative rights was established by the California Supreme Court in 1886.*

The riparian doctrine was applied in the eastern United States, eventually gaining recognition in some western states, including California. In 1850, the first legislature in California passed the Act of April 13, 1850 which stated that—

> The common law of England, so far as it is not repugnant to or inconsistent with the constitution of the United States, or the constitution or laws of this state, is the rule of decision in all the courts of this state. *Gin Chow,* page 695.

Because of this provision, several early court decisions recognized riparian rights based upon private ownership of land. (*Los Angeles v. Baldwin* (1879) 53 Cal. 469; *Pope v. Kinman* (1879) 54 Cal. 3; *Cave v. Crafts* (1878) 53 Cal. 135.)

Appropriative rights, recognized by the California Supreme Court in the early case of *Irwin v. Phillips* (1855) 5 Cal. 140, 145-147, also existed at this time, primarily as a practice of miners. The custom arose in mining camps on public lands because no one could own the land, and thus no one could get a riparian right. The California legislature regulated water rights in 1872 through the enactment of Civil Code provisions, codifying customs such as prior appropriation. Civ. Code §§ 1410-22 (1872, 1913); §§ 1410b-1413 have been repealed. Specifically, Civil Code Section 1410 stated that "[t]he right to use running water flowing in a river or stream, or down a canyon or ravine may be acquired by appropriation." Civ. Code § 1410 (1872). Civil Code Section 1422 stated that "[t]he rights of riparian proprietors are not affected by the provisions of this title." Civ. Code § 1422 (1872); now repealed. Thus, battle lines were drawn between those opposing riparian rights (individuals without riparian land, typically miners operating on public domain property) and the riparians who worried about losing their water rights to upstream appropriators.

**Lux v. Haggin.** The conflict between riparian and appropriative rights was addressed by the Supreme Court in 1886 in the celebrated case of *Lux v. Haggin* (1886) 69 Cal. 255, when the court established the dual doctrine of riparian and appropriative rights. The case involved the water rights of a downstream riparian rancher and an upstream appropriator on the Kern River, each claiming a superior right to the use of water. The court, recognizing both the riparian and appropriative doctrines, found that riparian rights had been recognized in California since the 1850 Act, which had "operated a transfer" of California's water rights to riparian owners. *Lux,* page 338. The court explained that the United States held common law water rights in non-navigable watercourses that flowed through the public domain. Public domain lands, which comprised the majority of western lands, were transferred by federal patents and state grants to private ownership and included the transfer of riparian water rights. The court held that the Civil Code sections addressing water rights established riparian rights as "paramount" to the rights of nonriparians in certain instances. *Lux,* pages 345-374. The court also held that a riparian was limited to taking a reasonable quantity of water without harming other riparian owners.

In 1913, the legislature took additional action to clarify water rights law through the enactment of the Water Commission Act. Stat. 1913, ch. 586, p. 1012. The Act provided the exclusive method for acquiring *new* appropriative rights through the establishment of a commission to administer the Act. Water Code § 174 *et seq.* (The commission ultimately evolved into the State Board.) The Water Commission Act does not apply to groundwater, riparian rights, or appropriative rights acquired prior to its enactment. The role of the State Board is discussed more fully in chapter 6.

***Constitutional Amendment of 1928.*** The dual system of water rights recognized in *Lux v. Haggin* continued to exist, with riparian rights generally being paramount to appropriative rights. *Lux v. Haggin* required riparians to use water reasonably vis-à-vis other riparians but was silent with regard to whether the same obligation was owed to appropriators. The issue of whether a riparian was required to exercise reasonableness with regard to nonriparians was first addressed in 1926 when the California Supreme Court heard another dispute between a riparian and an appropriator. In *Herminghaus v. Southern California Edison Co.* (1926) 200 Cal. 81, the court held that a downstream riparian had the right to use the entire flow of the San Joaquin River to flood pastureland for the reclamation of soil and for irrigation, thus preventing the upstream development of a power project pursuant to an appropriative right. The riparian's use of water resulted in the waste of huge amounts of water, and the appropriator argued that the supply was adequate to meet the needs of both parties if the water was used more efficiently. Nonetheless, the California Supreme Court declared that although riparians were required to be reasonable with regard to one another, if a riparian's use of water was beneficial, the riparian was under no duty to an appropriator to use water reasonably or to utilize a reasonable method of diversion.

In direct response to the *Herminghaus* decision, the California Constitution was amended in 1928, broadening existing law to require all water to be used in a reasonable, beneficial manner. Cal. Const. art. X, § 2, originally Cal. Const. art. XIV, § 3 (1928, amended

*The 1928 constitutional amendment required riparian use to be reasonable vis-à-vis competing appropriative uses.*

1976). While preserving riparian rights, Article X, Section 2, declares that the right to the use or flow of water in or from any natural stream or watercourse in California is limited to water reasonably required for beneficial use. The 1928 amendment read, in pertinent part—

It is hereby declared because of the conditions prevailing in this State the general welfare requires that the water resources of the State be put to beneficial use to the fullest extent of which they are capable, and that the waste or unreasonable use or unreasonable method of use of water be prevented, and that the conservation of such waters is to be exercised with a view to the reasonable and beneficial use thereof in the interest of the people and for the public welfare. The right to water or to the use or flow of water in or from any natural stream or watercourse in this State is and shall be limited to such water as shall be reasonably required for the beneficial use to be served, and such right does not and shall not extend to the waste or unreasonable use or unreasonable method of use or unreasonable method of diversion of water. . . .

Specifically addressing riparian rights, the amendment continued—

Riparian rights in a stream or watercourse attach to, but to no more than so much of the flow thereof as may be required or used consistently with this section, for the purpose for which such lands are or may be made adaptable, in view of such reasonable and beneficial uses; provided, however, that nothing herein contained shall be construed as depriving any riparian owner of the reasonable use of water of the stream to which his land is riparian under reasonable methods of diversion and use. . . . Cal. Const. art. X, § 2.

As a result, riparian rights in a watercourse continued to exist, but riparian use was required to be reasonable with regard to other water users, whether riparian or appropriative. One court stated that—

The primary purpose of the amendment was to modify the existing riparian doctrine of this state, and apply the rule of reasonableness of use to water controversies between a riparian owner and an appropriator, thus extending the application of that rule to every water right and to every method of diversion. *State of California v. Hansen* (1961) 189 Cal.App.2d 604, 609.

### Nature and Extent of Riparian Right

***Waters to which the riparian right attaches.*** Water rights, termed "usufructuary rights," do not actually extend to ownership of the corpus of water as it flows in the stream, but extend only to the use of water. *Rancho Santa Margarita v. Vail* (1938) 11 Cal.2d, 501, 554-555. Riparian rights confer upon the owner of land contiguous to the watercourse the right to a reasonable and beneficial use of water on his land (*Shirokow,* pages 301, 307), but these rights attach only if the water is actually contiguous to the land. *Miller & Lux v. Enterprise Canal & Land Co.* (1915) 169 Cal. 415, 441.

Riparian rights apply to waters contained in natural watercourses as well as artificial channels that have been accepted by long use and acquiescence as a natural watercourse (*Chowchilla Farms v. Martin* (1933) 219 Cal. 1). Riparian rights may extend to non-navigable streams and rivers (*Fall River Valley Irr. Dist. v. Mt. Shasta Power Corp.* (1927) 202 Cal. 56, 58, 65); lakes and ponds (*Turner v. James Canal Co.* (1909) 155 Cal. 82, 87-88); the underflow of streams and rivers (*Rancho Santa Margarita* at 555); definite underground streams and rivers (*Prather v. Hoberg* (1944) 24 Cal.2d 549); and abandoned or escaped waters (*Lindblom v. Round Valley Water Co.* (1918) 178 Cal. 450, 457). The same riparian rules and priorities apply to lakes and are termed littoral rights. *Elsinore v. Temescal Water Co.* (1939) 36 Cal.App. 2d 116, 129-130. However, riparian rights do not apply to percolating groundwater, and groundwater is presumed to be percolating water. *Arroyo Ditch & Water Company v. Baldwin* (1909) 155 Cal. 280, 284.

*Riparian rights extend to waters contained in natural water courses, including lakes and the underflow of rivers and streams.*

A riparian right does not extend downstream after the water is used and passes the riparian's land. *Holmes v. Nay* (1921) 186 Cal. 231, 234, 235-237. Instead, after use by an upstream riparian, any water that remains must be returned to the natural watercourse for the use of the downstream riparians. *Seneca Consolidated Gold Mines v. Great Western Power Co.* (1930) 209 Cal. 206, 215-17. Additionally, water cannot be required to flow past a riparian's property for aesthetics. *Meridian, Ltd. v. San Francisco* (1939) 13 Cal.2d 424, 447. Riparian rights also do not attach to foreign or imported water (waters brought into an area from a different watershed). *Bloss v. Rahilly* (1940) 16 Cal.2nd 70.

**Lands to which the riparian right attaches.** A parcel of property must meet three criteria before a riparian right attaches to it. First, the property must be contiguous to the watercourse, except in the instance where a riparian right has been preserved in noncontiguous parcels after the land has been subdivided. The length of the property's frontage on the watercourse does not affect the riparian right. *Rancho Santa Margarita,* page 528. Because a riparian water right is "part and parcel" of riparian property, a document transferring such land typically transfers the riparian rights as well, unless it expressly provides that the rights do not go with the land. *Holmes v. Nay* (1921) 186 Cal. 231, 236. Land adjoining riparian land but not contiguous with the watercourse cannot become riparian simply

*The criteria for "riparian land"*

through common ownership, even if such land is located within the watershed of the stream. *Miller & Lux v. James* (1919) 180 Cal. 38, 51-52. Similarly, if land is severed and becomes noncontiguous to the water source, the property loses its riparian character. *Anaheim Union Water Co. v. Fuller* (1907) 150 Cal. 327, 331. However, property that overlies the subsurface portion of a stream which is not contiguous to the surface water does have riparian rights to the subsurface portion of the stream, but not to surface flow. *Peabody v. City of Vallejo* (1935) 2 Cal.2d 351, 375-376.

The second criteria is that the "riparian right extends only to the smallest tract held under one title in the chain of title leading to the present owner." *Rancho Santa Margarita,* page 529. The "source of title" rule means that the riparian parcel may never become larger than the original parcel size, but may become smaller through the severance of riparian rights from noncontiguous parcels when a riparian tract is subdivided. *Title Ins. and Trust Co. v. Miller & Lux, Inc.* (1920) 183 Cal. 71, 82.

Finally, the land must be within the watershed of the watercourse. *Rancho Santa Margarita,* pages 528-529; *Anaheim Union,* page 330. Property is within the watershed if the water used upon the land, or rain runoff from the land, naturally runs to the stream. *Duckworth v. Watsonville Water & Light Co.* (1915) 170 Cal. 425, 430-431. Thus, any unused water will return to the watercourse for the benefit of downstream riparian water users—

> The principal reasons for the rule confining riparian rights to that part of lands bordering on the stream which are within the watershed are, that where the water is used on such land it will, after such use, return to the stream, so far as it is not consumed.... *Anaheim Union,* page 330.

One California Supreme Court decision held that federally owned national forest land can have riparian rights. *In re Rights to Water of Hallett Creek Stream System* (1988) 44 Cal.3d 448, 467. However, the State Board in this statutory adjudication proceeding may subordinate the United States' unexercised riparian rights to appropriative and riparian rights currently being used. *Hallett Creek,* page 471.

***Holders of a riparian right.*** Riparian rights can be held both by governmental agencies and by private individuals. Thus, both the United States and California can have riparian rights to water running through lands they own.[4] *Palmer v. Railroad Commission* (1914) 167 Cal. 163, 168. However, the existence of federal riparian rights in

---

4   Rogers and Nichols, *Water for California,* 1967, § 167, pages 228-230.

public domain lands is in dispute. Municipalities can have riparian rights as a result of the ownership of riparian land, but a municipality cannot divert riparian water for use on nonriparian land.[5] The only way a city can use a riparian right is on its own riparian land, such as at a park or golf course. A city's riparian rights do not extend to its municipal water supply customers. *San Bernardino v. Riverside* (1921) 186 Cal. 7, 25. Additionally, city boundaries are irrelevant to the determination of riparian rights, so city boundaries which border a watercourse do not give a municipality a riparian right unless the city actually owns the property. *Antioch v. Williams* (1922) 188 Cal. 451, 456. If a city acquires property with riparian rights, these water rights can be acquired for public use by condemnation. *Lux,* page 300.

*A municipal water supplier holds appropriative rights and does not generally exercise the riparian or overlying rights of its inhabitant customers.*

### Acquisition and Loss of Riparian Rights

**Acquisition.** Riparian rights are typically acquired by ownership of riparian land. Because riparian rights run with the land and are not lost through nonuse, title to the rights is acquired as part of the property purchase. *Lux,* page 391. In a statutory adjudication of stream rights, however, an unused riparian right can be accorded a junior priority. *In re Rights to Waters of Long Valley Creek Stream System* (1979) 25 Cal.3d 339.

*A riparian right is not lost by nonuse but may be accorded a junior priority in a statutory adjudication.*

A property owner can reserve the riparian rights in a property transfer and subsequently use those rights on another parcel of riparian property. *Forest Lakes Mutual Water Co. v. Santa Cruz Land Title Co.* (1929) 98 Cal.App. 489, 495-496. However, this operates as an estoppel on the riparian land which lost its water rights, and use of the water elsewhere is not the exercise of a riparian right. If the conveyance does not reserve any riparian rights, such rights are automatically conveyed as part of the land. *Holmes,* pages 236-238.

#### Loss/severance of right

Conveyance of right. Riparian rights can be severed from the property and transferred to another party, leaving the former riparian land without riparian rights. *Duckworth v. Watsonville Water & Light Co.* (1907) 150 Cal. 520, 526. A riparian can convey all or a portion of the rights separately. *Holmes,* pages 236-237.

Loss of contiguity to water. Riparian rights can also be severed through the loss of contiguity of the land to the watercourse. *United States v. Fallbrook Pub. Util. Dist.* (1961) 193 F.Supp. 342, 347-348; *Rancho Santa Margarita,* page 538. This can occur by physical changes such as avulsion or by legal changes such as subdivision. However,

*A riparian right can be lost by severing the land from the river.*

---

[5]  Hutchins, page 207.

riparian rights are not severed if the parties to the sale intended to preserve the rights in the detached parcels, either through language in the sale agreement or by implication. *Hudson v. Dailey* (1909) 156 Cal. 617, 624-625. After riparian rights are severed from the land due to loss of contiguity, the rights will not be regained if the property is subsequently reconveyed into one ownership. *Anaheim Union,* page 331.

Condemnation. Riparian rights can also be severed from land through condemnation by a public agency for a public purpose. *Miller & Lux v. Madera Canal & Irr. Co.* (1909) 155 Cal. 59, 65. Article X, Section 5, specifically contemplates the condemnation of water rights for public uses. Cal. Const. art. X, § 5. Riparian rights can also be severed through inverse condemnation when a governmental agency takes water for a public use and fails to compensate the holder of the riparian rights. *Collier v. Merced Irr. Dist.* (1931) 213 Cal. 554, 563-564.

Prescription. Because riparian water rights are real property rights, these rights may be lost by prescription. *Pasadena,* pages 926-927. By definition, a prescriptive water right holder has a higher priority right than the original owner from whom the right is taken. If a water user takes water and thereby injures a lawful riparian right in a manner which is open, notorious, hostile, exclusive, continuous, and under claim of right, that use of water can result in a legal cause of action. Failure to sue on that cause of action for a period of five years can result in a legal determination that the riparian right has been lost. *Pasadena,* pages 926-927.

The amount of the riparian right lost by the riparian and gained by the prescriptor is the amount of water applied by the prescriptive user to a reasonable, beneficial use under reasonable methods of diversion and use. *E. Clemens Horst Co. v. Tarr Mining Co.* (1917) 174 Cal. 430. In order for prescription to run, there must be an invasion of a riparian's present reasonable, beneficial use, and prescription cannot run against surplus water. *Rank,* page 113. A prescriptive right cannot be gained by a downstream user of water against an upstream riparian because, once water has flowed past upstream riparian land, the downstream use would not cause any injury to the upstream user and therefore would not be adverse. *Orange Co. Water Dist. v. City of Riverside* (1959) 173 Cal.App.2d 137, 185. It is commonly stated that "prescription does not run upstream."

Abandonment/nonuse. Unlike some other water rights, riparian rights cannot be abandoned or lost through nonuse (except as the priority may be subordinated in a statutory adjudication).[6]

---

[6]   Hutchins, pages 285, 291.

*A prescriptive water right holder has a higher priority right than the original owner from whom the right is taken.*

Loss of priority. In the decision of *In re Rights to Waters of Long Valley Creek Stream System* (1979) 25 Cal.3d 339, a statutory adjudication proceeding, the California Supreme Court held that, while they cannot be extinguished in the statutory adjudication process, in certain situations unexercised riparian rights can be subordinated to all presently exercised riparian *and* appropriative rights. In this circumstance, when a riparian seeks to activate a dormant right, application must first be made either to the State Board or to the superior court. *Long Valley Creek,* page 359, fn. 15. Such rights will be incorporated into the court decree from the adjudication, but the date of priority will be the date of the riparian's application. Thus, the riparian right will be subordinate to all rights recognized in the original decree and to any rights granted after the original decree before the date of the riparian's application. *Long Valley Creek,* pages 358-359.

### Priority/Interrelationship with Other Rights

#### Rights between riparians

Correlative rights. Riparians do not have a right to a predetermined amount of water. *Prather,* pages 559-561. Instead, riparian rights in water are held in common with all riparian users on a watercourse. *Seneca Consolidated Gold Mines v. Great Western Power Co.* (1930) 209 Cal. 206, 220. These "correlative rights" allow the use of water on riparian land if the rights of the other riparians along the watercourse are not injured. *Gin Chow,* page 695; *Pabst v. Finmand* (1922) 190 Cal. 124, 129. Water shortages are shared by all riparian owners. *Harris v. Harrison* (1892) 93 Cal. 676, 681-682. Unlike appropriators, who are subject to a first-in-time, first-in-right doctrine, a riparian owner does not have a priority over other riparian owners along the same watercourse due to earlier use in time. *Gin Chow,* page 695.

*A riparian owner does not have a priority over other riparians due to earlier use of the water.*

#### Rights between riparians and appropriators. Traditionally, a riparian right has been "prior and paramount" to an appropriative right. *Meridian, Ltd. v. San Francisco* (1939) 13 Cal.2d 424, 445. In the past, in times of shortage, riparians were entitled to fulfill their needs before appropriators were entitled to any use of the water. *United States v. State Water Resources Control Board* (1986) 182 Cal.App.3d 82, 101-102.

*Generally, a riparian right is "prior and paramount" to an appropriative right.*

However, several cases decided after the 1928 constitutional amendment have limited a riparian's use of water against an appropriator under the reasonable use requirement. In *Peabody v. City of Vallejo* (1935) 2 Cal.2d 351, the California Supreme Court held that a riparian plaintiff did not have the right to use stream flow for the purpose of depositing silt and leaching salts on riparian land. The plaintiff had protested the defendant city's proposed storage of water during high-flow periods, since this upstream appropriation would damage his riparian use of water for leaching salts. The court held that the downstream riparian's use of stream flow was an unreasonable use of water that conflicted with the police powers of the state in conservation of its waters. *Peabody*, page 369. "The rule of reasonableness" therefore allowed the appropriation of water for domestic uses to prevail over the riparian's claim to the full flow of the stream. *Peabody,* pages 367-371.

In *Joslin v. Marin Municipal Water District* (1967) 67 Cal.2d 132, the court balanced the social utility of the municipal use of water against the use of water for the accumulation of gravel. In *Joslin*, the court reviewed a dispute between an appropriator of water for municipal purposes and a riparian owner who relied on the flow of the stream to deliver gravel to his land for use in a business. The court held that the use of water for gravel transport was unreasonable as a matter of law under Article X, Section 2, and that no right attaches to unreasonable use. *Joslin*, page 141.

*Reasonable use is a question of fact depending upon a case by case determination.*

The courts, including the *Joslin* court, have uniformly determined that reasonableness is a question of fact depending on a case-by-case determination. *Tulare,* page 567. Beneficial uses must be compared to determine the advantages of competing claims to a stream flow that cannot satisfy all needs. *Imperial Irr. Dist. v. State Water Resources Control Bd.* (1990) 225 Cal.App.3d 548, 570. The reasonableness of a riparian use cannot be determined without considering its effect "on the needs of those in the stream system," presumably including appropriators as well as other riparians. Moreover, reasonable use cannot be made "*in vacuo* isolated from statewide consideration of transcendent importance." *Long Valley,* page 354.

### Limitations on Exercise of Riparian Right

*Use of the water.* Riparians are limited in the method and location of use of water. The water may be used on or in connection with any portion of the riparian property, but it cannot be used off the property. *People v. Shirokow* (1980) 26 Cal.3d 301, 307. A riparian's use of water on nonriparian land would result in a trespass upon the rights of the lower riparians. *Moore v. California Oregon Power Co.* (1943) 22 Cal.2d 725, 734.

*A riparian right may not be exercised on nonriparian land.*

Additionally, riparian rights do not extend to the use of riparian water on other riparian lands, even if the tract is riparian to the same stream. *Parker v. Swett* (1922) 188 Cal. 474, 479. Neither do riparians have the right to injure other riparians by selling water outside the watershed. However, the riparian right is not lost by diverting water across nonriparian lands. *Fall River Valley Irr. Dist. v. Mt. Shasta* (1927) 202 Cal. 56, 71-72.

## Appropriative Water Rights

***Introduction.*** The second major doctrine governing surface water rights in California is the law of appropriative rights, which exists concurrently with the doctrine of riparian rights. *Lux v. Haggin* (1886) 69 Cal. 255.

An appropriative right is the right to divert and use a specific quantity of water for reasonable, beneficial use in a specific location. Unlike the riparian rights doctrine, the historic principle of the prior appropriation doctrine is "first-in-time, first-in-right." An individual who first appropriates and uses water for a reasonable, beneficial purpose has a right which is superior to that of later appropriators. *Irwin v. Phillips* (1855) 5 Cal. 140, 147; *Shirokow,* pages 307-308; Water Code § 1450.

*The traditional rule among appropriators is "first-in-time, first-in-right."*

When the amount of water available is insufficient to meet the needs of all appropriators, traditional case law holds that junior appropriators can be prevented from exercising their rights until the water rights of senior appropriators are satisfied. However, this rule seems impractical today, since the cities and water districts providing urban water supplies generally hold appropriative rights. *San Bernardino v. Riverside* (1921) 186 Cal. 7; *Orange County Water District v. City of Riverside* (1959) 173 Cal.App.2d 137. Because it is generally unrealistic to terminate such uses completely, courts can be seen to be moving away from a strict application of the first-in-time doctrine in order to protect established uses. *See Los Angeles v. San Fernando* (1975) 14 Cal.3d 199, 265, fn. 61.; *United States v. State Water Resources Control Bd.* (1986) 182 Cal.App.3d 82, 133.

The law of prior appropriation has been adopted by the legislature (*see* generally Water Code §§ 100 *et seq.*, §§ 120 *et seq.*, §§ 175 *et seq.*; Civil Code §§ 1410(a) *et seq.*) and the courts. *Yuba River Power Co. v. Nevada Irr. Dist.* (1929) 207 Cal. 521, 526; *Thayer v. California Development Co.* (1912) 164 Cal. 117, 125-126. *Temescal Water Co. v. Department of Public Works* (1955) 44 Cal.2d 90, 95. All waters in excess of the reasonable and beneficial needs of lawful users, including riparians, are considered unappropriated waters and are available for appropriation for beneficial use. *Stevinson Water Dist. v. Roduner* (1950) 36 Cal.2d 264, 269-270. Water that is diverted pursuant to an appropriative right may be used on or in connection with lands away from streams or outside a watershed, as well as on

Hydraulic gold mining more than 100 years ago—an early "appropriative" water right

lands contiguous to streams. *Gallatin v. Corning Irr. Co.* (1912) 163 Cal. 405, 413. However, this use may be governed by other provisions, such as area-of-origin limitations and the needs of fish and wildlife, which are now beneficial uses. Water Code §§ 10505, 11460, 11461.

### Development of the Appropriative Right in California

#### Appropriative rights prior to 1872.

Appropriative water rights were developed in California to satisfy the requirements of miners who moved to the state when gold was discovered in the mid-1800s. Miners typically did not own the land they worked, and water was often diverted to supply placer and hydraulic mining claims and other operations that were located far away from water supplies. Typically, they mined in federal public domain, unsurveyed and thus unpatentable at the time.[7] This lack of property ownership and use of water away from the watercourse prevented a claim of a riparian right. Because there was no official state government at that time, the miners developed their own custom of apportioning water based on the concept of "first in time, first in right." Under this custom, the first water user was entitled to divert all the water needed from a stream, and a later user could be forced to stop or reduce diversions if the supply were insufficient for all. The miners were required to act diligently and put water to beneficial use or they risked forfeiting their rights, which was known as the "use it or lose it" rule.[8]

*Before 1872, appropriative rights were developed under court rules.*

The customs and regulations of the miners were recognized and adopted by the California Supreme Court in one of its earliest decisions concerning water rights, *Irwin v. Phillips. Irwin,* page 146. In *Irwin,* the plaintiff owned a canal that diverted water to mining operations away from a stream. The defendants were miners who arrived in the area at a later point in time, setting up their mining operations on public domain land contiguous to a stream. The court found that the defendants who claimed riparian rights did not have the necessary ownership of the land and that the issue was controlled by appropriative rules. The court then decided the case according to the first-in-time, first-in-right, prior appropriation doctrine, holding that between two users of water on public domain lands the water user

---

[7]  Rogers and Nichols, § 4, pages 21-22.
[8]  Hutchins, pages 41-43.

who was first-in-time had a superior right, regardless of the location being contiguous or noncontiguous to a stream. *Irwin,* page 147.

The appropriation doctrine, which originally was applied only to the mineral regions of the state, was judicially expanded to cover other uses, establishing priorities between mining, agricultural, and other claims. *See Rupley v. Welch* (1863) 23 Cal. 452, 455-457; *Gillan v. Hutchinson* (1860) 16 Cal. 153, 156. Water was considered to be appropriated if diverted and used for the intended purpose before another user intervened and claimed a right to it. No notice of the claim was required to be posted or recorded. *De Necochea v. Curtis* (1889) 80 Cal. 397, 408. Miners did occasionally post a notice of appropriation, but this notice was invalid unless the appropriator constructed the diversion works and put the water to beneficial use. *Weaver v. Eureka Lake Co.* (1860) 15 Cal. 271, 274. Thus, although the priority was established as of the date of the notice, the right to appropriate did not vest until the diversion works were completed and the water was actually used. *Nevada County v. Kidd* (1869) 37 Cal. 282, 311.

**Appropriative rights from 1872 to 1914.** Before 1872, the appropriative rights doctrine evolved solely through court decisions. In 1872, the legislature formally recognized the prior appropriation doctrine through the enactment of Civil Code Sections 1410-1422. (This principle is still embodied in § 1414.) The code provided: "As between appropriators, the first in time is the first in right." Civ. Code § 1414 (1872). This legislation also codified an alternative appropriation procedure to the customs established earlier by the miners, although appropriation still depended upon the taking and possession of the water.

*In 1872, the California legislature established an alternate procedure for acquiring an appropriative right.*

The new appropriation procedure in place between 1872 and 1914 required a potential appropriator to both post a notice in a conspicuous place at the point of diversion and record the notice with the office of the county recorder within ten days of posting. The notice had to provide specific information, such as the amount of water to be diverted, the means of diversion, and the purpose and place of use. Civ. Code § 1415 (1872). The appropriator had to begin construction work within sixty days of posting the notice and to work diligently and continually to deliver water to the planned location of the use. Civ. Code §§ 1416-1417 (1872).

*The new procedure called for posting and recording notice; it did not replace earlier methods.*

No actual permission was required from the state to appropriate water under these Civil Code sections. Instead, the amount of water an appropriator could divert was limited to the amount that could be applied to beneficial use pursuant to reasonable methods of diversion and up to the amount stated in the notice. Holders of appropriative rights could change the point of diversion, the place of use, and the

*Under the new statutory procedure, no state permission was required in order to appropriate water.*

purpose of the use (for example, from agricultural to domestic) as long as other right holders were not injured by the change. *Ramelli v. Irish* (1892) 96 Cal. 214, 217.

If Civil Code provisions were followed, the priority of use of the water "related back" to the original time of posting the notice. Civ. Code § 1418 (1872). Since in some instances the entire amount of water intended to be used for a beneficial use could not be immediately utilized, the use could be established over time if the project were diligently pursued, but it could not exceed the amount stated in the notice. The priority for the entire amount of water then related back to the time the appropriation began. As between statutory and nonstatutory appropriators, only a nonstatutory appropriation completed before the posting of statutory notice had a right prior to one obtained through a notice procedure. *Yuba River Power Co. v. Nevada Irr. Dist.* (1929) 207 Cal. 521, 524-525.

Between 1872 and 1914, the statutory method was not the exclusive way to acquire water rights. Water could still be appropriated simply by taking water and putting it to reasonable use. *Lower Tule River Ditch Co. v. Angiola Water Co.* (1906) 149 Cal. 496, 499.

*Effective in 1914, the state established a permit system to appropriate stream flow.*

**Water Commission Act (1913).** The Water Commission Act, established in 1913 (Stat. 1913, ch. 586, p. 1012) (effective December 19, 1914), resulted in substantial changes in the method for appropriating water. This system is the basis for the appropriation procedure found today in the California Water Code. Water Code §§ 1200 *et seq.*

The Act provides that all water within the state is the property of the people of the state and that the right to use water can be acquired by law. Water Code § 102. A permit system was established to allow the Water Commission (now the State Water Resources Control Board) to allocate the state's unappropriated surface waters. These include subterranean streams flowing through known and definite channels as well as the underflow of surface streams. The Act's procedures have become the exclusive manner to obtain such new appropriative rights in California. *People v. Shirokow* (1980) 26 Cal.3d 301, 309. Although a valid appropriative right to such waters can now be acquired only by filing an application with proper state authorities and by pursuing the appropriation through the necessary steps required by the Act, pre-1914 rights obtained under the previous methods are still valid.

*This system does not invalidate pre-1914 rights but is the exclusive procedure for acquiring new rights.*

The Water Commission's authority to issue permits was originally ministerial; that is, if an application complied with all procedures and unappropriated water was available, the commission was obliged to issue the permit. *Tulare Water Co. v. State Water Commission*

(1921) 187 Cal. 533, 536. The commission was ultimately granted the discretion to refuse a permit if the diversion would be detrimental to the public welfare.

*Current appropriation requirements.* The existing procedures for acquiring appropriative rights are based upon the requirements in the Water Commission Act. The State Board is now responsible for the allocation of appropriative rights in the state. Water Code §§ 174 *et seq.* Only surface water and subterranean streams flowing through known and definite channels can be appropriated through Water Code procedures; percolating groundwater cannot. Water Code § 1200. Water that can be appropriated is limited to—

> All water flowing in any natural channel, excepting so far as it has been or is being applied to useful and beneficial purposes upon, or in so far as it is or may be reasonably needed for useful and beneficial purposes upon lands riparian thereto, or otherwise appropriated, is hereby declared to be public water of the State and subject to appropriation in accordance with the provisions of this code. Water Code § 1201.

The statutory procedures for appropriating water are discussed in chapter 4.

The State Board does not regulate nonpermitted water rights. However, to maintain records of water use in the state, diverters of surface water or subterranean water that flows in known channels pursuant to a riparian right, pre-1914 right, or any other nonpermitted right, must file statements of diversion with the State Board. Water Code §§ 5100 *et seq.* These statements must include the source, point of diversion, place of use, and the amounts of water diverted or stored, and must be updated every three years. Water Code § 5103-04. Failure to file the statements of diversion of surface flows does not result in any penal consequences, although willful misstatements are subject to misdemeanor prosecution. Water Code § 5107-5108. Such statements may help to establish water use, preventing forfeiture of a water right through nonuse.

*Riparians and pre-1914 rights holders are supposed to file statements of diversion with the State Board, but there are no penal sanctions for failure to file.*

### Nature and Extent of Right

*Water to which the right attaches.* Waters in excess of the existing reasonable, beneficial needs of lawful users, including riparians, may be lawfully appropriated. *Stevinson,* pages 269-270; *Pasadena,* pages 925-926; Cal. Const. art. X, § 2. These include—

- Water in a running stream and in a lake (*Duckworth v. Watsonville Water & Light Co.* (1907) 150 Cal. 520, 528-529, 530)

- Water flowing in a natural channel (Water Code § 1201)
- Underground waters constituting a subterranean stream flowing through known, definite channels (Water Code § 1200)
- Spring waters (*Ely v. Ferguson* (1891) 91 Cal. 187; *De Wolfskill v. Smith* (1907) 5 Cal.App. 175, 181)
- Waters in navigable and interstate streams (*Waterford Irr. Dist. v. Turlock Irr. Dist.* (1920) 50 Cal.App. 213, 220)

Temporary waters, such as water available only at select times of the year or part-time flows, are also appropriable. *Tulare,* page 569.

*An appropriative right does not require land ownership or use of the water within the watershed.*

**Land on which the water can be used.** A water user is not required to own land to acquire an appropriative right (*Pasadena,* pages 925, 927; *see Duckworth v. Watsonville Water & Light Co.* (1907) 150 Cal. 520, 530-531; *Joerger v. Pacific Gas & Electric Co.* (1929) 207 Cal. 8, 34), but the appropriator must have legal access to the water source. Cal. Code Regs., tit. 23, § 775 *et seq.*

In contrast to the riparian doctrine, there is no prohibition against diverting appropriated water outside the watershed. *Gallatin,* page 413. An appropriator is, however, entitled to protection against the actions of others that would materially impact water quality. *Joerger,* pages 25-26.

**Who may appropriate.** The ability to appropriate water is very broad. Individuals, firms, associations, organizations, partnerships, and state and federal agencies may all appropriate water. Water Code §§ 1252, 1252.5. Municipal corporations are also entitled to appropriate water. Water Code §§ 106.5, 1203, 1460-1464. However,

*Water may not be appropriated for instream purposes.*

water may not be appropriated for instream purposes, that is, to require that water be left in a stream as opposed to diversions for consumptive uses. Diversion from the stream and some physical control of the water remains an essential element of an appropriative right. *Fullerton v. State Water Resources Control Board* (1979) 90 Cal.App.3d 590.

### Priority/Interrelationship with Other Water Rights

**Rights among appropriators.** Appropriative rights can be limited by the rights of other appropriators in the same waters under the first-in-time, first-in-right rule. *United States v. State Water Resources Control Board* (1986) 182 Cal.App.3d 82, 101-102. Traditionally, the prior appropriator takes the full quantity of water that has been appropriated, having a preferred right to the exclusive use of a definite amount of flow. *Joerger,* page 26. This right may also be subject to priorities; for example, some uses, such as domestic ones, are considered "higher" than others. Water Code § 106. The priority clearly applies if applications are competing for the same water, but no case law controls its application during water shortages. However, in *Lake Don Pedro CSD v. Merced Irr. Dist.* (Mariposa County Sup. Ct. (1992) No. 7066), the court entered a temporary restraining order requiring the reduction of reservoir releases for agricultural uses in order to guarantee a municipal supply.

As between statutory appropriators (between 1872 and 1913) and later Water Code appropriators, the first to post and record the notice or to file the application for a permit prevails. Civ. Code §§ 1418-1419 (1872); Water Code § 1450.

As between statutory and nonstatutory appropriators from 1872 to 1914, the former had priority if the notice was posted and recorded before the nonstatutory appropriator actually diverted the water and put it to a beneficial use.[9] However, the nonstatutory appropriator had priority to the extent of water diverted and put to beneficial use before the statutory appropriator had posted and recorded the notice as required by code. *Haight v. Costanich* (1920) 184 Cal. 426.

Senior appropriators cannot extend their use or make substantial changes so as to interfere with the rights of junior appropriators. *Senior v. Anderson* (1900) 130 Cal. 290, 297. As between upper and lower appropriators, the first in time rule applies regardless of location on the watercourse. *Hill v. King* (1857) 8 Cal. 336, 337-338.

### Limitations on Appropriative Rights

*Diversion/due diligence.* To establish an appropriative right, the appropriation must be completed within the time required by the State Board permit, with due diligence applied to the construction of diversion works. Water Code §§ 1395-1398. Appropriative water rights attach only to water actually used. No appropriative rights attach before the completion of the appropriation, but often "inchoate" (or pending) rights do attach if there is due diligence in the construction of diversion works. Water Code §§ 1460, 1462-1464.

For appropriative rights acquired after 1914, the Water Code provides that actual construction work upon the project must begin within the time specified in the permit to appropriate water, not less than sixty days from the date of the permit. Construction of the diversion works and utilization of the water for beneficial purposes must be done with due diligence in accordance with the statute, the terms of the permit, and the rules and regulations of the State Board. Water Code §§ 1395-1398. Diligence is primarily a question

*Appropriative rights require due diligence in the construction of necessary facilities and the use of the water.*

9   Rogers and Nichols, § 209, pages 301.

of fact to be decided on a case-by-case basis. *Haight,* page 435. Additionally, diligence depends on many factors such as the type of terrain, climate, construction difficulties, time requirements, and the time that water can be used. *Kimball v. Gearhart* (1859) 12 Cal. 27, 30. Municipalities have higher priorities in the use of water, and a less stringent standard of diligence in the construction of diversion works. Water Code §§ 1460, 1462-1464.

### Loss/severance of rights

Condemnation/prescription. An appropriative right can be lost in several ways, including through eminent domain or inverse condemnation. *San Joaquin & Kings River Canal Co. v. Stevinson* (1912) 164 Cal. 221, 225-227.

Prescription. Traditionally, a right may also be lost by prescription. If a continuous use of water is made which is adverse to an existing right, is uninterrupted for five years, and is open, notorious, exclusive, and under claim of right, the prior right may be lost. However, a right held by a public entity, including the state and the federal government, may not be lost by prescription. Civ. Code § 1007.

*Since 1914, a right to store water can be obtained against the state only through the permit process.*

Whether it has been legally possible since 1914 to acquire a diversion right by prescription—that is, by use alone without going through the permit process—has been the subject of litigation. In *People v. Shirokow* (1980) 26 Cal.3d 301, the California Supreme Court held that the permit process is the only means of acquiring an appropriative right (in this case to store water) against the state. However, it did not consider the issue of whether prescriptive rights may still exist as between private parties where the statutory appropriation procedure has not been followed. The court left undecided the issue of whether the prescriptive rights doctrine was valid among private parties.[10]

Abandonment. Appropriative rights may be lost by abandonment. *Wood v. Etiwanda Water Co.* (1905) 147 Cal. 228, 233-234. Once water rights are abandoned, there can be no reversion to the appropriator because the rights cease to exist. The water becomes part of the watercourse subject to future water claims. *Smith v. Hawkins* (1895) 110 Cal. 122, 126. There are two requirements for abandonment: (1) relinquishment of possession; and (2) the permanent intent to abandon the water. The intent to abandon must be permanent and the appropriator must have no intention to repossess. *Wood,* page 234.

[10] Atwater and Markle, "Overview of California Water Rights and Water Quality Law," 1988, 19 *Pacific L.J.* 957, 983-984.

Forfeiture. All or part of an appropriative right may also be lost if the water is not put to a reasonable, beneficial use. Water Code § 1240. A right which has been acquired under the current appropriation permit system may be lost by five years of nonuse, after which the water may be appropriated by another party. Water Code § 1241. Appropriative rights held under the Civil Code were also determined to be lost if not used over a five-year period. *Smith v. Hawkins* (1895) 110 Cal. 122, 127. Currently a hearing is required prior to forfeiture.

Statutory adjudication procedure. A statutory procedure exists for adjudicating the rights of all claimants to the use of water in a stream system for both riparian and appropriative rights. Water Code § 2500 *et seq*. The purpose of an adjudication process is to allow the State Board to make a determination of the rights to a stream system, which includes streams, lakes, or other bodies of water and tributaries. Water Code § 2500. The proceeding is triggered by a petition from a water right holder on the stream system. Water Code § 2525. The State Board, if it agrees to the adjudication, eventually adopts an order establishing rights to the water. Water Code § 2700. The superior court then conducts a hearing and issues a decree establishing all rights to use of the water in the stream, the priority of the right, and the place of use. Water Code § 2769. Any claimant who does not submit a proof of claim during the adjudication process is prevented from subsequently asserting rights, leading to a forfeiture of rights not reflected in the court's decree. (Water Code § 2774.)

## Underground Water Rights

*Introduction.* Groundwater contributes approximately 15 million acre-feet annually to satisfy California's water needs. However, it is estimated that state groundwater basins are annually overdrafted by some 1.3 million acre-feet.[11] Overdraft means that the amount of water extracted from a groundwater basin is beyond the "safe yield" of the basin, which is typically equivalent to the long-term recharge.

Despite the severe overdraft of many basins in California, groundwater is not regulated under a statewide permit system, in contrast to the procedures for appropriating surface water. Most property owners with land overlying groundwater can simply drill wells and extract water. No state permission is required. These users then share the use of the groundwater supply with the other overlying

*Groundwater supplies account for about 15 million acre-feet of California's annual water needs.*

*The state's groundwater basins are being overdrafted by approximately 1.3 million acre-feet a year.*

*State permission is not required to drill a well and pump groundwater.*

[11] *California Water Plan Update,* Department of Water Resources Bulletin 160-93, October 1994, volume 1, page 81.

users for reasonable, beneficial purposes, similar to riparian rights. *Katz v. Walkinshaw* (1903) 141 Cal. 116, 134-136. Groundwater uses are limited to extracting only the amount necessary for reasonable, beneficial uses on the overlying property. *Katz,* pages 135-136. However, groundwater that is surplus to the needs of overlying owners can be appropriated and used away from the overlying property. *Pasadena,* pages 925-926. Regulation of groundwater extraction has traditionally been left to the courts under common law principles.

**Definition of Groundwater.** California recognizes several legal classifications of groundwater (depending on its occurrence in various geologic formations) which govern the application of water rights laws. For legal purposes, underground waters are divided into three categories: (1) the underflow of a surface stream; (2) a definite underground stream; and (3) percolating waters. Since all underground water is generally presumed to be percolating water, the burden of proof is on the party seeking to prove that the water is underflow or a definite underground stream. *Arroyo Ditch & Water Co. v. Baldwin* (1909) 155 Cal. 280, 284.

*The underflow of a surface stream is subject to riparian or appropriative rules.*

**Underflow of a surface stream.** The underflow of a surface stream consists of the water in the soil, sand, and gravel in the bed of a stream in its natural state and essential to its existence. *City of Los Angeles v. Pomeroy* (1899) 124 Cal. 597, 623-635. To constitute underflow, the flow must be in a known and definite channel. Water Code § 1200. The underflow may include lateral extensions of the stream on each side of the surface channel if its movement and location can be determined. *Larsen v. Apollonio* (1936) 5 Cal.2d 440, 444; *Peabody,* page 375.

The party who owns the right to the surface flow has the same rights to the underflow. *Rancho Santa Margarita v. Vail* (1938) 11 Cal.2d 501, 556, 560-561; *Peabody,* pages 375-76; *Vineland Irr. Dist. v. Azusa Irr. Co.* (1899) 126 Cal. 486, 495.

**Underground streams.** Groundwater also includes an underground stream which flows in a known and definite channel in a subterranean watercourse. *Cave v. Tyler* (1905) 147 Cal. 454, 456; Water Code § 1200. A definite channel is defined as a "contracted and bounded channel" and knowledge must exist as to the course of the stream by "reasonable inference."[12] Proof of the existence of an underground stream is shown through the direction of flow, confinement within the watercourse banks, and flow within a defined channel. *Pomeroy,*

---

[12] Hutchins, pages 419-420.

pages 633-634. The same water rights are applicable to underground streams as surface water. *Pomeroy,* pages 630, 632; *Rank v. Krug* (1950) 90 F.Supp. 773, 787; Water Code §§ 1200-1201; *Prather v. Hoberg* (1944) 24 Cal.2d 549, 557-562.

**Percolating waters.** All underground waters other than underflow or underground streams are considered percolating waters. *Vineland,* pages 494-495; Water Code §§ 1200, 2500. Groundwater is presumed to be percolating. *Arroyo Ditch & Water Co. v. Baldwin* (1909) 155 Cal. 280, 284. Percolating waters include water in underground water basins and groundwaters that have escaped from streams. *Montecito Valley Water Co. v. Santa Barbara* (1904) 144 Cal. 578, 584.

*Groundwater, except for an underground stream or the underflow of a surface stream, is considered to be "percolating" water.*

Correlative rights doctrine. The use of percolating groundwater in California is governed by the doctrine of "correlative rights and reasonable use," which gives each overlying property owner a common right to the reasonable, beneficial use of the basin supply on the overlying land. *Katz,* pages 134-136. This doctrine differs from the English common law concept of groundwater first enunciated in *Acton v. Blundel. Katz,* page 141. The English court in *Acton* held that groundwater was covered by the rule that a landowner owns everything that lies beneath the surface of his or her land, including rock, soil, and water. Accordingly, a landowner had no cause of action against well interference caused by the pumping of another landowner. This common law rule failed to provide protection from those with deeper wells who could take unlimited quantities of water. *Katz,* pages 141-143.

*Most water pumped from groundwater basins is percolating water and is not subject to the state's permit system.*

In *Katz,* the California Supreme Court rejected the English common law doctrine of groundwater rights. *Katz,* page 116. In *Katz,* the plaintiffs were overlying landowners who had used the groundwater for twenty years for domestic and irrigation purposes. The defendant extracted groundwater and transported the water off the overlying basin for sale on distant land. The plaintiffs alleged that continuation of the defendant's water exportation had destroyed the artesian head of their wells, forcing them to spend money on pumping and effectively prohibiting their continued use of the property.

The court in *Katz* concluded that the English common law rule of absolute ownership of percolating groundwater was not suitable for the "natural conditions" in California. Instead, the court adopted the "rule of reasonable use of percolating waters," developing in the process the doctrine of correlative rights. As between landowners overlying a groundwater basin, all have equal rights to the water and all must share in any water shortages. *Katz,* pages 134-136.

*Owners of lands overlying a groundwater basin have a common right to pump from the basin for use on their lands.*

*The rights of overlying owners are "correlative," that is, shared rights in the basin supply.*

The correlative rights doctrine of *Katz* is now firmly established as governing overlying uses of groundwater. In disputes between landowners regarding the use of water on their overlying lands, all have equal rights and, if the supply of water is insufficient for all needs, each user is entitled to a fair and just proportion of the water.[13] *Katz,* pages 134-136. However, some uses of groundwater on land overlying the basin have been held to constitute appropriative uses. For example, the public use of groundwater is typically not an overlying use. Municipalities generally have appropriative rights, not overlying rights, to the water pumped from a groundwater basin to supply their customers. That is, they do not exercise the overlying rights of their inhabitants. *San Bernardino v. Riverside* (1921) 186 Cal. 7, 25.

*An overlying right is analogous to a riparian right.*

Correlative rights of overlying owners, like those of riparians, are held in common to be determined relative to the needs of others. *Pasadena,* page 926. An overlying owner is considered to have a water right that is analogous to a riparian right. Unlike appropriators, there are no junior or senior overlying users who gain priority by being the first to pump groundwater. *Tehachapi-Cummings County Water District v. Armstrong* (1975) 49 Cal.App.3d 992, 1001. "Overlying beneficial uses are regarded in law as akin to riparian beneficial uses and are given similar protection." *United States v. 4.105 Acres of Land* (1946) 68 F.Supp. 279, 288.

Water that is surplus to the needs of overlying owners is available for appropriation for uses outside the basin. *Katz,* pages 135-136; *Tehachapi-Cummings,* pages 1000-1001. However, water use on overlying lands for a reasonable, beneficial purpose has preference over the appropriation of water for use on other property. *Montecito Valley,* pages 584-585; *Corona Foothill Lemon Co. v. Lillibridge* (1937) 8 Cal.2d 522, 525.

### Acquisition of Rights

***Overlying rights.*** An overlying right is dependent upon land ownership overlying groundwater and is exercised merely by extraction and use of the water. No state permit is required in order to drill a well and pump groundwater. Unless the basin has been adjudicated or other local ordinances apply, no discretionary governmental permission is required to produce groundwater. Regulation is generally left to the courts. However, ministerial permits may be required in regard to the construction of the well, for example, from the Department of Health Services or pursuant to local building ordinances.

*Unless local ordinances apply, regulation of groundwater pumping has been left to the courts.*

[13] Hutchins, pages 431-436.

***Appropriative rights in underground water.*** Underground water is subject to appropriation whether it is underflow, an underground stream, or percolating water. Underflow and underground streams are appropriated in the same manner as surface water, that is, pursuant to the procedures in the Water Code. Percolating groundwater, on the other hand, is appropriated by taking the water. There is no statutory procedure for the appropriation of percolating groundwater. Water Code §§ 1200 *et seq.*; *Katz,* pages 134-135; *Pasadena,* page 926. However, only water that is surplus to the reasonable needs of overlying owners is available for appropriation. If overlying owners are putting the full safe yield to reasonable, beneficial use, then no surplus exists and no water is available for appropriative uses or for export from the basin. *Corona Foothill Lemon,* page 531; *Monolith Portland Cement Co. v. Mojave P.U. District* (1957) 154 Cal. App.2d 487, 494. The burden of proof is on the appropriator to prove that a surplus exists beyond prior vested-right uses. *Allen v. California Water & Tel. Co.* (1946) 29 Cal.2d 466, 481.

*Surplus groundwater may be appropriated merely by pumping and using the water; there is no statutory procedure for these appropriations.*

*Water that is surplus to overlying needs is subject to appropriation.*

Public agencies such as cities and water districts that operate their own water systems and pump groundwater do not exercise the overlying rights of their customers. Except for groundwater used on public lands like parks, the public purveyors of water exercise appropriative rights when producing groundwater. *San Bernardino v. Riverside* (1921) 186 Cal. 7, 25; *Orange County Water District v. Riverside* (1959) 173 Cal.App.2d 137, 165. Thus, public water supplies depending upon groundwater are technically limited to "surplus" water and are junior to the needs of overlying users. However, in overdrafted basins, unchallenged pumping by public agencies may establish prescriptive rights against private pumpers in the basin. *Los Angeles v. San Fernando* (1975) 14 Cal.3d 199, 294. In that situation, the prescriptive rights of such public agencies become paramount to the overlying rights of private pumpers.

*When pumping groundwater, public water suppliers are appropriators who are technically limited to "surplus" water.*

***Groundwater Storage Rights.*** Water imported into an area may be stored in underground basins. *Los Angeles v. San Fernando,* pages 251-259. The water may be percolated underground in spreading grounds, in natural river channels, or through the use of injection wells. Title to imported water may be retained even though the water is commingled underground with the natural supply in the basin. No statewide permit system exists for the allocation of underground storage capacity, nor is the permission of landowners overlying the storage area required in order to store imported water underground. In some adjudicated groundwater basins, however, storage of ground-

*Imported water may be stored in a groundwater basin; title is retained even though the imported water is commingled with the natural supply.*

water is controlled by a watermaster. *See,* for example, the judgment in *Chino Basin Municipal Water District v. City of Chino, et al.*, San Bernardino Superior Court, No. RCV 51010, formerly No. 164327.

In determining the safe yield of a groundwater basin, any stored imported water is distinguished from the supply native to the basin. *Los Angeles v. San Fernando,* page 279. The owner of stored water is entitled to pump an amount of water equivalent to that imported, less losses. This right of recapture is separate from any rights to produce native groundwater. To date, regulation of groundwater storage has been left to the courts on a case-by-case basis, and little precedent exists. Many potential issues have yet to be addressed and remained unresolved; for example: Must space be reserved for the normal water level fluctuations during wet and dry cycles? Do overlying entities have a priority over storage and use of water for distant areas if storage capacity is limited? Can local overlying water districts charge for the use of storage capacity underlying their areas? Can counties or other local agencies regulate the use of underground storage capacity? What happens if the imported water degrades the quality of the native supply? Must the recapture area bear some relationship to the areas where the water was put underground? Groundwater movement and the time in which recapture is permitted must also be addressed. Groundwater storage capacity becomes increasingly valuable as good surface sites are built upon or ruled out for environmental reasons. More regulation by the courts, the state legislature, or local government can be expected.

### Priority/Interrelationship with Other Water Rights

*Priorities between overlying owners.* Each overlying owner is entitled only to the quantity reasonably necessary and available. In cases of water shortage, all overlying owners are entitled to a fair and just proportion of the available waters. *Pasadena,* pages 925-926. The rights of overlying users are based solely on the owners' current reasonable and beneficial need for water, not past use or time pumping is commenced. *Tehachapi-Cummings,* page 1001.

*Priorities between overlying owners and appropriators.* Owners of land overlying percolating waters have paramount rights, which allow appropriative rights to attach only to surplus waters. *California Water Service Co. v. Edward Sidebotham & Son, Inc.* (1964) 224 Cal.App.2d 715, 725. The rights of the overlying owner to the quantity of water necessary for use on overlying land are paramount to an appropriation for use on distant land. *Katz,* pages 134-137. An appropriator must yield to an overlying user in the event of a shortage

*Many questions remain unresolved concerning the rights to store water underground.*

*In case of shortage, overlying owners must share the available supply according to need; earlier users do not have a priority.*

unless the appropriator has gained a prescriptive right. *Los Angeles v. San Fernando* (1975) 14 Cal.3d 199, 293. The right of an overlying owner to protect prospective use against an established appropriation was raised in *Burr v. Maclay Rancho Water Co.* (1908) 154 Cal. 428, 435-436. The court held that the overlying owner who has not yet used an overlying right can obtain a declaratory judgment protecting his or her paramount right. However, until the overlying owner's use of water takes all of the supply, an appropriator has the right to use any existing surplus. *Burr,* page 436. The court also confirmed the overlying user's right to reasonable protection against pumping which lowers groundwater levels in the overlying owners' wells. *Burr,* page 438.

*Overlying rights are prior to those of appropriators, unless prescription has occurred.*

### Limitations on Groundwater Rights

**Adjudication.** Groundwater rights can be determined, and pumping limited, through court adjudications. However, a statutory stream adjudication cannot include a determination of percolating groundwater rights. Water Code § 2500. The reference procedure applies to all water rights and allows a court to refer matters to the State Board as a referee on any or all matters involved in a lawsuit for the determination of rights to water. Water Code §§ 2000 *et seq.* The State Board may also initiate an adjudication to protect the *quality* of groundwater.

**Mutual prescription.** In 1949, the California Supreme Court issued a landmark decision that added a new principle to the long established correlative rights doctrine of California. In *Pasadena v. Alhambra,* most substantial pumpers in the Raymond Basin, both overlying and appropriators, were joined in a suit to determine rights to the groundwater basin. Groundwater levels in the basin had been declining for 22 of the 24 years prior to filing the suit. The plaintiffs claimed that the basin was in a condition of overdraft, and that extractions should be limited to the safe yield of the basin.

*The doctrine of "mutual prescription" eliminated priorities among overlying and appropriative rights in a long overdrafted groundwater basin.*

The court found that groundwater levels in the basin had been progressively falling through both wet and dry cycles and the basin was indeed being overdrafted. The annual safe yield was only about two-thirds of the then current pumping. If production were to be reduced to safe yield, the principal issue was how to curtail pumping. Based upon a stipulation accepted by most but not all parties, the court adopted a program of proportionate reductions. In so doing, the court developed the doctrine of "mutual prescription," whereby rights were essentially based on the highest continuous amount of pumping during five years following commencement of the overdraft.

*Under the mutual prescription doctrine, shortages were prorated.*

The court rejected the notion that water must be allocated strictly on the basis of priority of appropriation, noting that such application of appropriative rules would result in an unequal sharing of the burden of curtailing water use. Specifically, later appropriators (including public water suppliers) could be completely eliminated while earlier appropriators might not be impacted at all. Therefore, the court held that under the conditions of the overdraft all of the overlying and appropriative users had acquired prescriptive rights against each other, that is, mutual prescription, whereby all uses merged into prescriptive rights without priorities. *Pasadena,* pages 928-33.

*In the* Pasadena *case, mutual prescription achieved an "equitable apportionment" of the available supply.*

Unfortunately, the concept of mutual prescription can encourage greater groundwater pumping than may be necessary, "a race to the pumphouse" mentality. Where rights depend upon recent pumping, the incentive is to maintain high production in order to prevent loss of rights to others. However, groundwater rights in several Southern California water basins were subsequently adjudicated, by stipulation, on the basis of mutual prescription. These judgments provide permanent watermaster administration of groundwater extractions under judicially approved and supervised physical solutions. They may include authority to fund and operate programs to control groundwater overdrafts by replenishment with imported water.[14]

**Los Angeles v. San Fernando.** In 1975, the California Supreme Court significantly limited the mutual prescription doctrine. The court interpreted Civil Code section 1007 as preventing prescription of groundwater rights owned by public agencies and public utilities. *Los Angeles v. San Fernando,* page 274. This case began in 1955, when the City of Los Angeles brought suit against the Cities of San Fernando, Glendale, Burbank, and other pumpers to declare that it had a prior right to all groundwater in the upper Los Angeles river area and to enjoin them from extracting groundwater without Los Angeles' permission. Los Angeles relied upon its "pueblo rights," while the defendants urged that the *Pasadena* doctrine of mutual prescription gave them rights to proportionate shares of the groundwater supply.

*In 1975, the California Supreme Court severely limited the doctrine of mutual prescription, holding that the water rights of public agencies and public utilities were not subject to prescription.*

In a lengthy decision, Los Angeles' claims based upon its pueblo rights were upheld, but the court also reviewed groundwater law generally and overturned the trial court's application of mutual prescription, holding that public agencies could not lose water rights through prescription. Where public agencies or public utilities are involved, groundwater rights may no longer be adjudicated on the

[14] Schneider, "Groundwater Rights in California," Governor's Commission to Review California Water Rights, 1977, pages 19-25.

basis of mutual prescription. What principles will apply in the future (when a pueblo right does not control) remains uncertain. *Wright v. Goleta Water Dist.* (1985) 174 Cal.App.3d 74, 90-91; *Tehachapi-Cummings,* pages 1000-1002.

The *Los Angeles v. San Fernando* decision seems to indicate that prescription against overlying owners may be limited by the owners' "self help," that is, by exercising their rights and pumping water. 14 Cal.3d 293, fn. 101. It is not clear, however, whether overlying rights which have not been exercised can be lost by prescription. A cryptic footnote states that the prescriptive rights of appropriators (cities and public utility water companies) "would not necessarily impair the private defendants' rights to ground water for *new* overlying uses for which the need had not yet come into existence during the prescriptive period." *Los Angeles,* page 293, fn. 100, italics in original. One court has since ruled that it was improper to limit the un-exercised rights of overlying users in a groundwater basin adjudication. *Wright v. Goleta Water Dist.* (1985) 174 Cal.App.3d 74.

This decision also holds that prescription does not run until the affected owner is "on notice" that the overdraft exists. *Pasadena* found that the long-term lowering of water levels was sufficient to charge owners with notice of a deficiency rather than a surplus. However, in *Los Angeles v. San Fernando*, the hydrologic situation was more complex. During certain periods of time, the court found that a surplus existed, interrupting any prescriptive period. It may be only in similar circumstances that additional "notice" of overdraft is required. The classic definition of overdraft was modified to require that extractions must exceed not only the safe yield of the basin but also "any temporary surplus." The *Pasadena* definition of safe yield was confirmed, namely, that it is the "maximum quantity of water which can be withdrawn annually... without causing an undesirable result." *Los Angeles,* pages 278, 280, 282.

The court also reiterated the rule allowing the recapture of imported water, including the return flows from such deliveries, whether the water is sold for irrigation or urban uses. Imported water, and the return flows from imported water, must be separated from native waters in determining safe yield. *Los Angeles* pages 258-59, 288.

**Springs.** A spring is defined as a damp, marshy area where underground waters seep to the surface as a stream or small pool. *Harrison v. Chaboya* (1926) 198 Cal. 473, 476; *De Wolfskill v. Smith* (1907) 5 Cal.App. 175, 181. Rights in spring waters are considered rights in real property. *Stepp v. Williams* (1921) 52 Cal.App. 237,

*If tributary to a watercourse, a spring is considered part of the stream.*

253. If a spring is a tributary to a watercourse, it is part of the stream itself. *Gutierrez v. Wege* (1905) 145 Cal. 730, 734. The owners of the lands on which a spring arises have rights with other riparians or appropriators along the watercourse, and spring waters are subject to appropriation just like any other appropriable waters. *Simons v. Inyo Cerro Gordo Mining & Power Co.* (1920) 48 Cal.App. 524, 536. Thus, appropriation methods have been applied to spring waters. *De Necochea v. Curtis* (1889) 80 Cal. 397, 401-404. Riparian rights also apply both to a spring and to the watercourse into which it flows.

*Water district assessments to pay for replenishment of groundwater supplies*

**Water districts.** The replenishment of groundwater basins and the protection of groundwater supplies may be under the jurisdiction of any one of the many kinds of water districts that can be formed under state law. *See,* for example, water replenishment districts, Water Code § 60,000 *et seq.*; water conservation districts, Water Code § 74000 *et seq.*; county water districts, Water Code § 30,000 *et seq.*; municipal water districts, Water Code § 71,000 *et seq.* Typically such districts can engage in replenishment activities, protect groundwater quality, and participate in litigation affecting the common water supply of users within the district. Certain special act districts (for example, the Orange County Water District, Cal. Water Code App. § 40-1; the Desert Water Agency, Cal. Water Code App. § 100-1) can also impose assessments on groundwater pumped in order to regulate production and provide funds for basin replenishment and management.

Other special act districts created by the California legislature to provide local groundwater management include Honey Lake Ground Water Management District, Lassen County, Cal. Water Code App. §§ 129-101 to 129-1301 (West Supp. 1994), Sierra Valley Ground Water Management District, Sierra County, Cal. Water Code App. §§ 119-101 to 119-1302 (West Supp. 1994), Mono County Tri-Valley Ground Water Management District, Mono County, Cal. Water Code App. §§ 128-1 to 128-906 (West Supp. 1994), Mendocino City Community Services District, Mendocino County, Cal. Water Code §§ 10700 to 10717 (West 1992), Pajaro Valley Water Management Agency, Santa Cruz County, Cal. Water Code App. §§ 124-1 to 124-1108 (West Supp. 1994), Ojai Ground Water Management Agency, Ventura County, Cal. Water Code App. §§ 131-101 to 131-1201 (West Supp. 1994), Fox Canyon Ground Water Management Agency, Ventura County, Cal. Water Code App. §§ 121-102 to 121-1105 (West Supp. 1994), Monterey Peninsula Water Management District, Monterey County, Cal. Water Code App. §§ 118-101 to 118-901 (West

Supp. 1994). Such districts regulate many aspects of groundwater extraction, use, and export.

*Groundwater management districts.* Recently the legislature authorized the formation of local groundwater management districts under "AB 3030." Water Code § 10752 *et seq*; Stat. 1992, ch. 947. This authority is now being widely implemented. It remains to be seen, however, whether this approach will produce effective groundwater management and whether it will silence those who seek a statewide permit system for groundwater pumping. Any local agency whose service area includes a groundwater basin or portion of a groundwater basin that is not subject to groundwater management, pursuant to a judgment or other statute, may adopt or implement a groundwater management plan. Water Code § 10752 *et seq*. Additionally, a local agency that does not provide water service but provides flood control, groundwater quality management, or groundwater replenishment may also implement a water management plan. Water Code § 10753.

*"AB 3030"—Local groundwater management authority*

A groundwater management plan may include components relating to the control of saline water intrusion, the regulation of the migration of contaminated groundwater, mitigation of conditions of overdraft, and the replenishment of groundwater extracted by water producers. Water Code § 10753.7. However, these statutes do not authorize the local agency to make a binding determination of the water rights of any person or entity. Water Code § 10753.8(b). Neither does the statute authorize the local agency to limit or suspend extractions, unless the local agency has determined that groundwater replenishment programs or other alternative sources of water supply have proved insufficient or infeasible to lessen the demand for groundwater. Water Code § 10753.8(c).

The question of whether the state has preempted the field of groundwater regulation was raised in connection with a Tehama County ordinance. The court upheld the county's authority to regulate the pumping and use of groundwater under its police power, finding that state law did not preclude local regulation. *Baldwin v. County of Tehama* (1994) 31 Cal.App.4th 166.

## Prescriptive Water Rights

*Introduction.* A prescriptive water right is a permanent right to use water acquired when the essential elements for adverse use are met. To obtain a prescriptive water right in California, the use of nonpublic water must be for a reasonable and beneficial purpose (Cal. Const. art. X, § 2), open and notorious, adverse and hostile,

*Water rights may be established by prescription.*

continuous and uninterrupted for a period of five years (Code Civ. Proc. § 318), exclusive and under claim of right. *Saxon v. DuBois* (1962) 209 Cal.App.2d 713, 719.

***Extent of Right.*** An adverse user may acquire all or part of an existing water right, but need not prescribe the entire flow of a watercourse to gain title. A prescriptive right is usufructuary and applies only to waters actually taken into possession and put to reasonable and beneficial use. A prescriptive right cannot attach to waters that are merely diverted but not used. *Pabst v. Finmand* (1922) 190 Cal. 124, 133, 135.

The right is measured by the extent and manner of use at the time the right accrued and entitles the prescriber to use the water for a specific purpose and in a specific quantity. When use levels vary over the course of the prescriptive period, the quantity of prescripted water is measured by the highest maximum level used consistently over the five-year period. For example, if the use consisted of 25 acre-feet in the first year, 50 in the second, 100 in the third, and 150 in the fourth and fifth, the adverse user would gain title only to 25 acre-feet, the highest amount consistently used. Having obtained the right to a specific quantity of water, the adverse user has no right to increase this amount for future uses. *San Bernardino v. Riverside* (1921) 186 Cal. 7, 25, 31.

A prescriptive right may be forfeited if the water is not put to reasonable and beneficial use for five years. *Garbarino v. Noce* (1919) 181 Cal. 125, 130. Under Water Code § 1241, rights over waters subject to appropriation may be lost if not used for five years. The statute was amended in 1980 to extend the period of nonuse from three to five years, incidentally coinciding with the five-year statute of limitations for prescription. Stats. 1980, c. 933, p. 2955, § 5, Stats.1980, c. 1100, p. 3532, § 1, eff. Sept. 26, 1980.

In the case of *People v. Shirokow* (1980) 26 Cal.3d 301, the California Supreme Court rejected the claim of a prescriptive right raised against the state by a property owner who had impounded water behind a dam without obtaining an appropriative permit from the State Water Resources Control Board. The court held that the statutory permit procedures of the Water Code form the exclusive method for obtaining the right to appropriate water. *Shirokow,* pages 306, 309. The court went on to restate the principle that public rights cannot be lost by prescription, ruling that the impounded waters were property held in trust for the people by the state. *Shirokow,* page 311.

*Prescriptive rights are measured by the highest amount of water used continuously over a five-year period.*

**Waters Subject to Prescription.** An adverse user may acquire a prescriptive right to any water that can be put to reasonable and beneficial use and in which some other private owner has a valid prior right. This includes riparian and underground water rights. Certain counties including Riverside, San Bernardino, Ventura, and Los Angeles require that all groundwater users who extract in excess of 25 acre-feet a year must file records of groundwater extraction each year. Water Code §§ 4999-5108. After 1956, no prescriptive right shall accrue to any user required to file until the appropriate notice has been filed with the state. Water Code § 5003. Moreover, after 1959 the statute provides that failure to file shall be deemed equivalent "for all purposes to nonuse." Water Code § 5004. No case has determined the validity or impact of late, but retroactive, filings.

Prescriptive rights may not be acquired in surplus waters due to a lack of adversity. Individuals attempting to acquire prescriptive title must show that the water they are diverting is not surplus to the needs of the original owner. Potential adverse users should also note that a user cannot prescribe against a right that is not being exercised. For example, a riparian may choose not to use the water to which he is entitled for a period of time, thereby allowing the would-be prescriber to use the water for five or more years. Nevertheless, the user may not be able to acquire a prescriptive right because the use does not qualify as adverse.

**Acquisition of Right.** Prescriptive rights may be acquired by anyone— corporations, political subdivisions, public service corporations, and individual citizens. *Montecito Valley Water Co. v. Santa Barbara* (1904) 144 Cal. 578, 594. For example, a bottled-water corporation may acquire a prescriptive right to water it has pumped from an underground reservoir. Similarly, an upper riparian may divert water from a stream for nonriparian, appropriative uses and give the lower riparian notice of the adverse use. Downstream use by a lower riparian does not usually qualify as prescriptive unless the lower use interferes with the upper use, thereby giving the upper riparian a cause of action against the adverse user. *Cave v. Tyler* (1901) 133 Cal. 566, 567-570. Civil Code section 1007 prevents a prescriptive right from being acquired against a public agency or public utility.

**Reasonable and beneficial use.** Prescriptive rights, like all other water rights, are subject to the reasonable and beneficial use requirements of the Constitution and may benefit from the policy that the state's water resources be used "to the fullest extent of which they are capable." Cal. Const., art. X, § 2. The California Supreme Court

*Riparians and overlyers may be prescripted.*

*In certain Southern California counties, no prescriptive rights may be established by pumping until extraction records have been filed with the state.*

*Prescriptive rights are based on adverse use and may not be acquired by pumping or diverting surplus waters.*

has interpreted "reasonable and beneficial use" to include periodic or seasonal storage (*Moore v. California Oregon Power Co.* (1943) 22 Cal.2d 725, 734-735; *Colorado Power Co. v. Pacific Gas & Elec. Co.* (1933) 218 Cal. 559, 564-566) as well as rental and sale. *Joerger v. Pacific Gas & Elec. Co.* (1929) 207 Cal. 8, 34.

*Open and notorious use.* This requirement is intended to put the original owner on notice of an adverse claim. In order to satisfy this requirement, the claimant must show either that the owner had actual notice of the prescription or that the use was sufficiently open and notorious for the court to presume that the owner knew of its existence. *Copeland v. Fairview Land & Water Co.* (1913) 165 Cal. 148, 163-164. If it can be demonstrated that the owner had actual knowledge of an adverse claim, the claimant does not have to show that the use was open and notorious. *Fogarty v. Fogarty* (1900) 129 Cal. 46, 50. To demonstrate knowledge of an adverse claim, the claimant may impute the knowledge an agent shared with the agent's principal. *Montecito Valley,* page 597.

In *Pasadena v. Alhambra* (1949) 33 Cal. 2d 908, overdraft was found to have commenced in 1913-14, and thereafter the progressive lowering of groundwater levels was held sufficient to put pumpers on notice that no surplus existed and that the appropriations causing the overdraft were invasions of the rights of overlying owners and prior appropriators. However, in *City of Los Angeles v. City of San Fernando* (1975) 14 Cal.3d 199, the Supreme Court held that to establish the required element of adversity pumpers must be on notice that an overdraft exists—

> The findings that the takings from the basin were open and notorious and were continuously *asserted* to be adverse does not establish that the owners were on notice of adversity *in fact* caused by the actual commencement of overdraft. 14 Cal.3d, page 283.

No case has since determined what may be required to put users on notice of an existing overdraft. The fact that surplus water temporarily existed may have influenced the *Los Angeles* decision.

An open and notorious use cannot be concealed. Therefore the use of an underground pipeline has been held insufficient to satisfy this requirement. *Powers v. Perry* (1909) 12 Cal.App. 77, 83. Similarly, the construction of a diversion ditch does not qualify as open and notorious until the claimant actually uses it to divert the water. *Senior v. Anderson* (1896) 115 Cal. 496, 505-506. The courts have held that the use of the entire flow of a watercourse can constitute presumptive notice of an adverse claim unless the lower user has not used the water. *Sibbett v. Babcock* (1954) 124 Cal.App.2d 567, 570-571.

The requirement that the original owner have notice of any adverse claim has also been complicated by the appropriation provisions of the Water Code. Original owners of surface water rights may claim that the prescriptive user, in bypassing the Code's permit requirements, is not acting under a claim of right and has failed to give the owner proper notice of the adverse claim.

**Adverse and hostile use.** Prescriptive use begins with a trespass or invasion of the prior rights of another. In order to establish the required level of adversity, the prescriptive use must be wrongful and must injure the rights of the original owner, forming the grounds for a suit against the use of water. A diversion of water is not adverse if enough water exists in the watercourse to satisfy the needs of all diverters. Pumping is not adverse if a surplus exists in a groundwater basin. Because riparians and appropriators have a right only to that quantity of water which can be put to reasonable and beneficial use, any excess water is considered surplus and not subject to prescription.

*Prescription requires an invasion of the prior rights of another.*

Establishing adverse use, or an invasion of prior rights, does not require injury based upon an immediate inability to obtain water. Even though the original owner may have been able to obtain all the water needed, that owner may be injured by a reduction in "the long term sufficiency of the water supply." *OCWD v. City of Riverside*, 173 Cal.App.2d 137, 212-14. The injury may occur from "a gradual reducing of the total amount of stored water, the accumulated effect of which, after a period of years, would be to render the supply insufficient to meet the needs of rightful owners." *Pasadena v. Alhambra*, 33 Cal.2d 908, 929. Irreparable damage, hence adverse use, may be shown by whatever "makes the supply less dependable, less satisfactory in its quality or permanently more expensive." *OCWD*, 173 Cal.App.2d 137, 216.

*Injury to another does not mean that he or she cannot obtain the water needed.*

*Injury, and adverse use, may result from water use that reduces the "long term sufficiency of the water supply," or makes it "less dependable, less satisfactory in its quality or permanently more expensive."*

**Continuous and uninterrupted use.** The adverse use must be continuous and uninterrupted for the five-year prescriptive period. The statute of limitations on the use begins with the first adverse use of the water. During this time, the use must be adverse and hostile and exclusive of any other right. *San Francisco Bank v. Langer* (1941) 43 Cal.App.2d 263, 269. Sporadic interruptions which are immediately removed or secret interferences in the diversion do not break the continuity of the use. *Big Rock Mutual Water Co. v. Valyermo Ranch Co.* (1926) 78 Cal.App. 266, 272. The filing of a suit against a trespasser may stop the running of the statute of limitations. *Alta Land & Water Co. v. Hancock* (1890) 85 Cal. 219, 227-228. This holding does not extend, however, to suits brought against prescriptive users by third parties. *Montecito Valley,* page 593. Furthermore, a suit that has been dismissed or abandoned does not interrupt the running of the statute. *Yorba v. Anaheim Union Water Co.* (1953) 41 Cal.2d 265, 270.

Seasonal, intermittent, or partial use is considered continuous as long as the water is used when it is necessary, but the right acquired is limited by the extent and duration of the use. For instance, a diversion of 100 acre-feet of water every summer for five years can result in a prescriptive right to that quantity during those months only.

***Under claim of right.*** Finally, the adverse use must be under claim of right or, as it is sometimes referred to, under color of title. To establish this element, prescriptive users must show that they claimed the water as their own and that the original owner was aware of this claim and failed to act within the statutory period. A claim of prescriptive right asserted in good faith by a user who diverted water under the mistaken belief that he or she had title to it does not necessarily lack adversity and may ripen into a prescriptive right. *Wood v. Davidson* (1944) 62 Cal.App.2d 885, 888. A user who renounces any right to the use of the water in the future will not be allowed to later assert a prescriptive title over the water. An adverse user may establish claim of right in several ways. The user may post notice at the point of diversion, informing the original owner and any other potential claimants of his or her interest in the water. The user may also be required to pay taxes on the water, to the extent that these taxes have been assessed separately from the land. Above all, the user must act in such a way as to give notice to the original owner that the diversion and use are adverse to the original owner's claim and under claim of right.

***Limitations on the Right.*** Several limitations on the acquisition of prescriptive rights have already been discussed. One cannot prescribe against the state, which holds public waters in trust for the people of the state. Prescriptive rights may be lost by nonuse over five years (forfeiture) and may be abandoned. Abandonment can occur, for example, when the purpose for which the water was taken has been accomplished and the prescriptive users have dispersed. Once water has been abandoned, the rights to its use are lost immediately. In contrast, loss by forfeiture does not occur until after a five-year period of nonuse and a public hearing declaring the forfeiture. As with all water rights, prescriptive rights give title only to those waters which can be put to reasonable and beneficial use.

Finally, there is uncertainty about the prescriptive claims of users who divert or store surface waters without a state permit and who may have done so for many years. In *People v. Shirokow* (1980) 26 Cal.3d 301, the state sought to enjoin the storage of surface water that was done outside the statutory appropriation process. The owner claimed that a prescriptive right had been established, but this defense was rejected. As against the state, and after 1914, the statutory procedure is the exclusive method of acquiring rights to stream flow. Still unresolved, however, is the question of whether prescriptive rights can be established against the other users on the stream system without a state permit.

## Water Rights Remedies

### Introduction

A wide variety of relief is available to enforce water rights in the courts. Although administrative and statutory procedures are also available, final jurisdiction lies with the courts. Water Code §§ 2500-2900.

### Declaratory Relief

A party may be entitled to declaratory relief to protect water rights. Declaratory relief has often been used to protect underground water rights and to preclude the ripening of prescriptive rights. *Tulare Irr. Dist. v. Lindsay-Strathmore Irr. Dist.* (1935) 3 Cal.2d 489, 533; *San Bernardino v. Riverside* (1921) 186 Cal. 7, 15-16. It may also be used to protect a riparian's prospective or future uses. *Tulare,* pages 529-530. The declaratory judgment establishes a present and future right to the use of the water based upon existing rights.

*Declaratory relief may be obtained to protect the future use of a water right.*

### Injunction

Injunctions are often used to prevent injuries to water users when there is a threat of continued or future injury. *People v. Los Angeles* (1950) 34 Cal.2d 695; *Pasadena,* page 924. The threatened diversion or use of waters by another can be a basis for injunction. *Lodi v. East Bay Municipal Utility District* (1936) 7 Cal.2d 316, 346. An injunction can also be used to enjoin water pollution. *Thompson v. Kraft Cheese Company* (1930) 210 Cal. 171, 176. However, one court held that an injunction would not be allowed where a matter could be resolved with a physical solution and continuing jurisdiction. *Meridian, Ltd. v. San Francisco* (1939) 13 Cal.2d 424, 452. Some examples of situations in which courts have held that there was sufficient injury to issue an injunction include material lowering of the groundwater level, damage from irregularity of flow, export of non-surplus water, and permanent, threatened interference with the use

*Injunctive relief may be appropriate to protect the use of water rights.*

of water. *Corona Foothill Lemon Company v. Lillibridge* (1937) 8 Cal.2d 522, 524-525; *Phoenix Water Company v. Fletcher* (1863) 23 Cal. 481, 485; *Smith v. Wheeler* (1951) 107 Cal.App.2d 451, 455-456; *Bonetti v. Ruiz* (1910) 15 Cal.App. 7, 10.

Examples of situations where the injury was not sufficient to warrant injunctive relief include situations where enough water is available for all uses, the use to be protected is wasteful, or damages are only nominal. *San Bernardino v. Riverside* (1921) 186 Cal.7, 20; *Hufford v. Dye* (1912) 162 Cal. 147, 155-156; *Nevada County & Sacramento Canal Co. v. Kidd* (1869) 37 Cal. 282, 306-307.

***Parties Entitled to Relief.*** Any party with an interest in the water, or the wrongful use or diversion of the water, may bring an action for injunctive relief. Thus, an individual who has acquired the right to divert water from a stream through appropriation or prescription may enjoin the subsequent diversion of water from the stream at points above the place of diversion if it can be shown that the subsequent diversion will diminish the flow of the stream or would otherwise injure the water right. *Antioch v. Williams Irr. Dist.* (1922) 188 Cal. 451, 457.

Both riparians and owners of underground water rights can bring an action for injunctive relief. *Tulare*, pages 533-535; *Pasadena*, pages 930-931. Consumer groups and governmental entities can also bring an action for injunctive relief, but an injunction will not be granted if the injury can be redressed in another manner or is insubstantial. *Lamb v. California Water & Tel. Co.* (1942) 21 Cal.2d 33, 44.

*Today, most significant water rights lawsuits involve either public agencies or environmental groups, or both.*

Today, however, most significant water rights lawsuits are brought either by public agencies to enforce their own rights or in a representative capacity on behalf of their inhabitants, or by environmental groups. *See,* for example, *U.S. v. Fallbrook Public Utility District* (1965) 347 F.2d 48; *Orange County Water District v. Riverside* (1959) 173 Cal.App.2d 137; *National Audubon Society v. Superior Court* (1983) 33 Cal.3d 419. The relatively liberal standing requirements and the ability of environmental groups to collect attorneys' fees have increased this type of water rights litigation. Because of the complexity and expense of this litigation, many suits result finally in a stipulated judgment. *See,* for example, *Orange County Water District v. City of Chino, et al.,* (1969) Orange County Superior Court, No. 117628, settling downstream claims to waters in the Santa Ana River system after some six years of litigation.

Settlement also allows the development of innovative and finely tailored provisions that best meet the needs of a local area. The stipulated judgment in *Chino Basin Municipal Water District v.*

*City of Chino, et al.*, (1978) San Bernardino Superior Court, No. RCV 51010, formerly No. 164327, illustrates this point. There, the pumpers were divided into three separate "pools" (agricultural overlying, nonagricultural overlying, and appropriative). Each pool was allocated a share of the total basin supply and treated quite differently with respect to the determination of rights, cutbacks, replenishment charges, and transfers.

## Physical Solutions

A "physical solution" is a practical type of relief. This doctrine permits a court to order the implementation of a water plan designed to meet the needs of the parties in the most efficient and economical way, to maximize the use of available water for all, and to avoid the waste that might otherwise result from a technical and strict enforcement of rights. The essence of any prior rights, however, must still be protected. *Lodi,* pages 339-40. Physical solutions extend to percolating waters as well as to watercourses.

Physical solutions are usually in the form of a conditional injunctive decree. *Gerlach Livestock Co. v. United States* (1948) 76 F.Supp. 87, 94-95. California courts favor this approach to water rights, and a trial court is bound to seek a physical solution if it is available. *Lodi,* pages 339-340. Physical solutions are enforceable by the courts and do not require consent of all parties. *Lodi,* page 341. Physical solution is discussed more fully in chapter 6.

## Adjudication of Water Rights

There are three procedures under which rights to the use of water may be adjudicated: (1) a civil action in which there is no participation by state officials (unless the state is a party to the action); (2) civil actions in which reference is made by the court to the State Board pursuant to statutory authorization; and (3) a statutory adjudication procedure which includes an administrative determination of water rights by the State Board and a subsequent court adjudication in a civil action.

***Statutory Adjudication Procedure.*** A statutory adjudication begins with an administrative determination by the State Board. This procedure applies to watercourses and their tributaries, but specifically excludes percolating groundwaters. Water Code § 2500 *et seq.* Any water rights claimant may petition the State Board to commence a general adjudication of the stream system in which a right is claimed. The State Board proceeds, after giving notice to all interested parties, by receiving claims, conducting an investigation, holding hearings, and making an order of determination. Water Code § 2525-2783.

*"Statutory adjudications" are before the State Board and confirmed by a court.*

*Statutory adjudications are confined to streams; the procedure excludes percolating groundwater.*

The State Board initially adopts an order of determination that is then filed with the court, which issues a final decree. Water Code § 2750-2783. The decree of the court is the final adjudication of the rights of all existing claimants to waters in the system. Water Code § 2768. The decree declares the water rights of each party, including the priority and amount, point of diversion, and season, purpose, and place of use. Water Code § 2769. The decree may also make allowances for incomplete appropriations for which the rights can be confirmed in the supplemental decree. Water Code § 2801. Statutory adjudication proceedings have been upheld as constitutional. *Wood v. Pendola* (1934) 1 Cal.2d 435, 442-444. The California Supreme Court has stated that a claimant, for the purposes of statutory adjudication, may include persons seeking recognition of public trust uses on a stream-wide basis. *National Audubon Society v. Superior Court* (1983) 33 Cal.3d 419, 431, fn. 11.

*A court may refer a water rights case to the State Board for a report on the facts or on all issues.*

**Reference Procedure.** The Water Code authorizes both the state and federal courts to request the State Board to act as referee in any dispute involving water rights. Water Code § 2000 *et seq*. The request for a reference is usually done by motion of one or more of the parties and may be opposed. An order of reference may cover all issues, in which case the State Board is asked to decide the case, or the order of reference may request only an investigation of any or all of the physical facts. Water Code § 2001. The State Board may control its own investigation and report procedures without interference by the referring court. Water Code § 2010; *Pasadena,* page 918.

After its investigation, the State Board produces a report that contains its findings on the law and the facts. Water Code § 2010. The parties may take exceptions to the report, which are then determined by the court in a *de novo* trial. Delay is often an advantage to some of the parties in water rights litigation, and a motion for reference may *Recent cases raise questions about the* be made for that purpose. There is also some question about the efficiency of the reference procedure. In two recent cases, despite several years spent before the State Board pursuant to a reference order, lengthy trials were still required. *Los Angeles v. San Fernando* (1975) 14 Cal.3d 199; *Environmental Defense Fund v. East Bay Municipal Utility District* (Superior Court Alameda Co. (1990) No. 425955).

*Recent cases raise questions about the efficiency of the reference procedure.*

### Dedication to Public Use

A public entity requiring water may secure water rights through eminent domain proceedings. With the doctrine of intervening public use, water appropriated for public use may also become dedicated to public use without the owner's actual consent. This requires the water to be appropriated, the beneficiaries to rely upon and change position based upon continued appropriation, the owner's knowledge of the right to the dedication and appropriation, and failure to make objections. *Miller & Lux v. Enterprise Canal & Land Co.* (1915) 169 Cal. 415, 429-430.

Inverse condemnation, which allows the original owner to obtain compensation for the loss while at the same time protecting governmental interests in the use of water, is usually based upon intervening public use of private water rights made without obtaining title. *Los Angeles v. Glendale* (1943) 23 Cal.2d 68, 80. Typically, the award of damages rather than injunctive relief is available, since inverse condemnation is considered a taking of private property for which compensation must be made. *Natural Soda Products Co. v. Los Angeles* (1943) 23 Cal.2d 193, 204. However, injunctive relief against governmental action can be granted if the entity invoking the doctrine of inverse condemnation fails to obey court orders or pay the damages, or if the court is unable to determine damages fairly. *Peabody,* pages 377-378; *Pasadena,* page 920.

Under the California Code of Civil Procedure, property necessary for conducting, storing, or distributing water for the use of a governmental entity may also be condemned. *See* Code Civ. Proc. §§ 1238, 1242-1244. The power of eminent domain can be exercised by any person or organization within the state furnishing water to the public for public use, including municipalities, corporations supplying water to the public, public utilities, or water companies, although some enabling acts place restrictions on the use of the power. Code Civ. Proc. §§ 1245.210 *et seq.* Compensation must be made to the owner of water rights when these rights are condemned. The measure of damages in an eminent domain proceeding is the market value of the property at the time the summons is issued, together with any detriment suffered by its severance from property not taken. *Los Angeles v. Pomeroy* (1899) 124 Cal. 597, 641-644; *People by and through Dept. of Public Works v. Lynbar, Inc.* (1967) 253 Cal.App.2d 870, 880-882.

## The California Water System—A Capsule View

California's system for managing its water resources is unique among western states. A highly complex and uncoordinated system that has evolved in piecemeal fashion over more than a century, it certainly would never have been invented in its present form. From 1850, when California became a state, until 1914, the regulation of water use was left entirely to the courts. Early water "law" came

*California's system for managing its water resources would never have been invented in its present form.*

from judicially developed doctrines, some derived from the English common law, and some adapted to meet current conditions such as the appropriations of stream flow for mining operations. Even today, groundwater law continues to be largely court-made, based upon decisions in individual cases.

There was no state statutory system for the allocation and regulation of water until 1914, and then it applied only to stream flow, excluding groundwater. Yet before that time, substantial development of surface waters had already occurred (for example, the construction of the first Don Pedro Dam on the Tuolumne River by the Modesto and Turlock Irrigation Districts and the development of their extensive irrigation systems). Water rights to stream flow acquired before 1914 continue today to be exempt from the state permit system.

Today, water allocation and use is further controlled by numerous local agencies and by the laws governing the massive water projects that move water throughout the length and breadth of the state. More recently, both state and federal environmental laws have overridden traditional water "rights" and controlled diversions and use of water.

Despite this history, in 1978 the Governor's Commission to Review California Water Rights found that "The existing system performed in much better fashion than might have been anticipated during two of the driest years [1976-1977] in California history."[15] The Commission recommended specific improvements to the state's water rights system but rejected proposals for sweeping changes such as adjudicating the amount and priority of all water rights or bringing all existing groundwater pumping under the state permit system. There is no assurance that a system of bureaucratic state control would produce better results. Until the last 15 years or so, the state's water system, hodgepodge though it may be, continued to meet the water demands of an ever-growing economy and population. To be sure, the system has functioned in the past partially because potential shortages and conflicts among users could be resolved by the development of new and additional water supplies. When pumping was limited by court decree to prevent continued overdraft in a number of Southern California groundwater basins, supplemental water from the Metropolitan Water District of Southern California was available to offset the cutbacks and provide for future growth. Certainly this approach will be more difficult in the future. Indeed, we have recently

*For most of the state's history, the system has functioned to provide the water needed for an ever-growing economy and population.*

*In the past, potential shortages and conflicts over the allocation of water could be resolved by the development of new and additional water supplies.*

[15] Governor's Commission to Review California Water Rights, 1978, Final Report, page 12.

seen the application of environmental considerations reduce the amounts of water previously available from the State Water Project, the Central Valley Project, and Los Angeles' Mono Lake system.

However, it has become apparent in recent years that the water system did not adequately provide for the consideration of instream and environmental values. These values were generally not considered in the myriad of court decisions that shaped our water law. Instead, the emphasis was on private property rights over public rights, reflecting the prevalent thinking of the time. The system lagged behind the public's changing values, and it took the intervention of the California Supreme Court in *Audubon* to give environmental values a significant place in the rules governing water allocation. Also, despite the lofty language in the statutes and elsewhere, the water system has not been able to smoothly integrate considerations of quality and quantity. The decade-long dispute before the State Board in the Bay-Delta proceedings attests to this problem.

Even so, the system has demonstrated a remarkable ability to adapt to society's changing needs, and there is no reason in the future to expect less from our courts, our legislators, and our institutional leaders. Water "law" requires a measure of stability, but it cannot remain static. Looking ahead, the structure exists to resolve disputes over the allocation of water, recognizing current values. For example, the Constitution requires that all uses of water must be "reasonable," and the Supreme Court has not found it necessary to decide whether that language means only that wasteful uses of water are prohibited or whether the optimal use of water is required.[16] Yet the doctrine of reasonable use has enormous potential to direct the future allocation of our water resources as changing conditions require.

The recent agreement between the state and federal governments on the Bay-Delta[17] may also portend a future approach that reconciles the need for a reliable water supply with the restoration and protection of instream values. This agreement provides in part for financing fish and wildlife improvements that do not call for more water. Moreover, if more water is necessary, it is to be provided, not taken by regulation.

*In recent years, however, it has become apparent that the system has not adequately met the public's changing concerns for the protection of instream values.*

*Water "law" requires a measure of stability, but it cannot remain static. Though we have an eclectic, even hodgepodge, system of water resource management, the structure is capable of continuing to regulate water allocation, recognizing current values.*

[16] In *National Audubon Society v. Superior Court* (1983) 33 Cal.3d 419, the court did not resolve the issue of whether "unreasonable use" refers only to inordinate and wasteful use of water or to any use which is "less than the optimum allocation of water." Fn. 28, page 447.

[17] *See* chapter 4 for a discussion of this accord.

Finally, a settlement of Bay-Delta standards may open the way for new facilities that will improve both the conditions for fish and the reliability of water supplies for cities and farms. But no such facilities can be built quickly, and in the interim at least water transfers must play a role in meeting such needs.[18]

[18] Transfers are discussed in chapter 8.

CHAPTER THREE

# The Allocation of Water Between Consumptive and Environmental Uses

## Introduction

For many years competition between consumptive and instream uses of water did not exist. It was partly because people thought there was enough water for all purposes, and partly because society generally was not sensitive to specific environmental needs for water, nor to the continuing decline in fish and wildlife resources. The primary issue was whether new water supplies could be developed at reasonable costs and in a timely way to meet burgeoning water demands. This changed dramatically with the emergence of the environmental movement in the late 1960s.

In the last two decades, a number of different mechanisms have been used to effect a reallocation of water between consumptive and environmental uses: (1) the public trust doctrine; (2) Article X, Section 2, of the California Constitution; (3) Sections 5937 and 5946 of the California Fish and Game Code; (4) legislation for wild and scenic rivers, and the Central Valley Project Improvement Act; (5) application of the Endangered Species Act; and (6) the National Environmental Policy Act (NEPA) and the California Environmental Quality Act (CEQA).

This chapter will focus on the public trust doctrine, Article X, Section 2, and Fish and Game Code Sections 5937 and 5946. The public trust doctrine is of ancient origin and has been brought into modern law through court decisions. Article X, Section 2, was adopted as an amendment to the California Constitution in 1928 and provides that the water resources of the state must be put to reasonable and

*Recently, a number of court decisions and state and federal laws have been used to reallocate water between consumptive and environmental uses.*

**NEPA = National Environmental Policy Act**

**CEQA = California Environmental Quality Act**

beneficial use to the fullest extent possible. The requirement of reasonable use has modified many uses of water in California. Because of this concept, a use cannot simply be beneficial but must also be reasonable considering the alternative uses that can be made of the water. A user with a higher priority can be forced to share water with a junior user if all of the senior's use is not reasonable.

Fish and Game Code Sections 5937 and 5946 have been significant primarily in the litigation surrounding the diversions by the Los Angeles Department of Water and Power. However, they are applicable to many streams and rivers in the state.

A satisfactory method for resolving the competing demands for water between consumptive and environmental users has not been found. Currently, these disputes are resolved through litigation, a process examined in the context of the decision in *Environmental Defense Fund v. East Bay Municipal Utility District.* Super. Ct. Alameda County, 1990, No. 425955.

## The Public Trust Doctrine

*The public trust doctrine applied to water law was a legal theory whose time had come.*

The application of the public trust doctrine in modern water law is a direct result of the work of Professor Joseph Sax, formerly a professor of law at Boalt Hall, University of California at Berkeley. In 1970, Professor Sax wrote an article entitled "The Public Trust Doctrine in Natural Resource Law: Effective Judicial Intervention" (Volume 68, *Mich. L.Rev.* 471). Between 1970 and 1985, approximately 100 cases were reported involving the public trust doctrine, many of which cited Professor Sax's article.[1] It is hard to imagine a more intense judicial response to a single article; the public trust doctrine was a legal theory whose time had come.

In his article, Professor Sax frankly described his interest in the public trust doctrine—

> Of all the concepts known to American law, only the public trust doctrine [citation omitted] seems to have the breadth and substantive content which might make it useful as a tool of general application for citizens seeking to develop a comprehensive legal approach to resource management problems. If that doctrine is to provide a satisfactory tool, it must meet three criteria. It must contain some concept of a legal right in the general public; it must be enforceable against the government (footnote omitted); and it must

[1] Lazarus, "Changing Conceptions of Property and Sovereignty in Natural Resources: Questioning the Public Trust Doctrine," 1968, 71 *Iowa L.Rev.,* pages 631, 644.

be capable of an interpretation consistent with contemporary concerns for environmental quality.[2]

The public trust doctrine has certainly proven to have all of these attributes. In the past twenty years it has been used very effectively against the government in a manner consistent with environmental quality concerns. Because it has become such an integral component of California water law, it is the subject of a fairly lengthy discussion here.

## The Public Trust Doctrine Comes to the United States

The public trust doctrine arises from the belief that certain properties should not be owned by private parties. Rather, they should be held by the government for the benefit of all its citizens.

*The public trust doctrine is based on the premise that certain things should be held by the government for the benefit of all its citizens.*

Professor Sax described the public trust doctrine in the following manner—

> . . . no grant may be made to a private party if that grant is of such amplitude that the state will effectively have given up its authority to govern, but a grant is not illegal solely because it diminishes in some degree the quantum of traditional public uses.[3]

The origins of the public trust doctrine are found in the work of Justinian, whose statement of the principles of Roman law included the following concept—

> By the law of nature these things are common to mankind—the air, running water, the sea and consequently the shores of the sea.[4]

These things were held in trust by the state for the benefit of all people, and this concept of common ownership ensured unlimited public rights for commerce, fishing, and navigation.

The starting point of the public trust doctrine in the United States is generally considered to be *Arnold v. Mundy* (1821) 1 Halsted, 1; 6 N.J.L.1,[5] a case centered around the rights to an oyster bed in Raritan Bay, New Jersey. Mundy claimed that he had a public right to take oysters from beneath the navigable waters of the bay, while Arnold, who owned property adjacent to the oyster bed, claimed the sole right to do so. In supporting Mundy's claim, the court developed

*The starting point of the public trust doctrine in the United States is an 1821 court decision.*

---

[2]  Sax, "The Public Trust Doctrine in Natural Resource Law: Effective Judicial Intervention," Volume 68, *Mich. L.Rev.,* page 471.

[3]  Sax, pages 488-489.

[4]  The Institute of Justinian 2.1.1, T. Cooper Translation, 2nd Edition, 1841.

[5]  Dunning, "The Public Trust Doctrine in Western Water Law: Discord or Harmony," 1984, 30 *Rocky Mt. Min. L. Inst.,* page 17-6.

three principles: (1) that certain types of property are unique and should not be privately owned; (2) that the state holds these types of properties as sovereign for the benefit of all people; and (3) that portions of trust property may be disposed of if it furthers the public interest. In the words of the court—

> I am further of opinion, that, upon the revolution, all these royal rights became vested in the people of New Jersey, as the sovereign of the country, and are now in their hands; and that they, having themselves, both the legal title and the usufruct, may make such disposition o them, and such regulation concerning them, as they may think fit; that this power of disposition and regulation must be exercised by them in their sovereign capacity; that the legislature is their rightful representative in this respect, and, therefore, that the legislature, in the exercise of this power, may lawfully erect ports, harbors, basins, docks, and wharves on the coasts of the sea and in the arms thereof, and in the navigable rivers; that they may bank off those waters and reclaim the land upon the shores; that they may build dams, locks, and bridges for the improvement of the navigation and the ease of passage; that they may clear and improve fishing places, to increase the product of the fishery; that they may create, enlarge, and improve oyster-beds, by planting oysters therein in order to procure a more ample supply; that they may do these things, themselves, at the public expense, or they may authorize others to do it by their own labor, and at their own expense, giving them reasonable tolls, rents, profits, or exclusive and temporary enjoyments; but still this power, which may be thus exercised by the sovereignty of the state, is nothing more than what is called the *jus regium,* the right of regulating, improving, and securing for the common benefit of every individual citizen. The sovereign power itself, therefore cannot, consistently, with the principles of the law of nature, and the constitution of a well-ordered society, make a direct and absolute grant of the waters of the state, divesting all the citizens of their common right. It would be a grievance which never could be long borne by a free people. *Arnold,* pages 369-370.

The United States Supreme Court relied on this decision in *Martin v. Lessee of Waddell,* (1842) 41 U.S. (16 Pet.) 367, a case that also involved the use of oyster beds in New Jersey. Waddell claimed the exclusive right to take oysters by virtue of his grant from the Duke of York. The court arrived at the same conclusion as the court in *Arnold v. Mundy*—

... the shores, and rivers, and bays, and arms of the sea, and the land under them, ... [are to be] held as a public trust for the benefit of the whole community, to be freely used by all for navigation and fishery... *Waddell,* page 413

The court concluded that the state of New Jersey owned the beds of navigable waters in its sovereign capacity. *Waddell,* page 410.

The idea that a state owns its resources in a "sovereign capacity" is a key element of the public trust doctrine. This is important primarily because it greatly restricts the state's ability to dispose of its resources.[6]

However, this restriction is not a complete prohibition against the disposition of trust properties. A state may even make large-scale grants of trust properties, although courts usually interpret these grants quite restrictively and apply a more rigorous standard when the conveyances are to private parties.[7] *See People v. California Fish Company* (1913) 166 Cal. 576. Authorities suggest that the disposition of trust properties for public water projects fits within the standard for an appropriate grant of trust property.[8] This is especially important in California, since virtually all of the state's major water projects impact trust properties.

## The *Illinois Central* Case

Although *Martin v. Waddell* made the public trust part of federal law, the most significant Supreme Court public trust decision came in *Illinois Central Railroad Company v. Illinois.* (1892) 146 U.S. 387 [36 L.Ed. 1018]. Professor Sax described this case as the "lodestar" of American public trust law, and as perhaps the single most influential public trust case.[9]

*The "lodestar" of American public trust law is the 1892 Supreme Court decision in Illinois Central Railroad Co. v. Illinois.*

This case arose after the Illinois legislature granted submerged lands, in fee simple, to the Illinois Central Railroad. This grant included lands underlying Lake Michigan and comprised virtually the entire commercial waterfront of the city of Chicago. In 1873, when the legislature realized that it might not have been wise to have given away what was becoming extremely valuable commercial real estate, it repealed the 1869 grant and brought an action to declare the original grant invalid.

6  Lazarus, page 637.
7  Sax, page 486.
8  *See* Dunning, "The Significance of California's Public Trust Easement for California's Water Rights Law," 1980, 14 *U.C. Davis L.Rev.* 391; Littleworth, "The Public Trust v. The Public Interest," 1988, 19 *Pacific L.J.* 1219-1221.
9  Sax, page 489.

The United States Supreme Court upheld Illinois' action, ruling that the express conveyance of trust lands was beyond the power of the legislature. Although the decision did not prohibit the disposition of trust lands to private parties, it prohibited a state from divesting itself of the authority to govern an area over which it has responsibility to exercise its police power. In this particular case, by granting such a large portion of the waterfront, the legislature had relinquished its control over navigation, a public trust use over which it was required to have authority.[10]

Expanding on the opinion in *Arnold v. Mundy*, the court articulated the limited purposes for which property subject to the trust may be disposed of—

> The interest of the people in the navigation of the waters and in commerce over them may be improved in many instances by the erection of wharves, docks and piers therein, for which purpose the State may grant parcels of the submerged lands; and, so long as their disposition is made for such purposes, no valid objections can be made to the grants. It is grants of parcels of lands under navigable waters, that may afford foundation for wharves, piers, docks, and other structures in aid of commerce, and grants of parcels which, being occupied, do not substantially impair the public interest in the lands and water remaining, that are chiefly considered and sustained in the adjudged cases as a valid exercise of legislative power consistently with the trust to the public upon which such lands are held by the State. *But that is a very different doctrine from the one which would sanction the abdication of the general control of the State over lands under the navigable waters of an entire harbor or bay, or of a sea or lake. Such abdication is not consistent with the exercise of that trust which requires the government of the State to preserve such waters for the use of the public.* The trust devolving upon the State for the public, and which can only be discharged by the management and control of property in which the public has an interest, cannot be relinquished by a transfer of the property. *The control of the State for the purposes of the trust can never be lost, except as to such parcels as are used in promoting the interests of the public therein, or can be disposed of without any substantial impairment of the public interest in the lands and waters remaining. Illinois Central, pages 452-453; emphasis added*

*"The control of the State for purposes of the trust can never be lost..."*

[10] Sax, page 489.

The court held that public trust lands may only be disposed of for public purposes—

A grant of all the lands under the navigable waters of a State has never been adjudged to be within the legislative power; and any attempted grant of the kind would be held, if not absolutely void on its face, as subject to revocation. *The State can no more abdicate its trust over property in which the whole people are interested, like navigable waters and soils under them, so as to leave them entirely under the use and control of private parties*, except in the instance of parcels mentioned for the improvement of navigation and use of the waters, or when parcels can be disposed of without impairment of the public interest in what remains, *than it can abdicate its police powers in the administration of government and the preservation of the peace*. In the administration of government the use of such powers may for a limited period be delegated to a municipality or other body, but there always remains with the State the right to revoke those powers and exercise them in a more direct manner, and one more conformable to its wishes. *So with trusts connected with public property, or property of a special character, like lands under navigable waters, they cannot be placed entirely beyond the direction and control of the State. Illinois Central,* pages 453-454; emphasis added

The *Illinois Central* decision emphasizes the significance of the state holding trust property in its sovereign capacity: A state must hold trust property for the benefit of its citizens, and the reasons it may dispose of it are carefully circumscribed. *Illinois Central* makes it apparent that states have special obligations in managing trust property. California courts have expanded this doctrine well beyond the parameters already outlined, and this is the topic of the next section.

## The Public Trust Doctrine in California

*Eldridge v. Cowell*, (1854) 4 Cal. 80, was the first California case to address the public trust doctrine. *Eldridge* involved the filling of lots along San Francisco Bay pursuant to a grant by the state of California to the city and county of San Francisco. The filling of one of these lots blocked the direct bay access of a neighboring lot. The owner who had lost direct access to the bay argued that the navigable waters of the bay could not be privately appropriated in a manner interfering with the public right of navigation. *Eldridge,* page 85.

The court held that pursuant to the public trust doctrine the state has an obligation to preserve the right of navigation. However, the court found that the legislature had established a waterfront

N

**Wild and Scenic Rivers
in California**

No.
Mid.
Smith
Klamath R.
Scott R.
River
Clair Engle
Lake
Pit
Trinity R.
Van Duzen R.
South Fk.
Shasta
Lake
Cottonwood
Eel R.
South Fk.
Sacramento River
Mid. Fk.
Russian R.
Cache Ck.
Putah
Feather R.
American R.
No. Fk.
Creek
E. Fk. Carson R.
W. Fk. Walker R.
Mokelumne R.
Stanislaus R.
Tuolumne R.
Merced
So. Fk.
San Joaquin R.
Kings R.
Mid Fk.
So. Fk.
Salinas
Kaweah R.
River
Big Sur R.
Tule R.
No. Fk.
So. Fk.
South Fk.
Kern R.
Sisquoc R.
Sespe
Creek
Santa Clara R.

⌒ Federal Designation
⌒ State Designation Only

boundary in San Francisco Bay behind which development could occur, and that the filling that was the subject of the lawsuit had occurred behind that line. The court ruled that to serve the public good the legislature could destroy the easement and allow the land to pass to private ownership. *Eldridge,* page 87. This decision established the principle, developed more fully in *Illinois Central*, that the legislature may dispose of public trust properties when it serves the public good.

A landmark California public trust decision, *People v. California Fish Co.* (1913) 166 Cal. 576, helped clarify the inherent tension between the state's obligation to protect trust values and the rule of *Eldridge v. Cowell* that the state could dispose of trust resources. In *California Fish*, the Supreme Court ruled against grantees asserting that they owned title to tidelands free of the public trust, holding that a patent for tidelands passed "at most, only the title to the soil subject to the public right of navigation." *California Fish,* page 588. Although it was not the case in *California Fish*, the court noted that absolute title could be granted to private individuals to "adapt the land to the use for navigation in the best manner." *California Fish,* page 597. In the absence of such a grant, the grantees owned the soil—

> ...subject to the easement of the public for the public uses of navigation and commerce, and to the right of the state, as administrator and controller of these public uses and the public trust therefor, to enter upon and possess the same for the preservation and advancement of the public uses and to make such changes and improvements as may be deemed advisable for those purposes. *California Fish,* page 599.

Most importantly, *California Fish* set forth guidelines for determining the validity of statutes authorizing the granting of tidelands—

*Guidelines for determining the validity of statutes disposing of assets subject to the trust.*

> [S]tatutes purporting to authorize an abandonment of...public use will be carefully scanned to ascertain whether or not such was the legislative intention, and that intent must be clearly expressed or necessarily implied. It will not be implied if any other inference is reasonably possible. And if any interpretation of the statute is reasonably possible which would not involve a destruction of the public use or an intention to terminate it in violation of the trust, the courts will give the statute such interpretation. *California Fish,* page 597.

Thus, the court created a presumption against disposing of trust lands and left open the possibility of invalidating legislation if it would cause the destruction of the public easement without an appropriate necessity.

Dedication of LADWP Aqueduct bringing Owens Valley water into Los Angeles

These principles were applied in *City of Berkeley v. Superior Court* (1980) 26 Cal.3d 515, in which a private company had acquired land within the city of Berkeley. The title to these lands was traceable to grants made by the Board of Tideland Commissioners (which was created by the legislature to oversee tideland development), and the issue was whether this sale of land pursuant to an 1870 act of the legislature had terminated the public trust so that the land was now held free of the public trust.

Following the *California Fish* guidelines set forth above, the court examined the grant to determine if it was made in promotion of navigation, commerce, or fisheries. *Berkeley,* page 525. Under *Eldridge,* the state could absolutely dispose of tidelands for these purposes. *Eldridge,* page 87. The court found that the grants were not made for these purposes, but rather that they may have been made for revenue-raising purposes. *Berkeley,* page 530. In light of this evidence, the court followed *California Fish* and strictly construed the statute not to constitute an absolute grant of land free of the public trust. *Berkeley,* pages 528, 532.

In determining the existing title to the property, the court, unlike the court in *California Fish*, did not rule that all the lands were subject to the public trust—

> We choose, instead, an intermediate course: the appropriate resolution is to balance the interests of the public in tidelands conveyed pursuant to the 1870 act against those of the landowners who hold property under these conveyances. In the harmonizing of these claims, the principle we apply is that the interests of the public are paramount in property that is still physically adaptable for trust uses, whereas the interests of the grantees and their successors should prevail insofar as the tidelands have been rendered substantially valueless for those purposes.

> In keeping with this principle, we hold that submerged lands as well as lands subject to tidal action that were conveyed by board deeds under the 1870 act are subject to the public trust. Properties that have been filled, whether or not they have been substantially improved, are free of the trust to the extent the areas of such parcels are not subject to tidal action. *Berkeley,* page 534, fn. omitted

Although the court upheld the principles of *California Fish* and *Illinois Central* by limiting the legislature's ability to convey tidelands, its opinion introduced the concept of "balancing" to the public trust. The court acknowledged that although it could absolutely divest all landowners who held property pursuant to conveyances made under the 1870 act, it could only do so if it compensated those owners. *Berkeley,* pages 533-534.

The reason it chose this intermediate course is obvious. The lands which had already been developed were valueless for public trust purposes. Conceivably, the court could have taken the extreme position that these lands should be restored so they could be used for trust purposes. However, by choosing the middle ground and balancing the interests involved, the court set a precedent for resolving future trust disputes.

## Types of Waters and Uses to Which the Public Trust Doctrine Applies

Historically, although apparent that the California public trust doctrine applied to tidelands, navigation, commerce, and fisheries, its application to other waters and other purposes was uncertain. Two cases alleviated much of that uncertainty. In *People v. Gold Run Ditch & Mining Co.* (1884) 66 Cal. 138, 151-52, the court applied the public trust doctrine to inland waters. In *Marks v. Whitney,* (1971) 6 Cal.3d 251, 259-60, the court expanded the scope of the public trust beyond the traditional purposes of navigation, commerce, and fisheries to include environmental and aesthetic purposes.

*The courts have now expanded the scope of the public trust beyond the traditional purposes of navigation, commerce, and fisheries to include environmental and aesthetic purposes.*

*Gold Run Ditch* was a very significant case, as much for its social as its legal impact. The case involved hydraulic mining on the American River and was the death knell for the hydraulic mining industry in California. Hydraulic mining involved spraying water at a high velocity from water cannons against a hillside in order to wash down gravel from which gold was recovered, but most of the sand and gravel tailings washed into rivers, in this case the north fork of the American River. These tailings amounted to nearly 5,000 cubic yards of boulders, sand, and gravel each day. *Gold Run Ditch,* page 144.

The impact of the discharge of these tailings had been dramatic. The beds of both the American River and the Sacramento River (below its confluence with the American River) had risen 6 to 12 feet, increasing the possibility of flooding. Navigation was severely impaired, and the water of the American River was no longer fit for domestic consumption. *Gold Run Ditch,* page 145. Faced with these facts, the court upheld the lower court's injunction of the company's discharge of debris into the river. *Gold Run Ditch,* page 152.

The court was aware that hydraulic mining was not economically feasible if streams could not be used for the discharge of debris.

*Gold Run Ditch,* page 151. When the injunction was issued, hydraulic mining was producing $10 million worth of gold per year.[11] The decision, relying on the public trust doctrine, marked California's transition from a mining economy to a commercial and agricultural economy (33 Cal.3d, page 436)—

> As we have already said, the rights of the people in the navigable rivers of the State are paramount and controlling. The State holds the absolute right to all navigable waters and the soils under them, subject, of course, to any rights in them which may have been surrendered to the general Government. (Citation omitted.) The soil she holds as trustee of a public trust for the benefit of the people; and she may, by her legislature, grant it to an individual; but she cannot grant the rights of the people to the use of the navigable waters flowing over it; these are inalienable. Any grant of the soil, therefore, would be subject to the paramount rights of the people to the use of the highway. And such was the doctrine of the common law. 'The *jus privatum*,' says Lord Hale, in *De Jure Maris*, p. 22, 'must not prejudice the *jus publicum*, wherewith public rivers and arms of the sea are affected to public use.' It is, therefore, beyond the power of legislatures to destroy or abridge such rights, or to authorize their impairment. *Gold Run Ditch,* pages 151-152.

The *Gold Run Ditch* opinion took on added significance when the court in *National Audubon Society v. Superior Court*, (1983) 33 Cal.3d 419, relied on it to expand the application of the public trust doctrine to non-navigable streams. Although the *Gold Run Ditch* case did not involve the diversion of water, the court interpreted its principles to apply to a situation in which diversion from a non-navigable tributary impairs the trust values of a downstream river or lake. The court stated that, if it applied to fills which impaired trust values (as was the case in *Gold Run Ditch*), the public trust doctrine also applied to extractions of waters that impair trust values. *Audubon,* page 436.

In *Marks v. Whitney*, (1971) 6 Cal.3d 251, the California Supreme Court expanded the public trust beyond the three traditional uses of navigation, commerce, and fisheries. *Marks* was a "quiet title" action involving a boundary dispute. The defendant was an owner of tidelands and sought to fill and develop them. Plaintiff argued that this development would cut off his right, as a member of the public,

*The* Audubon *case expanded the application of the public trust to include non-navigable tributaries to a navigable body of water.*

---

[11] Dunning, "The Significance of California's Public Trust Easement for California's Water Rights Law," page 367.

to the land and the navigable waters that covered it. *Marks,* page 256. The *Marks* court stated that traditionally the public trust doctrine had been applied to rights such as fishing, hunting, bathing, swimming, boating, and general recreational purposes in the navigable waters of the state. However, the court stated that public uses of tidelands are flexible enough to encompass changing public needs. Thus, the state as trustee is not limited to an "outmoded classification" in determining which utilizations are appropriate. *Marks,* page 259. The court wrote—

> There is a growing public recognition that one of the most important public uses of the tidelands—a use encompassed within the tidelands trust—is the preservation of those lands in their natural state, so that they may serve as ecological units for scientific study, as open space, and as environments which provide food and habitat for birds and marine life, and which favorably affect the scenery and climate of the area. It is not necessary to here define precisely all the public uses which encumber tidelands. *Marks,* pages 259-260.

*Uses currently embraced within the protection of the public trust.*

This holding significantly expanded the scope of protection offered by the public trust doctrine, since the diversions from streams may adversely impact these natural values, even if navigation, commerce and fishing are not affected.[12]

For some time there has been controversy over whether the public trust doctrine applies to water stored behind dams. Because so much of California's water supply is stored behind dams, this is an issue of tremendous importance. As yet, no court has ruled on this issue, although, in the case of a non-navigable stream, one court held that the water behind a dam is not subject to the public trust doctrine. *Golden Feather Community Association v. Thermalito Irrigation District* (1989) 209 Cal.App.3d 1276.

*Whether the public trust applies to water stored behind dams remains an unsettled question.*

The real question is whether the legislature's direct authorization of a water project involving the construction of reservoirs and the storage and diversion of water for consumptive uses is a disposition of public trust values. As noted earlier, the legislature, at the exercise of its discretion, has the power under certain circumstances to dispose of property free of any public trust obligations. Under such circumstances, the legislative determination is "conclusive upon the courts." Of course, the legislative intention must be clearly expressed

---

[12] Dunning, "The Public Trust Doctrine in Western Water Law: Discord or Harmony," pages 17-20 to 17-21.

or necessarily implied, and will not be implied if any other inference is reasonably possible. *California Fish,* page 597.

The State Water Project is an example of this issue. After many studies of California's water needs, the State Water Project was approved by the legislature, with a yield of 4.2 million acre-feet annually. Project facilities were designed and constructed to produce that yield, and contracts were entered into to supply that maximum entitlement. The size of the project, the various facilities to be constructed, and its financing were all before the legislature and the voters when the project was approved in 1959-1960. *Goodman v. County of Riverside* (1983) 140 Cal.App.3d 900, 908. Specific water rights for the project were to be issued by the State Board, and construction of the project was well under way before the first water rights permits were issued.[13]

*By approving the State Water Project, did the California legislature make a valid disposition of trust assets that exempts the water supply of the SWP from public trust obligations?*

By its action, did the legislature make a disposition of trust assets that exempts the water supply of the State Water Project from any public trust obligations? The legislature has the power to sanction one public trust use at the expense of another. *Colberg, Inc. v. California Dept. of Public Works* (1967) 67 Cal.2d 408 (cited with approval in *Audubon,* page 439 fn. 21). This could occur in the case of a dam that enhances navigation and recreation but adversely impacts spawning habitat or the ability of fish to spawn upstream. However, not all public uses served by a water project are trust uses. In *Audubon,* the California Supreme Court specifically rejected the contention that the state can abrogate the public trust merely by authorizing a use inconsistent with the trust. *Audubon,* page 439 fn. 21. Furthermore, the contention that all public uses are "trust uses" and thus there are no restrictions on the state's ability to allocate trust property was also rejected. *Audubon,* page 440. This holding creates some uncertainty as to the limits of the state's ability to dispose of trust resources.

The critical issue is whether the intended yield of the State Water Project is subject to reduction in order to provide water for public trust uses. *Audubon* seems to hold that water rights "expressly conferred by the legislature would not be limited by the public trust doctrine." *Audubon,* page 445 fn. 24. If that is true, it seems that an action by the State Board should be nothing more, insofar as the public trust is concerned, than the administrative procedure for implementing the legislature's directive. On the other hand, the various State Water Project contracts do not guarantee a

---

[13] *See* S.W.R.C.B. Decision 1275 (1967) and S.W.R.C.B. Decision 1291 (1967); cited in Littleworth, "The Public Trust v. The Public Interest," page 1220, fn. 97.

yield equal to their aggregate entitlements. Each contract provides for the possibility of shortage. And each contract provides only that the state "shall make all reasonable efforts to perfect and protect water rights necessary... for the satisfaction of water supply commitments under this Contract."[14]

The court in *EDF v. EBMUD* (1990) Super. Ct. Alameda County, No. 425955 (discussed later in this chapter), rejected the argument that the public trust doctrine does not apply to stored water on the grounds that there were public trust values in the American River prior to the construction of Folsom Dam and that these values, even if they had been modified, still deserved protection. Because the case was not appealed, there is still no controlling authority on the issue of whether the public trust doctrine applies to artificially stored water.

### *National Audubon Society v. Superior Court*

At the beginning of the 1980s, it was clear that the public trust required the protection of trust values in navigable waters whenever possible. The protected trust values extended to ecological values, as well as to navigation, commerce, and fishing. Left unresolved, however, was the issue of whether the public trust doctrine applied to water rights. Water users firmly believed that water rights were vested rights whose utilization could not be impacted by the public trust doctrine.

*Until* Audubon, *the question of whether the public trust doctrine applied to water rights was unresolved.*

This matter was finally addressed by the California Supreme Court in 1983 in one of the most important California water rights decisions in this century. In *Audubon* the court found that the public trust doctrine applied to the tributary streams of Mono Lake, and prevented the Los Angeles Department of Water Power (LADWP) from maintaining a vested right to divert these waters if the diversion would harm public trust values. *Audubon,* page 426.

**LADWP = Los Angeles Department of Water Power**

The underlying facts in *Audubon* are essential to understanding the court's decision. Mono Lake, a saline lake and the second-largest lake in California, is located at the eastern entrance to Yosemite National Park. It contains no fish but supports a large population of brine shrimp. These brine shrimp feed vast numbers of nesting and migratory birds. Islands in the lake are home to a large breeding colony of California Gulls. Although Mono Lake receives water from rain and snow, most of its supply comes from the runoff from snow melt in the Sierra Nevada. It is fed by five fresh water streams: Mill, Lee Vining, Walker, Parker, and Rush Creeks. *Audubon,* page 424.

*The facts underlying the* Audubon *decision*

---

[14] State Water Contract Provision 16(b), Water Supply contract with the California Department of Water Resources.

Mono Lake

In 1940, the Division of Water Resources (the forerunner of the State Water Resources Control Board), granted the LADWP a permit to appropriate almost the entire flow of four of the five streams tributary to the lake. *Audubon,* page 424. The Water Board granted LADWP's water rights without any consideration of the impact those rights have on public trust resources. The Board, interpreting the law as it stood in 1940, concluded that although LADWP's diversions would impact the natural values of Mono Basin, it could do nothing about those impacts. *Audubon,* pages 427-428. In 1974, these permit rights were confirmed in a license issue by the Water Board, again without consideration of any impacts on Mono Lake.

As a result of LADWP's diversions, the level of Mono Lake decreased substantially—its surface area diminished by one-third and one of the two principal islands in the lake became a peninsula. This exposed the California Gull rookery to coyotes and other predators, resulting in the gulls' abandoning the exposed island. *Audubon,* page 424. Plaintiffs filed suit to enjoin the LADWP diversions on the theory that the shores, bed and waters of Mono Lake were protected by the public trust. *Audubon,* page 425.

The Supreme Court concluded that water rights in the Mono Basin should be reevaluated. The *Marks* court's recognition that the public trust protects environmental and recreational values had set the stage for a conflict between the appropriative water rights system and the public trust doctrine—

> They meet in a unique and dramatic setting which highlights the clash of values. Mono Lake is a scenic and ecological treasure of national significance, imperiled by continued diversions of water; yet, the need of Los Angeles for water is apparent, its reliance on rights granted by the board evident, the cost of curtailing diversions substantial. *Audubon,* page 425

*The Supreme Court held that the public trust doctrine and the appropriative water rights system both had to be accommodated.*

Although the public trust doctrine and the appropriative water rights system developed independently of each other, the court believed that both doctrines had to be accommodated in order to avoid an unbalanced structure. The result of choosing one over the other would be either to invalidate appropriations essential to the economic development of the state, or not to provide protection of public trust values. *Audubon,* page 445. In the words of the court—

The population and economy of this state depend upon the appropriation of vast quantities of water for uses unrelated to in-stream trust values. [Footnote omitted.] California's Constitution (*see* art. X, § 2), its statutes [citations omitted], decisions [citations omitted], and commentators (citations omitted) all emphasize the need to make efficient use of California's limited water resources: all recognize, at least implicitly, that efficient use requires diverting water from in-stream uses. Now that the economy and population centers of this state have developed in reliance upon appropriated water, it would be disingenuous to hold that such appropriations are and have always been improper to the extent that they harm public trust uses, and can be justified only upon theories of reliance or estoppel.

The state has an affirmative duty to take the public trust into account in the planning and allocation of water resources, and to protect public trust uses whenever feasible. [Footnote omitted.] Just as the history of this state shows that appropriation may be necessary for efficient use of water despite unavoidable harm to public trust values, it demonstrates that an appropriative water rights system administered without consideration of the public trust may cause unnecessary and unjustified harm to trust interests. [Citations omitted.] As a matter of practical necessity the state may have to approve appropriations despite foreseeable harm to public trust uses. In so doing, however, the state must bear in mind its duty as trustee to consider the effect of the taking on the public trust [citation omitted], and to preserve, so far as consistent with the public interest, the uses protected by the trust. *Audubon,* pages 446-447

The court realized that the public trust rules which had evolved in tideland and lakeshore cases had to be modified to apply to flowing waters—

> The prosperity and habitability of much of this state requires the diversion of great quantities of water from its streams for purposes unconnected to any navigation, commerce, fishing, recreation, or ecological use relating to the source stream. The state must have the power to grant nonvested usufructuary rights to appropriate water even if diversions harm public trust uses. Approval of such diversion without considering public trust values, however, may result in needless destruction of those values. Accordingly, we believe that before state courts and agencies approve water diversions they should consider the effect of such diversions upon interests protected by the public trust, and attempt, so far

Sunset over Mono Lake

*"The State has an affirmative duty... to protect public trust uses whenever feasible."*

*However, the state must have the power to grant nonvested rights to appropriate water "even if diversions harm public trust uses."*

as feasible, to avoid or minimize any harm to those interests. *Audubon,* page 426

*The public trust imposes a duty of continuing supervision, and prior allocation decisions may be reconsidered.*

Even after an appropriation has been approved, the public trust imposes a duty of continuing supervision. The state has the power to reconsider allocation decisions, even if those decisions were made after their impact on public trust values were considered. *Audubon,* page 447. However, the court noted that the case for reconsidering a particular decision is stronger when that decision has failed to weigh and consider public trust uses. *Audubon,* page 447. In the Mono Lake situation, the court concluded that a responsible body should reconsider the allocation of the waters of the Mono Basin and that no vested rights prevented such a reconsideration.

The dominant theme in the *Audubon* opinion is the state's sovereign power and duty to exercise continued supervision over public trust resources. As a consequence, parties acquiring rights in trust property hold those rights subject to the trust and cannot assert a vested right to use those rights in a manner harmful to the trust. *Audubon,* page 437. Thus, the public trust is an affirmation of the duty of the state to protect the common heritage of streams, lakes, marshlands, and tidelands, surrendering that right of protection only when the abandonment of that right is consistent with the purposes of the trust. *Audubon,* page 441.

With the *Audubon* decision, the die was cast for the ongoing controversy over water allocation in California. After the Supreme Court's decision in *Audubon*, it was clear that the right to water use is somewhat different than other vested property rights. Someone who has enjoyed a water right for many years may have the right altered by the application of public trust doctrine. However, the movement of large quantities of water is a necessity for the state of California, which *Audubon* acknowledges, holding that sometimes trust resources may have to give way to consumptive uses.

1962 Benchmark Tufa in Mono Lake

It is not logical to assume from *Audubon* that all water users are apt to be divested of their consumptive rights. All public trust uses are subject to the doctrine of reasonable use. *Audubon,* pages 442-443. Public trust uses do not have a priority over other water uses, and all competing uses of water must be balanced. *Audubon,* pages 445-447. The future of the public trust doctrine lies in this balancing. It will be up to the courts, on a case-by-case basis, to reconcile the protection of public trust values with the equally important need to provide water to our cities and farms.

## The Law of Reasonable Use

### *Herminghaus* and Article X, Section 2

For most of this century, California water law has been evolving from a system of vested rights to a system of use rights. This evolution has seen beneficial uses become unreasonable and has significantly eroded the priority system in California water law. This evolution has changed the standard by which courts evaluate claims of absolute priority. It is now far less likely than in the past that a claim of absolute priority will be upheld.

The primary force in this evolution has been Article X, Section 2, of the California Constitution, the role of which has been particularly evident in the conflict between consumptive and beneficial uses. Cases such as *EDF V. EBMUD* (Super. Ct. Alameda County, 1990, No. 425955) (discussed later in this chapter) and *United States v. State Water Resources Control Board* (1986) 182 Cal.App.3d 82 (the *Racanelli* decision), have wrestled with the application of Article X, Section 2, to this conflict. In *Racanelli,* the court wrote that reasonable use was the "cardinal principle" of California water law. *Racanelli,* page 105. The opinion concluded that reasonableness is not a static concept and that the State Board must balance competing consumptive and instream needs—

*Reasonable use is the "cardinal principle" of California water law.*

> Here, the Board determined that changed circumstances revealed in new information about the adverse effects of the projects upon the Delta necessitated revised water quality standards. Accordingly, the Board had the authority to modify the projects' permits to curtail their use of water on the ground that the projects' use and diversion of the water had become unreasonable...
>
> We conclude, finally, that the Board's power to prevent unreasonable methods of use should be broadly interpreted to enable the Board to strike the proper balance between the interests in water quality and project activities in order to objectively determine whether a reasonable method of use is manifested. [Footnote omitted.] *Racanelli,* page 130

1994 Benchmark Tufa in Mono Lake

The reasonable use doctrine has been present in California water law at least since *Lux v. Haggin* (1886) 69 Cal. 255. That case set forth the basis of the current doctrine of reasonable use—

> The reasonable usefulness of a quantity of water for irrigation is always relative; it does not depend on the convenience of or profitable results to the

particular proprietor, but upon the reasonable use, reference being had to the needs of all the other proprietors on the stream. It depends, in other words, on all the circumstances. *Lux,* page 408.

However, the evolution of the reasonable use doctrine is generally traced to the Supreme Court's decision in *Herminghaus v. Southern California Edison Company* (1926) 200 Cal. 81. The decision in *Herminghaus* prompted the adoption of an amendment to the California Constitution, which is now codified as Article X, Section 2. *Herminghaus* involved a dispute between an upstream power company which sought to build a large reservoir on the San Joaquin River and a downstream riparian ranch. The ranchers used the peak flows of the unregulated San Joaquin River to overflow and inundate their lands and foster grass production. *Herminghaus,* page 93. The construction of the dam would have regulated these peak flows and prevented the river from overflowing onto the riparian lands.

The power company, claiming that the ranchers' large flow requirements were unreasonable, argued that the amount of water needed to raise the San Joaquin River's level to a height sufficient to inundate the riparian lands was a waste of water and that irrigation water could be supplied without this waste through the construction of irrigation works. *Herminghaus,* pages 105-108.

The court held that the rule of reasonable use did not apply between a riparian and an appropriator. A riparian had an absolute priority over an appropriator, regardless of the reasonableness of the riparian's use. *Herminghaus,* pages 100-101. The court rejected the argument that it should reallocate water from the riparians to the appropriator because a greater social benefit would come from the appropriator's use—

> It may be that, if nonriparian owners are permitted to intercept the winter flow of streams, in order to irrigate nonriparian lands, or to develop power, the water so taken will permit the cultivation of more land and benefit a greater number of people than will be served if the flow continues in its accustomed course... Neither a court nor the legislature has the right to say that because such water may be more beneficially used by others it may be freely taken by them. Public policy is at best a vague and uncertain guide, and no consideration of policy can justify the taking of private property without compensation. If the higher interests of the public should be thought to require that the water usually flowing in streams of this state should be subject to appropriation in ways that will deprive the riparian proprietor of its benefit, the change

sought must be accomplished by the use of the power of eminent domain. *Herminghaus,* page 101

This absolute protection of the vested nature of riparian rights prompted the passage of the 1928 constitutional amendment, which is now Article X, Section 2, of the California Constitution. This amendment made the rule of reasonable use applicable to all water users.[15]

Article X, Section 2, changed the nature of a water right. No longer did riparians have an absolute priority over appropriators. And the erosion of the traditional priority system in California water law had begun. Since the adoption of Article X, Section 2, claims of absolute priority have often been rejected by courts.

In *Gin Chow v. City of Santa Barbara* (1933) 217 Cal. 673, the city of Santa Barbara constructed the Gibraltar Dam upstream from Chow's property. *Gin Chow,* pages 677-678. It was uncontested that Chow had a valid riparian right by virtue of his land ownership, and Chow brought an action to prevent the city from impounding or diverting any waters of the Santa Ynez River above his property. *Gin Chow,* page 680. Relying on the ruling in *Herminghaus,* Chow argued that he was entitled to the use of all of the waters of the river and that the city should be enjoined from diverting any waters. *Gin Chow,* pages 695-696.

The court characterized this as a controversy between the public, represented by the city, and property owners asserting an interest against the exercise of power on behalf of the public. *Gin*

*The 1928 constitutional amendment, now Article X, Section 2, changed the nature of a water right.*

---

[15] It is hereby declared that because of the conditions prevailing in this State the general welfare requires that the water resources of the State be put to beneficial use to the fullest extent of which they are capable, and that the waste or unreasonable use or unreasonable method of use of water be prevented, and that the conservation of such waters is to be exercised with a view to the reasonable and beneficial use thereof in the interest of the people and for the public welfare. The right to water or to the use or flow of water in or from any natural stream or water course in this State is and shall be limited to such water as shall be reasonably required for the beneficial use to be served, and such right does not and shall not extend to the waste or unreasonable use or unreasonable method of use or unreasonable method of diversion of water. Riparian rights in a stream or water course attach to, but to no more than so much of the flow thereof as may be required or used consistently with this section, for the purposes for which such lands are, or may be made adaptable, in view of such reasonable and beneficial uses; provided, however, that nothing herein contained shall be construed as depriving any riparian owner of the reasonable use of water of the stream to which the owner's land is riparian under reasonable methods of diversion and use, or as depriving any appropriator of water to which the appropriator is lawfully entitled. This section shall be self-executing, and the Legislature may also enact laws in the furtherance of the policy in this section contained. California Constitution, Art. X, Section 2.

*Chow,* pages 703-704. A similar characterization was later used in *Joslin v. Marin Municipal Water District* (1967) 67 Cal.2d 132, 140. In *Gin Chow,* the court contravened *Herminghaus* and ruled against Chow. One basis for the court's ruling was the new 1928 constitutional amendment, although the court did not base its decision solely upon the reasonable use provision of the constitutional amendment. The court found that Chow was getting very little benefit from the extraordinary floodwaters of the Santa Ynez and that it was a waste of water. *Gin Chow,* page 706. The court quoted Justice Shaw's famous concurring opinion in *Miller v. Bay Cities* (1910) 157 Cal. 256—

> In many parts of the state, especially in the large interior valleys, practically all the flood waters are waste waters. They contribute little or nothing to the saturation of any subterranean gravel beds which are resorted to for a supply of water for useful purposes. They rush in great volume to the sea, carrying destruction in their path and overflowing the low lands to the great damage of the owners, serving no useful purpose whatever. If they were stored in reservoirs they might be made to serve a triple purpose. The extreme floods and consequent overflow and destruction would be prevented; the stored water could be used to irrigate large areas of valley land, now left unproductive for lack of water; if distributed upon the plains, for irrigation, a large portion of these waters would in due course of time find their way by seepage and percolation to the channels of the streams, giving an increased and more regular flow in the summer months, increasing the amount available for irrigation in the smaller streams and bettering the navigation of the large rivers; all of which would add tremendously to the growth, prosperity and wealth of the state and to its ability to support the large population which its climate and productions attract. The question of the right to store such flood waters and the terms upon which it can be obtained or exercised is of the greatest importance to the future welfare of the state. *Gin Chow,* page 701, citing *Miller,* page 287

*The first application of the 1928 constitutional amendment was to subject riparian rights to the requirement of reasonable use.*

Because the court recognized the need to modify the riparian doctrine to meet these modern conditions, the *Gin Chow* opinion had a significant impact on the reasonableness doctrine—

> ...what is an unreasonable use is a judicial question depending upon the facts in each case. Likewise, what is a reasonable or unreasonable use of water is a judicial question to be determined in the first instance by the trial court. *Gin Chow,* page 706.

The significance of the *Gin Chow* case was twofold. First, unlike *Herminghaus*, it did not blindly uphold the riparian's right because it was superior to the appropriator's. Rather, it recognized that the riparian was receiving very little benefit from the exercise of his right, and judicial enforcement must take that factor into account. Second, it held that reasonableness was not a fixed concept but a finding based on the facts of each case.

*City of Lodi v. East Bay Municipal Utility District*, (1936) 7 Cal.2d 316, further undermined the priority system. In this case, the city of Lodi, which was using well water replenished by river flows, sued the East Bay Municipal Utility District (EBMUD) for an injunction to prevent EBMUD from holding the waters of the Mokelumne River behind the Pardee Dam. EBMUD had constructed this reservoir to provide a water supply for its service area in Alameda and Contra Costa counties. *Lodi,* pages 320, 323.

*Application of Article X, Section 2, between two municipal appropriators*

**EBMUD = East Bay Municipal Utility District**

Prior to the adoption of Article X, Section 2, the appropriator would have been entitled to a judgment fixing releases from Pardee Reservoir at a point that would substantially maintain the water table as it would have existed if EBMUD had not built the reservoir. *Lodi,* page 337. After the amendment, the city was no longer entitled to this relief. Rather, the city could limit upstream appropriations only when water levels dropped to a point that significantly impacted its pumping. In the absence of a significant impact, Lodi was not entitled to an injunction against EBMUD. *Lodi,* page 344. Basing its holding on the concept of reasonable use defined in Article X, Section 2, the court concluded that the trial court should determine what well levels were reasonable. *Lodi,* page 343.

*Peabody v. Vallejo* (1935) 2 Cal.2d 351 is the best articulation of the impact of Article X, Section 2. The facts in *Peabody* were similar to those in *Gin Chow.* The city of Vallejo constructed a dam on a tributary that contributed about 35 percent of the flow of Suisun Creek. *Peabody,* pages 358-360. Plaintiffs were riparian owners on Suisun Creek and alleged that they were making beneficial use of all the waters of Suisun Creek because the waters from the stream deposited silt on their lands, repelled saline waters from the ocean, and saturated their land. *Peabody,* page 362.

The court found no damage to plaintiff's lands in allowing Vallejo's reservoir to impound water. Under Article X, Section 2, the court limited plaintiffs to the amount of water needed for reasonable use. The court found that requiring more than 13,000 acre-feet of water to flow into the San Francisco Bay in order to make an insignificant contribution to the plaintiff's underground water supply

*The demands of a downstream riparian will be examined for reasonableness.*

was an unreasonable waste of water. *Peabody,* page 376. The court remanded the case for a determination of whether Vallejo's dam impacted the amount of water needed for plaintiff's reasonable uses. *Peabody,* page 383.

*Tulare Irrigation District v. Lindsay-Strathmore Irrigation District* (1935) 3 Cal.2d 489 explicitly held that a beneficial use could be unreasonable and broadened the reasonable use concept to include consideration of the needs of others. Lindsay-Strathmore had purchased land in the Kaweah Delta and sought to pump and transport water out of the Delta to lands within its boundaries. Plaintiffs were a group of appropriators, riparian owners, and overlying owners holding water rights in the Delta. The trial court found that Lindsay-Strathmore's pumping had injured the plaintiffs. The court also found that plaintiffs' appropriative rights antedated Lindsay-Strathmore's and that the riparians and overlying owners had valid rights. Thus, Lindsay-Strathmore was junior to all of the other users. *Lindsay-Strathmore,* pages 509, 573.

The court concluded that determining a reasonable use requires the consideration of: (1) all of the needs of parties who may take water from a particular area; (2) the uses being made of the waters; and (3) all factors involved. In the words of the court—

> Under this new doctrine, it is clear that when a riparian or overlying owner brings an action against an appropriator, *it is no longer sufficient to find that the plaintiffs in such action are riparian or overlying owners, and, on the basis of such finding, issue the injunction. It is now necessary for the trial court to determine whether such owners, considering all the needs of those in the particular water field, are putting the waters to any reasonable beneficial uses, giving consideration to all factors involved, including reasonable methods of use and reasonable methods of diversion.* From a consideration of such uses, the trial court must then determine whether there is a surplus in the water field subject to appropriation. *Lindsay-Strathmore,* pages 524-525, emphasis added.

The court held that the trial court's finding that every riparian was putting underground flow to beneficial uses was insufficient and that on retrial it would be necessary to determine if those beneficial uses were reasonable. *Lindsay-Strathmore,* page 531. The court wrote—

> Preliminarily, it should be stated that, whatever quantity an appropriator has actually diverted in the past, he gains no right thereto unless such water is actually put to a reasonable beneficial use. (Citation omitted.) What is a beneficial use, of course, depends

*The concept of reasonable use has been extended to include consideration of the needs of others who share the common supply.*

upon the facts and circumstances of each case. What may be a reasonable beneficial use, where water is present in excess of all needs, would not be a reasonable beneficial use in an area of great scarcity and great need. What is a beneficial use at one time may, because of changed conditions, become a waste of water at a later time. *Lindsay-Strathmore,* page 567.

The court noted that in an area of great water need and scarcity such as the Kaweah Delta the use of the entire flow of a stream for subirrigation and the killing of gophers was not a reasonable, beneficial use of water. *Lindsay-Strathmore,* pages 526, 568. The court remanded the case to the trial court for a determination of whether there was a surplus over the reasonable, beneficial needs of plaintiffs. *Lindsay-Strathmore,* pages 582-583.

Thus, in a ten-year period the California legislature and courts redefined the nature of a water right. The concept of an immutable, vested right with an absolute priority was replaced with a flexible, context-related right. The limits of the new right were contingent on supply, competing uses of water, and the amount of benefit obtained from exercising the right. Against this background, the application of the public trust doctrine to rights seems less startling. As discussed below, recent cases have amplified this change even further.

*The concept of immutable vested rights with an absolute priority has given way under Article X, Section 2, to more flexible and context-related rights.*

## Article X, Section 2, in the Modern Day:
## Reallocating Water as a Matter of Public Policy

The next major decision interpreting reasonable use was *Joslin v. Marin Municipal Water District* (1967) 67 Cal.2d 132, which added the consideration of statewide conditions of transcendent importance to the doctrine. In *Joslin*, plaintiffs were riparians operating a rock and gravel business on their property. Plaintiffs relied upon the normal flow of the waters of Nicasio Creek to deposit rock, sand, and gravel on their land. The defendant water district constructed a dam across the stream that obstructed the "normal and usual replenishment of rocks and gravel" upon plaintiffs' land. *Joslin,* pages 134-135. The court reviewed the case in the context of reasonable use—

*Determining reasonable use must also take into account "statewide conditions of transcendent importance."*

> Although, as we have said, what is a reasonable use of water depends on the circumstances of each case, such an inquiry cannot be resolved *in vacuo* isolated from statewide considerations of transcendent importance. Paramount among these we see the ever increasing need for the conservation of water in this state, an inescapable reality of life quite apart from its express recognition in the 1928 amendment (footnote omitted). *Joslin,* page 140.

The court held that it was not reasonable that water from streams should be used in amassing sand and gravel, which in the court's view served no public policy—

> We cannot deem such a use to be in accord with the constitutional mandate that our limited water resources be put only to those beneficial uses "to the fullest extent of which they are capable," that 'waste or unreasonable use' be prevented, and that conservation be exercised "in the interest of the people and for the public welfare." Cal. Const. art. XIV, § 3 [now art. X, § 2]; *Joslin,* pages 140-141.

The *Joslin* court expanded the doctrine of reasonable use by reviewing not only the circumstances of the particular case, but the water situation in the state as a whole, and by determining the reasonableness of plaintiffs' use on that basis. It also fully articulated the idea that a beneficial use could be unreasonable and that this judgment must be based on the facts of each case. Finally, it essentially repudiated the *Herminghaus* court's statement that water could not be reallocated for public policy reasons. The court found plaintiffs' use unreasonable on the grounds that it served no "public policy." *Joslin,* pages 140-141.

If there was any doubt after *Joslin* that water could be reallocated based on public policy considerations, it was dispelled in *People ex rel. State Water Resources Control Board v. Forni* (1976) 54 Cal. App.3d 743. *Forni* followed *Joslin* in holding that a beneficial use could nonetheless be unreasonable. In *Forni,* the State Board enjoined vineyard owners in the Napa Valley from taking water from the Napa River between March 15 and May 15 for frost protection, because this use dried up the river and made water unavailable to other vineyards with junior appropriative rights.

The court held that the overriding principle in California water law was that the use of water be reasonable, and that it was "readily apparent" that the use of water during this period was unreasonable because it created an unnecessary water shortage for the appropriators who needed water for the same purpose. *Forni,* page 750. The State Board found that the only way for the riparians to reasonably exercise their right was for them to build storage reservoirs. *Forni,* pages 747 fn. 2, 750. The court upheld this finding, stating that to achieve the reasonable use of water, senior users (riparians in this case) could be required to endure "some inconvenience or to incur reasonable expenses." *Forni,* pages 751-752. Thus to maximize beneficial use, senior users were required to build reservoirs so that more users could share in the scarce supply.

*Senior right holders may be required to endure "some inconvenience or to incur reasonable expenses."*

In a subsequent case, *In re Waters of Long Valley Creek Stream System* (1979) 25 Cal.3d 339, the court upheld the power of the State Board to redefine the unexercised right of a riparian owner. *Long Valley,* page 351. The decision in *Long Valley* was dramatic, because there was a long line of precedent, including *Peabody v. City of Vallejo*, which stated that a dormant riparian right was paramount to an active appropriative right. The court in *Long Valley*, basing its holding on Article X, Section 2, upheld the State Board's determination that, not only might an unexercised riparian right have a lower priority than existing appropriative rights, it might even have a priority below future authorized appropriative uses. *Long Valley,* pages 358-359. The primary basis for this decision was the court's belief that users suffered too much from the uncertainty created by granting an unexercised riparian right a high priority. *Long Valley,* pages 354-355. This rule has been applied only in statutory adjudications but shows the willingness of courts to subordinate a higher priority right to lower priority right, at least in certain instances.

*Under Article X, Section 2, a dormant riparian right has been subordinated in priority to existing appropriative uses of water.*

In the most recent decision on reasonable use, *Imperial Irrigation District v. State Water Resources Control Board* (1990) 225 Cal.App.3d 548, the court held that the State Board had the jurisdiction to determine whether the irrigation practices of Imperial were reasonable. *Imperial Irrigation,* page 561. In the words of the court—

> Put simply, IID does not have the vested rights which it alleges. It has only vested rights to the 'reasonable' use of water. It has no right to waste or misuse water. The interference by the Board with IID's misuse (this finding of fact by the Board being accepted for purposes of the present issue) does not constitute a transgression on a vested right. *Imperial Irrigation,* pages 563-564

The court then made the most expansive judicial statement to date on the modern water use right—

> All things must end, even in the field of water law. It is time to recognize that this law is in flux and that its evolution has passed beyond traditional concepts of vested and immutable rights. In his review of our Supreme Court's recent water rights decision in *In re Water of Hallett Creek Stream System* (1988) 44 Cal.3d 448 [243 Cal.Rptr. 887, 749 P.2d 324], Professor Freyfogle explains that California is engaged in an evolving process of governmental redefinition of water rights. He concludes that 'California has regained for the public much of the power to prescribe water use practices, to limit waste, and to sanction water transfers.' He asserts that the concept that 'water use entitlements are clearly and permanently

*"Everything is in the process of changing or becoming in water law."*

defined,' and are 'neutral [and] rule-driven,' is a pretense to be discarded. It is a fundamental truth, he writes, that 'everything is in the process of changing or becoming' in water law (footnote omitted).

In affirming this specific instance of far-reaching change, imposed upon traditional uses by what some claim to be revolutionary exercise of adjudicatory power, we but recognize this evolutionary process, and urge reception and recognition of same upon those whose work in the practical administration of water distribution makes such change understandably difficult to accept. *Imperial Irrigation,* page 573.

Yet another example of a way in which the priority and vested right system has been eroded is found in a recent riparian right decision. As mentioned earlier, under the traditional California water rights hierarchy, riparian rights were always at the top. The priority of a riparian right was not determined by whether or not it had been exercised. In other words, a riparian with an unexercised right would still have a higher priority when it began using the water than would any appropriator.

The California Supreme Court's decision in *In re Water of Hallett Creek Stream System* (1988) 44 Cal.3d 448 further undermined the priority of the riparian right. In that case, the court ruled that the federal government held unexercised riparian rights on reserved lands. *Hallett Creek,* page 470. However, the court severely circumscribed these rights. The court stated that, when the federal government asked the State Board for permission to begin a new riparian use, the State Board could "evaluate the proposed use in the context of other uses and determine whether the riparian use should be permitted in light of the state's interest in promoting the most efficient and beneficial use of the state's waters (footnote omitted)." *Hallett Creek,* page 472. Thus the value of the riparian right on reserved land is limited. Indeed, after the decisions in *Long Valley* and *Hallett Creek,* an unexercised riparian user may find itself with a lower priority than a junior appropriator.

## Fish and Game Code Sections 5937 and 5946

Two California Fish and Game Code sections have had a significant impact on water allocations. Unlike the public trust doctrine, these statutes do not provide for balancing but are effectively a legislative determination that certain fishery uses must receive sufficient water. In addition to these provisions, criminal prosecutions for water quality violations have included counts under the public nuisance provisions of Penal Code Section 372.

Fish and Game Code Section 5937 requires that the owner of a dam allow sufficient water to pass through a fishway or dam, to keep in "good condition" any fish that may be planted or exist below the dam. Section 5946 requires the State Board, when it is issuing permits and licenses to appropriate water in District 4½ (including Mono Lake and its tributaries), to impose terms that order full compliance with Section 5937. This section also requires the Department of Water Resources to condition dam approval in that district upon adequate provisions for compliance.

*The California legislature has required that the owner of a dam allow sufficient water to pass in order to keep downstream fish in "good condition."*

Two decisions arising from litigation involving Mono Lake are primarily responsible for the impact of Sections 5937 and 5946 on water allocation. Four lawsuits challenged Los Angeles' longstanding diversions of water from streams tributary to Mono Lake: *Dahlgren et al. v. City of Los Angeles* (regarding Rush Creek) and *Mono Lake Committee v. Department of Water and Power* (regarding Lee Vining Creek), both seeking to impose Section 5937 conditions; and *California Trout, Inc. v. State Water Resources Control Board* and *National Audubon Society v. State Water Resources Control Board*, both seeking to impose Section 5946 conditions.

The Los Angeles Department of Water and Power applied to appropriate the entire flow of Lee Vining, Rush, Walker, and Parker Creeks in 1923, all of which are tributaries to Mono Lake. In 1935, the LADWP applied for a permit from the state to build Grant Lake Reservoir. The Fish and Game Commission determined that to comply with Section 520.5 of the Fish and Game Code (which is now 5937) LADWP would be required to provide an "alternate fish culture." In 1940, to provide "alternate fish culture," the LADWP and the California Fish and Game Commission entered into the Hot Creek Fish Hatchery Agreement. LADWP believed that this agreement brought it into full compliance with Section 5937.

*Los Angeles has been required to release water from Grant Lake Reservoir, though it had earlier financed a new fish hatchery in lieu of releases.*

In 1940, LADWP received permits to appropriate the full flows of Rush, Lee Vining, Walker, and Parker Creeks. In 1941, LADWP began diverting water, and these diversions eventually resulted in the elimination of the fisheries in these creeks.

Fish and Game Code Section 5946, which provided that no permit or license to appropriate water in District 4½ could be issued after its enactment unless conditioned on full compliance with Section 5937, was enacted in 1953. The chief counsel of the Water Board opined that 5946 did not apply to licenses based on permits issued prior to 1953 and that it did not give fish priority over domestic uses. Furthermore, the Attorney General, in unpublished opinions, stated that the Hot Creek Fish Hatchery Agreement was

Lee Vining Creek, one of the tributaries to Mono Lake

valid and binding on the state. In 1974, the State Board granted licenses confirming the vesting of LADWP's right to divert and use water from the four Mono Basin streams. These licenses did not include any conditions requiring compliance with Section 5937.

In 1984, a lawsuit was filed against LADWP when it sought to resume normal operations after heavy precipitation in the Mono Basin had forced releases from Grant Lake Dam down Rush Creek. These releases had created a fishery in Rush Creek. In the litigation, *Dahlgren v. City of Los Angeles Department of Water and Power*, Mono County Superior Court No. 8092 (Rush Creek), plaintiffs argued that the public trust doctrine protected the fishery resources of Rush Creek and that Fish and Game Code Section 5937 imposed an overriding duty on the city to release water for fish below Grant Lake Dam. In November 1984, a temporary restraining order was granted that compelled the release of 19 cubic feet per second (cfs). LADWP agreed to a preliminary injunction. Its motion for summary judgment to terminate the preliminary injunction was denied in August 1985. Ignoring LADWP's argument that Section 5937 was inapplicable, the Superior Court held that the fishery was a public trust resource protected by the public trust doctrine.

In 1986, heavy precipitation caused water to spill (below the city's diversion facilities) into Lee Vining Creek. This created a fishery in Lee Vining Creek. In August 1986, the Mono Lake Committee sought a temporary restraining order for a minimum flow of 20 cfs in Lee Vining Creek and obtained a temporary restraining order compelling the release of 10 cfs. *Mono Lake Committee v. Los Angeles Department of Water and Power*, Mono County Superior Court No. 80608 (Lee Vining Creek). The court subsequently issued a preliminary injunction requiring the release of approximately 4 cfs.

*The impact of Fish and Game Sections 5937 and 5946 on the City of Los Angeles*

In *California Trout v. State Water Resources Control Bd.* (1989) 207 Cal.App.3d 585 (*Cal Trout I*), environmental groups sought writs of mandate to compel the State Board to require compliance with Fish and Game Code Section 5937 as a condition of LADWP's licenses. LADWP argued that 5946 was not intended to apply to its water rights license, which was issued on permits granted prior to the statute's 1953 enactment. LADWP also argued that 5946 could not be applied to impose the requirements of 5937 in violation of the Hot Creek Hatchery Agreement. Finally, LADWP argued that the statute could not be constitutionally interpreted to apply to rights that vested before its enactment. *Cal Trout I,* page 592. The State Board also argued that an action to review its 1974 decision to issue licenses was barred by the statute of limitations. *Cal Trout I,* page 593. Agreeing with LADWP that 5946 did not apply to the appropriation of water by diversion from dams constructed before 1953, the trial court denied the petitions.

In *Cal Trout I* the appellate court reversed the superior court and ordered the State Board to modify the licenses held by the city of Los Angeles to appropriate water from the Mono Lake Basin. *Cal Trout I,* page 593. The court ordered the State Board to follow Fish and Game Code Section 5946 and insert license terms requiring LADWP to comply with Section 5937. *Cal Trout I,* pages 632-633.

The court rejected LADWP's claim that Section 5946 did not apply to licensees whose permits had been issued before the statute's effective date, holding that it applied only to licenses predicated on permits issued before 1953. According to the court, applying Section 5946 did not retroactively alter rights acquired under permits that had been issued prior to 1953, because: (1) the city had not acquired a vested right prior to the enactment of Section 5946; and (2) the right to appropriate 50,000 acre-feet of water could not have vested until completion of the second Los Angeles Aqueduct in the early 1970s, because until that time LADWP was incapable of taking the water. *Cal Trout I,* page 620. Furthermore, applying Section 5946 was not a violation of Article X, Section 2, because that section granted the legislature authority to enact statutes determining reasonable uses of water. The court also rejected LADWP's claim that the statute improperly gave fishery uses of water a priority over domestic uses, concluding that Section 5946 was a legislative choice between competing uses of water. *Cal Trout I,* page 622, 625. Finally, the court rejected the argument that the Hot Creek Hatchery Agreement acted as an estoppel, because allowing such an estoppel would impair the power of the legislature.

The State Board and LADWP did not interpret *Cal Trout I* to require the immediate restoration of water to the four streams tributary to Mono Lake. The superior court denied a request by environmental groups for interim relief, instead supporting LADWP and the State Board's position that the licenses should not be amended to require minimum flows until studies determining the amount of flow needed to comply with Section 5937 had been completed. The appellate court agreed to review this decision.

In *California Trout v. Superior Court* (1990) 218 Cal.App.3d 187 (*Cal Trout II*), the appellate court again overruled the superior court and ordered it to set interim flow releases for the four Mono Lake tributaries covered by the City's licenses. *Cal Trout II,* page 212. The court rejected the State Board's request to delay compliance with Section 5946 until after the State Board completed a comprehensive review of the Mono Lake basin area. The court directed the Superior Court to order the State Board to immediately amend the city's licenses. It also directed the Superior Court to conduct an evidentiary hearing to determine the flows to be released pending establishment of permanent flows by the Water Board. *Cal Trout II,* pages 212-213. After an evidentiary hearing, the court ordered specific flows.

The impact of these two sections in other areas of California has been limited. However, because environmentalists have been successful in these cases, the arguments will certainly appear in other matters and have already appeared in State Board proceedings involving the Santa Ynez River.

### The State Board's Mono Lake Decision

*The end of a long battle: diversions of no more than 16,000 acre-feet annually for many years; Los Angeles' previous diversions averaged 83,000 acre-feet a year.*

In September 1994, the State Water Resources Control Board issued Decision 1631 ("D-1631") which amended LADWP's licenses, severely restricting its diversions from the streams tributary to Mono Lake. LADWP announced that it would not appeal the decision to the courts. D-1631 prohibits any exports until Mono Lake rises to a level of 6,377 feet. It then allows exports of 4,500 acre-feet annually at times when the lake elevation is between 6,377 and 6,380 feet; and exports of up to 16,000 acre-feet annually when the lake is between 6,380 feet and 6,391 feet. Above 6,391 feet LADWP is allowed to export about 31,000 acre-feet annually from the Mono Basin. The State Board believes that this level will protect the full range of public trust resources, although 6,391 feet is 26 feet below the 1941 lake level of 6,417 feet.[15]

LADWP will probably be limited to 16,000 acre-feet for some time, since it has been estimated that it will take twenty years for the lake level to rise to 6,391 feet.[16] Between 1974 and 1989 Los Angeles' diversions from the Mono Lake Basin averaged about 83,000 acre-feet annually.

### Consumptive and Instream Uses in the Litigation Context: A Case Study of *EDF v. EBMUD*

*EDF v. EBMUD—a case study of a controversy between instream and consumptive uses*

An example of litigation involving consumptive and instream uses was *EDF v. East Bay Municipal Utility District* (Super. Ct. Alameda County, 1990 No. 425955). A review of this case provides considerable insight into how cases involving competing demands for consumptive

---

[15] Dunning, "The End of the Mono Lake Basin Water War: Ecosystem Management, Fish and Fairness to a Water Supplier," *California Water Law and Policy Reporter,* November, 1994, page 27.

[16] Birmingham, "Mono Lake: A Retrospective," February 2-3, 1995, Proceedings of the 13th Annual ABA Water Conference, page 3.

and environmental uses may be litigated. Typical of these types of cases, the issues were complex, involving both environmental and public health considerations. The case involved a great deal of expert testimony, numerous procedural battles, a reference to the State Board, and a trial court decision with continuing jurisdiction.

### Summary

The issue at the center of 17 years of litigation was whether EBMUD, pursuant to a 1970 contract with the United States Bureau of Reclamation (USBR), could divert 150,000 acre-feet of water from the Folsom Reservoir at the Folsom-South Canal, or whether Article X, Section 2, of the California Constitution and the public trust doctrine required that the diversion be located below the confluence of the American and Sacramento rivers. Plaintiffs and intervenors (Environmental Defense Fund (EDF), Save the American River Association (SARA) and the county of Sacramento)[17] contended that EBMUD's diversion, alone and combined with future proposed diversions, would cause substantial ecological harm to riparian habitat, fisheries, and the recreational resources of the American River.

**USBR = United States Bureau of Reclamation**

**EDF = Environmental Defense Fund**

**SARA = Save the American River Association**

EBMUD argued that (1) its diversion would not cause harm to public trust values, (2) California water law required the recognition and implementation of its contract rights, (3) sound public policy required that high-quality drinking water be obtained from the best available source, and (4) the Folsom Dam was constructed pursuant to congressional objectives and purposes, thus preempting state interference. *East Bay MUD,* page 2.

The court concluded that EBMUD's contract was valid and that providing high-quality drinking water was a significant public policy objective furthered by EBMUD's upstream diversion at the Folsom-South Canal. However, the court held that specific conditions must be applied to that diversion in order to protect public trust values. The court fashioned a physical solution to accommodate the competing concerns. *East Bay MUD,* Statement of Decision, January 2, 1990, pages 1-2.

### Background

In 1944, Congress authorized the construction of Folsom Dam. It was reauthorized in 1949, and water storage behind the dam began in 1956. In March 1958, the State Water Resources Control Board (SWRCB) issued Decision 893 (D-893), granting permits to the United

---

[17] Later, the California Department of Fish and Game and the State Lands Commission also intervened on behalf of the plaintiffs.

Folsom Dam and Reservoir
on the Lower American River

**SWRCB = State Water
Resources Control Board**

**EIS = Environmental
Impact Statement**

*Pursuant to its state permits, the United States contracted with EBMUD for the delivery of 150,000 acre-feet annually, to be taken from the Folsom-South Canal.*

*The Lower American River chinook salmon run is one of the state's most valuable fisheries.*

States Bureau of Reclamation for storage of water at Folsom. The USBR's permits were subject to minimum flows for fisheries resources, as provided for in a memorandum between the USBR and the California Department of Fish and Game (250 cfs from January 1 through September 14, and 500 cfs from September 15 through December 31). *East Bay MUD,* page 3.

In 1965, Congress authorized the Auburn-Folsom South Unit, the main features of which were the Auburn Dam and Reservoir and the Folsom-South Canal. Construction of the Folsom-South Canal began in 1968, and 27 miles of the canal were completed. A lawsuit filed in 1972 by certain environmental groups, including SARA and EDF, challenged the USBR's decision to proceed with the Auburn-Folsom South project, charging that the Environmental Impact Statement (EIS) was inadequate. *See NRDC v. Stamm* (1974) 6 ERC 1525. An injunction was issued and, because the Department of the Interior has not completed an EIS for the contracting of additional American River water, as of early 1995 no additional work has been done on the Folsom-South Canal. *East Bay MUD,* pages 3-4.

In April 1970, the State Board issued Decision 1356 (D-1356), granting the USBR water rights permits for Auburn Dam. The State Board also reserved jurisdiction for the purpose of formulating terms and conditions relative to flows to be maintained in the lower American River for recreational purposes and the protection and enhancement of fish and wildlife. *East Bay MUD,* page 4. On December 2, 1970, EBMUD entered into its contract with the USBR for the delivery of 150,000 acre-feet of American River water from the Folsom-South Canal. *East Bay MUD,* page 6.

In 1971, the State Board issued Decision-1400 (D-1400) setting flows for fisheries at 1250 cfs from October 15 through July 14, and at 800 cfs from July 15 through October 14. These flows were recommended by the California Department of Fish and Game and were higher than those set under D-893. Minimum recreation flows were set at 1500 cfs; however, these flows could be eliminated and fishery flows reduced during dry years. *East Bay MUD,* page 6.

The lower American River is home to 41 species of fish, of which 9 are anadromous (they live mainly in salt water but enter freshwater rivers to spawn). The most abundant anadromous game fish in the river are chinook salmon, striped bass, American shad, and steelhead trout. The lower American River chinook salmon run is one of the state's most valuable fisheries, supporting significant commercial and sport fisheries in the Pacific Ocean and in the lower American River. Although some adult salmon may be found in the river year-round, the population is mainly the fall-run species. The fall-run adult salmon begin to enter the river in September. Spawning occurs through January, and the juvenile salmon typically leave for the ocean during the spring season. *East Bay MUD,* pages 15-16.

Chinook Salmon from the Lower American River; primarily a fall-run species, and not endangered

Like many water cases, this litigation had a long judicial history. Over a period of 17 years the case went, based on procedural issues, to the California Supreme Court twice and to the United States Supreme Court once. Although the trial began in 1984, the case was referred to the State Water Resources Control Board as referee. The Reference proceedings went on for three and a half years and resulted in a five-volume report, to which plaintiffs and intervenors took voluminous exceptions. *East Bay MUD,* page 17.

*This case involved 17 years of judicial proceedings and reached the California Supreme Court twice before the trial even began.*

The original complaint was filed in 1972 and was based on Article XIV, Section 3 (now Article X, Section 2) of the California Constitution and Water Code Sections 100 and 13500 *et seq.* Plaintiffs challenged (1) EBMUD's decision not to develop facilities to reclaim wastewater to supplement its existing water supplies and to assist in meeting its future water requirements; and (2) EBMUD's decision to seek a supplemental supply of water from the American River. *East Bay MUD,* page 17.

A demurrer to plaintiffs' complaint and a demurrer to plaintiffs' amended complaint were both sustained without leave to amend, and an appeal followed. The California Supreme Court affirmed the judgment in favor of EBMUD (*Environmental Defense Fund, Inc. v. East Bay Municipal Utility District* (1977) 20 Cal.3d 327 (*EDF I*)), holding that the reclaimed wastewater issue must be presented in the first instance to the State Board. *See* discussion in chapter 6. Plaintiffs chose not to do so, and the issue was dropped from subsequent complaints. *East Bay MUD,* pages 18-19.

The Supreme Court held that the remaining allegations were preempted by federal law. The court stated—

> Insofar as the complaints challenge construction of the canal and the choice of diversion point on the basis of state law, they fail to state a cause of action because they attempt to use state law to determine a matter within the authority of the federal agency. *EDF I,* 20 Cal.3d, page 334

Plaintiffs filed a petition for certiorari with the United States Supreme Court. In 1978, the court vacated the judgment in *EDF I* and remanded the case to the California Supreme Court for further consideration in light of the United States Supreme Court's decision in *California v. United States* (1978) 438 U.S. 645. *Environmental Defense Fund, Inc. v. East Bay Municipal Utility District* (1978) 439 U.S. 811; *East Bay MUD*, page 19.

On remand, the California Supreme Court reversed itself. *Environmental Defense Fund, Inc. v. East Bay Municipal Utility District* (1980) 26 Cal.3d 183 (*EDF II*). The Supreme Court reaffirmed its earlier ruling that there was federal preemption as to the complaint's challenge to EBMUD's contract on the ground that the construction of the Auburn Dam and the Folsom-South Canal would constitute a violation of state law. *EDF II*, page 193. However, the court also held that to the extent the complaints "challenge the location of the diversion point as being violative of California law, there is no federal preemption." *EDF II*, page 193. Accordingly, plaintiffs and intervenor were allowed to amend their complaints to "allege that diversion of EBMUD's water through the Folsom-South Canal constitutes an unreasonable method of diversion." *EDF II*, page 200.

After *EDF II*, plaintiffs filed their Second Amended Complaint in September 1980, and Sacramento County filed its First Amended Complaint in Intervention in November 1980. Both complaints alleged that EBMUD's "decision" to seek a supplemental supply of water from the American River to be diverted in a manner which would not allow the water to flow down the lower American River constituted an abuse of discretion and an unreasonable diversion and use of water. Plaintiffs argued that this diversion would harm the fisheries and recreational opportunities on the lower American River. *East Bay MUD*, page 20.

Trial began on April 9, 1984, in the Alameda County Superior Court, but on plaintiffs' motion the case was referred to the State Board as referee. The State Board staff interviewed some 60 technical witnesses and reviewed more than 200 exhibits and reports submitted by the parties. In November 1985, the court granted leave to the California Department of Fish and Game to intervene for the limited purpose of addressing issues related to the protection and enhancement of the state's fish, wildlife resources, and associated recreational activities in the lower American River. In June 1986 the California State Lands Commission was also granted leave to intervene on a limited basis related to riparian issues. *East Bay MUD*, pages 21-22.

In its Report of Referee, the State Board made these findings—

■ Delivery to EBMUD of 150,000 acre-feet from the Folsom-South Canal "will not cause significant harm to reasonable uses made

*The plaintiffs were finally allowed to "challenge the location of the diversion point [Folsom-South Canal] as being violative of California law."*

*Reference to the State Board*

*The State Board found that deliveries to EBMUD under its federal contract would not cause "significant harm to reasonable uses made of the lower American River."*

of the lower American River"; further, the maximum diversion "will not significantly harm reasonable public trust uses of the lower American River." Final Report of Referee, page 11.

■ Under current Bureau of Reclamation operations, "the supply of water available in the lower American River is sufficient to meet existing and projected demand and to provide a reasonable level of protection to public trust uses." Final Report of Referee, page 11.

■ None of the alternatives suggested by plaintiffs is as feasible as the Folsom-South Canal, and "[s]ubstantial additional effort would be required to determine if any alternative is feasible and cost effective from a social, engineering and environmental standpoint." Final Report of Referee, page 13; Final Technical Report, page 259, 243.

■ Of the three sources, namely, the American River, the Sacramento River and the Delta, ". . . water from the American River has the highest quality, with the least potential for degradation and the lowest risk to public health" and further, "[p]rudence requires that public water suppliers should minimize treatment uncertainties by seeking water from the best available source and as removed from the potential for degradation as possible." Report of Referee, pages 14, 15.

■ Finally, the Folsom-South Canal diversion point is not unreasonable, within the meaning of Article X, Section 2, of the Constitution. Final Report of Referee, page 17.

Despite these findings, the case was far from over. Indeed, it calls into question the value of a State Board Reference, since the entire process was repeated by the trial court after plaintiffs and intervenors filed extensive exceptions to the Final Report. A trial addressing those exceptions began on March 6, 1989, and continued for nine weeks.

*The lengthy trial that followed the State Board reference calls into question the value of the reference procedure.*

### The Trial Court's Opinion

The main issues at trial, which was held in front of Judge Richard Hodge, concerned the comparative impacts on public trust uses of allowing EBMUD to divert according to its federal contract from the Sacramento River or the Delta and the comparative public health impacts of taking a drinking water supply from the best available source (American River and the Folsom-South Canal) as opposed to being required to divert from the Sacramento River or the Delta.

The court found balancing to be essential in its application of the public trust doctrine. Both *Audubon v. Superior Court* (1983) 33 Cal.3d

*The primary issue: to take water downstream in order to allow greater flows in the lower American River for fish, recreation, and riparian habitat; or to take water upstream in order to provide the highest quality and the least risk to the public health.*

419 and *United States v. State Water Resources Control Board* (1986) 182 Cal.App.3d 82 provided authority for the importance of balancing competing public water uses without any priority for instream uses and without establishing artificial priorities. *East Bay MUD*, page 24. The court rejected EDF's argument that *Audubon* made protection of public trust resources the first priority in the allocation and use of water resources. *East Bay MUD*, pages 24-25. However, the court did find that public trust values were not just another beneficial use co-equal with irrigation, power production, and a municipal water supply. *East May MUD*, page 26. The court also found that drinking water quality was a public trust value. *East Bay MUD*, page 26. Finally, although municipal use of water and the health-related quality of that water do not fall into a specific category under *Audubon*, the court interpreted *Audubon* to require that they receive full credit in any constitutional balancing evaluation. *East Bay MUD*, page 27. The court attempted to balance all of these competing interests, not to protect public trust uses absolutely, but to preserve them so far as was consistent with the public interest. *East Bay MUD*, page 26.

*Drinking water quality is a value to be balanced against public trust uses.*

Plaintiffs argued against EBMUD's diversion, pointing out that *Audubon* required that, in the allocation of water resources, the state has a duty "to protect public trust uses whenever feasible," and "to attempt, so far as feasible, to avoid or minimize any harm to those interests" because, according to plaintiffs, EBMUD had "feasible" alternative diversion sites and therefore could not divert water at the Folsom-South Canal.

The court rejected this argument because it believed there were a variety of ways to protect public trust values besides relocating the diversion point below the confluence of the American and Sacramento Rivers. In the words of the court—

> . . . if protection of public trust values can be accomplished consistently with the diversion at Folsom-South Canal, then plaintiffs and intervenors can have no sustainable complaint. In the absence of an unnecessary diminution of public trust values, plaintiff's demand for a different diversion site has no supportable legal foundation. In the absence of harm, plaintiff is not entitled simply to achieve a different diversion site as a question of policy or preference. *East Bay MUD*, page 28

Thus, the feasibility of protecting a particular public trust value, regardless of the social cost involved, is only one factor in the balancing process. Proving that the diversion of drinking water from the Delta can be physically accomplished does not establish that diversion at the Folsom-South Canal is constitutionally impermissible. Only if a Delta or Sacramento River diversion could be accomplished at reasonable cost and without compromising the long-term health requirements of the East Bay community might the American River diversion be found constitutionally impermissible. *East Bay MUD*, page 29.

Drinking water quality was a significant factor in the court's decision. The court believed that the evidence presented demonstrated that EBMUD's customers would face an increased health risk if they were required to drink Delta or Sacramento River water instead of American River water. As the court wrote—

> To this court, the establishment of 'slight' or 'moderate' risks with respect to certain pollutants assumes a higher level of significance given the substantial unknown factors which have also been demonstrated. Developing chemical technologies continue to increase the pollutant load on the waterways, while the technology of effective detection has not kept apace. Further, it [is] entirely likely that the existence of deadly carcinogens may first be conclusively determined only through epidemiological studies which are successful in charting patterns of illness only after substantial illness has occurred throughout the population. It is the respect for the unknown which dictates the continuing validity of the sanitary survey as one of the legitimate bases for public health decisions. And if defendant's risk assessment proves prophetic, then it would have been a judicial act of exceptional irresponsibility not to have taken the safer course. This is particularly true given the formulation of a physical solution which can, in this court's view, protect the public trust values which have been advanced as the other side of the equation. *East Bay MUD*, pages 72-73

The court stated that drinking water quality was EBMUD's strongest issue, and without it plaintiffs' argument that multiple uses of the waters of the American River water are the most reasonable and highest beneficial use under Article X, Section 2, might have prevailed. *East Bay MUD*, pages 72-73.

In evaluating the alternatives in its balancing process, the court also rejected plaintiffs' position that the existence of feasible alternatives prevented diversions through the Folsom-South Canal. *East Bay MUD*, page 105. The court noted that no point of diversion is without ecological consequences—

> It is simply not the case that diversion at the Folsom-South Canal creates an environmental disaster, while diversion on the Sacramento River or Delta poses only inconsequential hazards. The

Delta and Sacramento River waterways are part of a complex natural and artificial water system replete with dikes, channels, aqueducts, pipes and an elaborate pumping system so powerful that the very flow of the San Joaquin River can be reversed. In some instances, the Delta environment is so precarious for fish survival, that salmon and striped bass from the Nimbus Hatchery must be transported around the Delta and deposited in the Carquinez Straits to ensure their survival. *East Bay MUD,* page 105.

*The court recognized its obligation to protect public trust values "whenever feasible." It did so by fashioning a physical solution that permitted EBMUD to take water under its contract, but only when certain minimum flows designed to protect public trust uses were present in the river.*

Ultimately, the court's Physical Solution provided, in part, the following—

- EBMUD could not divert more than 150,000 acre-feet annually (AFA) from the Folsom-South Canal pursuant to its contract of December 22, 1970, with the U.S. Bureau of Reclamation. *East Bay MUD,* page 108.

- Certain instream flow requirements had to be met throughout the lower American River as a condition of diversion—
  - October 15 through February, 2000 cfs
  - March through June, 3000 cfs
  - July through October 15, 1750 cfs

- An additional 60,000 acre-feet of water would be reserved at the Folsom Reservoir from mid-October through June for release upon the recommendation of the Department of Fish and Game in response to specific fishery requirements.

- EBMUD would use its best efforts to divert as much water as possible during those times when instream flows are least required for the protection of environmental interests and public trust values.

- The instream flow conditions were not intended to be operational flows to be met in every month of every year without regard to the hydrologic conditions that might prevail at any given time. The court anticipated the establishment of operational criteria based upon the various hydrologic year types (critically dry, dry, below normal, above normal, and so on) to ensure that Folsom Reservoir is not emptied and that there are flows available in the river whenever possible. However, the court did intend for the instream flow requirements to be an absolute limit on EBMUD's ability to divert water from the Folsom-South Canal. If the instream flow requirements cannot be met, EBMUD may not divert any part of its appropriation. *East Bay MUD,* page 109.

*The court appointed a Special Master to supervise continuing studies to determine if any modifications should be made to the minimum flow requirements.*

- All parties were required to cooperate in the development and implementation of scientific studies pertaining to the fish, wildlife, and habitat issues which have been identified in this litigation. These studies are supervised by a Special Master. EBMUD is required to contribute its fair share of the cost of programs to maintain a viable fishery and riparian habitat in the lower American River.

Salmon spawning grounds in Lower American River at Goethe Park

- The court retained jurisdiction to implement the physical solution and modify it as needed.
- Notwithstanding any other provision of the Physical Solution, the court anticipated that during certain "dry year" periods modification of the flow regimens therein might be permitted in limited circumstances to accommodate EBMUD. At such times of crisis, and with the guidance of the Special Master, the court may temporarily modify the flow regimen if such modification can be effected without substantial harm to the fishery, habitat, and other public trust values identified herein. Any such modification will be temporary and only in response to a showing of significant, specific, and immediate health risks to EBMUD. In evaluating circumstances in which a modification may be indicated, recreational interests may be accorded a lower priority than they would otherwise have been. *East Bay MUD,* pages 110-111.

Under the continuing jurisdiction of the court, and with the assistance of a court-appointed Special Master, additional studies on the lower American River are being conducted at the expense of the parties. The purpose of these extensive studies is to determine whether any modifications should be made to the court's minimum-flow requirement. As this book is being written, there is still no resolution of the jurisdictional questions related to these minimum flows. The State Water Resources Control Board has the legal authority to modify the releases currently required of the Bureau of Reclamation in the operation of Folsom Reservoir, but has not done so, either by accepting the court's minimum flows, or otherwise. The Bureau was not a party to the case, and so technically it is not bound by these minimum flows. However, the court views the original minimum flow requirements, and the work being done to confirm or modify these numbers, as a prototype application of the law and science that should be adopted by all interested parties.

## CHAPTER FOUR

# The Role of the State Water Resources Control Board in Controlling the Use and Allocation of Water

## Origin

The State Water Resources Control Board ("State Board") was formed in 1967 to replace the State Water Rights Board.[1] In addition to taking over the water rights duties of the State Water Rights Board, the State Board also assumed the water pollution planning and control duties of the State Water Quality Control Board. The integration of water rights and water quality authority was seen as a timely joinder as water quality and quantity issues steadily became more intertwined.

**SWRCB or State Board = California State Water Resources Control Board**

In 1969 the California legislature adopted the Porter-Cologne Water Quality Control Act, and in 1972 Congress enacted the Water Pollution Control Act Amendments (better known as the Clean Water Act). The problem inherent in separate water quality and water rights agencies was expressed in the following excerpt from hearings before the California Assembly Interim Committee on Water—

**Clean Water Act = Federal Water Pollution Control Act Amendments**

> When the State Water Rights Board approves an application to appropriate water, it is not necessarily concerned with the downstream effect on water quality. The downstream water users with vested rights may protest the upstream application, [but] . . . [t]he administrative mechanism to demonstrate this adverse effect is essentially undeveloped in California. A prime example of this deficiency occurred in the application of the Bureau of Reclamation to appropriate waters in the Delta. After having recognized the need to protect water quality as a part of the rights of existing Delta

[1] The Water Rights Board was established in 1956 to administer California's system of acquiring appropriative water rights.

users, the Water Rights Board found itself unable to take . . . steps [in Decision 990 of 1961] to protect those rights. [fn. 152. Cal. Assembly Interim Comm. on Water, "A Proposed Water Resources Control Board for California," 25-26 (1966)]

The Porter-Cologne Act set out the functions of the State Board with respect to water quality control, encouraged state planning, and incorporated additional water quality considerations into the procedures governing the acquisition of water rights permits. The Porter-Cologne Act gave the State Board full authority over the State's rivers and their use.[2] As the California Supreme Court wrote—

> In obvious recognition of our public policy to require water resources be put to beneficial uses and not wasted, the complexity of the problems presented, the numerous persons affected by water development projects and the necessity of continued regulation to meet changing circumstances, the Legislature has provided a comprehensive system for development, issuance, and administrative regulation of appropriative water rights.
>
> *Environmental Defense Fund v. East Bay Municipal Utility District* (26 Cal.3d 183, 195).

*The State Board is the centerpiece of California's comprehensive system to control water use.*

The State Board is the centerpiece of this comprehensive system. It bears responsibility for the "exercise [of] the adjudicatory and regulatory functions of the state in the field of water resources." Water Code § 174. The Board consists of five members appointed by the governor and must include an attorney specializing in water supply and water rights; a civil engineer knowledgeable in water supply and water rights matters; a sanitary engineer skilled in the water quality field; a water quality expert; and a member of the public. One of these five must have additional expertise in the field of water supply and water quality relating to irrigated agriculture. Water Code § 175. The Board grants, enforces, and reviews all permits to appropriate water within the state.

## The Appropriation of Water

Any person or entity wishing to appropriate water in California must file an application with the State Board. Water Code § 1252. This includes public agencies, cities, counties, and the state and federal

---

2   The jurisdiction of the State Board is limited to surface water and subterranean steams flowing through known and definite channels. Water Code §§ 1200, 1201. The acquisition and exercise of riparian rights and overlying rights to groundwater not part of the underflow of a stream remain outside the Board's control.

governments. Before a permit can be obtained, several conditions must be met: (1) there must be a specific applicant or water user; (2) the applicant must file an application with the Board; (3) the applicant must intend to put the water to beneficial use; and (4) there must be enough unappropriated water to supply the proposed use. The appropriation system applies to surface waters flowing in any natural channel which are not needed to satisfy the reasonable needs of riparian landowners. Water Code § 1201. The appropriative permit process does not apply to riparian rights or to claims for percolating groundwater.

Only unappropriated waters are available for appropriation. These are defined in Section 1202 of the Water Code and include: (1) water which has never been appropriated; (2) water which has been appropriated and subsequently abandoned after the appropriator failed to put it to beneficial use; and (3) water which, once it has been appropriated, flows back into an underground channel or any surface water body.

South fork of the Smith River, part of the Wild and Scenic System

After an application is filed, the Board is required to give notice of the application. Publication of notice triggers a protest period, during which any person with good cause may protest against the approval of the application. Water Code § 1330. Under Section 1243 of the Water Code, the State Board is specifically required to notify the California Department of Fish and Game of all applications to appropriate water. The Department of Fish and Game then must recommend the amount of water, if any, required to preserve and enhance fish and wildlife resources. Water Code § 1243. (Under Fish and Game Code Sections 1601 and 1603, the Department of Fish and Game also has the statutory right to be notified of planned diversions independently of the water rights process and to propose measures to mitigate anticipated adverse impacts on fish and wildlife resources.)

*The Department of Fish and Game must be notified of all applications to appropriate water.*

If the application is not protested, no hearing is required. Water Code § 1351. If a protest is filed, applicants are entitled to an administrative hearing. Water Code §§ 1330, 1331, and 1340. After the State Board makes a decision, parties have several options if they wish to challenge the outcome. Within 30 days a petition may be filed with the State Board for reconsideration of its decision, and the State Board has 90 days to determine whether or not to grant the petition. Water Code § 1357. If the State Board grants the petition, it may reconsider its decision, and the Board has the option of asking the parties to submit new arguments and additional evidence. Water Code § 1358.

The parties may also seek a writ of mandate in the state Superior Court within 30 days of the State Board's decision. This option is available whether or not the parties petition the State Board for reconsideration. The court does not independently review the merits of the State Board's decision. Instead, the court examines the administrative record to determine if the decision was based on "substantial evidence" presented to the State Board. If the decision is supported by substantial evidence, it will be upheld. If not, the court usually remands it to the State Board for reconsideration or additional fact finding. Code of Civ. Proc. § 1094.5; Water Code § 1360.

All water rights in California are subject to the state constitutional limitation of the principles of Article X, Section 2. These are embodied in Water Code Section 100. However, beyond these requirements, several other determinations must be made. First, the State Board must find that the proposed use of water will be beneficial. Water Code §§ 100, 1240, 1375. A list of beneficial uses is found in the California Code of Regulations, Title 23, Section 659 *et seq.* These uses are: (1) domestic use; (2) irrigation; (3) power; (4) frost protection; (5) municipal; (6) mining; (7) industrial; (8) fish and wildlife preservation and enhancement; (9) aquaculture; (10) recreational; (11) water quality; (12) stockwatering; and (13) heat control. Additionally, the Water Code specifically identifies as a beneficial use the storing of water underground, the release of water to control water quality, and the use of water for recreation and the preservation of fish and wildlife. Water Code §§ 1242, 1242.5, 1243.

One clear requirement of beneficial use is that water must be diverted from the stream, or its flow in some way physically altered. Simply leaving water in a stream for instream uses does not constitute a beneficial use. *California Trout v. State Water Resources Control Board* (1979) 90 Cal.App.3d 816.

A second requirement is that unappropriated water must be available for the applicant's use. Water Code § 1375(d). The State Board has published a list of fully appropriated streams from which no further appropriations are allowed. Order No. 89-25, November 16, 1989, and Order No. 91-07, August 22, 1991. Applications on these streams will not be accepted for filing unless the Board's finding is modified. The State Board must also determine if the water has been appropriated by someone else and whether other beneficial uses, such as the control of water quality, recreation, and the preservation of fish and wildlife, limit or preclude the appropriation. Finally, the State Board must consider the public interest in its decision to allow appropriations and must reject applications that are not in the public interest. Water Code §§ 1253, 1255.

## The Evolution of the State Board's Authority

Today, the State Board occupies a central role in the allocation of the State's water resources. Initially, however, the State Board's predecessor agencies took a much narrower view of their authority— that is, simply to determine if unappropriated water was available. If it was available, and no competing appropriator submitted a claim, the water board granted a permit as a ministerial act. *National Audubon Society v. Superior Court* (1983) 33 Cal.3d 419, 442. The evolution of the State Board's authority has occurred gradually—

> Thus, the function of the Water Board has steadily evolved from the narrow role of deciding priorities between competing appropriators to the charge of comprehensive planning and allocation of waters. This change necessarily affects the board's responsibility with respect to the public trust. The board of limited powers of 1913 had neither the power nor duty to consider interests protected by the public trust; the present board, in undertaking planning and allocation of water resources, is required by statute to take those interests into account.
>
> *Audubon,* page 444.

## Exclusive vs. Concurrent Jurisdiction

A pivotal case in the development of the State Board's authority was *Environmental Defense Fund v. East Bay Municipal Utility District* (1977) 20 Cal.3d 327 (*EDF I*). In *EDF I*, the court concluded that the State Board had exclusive jurisdiction over wastewater issues. Such issues could not be taken directly to the courts without plaintiffs first having exhausted the State Board process. The court's conclusion was based on its interpretation of the legislature's statutory scheme for water quality—

*EDF I = Environmental Defense Fund v. East Bay Municipal Utility District (1977)*

> Permitting our superior court's concurrent jurisdiction in this difficult area would impair the comprehensive administrative system established by the Legislature to guarantee reasonable water use and purity. The scope and technical complexity of issues concerning water resource management are unequalled by virtually any other type of activity presented to the courts. What constitutes reasonable water use is dependent upon not only the entire circumstances presented but varies as the current situation changes. As this court noted in *Joslin v. Marin Mun. Water Dist.* (1967) 67 Cal.2d 132, 140 [60 Cal.Rptr. 377, 429 P.2d 889],

'what is a reasonable use of water depends on the circumstances of each case, such an inquiry cannot be resolved *in vacuo* from statewide considerations of transcendent importance.'

The question whether available economic resources should be devoted to waste water reclamation or development of other water supplies is basically a legislative one. The necessity of considering the entire circumstances is obviously increased when, as here, a court is called upon to adjudicate the reasonableness of a decision not to reclaim waste water in the context of a long term procurement of water supplies for over a million people. The issues are far more complex and different both in kind and degree from those presented when a court adjudicates only between two competing users. (For example, *Joslin v. Marin Mun. Water Dist.*, *supra*, 67 Cal.2d 132 [reasonableness of municipal water supply as opposed to availability of sand, gravel, and rock]; *Peabody v. City of Vallejo* (1935) 2 Cal.2d 351 [40 P.2d 486] [reasonableness of municipal use versus water flow over land to deposit silt and wash out salt deposits].) The matter is still further complicated when, as here, transcendent interests of public health and safety beyond normal water use are involved.

When as in the instant case the statutory pattern regulating a subject matter integrates the administrative agency into the regulatory scheme and the subject of the litigation demands a high level of expertise within the agency's special competence, we are satisfied that the litigation in the first instance must be addressed to the agency.

*EDF I,* pages 343-344.

*The State Board has exclusive jurisdiction over wastewater issues but shares jurisdiction with the courts over other water issues.*

**EDF II = Environmental Defense Fund v. East Bay Municipal Utility District (1980)**

Although the State Board has exclusive jurisdiction over wastewater, courts rejected the argument that it should have exclusive jurisdiction over all water issues. In *Environmental Defense Fund v. East Bay Municipal Utility District* (1980) 26 Cal.3d 183 (*EDF II*), the California Supreme Court distinguished the State Board's exclusive jurisdiction over wastewater from its concurrent jurisdiction in actions involving unreasonable water use. The court based its decision on the fact that claims of unreasonable use do not involve the type of complex issues of public health and safety present in wastewater reclamation issues—

Apart from overriding considerations such as are presented by health and safety dangers involved in the reclamation of waste water, we are satisfied that the courts have concurrent jurisdiction with the legislatively established administrative agencies to enforce the self-executing provisions of article X, section 2. Private parties thus may seek court aid in the first instance to prevent unreasonable water use or unreasonable method of diversion.

The fact that the board has retained jurisdiction to consider the diversion point of appropriated water does not deprive the superior court of jurisdiction. Express retention of jurisdiction of a matter not previously determined is merely express recognition of its statutorily granted concurrent jurisdiction. The board has not determined whether diversion of the EBMUD water through the Folsom-South Canal rather than diversion at Hood constitutes an unreasonable method of diversion.

*EDF II,* page 200.

*Audubon* also addressed the concurrent jurisdiction issue raised by the courts in *EDF I* and *EDF II*. Clearly the court was tempted to vest the Board with exclusive jurisdiction, but finally did not.

Audubon *upheld the concurrent jurisdiction of the courts and the State Board but recommended using the reference procedure to take advantage of the State Board's expertise.*

The present case involves the same considerations as those before us in the *EDF* cases. On the one hand, we have the board with experience and expert knowledge, not only in the intricacies of water law but in the economic and engineering problems involved in implementing water policy. (Footnote omitted.) The board, moreover, is charged with a duty of comprehensive planning, a function difficult to perform if some cases bypass board jurisdiction. . . .

We have seriously considered whether, in light of the broad powers and duties which the Legislature has conferred on the Water Board, we should overrule *EDF II* and declare that henceforth the board has exclusive primary jurisdiction in matters falling within its purview. We perceive, however, that the Legislature has chosen an alternative means of reconciling board expertise and judicial precedent. Instead of granting the board exclusive primary jurisdiction, it has enacted a series of statutes designed to permit state courts, and even federal courts, to make use of the experience and expert knowledge of the board.

. . .

These statutes necessarily imply that the superior court has concurrent original jurisdiction in suits to determine water rights, for a reference to the board as referee or master would rarely if ever be appropriate in a case filed originally with the board. The court, however, need not proceed in ignorance, nor need it invest the time required to acquire the skills and knowledge the board already possesses. When the case raises issues which should be considered by the board, the court may refer the case to the board. Thus the courts, through the exercise of sound discretion and the use of their reference powers, can substantially eliminate the danger that litigation will bypass the board's expert knowledge and frustrate its duty of comprehensive planning. (Footnote omitted.)

*Audubon,* pages 450-451.

As a practical matter, the reference procedure on which the Supreme Court relies has not worked well in recent years. The Board's workload has been overwhelming, and it has not been able to act with dispatch. A reference motion becomes a convenient tool for delay by parties who do not want an early decision. Three to five years is not an unusual time for a reference. Even after a reference is completed, a trial can be conducted on exceptions taken to the reference report. Water Code § 2017. The losing party in the reference can take exception to everything in the report, thus essentially requiring the trial court to conduct a *de novo* review.

## Reasonable Use Considerations

Article X, Section 2, has been used as the basis from which legislative and judicial actions have increased the power of the State Board to review the reasonable use of water. *Audubon*, pages 443-444. These include the legislative adoption of Water Code Sections 1243, 1243.5 and 1257 and the finding that the State Board's decision to grant an application to appropriate water is a quasi-judicial decision, not a ministerial act. *Audubon*, page 444.

For example, the court in *People v. Shirokow* (1980) 26 Cal.3d 301 expanded the State Board's authority by allowing it to prevent the diversion of water by the owner of a prescriptive right who would not comply with water conservation programs. It ruled the State Board had jurisdiction over this matter even though the diverter's right was not based on a State Board license. *Audubon*, page 444. The *Audubon* decision broadened the State Board's authority further, because it construed Water Code Section 2501 (which provides for all the rights to water of the stream system to be determined after a petition filed by a claimant to water) to encompass an action such as the Mono Lake case.

The case of *Imperial Irrigation District v. State Water Resources Control Board* (1986) 186 Cal.App.3d 1160 (*IID I*) further strengthened the State Board's authority. This case arose as a result of a State Board decision declaring that the Imperial Irrigation District's (IID) failure to implement water conservation measures was unreasonable

*As a practical matter, the reference procedure may not achieve the prompt, expert, and final decision that is intended.*

*The State Board may determine the reasonableness of water use.*

**IID I = Imperial Irrigation District v. State Water Resources Control Board (1986)**

and constituted a misuse of water under Article X, Section 2, of the California Constitution and Section 100 of the Water Code. The trial court ruled that this adjudicatory decision was not binding on IID. The trial court reasoned that the statutory scheme did not authorize the State Board to determine unreasonable use issues—rather that the State Board's remedy was found in Water Code Section 275, which allows such a matter to be referred to the attorney general for legal proceedings before the Superior Court. The appellate court over-turned this decision, ruling that the State Board had the power to adjudicate the constitutional issue of the unreasonable use of water. *IID I*, pages 1162-1163, 1171.

The battle between IID and the State Board did not end with this case. After the decision in *IID I*, the case was returned to the Superior Court, where the Superior Court determined that the State Board's findings were supported by the evidence and that the decision was a reasonable way of achieving compliance with Article X, Section 2. IID appealed this decision. Again, the appellate court supported the Board, concluding that the State Board had the power to establish standards of reasonableness and to determine whether the irrigation practices of IID were reasonable or wasteful. *Imperial Irrigation District v. State Water Resources Control Board* (1990) 225 Cal.App.3d 548, 561 (*IID II*). The court also rejected IID's argument that the State Board could not interfere with its vested rights. The court held that IID had no vested right to waste or misuse water, and that therefore the State Board's determination did not constitute a violation of IID's vested water right. *IID II*, pages 563-564.

*IID II = Imperial Irrigation District v. State Water Resources Control Board (1990)*

These court decisions demonstrate the significant change in the State Board's role in California water law and policy. The State Board has moved from an agency with limited powers to perhaps the most significant participant in water issues. This is evident in two other areas: water quality and the Bay-Delta process.

## Water Quality Control

### California's Role

California's major water quality protection legislation, the Porter-Cologne Water Quality Control Act, was adopted in 1969. Stats. 1969, Ch. 482, § 18, p. 1051. This pre-dated the Federal Water Pollution Control Act Amendments of 1972. The Porter-Cologne Act sets the goal of regulating activities in California to achieve the high-est reasonable water quality. Reasonableness is determined after considering the demands being made on the waters and all of the values involved. Water Code § 13000. Under the Porter-Cologne

Act, the State Board has the ultimate authority over state water quality policy. Water Code § 13146. However, the Act also establishes nine regional water quality boards to oversee water quality at more local levels. These boards govern the following regions: (1) North Coast; (2) San Francisco Bay; (3) Central Coast; (4) Los Angeles; (5) Santa Ana; (6) San Diego; (7) Central Valley; (8) Lahonton region; and (9) Colorado River Basin. Water Code § 13200. Each regional board has nine members. Water Code § 13201(a).

*The nine regional water quality control boards*

Regional boards engage in a number of tasks related to water quality within their respective regions. One of the most important is preparing a water quality plan for all areas within the region. Water Code § 13240. (As discussed below, regional boards also are responsible for establishing waste discharge requirements.) The regional board must hold a hearing before the adoption of a water quality plan, and the State Board must approve the plan. Water Code §§ 13244 and 13245. These plans, also known as basin plans, have three components: (1) beneficial uses to be protected; (2) water quality objectives; and (3) an implementation program to meet the water quality objectives. Water Code § 13050(j). The beneficial uses that may be protected against degradation include, but are not limited to, "domestic, municipal, agricultural and industrial supply, power generation, recreation, aesthetic enjoyment, navigation, and preservation and enhancement of fish, wildlife, and other aquatic resources or preserves." Water Code § 13050 (f).

Once beneficial uses have been identified, the Porter-Cologne Act requires the state to develop water quality objectives. These objectives are the limits or levels of water quality constituents and characteristics that are established for the reasonable protection of beneficial uses or the prevention of nuisance. Water Code § 13050 (h).

*Water quality plans must consider all demands upon the water source.*

This process requires a balancing of all competing needs for water—

> Each regional board shall establish such water quality objectives in water quality control plans as in its judgment will ensure the *reasonable protection* of beneficial uses . . . .
>
> Water Code § 13241, emphasis added.

As described by the California Court of Appeal in *United States v. State Water Resources Control Board* (1986) 182 Cal. App.3d 82—

> We think this statutory charge ["reasonable protection of beneficial uses"] grants the Board broad discretion to establish reasonable standards consistent with the overall statewide interest. The Board's obligation is to attain the highest reasonable water quality 'considering all demands being made and to be made on those

*waters* and the total values involved, beneficial and detrimental, economic and social, tangible and intangible.'

182 Cal. App.3d, page 116, emphasis in original.

In order to achieve this balance, the regional boards are required to consider the following issues when they establish water quality objectives— *Statutory considerations in establishing water quality objectives*

- Past, present, and probable future beneficial uses of water
- Environmental characteristics of the hydrographic unit under consideration, including the quality of water available thereto
- water quality conditions that could reasonably be achieved through the coordinated control of all factors which affect water quality in the area
- Economic considerations
- The need for developing housing within the region
- The need to develop and use recycled water

Water Code § 13241.

Thus, once the beneficial uses are designated, the balancing occurs when the state determines what objectives will reasonably protect those uses.

The implementation plan must contain a description of the nature of specific actions that are needed to achieve the water quality objectives, a time schedule, and a plan for monitoring compliance. Water Code § 13242.

## The Federal Role

The Clean Water Act also requires that states prepare water quality standards and submit them to the Environmental Protection Agency (EPA) for approval. 33 U.S.C. § 1313(a). In California, the State Board adopts the water quality control plans needed to meet this requirement. Water Code § 13170. **EPA = Environmental Protection Agency**

The Clean Water Act requires that state water quality standards specify "appropriate water uses to be achieved and protected." 40 C.F.R. § 131.10 (a). These uses are called "designated uses" under the Clean Water Act. When classifying state waters for the purpose of designating uses, the state must consider "the use and value of water for public water supplies, propagation of fish and wildlife, recreational purposes, and agricultural, industrial, and other purposes, and also take into consideration their use and value for navigation." 33 U.S.C. § 1313 (c)(2)(A). Thus, EPA has taken the position that in the federal process the balancing between competing water uses occurs at the use designation stage.

Water quality standards are required to contain not only designated uses but also "water quality criteria" based upon such uses. 33 U.S.C. § 1313(c)(2)(A). Criteria are defined by regulations developed by EPA as elements of water quality standards, expressed as "constituent concentrations, levels, or narrative statements, representing a quality of water that supports a particular use." 40 C.F.R. § 131.3 (b). Criteria "must be based upon sound scientific rationale and must contain sufficient parameters or constituents to protect the designated use." 40 C.F.R. § 131.11. EPA interprets this to mean that there is no balancing in the adoption of criteria.

*Both federal and state law include a balancing process in setting water quality standards. The difference lies in the timing.*

The crucial difference in the development of "water quality standards" pursuant to the Clean Water Act and the development of "water quality plans" under California's Porter-Cologne Act is one of timing. While both processes incorporate a balancing process that takes competing water uses into consideration, the balancing occurs at a different time depending upon whether it is EPA's process or the California process which is followed. Thus, if it is EPA's process of developing "water quality standards" which is used, the consideration of competing water uses occurs up-front, when uses are designated. Under California's Porter-Cologne Act, on the other hand, the balancing of competing water uses occurs at the end, when the State decides how to "reasonably protect" previously developed "beneficial uses."

*Federal and state antidegradation policies*

The Clean Water Act requires state water quality standards to contain an antidegradation policy that is consistent with the federal policy. The federal requirements call for different levels of protection based upon three classifications of water bodies: (1) all existing instream uses (uses that actually existed in a water body on or after November 28, 1975 (40 C.F.R. § 131.3(e) (1992)) must be maintained and protected; (2) water bodies that are of sufficient quality to support the propagation of fish, shellfish, wildlife and recreation cannot be degraded below the level necessary to support those uses; and (3) high-quality waters that are outstanding natural resource waters must be maintained and protected. 40 C.F.R. §131.12 (a)1,2,3 (1992).

The State Board complied with this directive by adopting Resolution No. 68-16, "Statement of Policy with Respect to Maintaining High Quality Waters of California." Resolution No. 68-16 requires that high quality be maintained and protected unless: (1) allowing some degradation is clearly in the best interests of the people of California as a whole; (2) such allowable degradation does not preclude an identified (present or future) beneficial use; and (3) the applicable basin plan or some statewide policy takes note of the change in question and concedes that it is appropriate.

## Regional Board Enforcement

The regional board has the authority to regulate any waste discharge that may affect either surface or ground waters. Water Code §§ 13050(e), 13260, 13263. Waste is broadly defined under the Porter-Cologne Act and includes sewage and all other waste associated with human habitation, of human or animal origin, or from any producing, manufacturing, or processing operation. Water Code § 13050(d). Any person proposing to discharge waste within any region must file a report with the appropriate regional board. Water Code § 13260(a)(1). After filing the report, no discharge may take place until: (1) a waste-discharge requirement is issued; (2) a waiver of the waste discharge requirement is issued; (3) 120 days have passed since complying with the Water Code Section 13260 reporting requirements. Water Code § 13264(a). The waste-discharge requirements must comply with the appropriate water quality control plans, and the regional board has the power to prohibit the discharge if necessary. Water Code § 13264. The waste-discharge requirements must implement the water quality control plan for the area and consider the beneficial uses to be protected. Water Code § 13263(a).

*Waste discharge requirements*

The National Pollution Discharge Elimination System (NPDES) was established by the Clean Water Act to establish permit requirements for point-source surface discharges. 33 U.S.C. § 1342. The waste-discharge requirements under the Porter-Cologne Act are the equivalent of NPDES permits, and they must be consistent with the applicable provisions of the Clean Water Act. 23 Cal. Code Regs., tit. 23, §§ 2235.1, 2235.2. Of course, waste discharge requirements must also comply with applicable state regulations. 23 Cal. Code Regs., tit. 23, § 2235.3. The State Board and EPA have entered into a Memorandum of Understanding (MOU) whereby the NPDES program in California is administered by the state and regional boards. *See* 40 C.F.R. § 123.24.

**NPDES = National Pollution Discharge Elimination System**

**MOU = Memorandum of Understanding**

Enforcement of water quality requirements is a responsibility shared by the state and regional boards. Both entities monitor discharges and surface water quality, and both have the authority to require monitoring by the dischargers. Water Code §§ 13377, 13383(a), (b). Regional boards are at the forefront of the enforcement process. Regional boards may issue cease-and-desist orders, which require a party to stop discharging if the board finds that the discharge is taking place or threatening to take place in violation of the controlling requirements. The cease-and-desist order requires the discharger to comply immediately or within a time schedule set by the board, or to take appropriate corrective action. Water Code § 13301.

The regional board may also enter cleanup or abatement orders. Water Code §§ 13223, 13304. These orders are used to regulate problems caused by unregulated discharges and usually require a discharger to clean up waste, abate its effects, or take other needed remedial action. If the discharger fails to comply with the cleanup and abatement order, the board may ask that the attorney general petition the superior court to issue an injunction to achieve compliance. Water Code § 13304(a). The regional board also has the authority to undertake the cleanup work itself and obtain reimbursement from the discharger. Water Code §§ 13050(l),(m), 13304(c). Finally, the regional board may enforce the Porter-Cologne Act through the assessment of administrative civil liability. This is a monetary assessment that may be levied against persons who violate the Act. Water Code §§ 13323-13327.

The State Board has the authority to review the regional board's actions. Water Code § 13320. The State Board may uphold the actions or may stay the regional board's decision, in whole or in part. Water Code § 13321(a).

## The Bay-Delta Hearing Process

The Sacramento River and the San Joaquin River meet in the Central Valley to form the Sacramento-San Joaquin Delta. As they flow jointly toward the ocean, they merge with smaller rivers to form a 700-mile-long area of rivers and sloughs, surrounding 57 islands. The "Delta," as the area is known, has been radically altered since it was discovered by early explorers. At that time it was a vast tidal marshland largely covered by vegetation, predominantly tules. In the late 1800s, farmers discovered the fertile soil of the Delta, and began building levees and channels to facilitate farming in this area. By 1930, more than 1,000 miles of levees had been built, and 500,000 acres of farmland had been reclaimed and were under cultivation.

The river flows and tidal influences in the Delta area have always been subject to major changes. Prior to any human alteration of the Delta environment, saline ocean water at times reached far into the Delta area. Indeed, during the severe drought of the early 1930s, salt water came as far inland as Sacramento. At the other end of the spectrum, a great flood in the 1860s resulted in a significant amount of fresh water in San Francisco Bay.[3]

---

[3]  "Unresolved Issues in Water Marketing," May/June 1992, *Western Water,* page 5, hereafter *Western Water.*

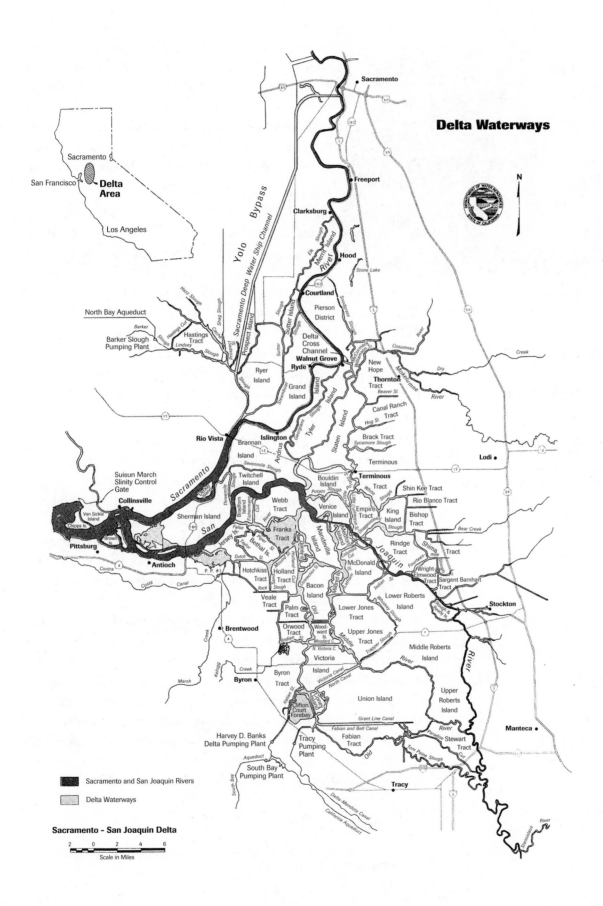

**Delta Waterways**

Delta Area

Sacramento

San Francisco

Los Angeles

N

Sacramento
Freeport
Clarksburg
Hood
Courtland
Pierson District
Walnut Grove
Ryde
Islington
Rio Vista
Thornton Tract
New Hope
Canal Ranch Tract
Brack Tract
Terminous
Lodi

North Bay Aqueduct
Barker Slough Pumping Plant
Hastings Tract
Ryer Island
Grand Island

Suisun March Slinity Control Gate
Collinsville
Pittsburg
Antioch
Twitchell Island
Bradford Island
Sherman Island
Webb Tract
Franks Tract
Bethal Is.
Holland Tract
Bacon Island
Hotchkiss Tract
Veale Tract
Palm Tract
Orwood Tract
Brentwood
Byron
Victoria Island
Byron Tract
Union Island
Clifton Court Forebay
Harvey D. Banks Delta Pumping Plant
Tracy Pumping Plant
South Bay Pumping Plant
Tracy
Fabian Tract

Bouldin Island
Venice Island
Empire Tract
King Island
Mandeville Island
McDonald Island
Lower Jones Tract
Upper Jones Tract
Middle Roberts Island
Lower Roberts Island
Shin Kee Tract
Rio Blanco Tract
Bishop Tract
Rindge Tract
Wright-Elmwood Tract
Sargent Barnhart Tract
Stockton
Shima Tract
Upper Roberts Island
Manteca
Stewart Tract

San Joaquin River
Sacramento River

**Sacramento and San Joaquin Rivers**

Delta Waterways

**Sacramento - San Joaquin Delta**

2  0  2  4  6
Scale in Miles

The Delta, a few miles southeast of Antioch

**CVP = Central Valley Project**

**SWP = State Water Project**

*D-1379, adopted in 1971, set Delta standards for salinity and protection of fish and wildlife, without regard to the priorities between the CVP and the SWP.*

As diversions by the Central Valley Project and the State Water Project have increased, less water has remained in the Delta, and thus less Delta water has flowed into San Francisco Bay. The average annual outflow of the Delta is 13 million acre-feet, although it can range from 4 million acre-feet to 40 million acre-feet, depending upon patterns of precipitation.

### D-1275

The State Board first turned its attention to the Delta in the late 1960s. Its earliest decisions on Delta waters, Decision 990 (D-990) and Decision 1275 (D-1275), did not impose specific salinity-control terms on the Central Valley Project (CVP), but reserved jurisdiction to allow for a mutual agreement among all Delta water users. In 1969, the State Board began hearings involving the water rights of the State Water Project (SWP) and the CVP in order to coordinate the operations of these projects and provide salinity protection for the Delta. In 1971, the State Board issued Decision 1379 (D-1379).

### D-1379

The State Board's D-1379 integrated water rights and water quality, and found that the State Board's jurisdiction encompassed not only the uses adopted for protection in the Clean Water Act, which included agricultural supply, protection of fish and wildlife, and municipal and industrial supply, but all beneficial uses of the Delta. D-1379, page 41. Significantly, D-1379 required both projects to meet its standards without regard to the relative priority of their water rights.[4] The State Board concluded that not only could project operators be required to refrain from interference with the natural flows required for proper salinity control and for fish and wildlife in the Delta, but they could also be required to provide a reasonable quantity of water conserved by storage for these purposes under the terms of their permits. D-1379, page 26. D-1379 placed all the burden for the protection of these uses on the state and federal projects, even though other water rights holders contributed to the depletion of Delta supplies. Indeed, the burden for protecting these uses still falls solely on the projects. However, the implementation of D-1379 was stayed in October 1971 as a result of litigation originated by the Central Valley East Side Project Association and the Kern County Water Agency. Decision 1485, page 4.

---

[4]  Robie, "The Delta Decisions: the Quiet Revolution in Water Rights," 19 *Pacific L. J.* 1111, 1128.

## D-1485

D-1379 was intended as an interim decision, and hearings were to be reopened no later than July 1, 1978. D-1379, page 63. These new hearings actually began on April 29, 1976. In August 1978, the State Board issued Decision 1485 (D-1485) and at the same time adopted a water quality control plan for the Sacramento-San Joaquin Delta and Suisun Marsh.

In D-1485 the State Board sought to protect vested water rights and the public interest. D-1485, page 9. The State Board identified the beneficial uses of the Delta and Suisun Marsh as: (1) fish and wildlife; (2) agriculture; and (3) municipal and industrial. The water quality standards established by the State Board were to ensure the protection of each of these interests. The underlying principle of D-1485 was that water quality in the Delta should at least be equal to the levels that would have been available if the state and federal projects had not been constructed. D-1485, page 10. D-1485 modified the permits held by the Bureau of Reclamation and the Department of Water Resources and compelled the two projects to adhere to water quality standards set out in the plan. D-1485, pages 21-30. In D-1485 the State Board again placed all of the burden of meeting the standards on the projects, without establishing priority between the two, because it concluded that the Delta Protection Act accorded first priority to satisfying vested rights and relegated all exports of water to a lesser priority. Furthermore, the State Board concluded that the projects must be operated so as not to cause material deterioration of water quality which would limit its reasonable beneficial uses for senior water rights holders. D-1485, page 9.

*D-1485 set Delta standards for the CVP and SWP based upon "without project" conditions.*

The Board concluded D-1485 by once more promising to reopen hearings on Delta issues within eight years. Although the Board believed the level of protection afforded by D-1485 was reasonable, it scheduled the future hearings because of the uncertainty connected with possible future project facilities and the need for further information. D-1485, pages 8, 18.

### The *Racanelli* Decision

The requirements of D-1485 were challenged in the case *United States v. State Water Resources Control Board* (1986) 182 Cal.App. 3d 82 (the *Racanelli* decision). *Racanelli* held that the D-1485 standards were invalid for three primary reasons.

*Racanelli overturned D-1485 as not providing sufficient Delta protection.*

First, the court held that the State Board's use of "without project" conditions as the measure of flows needed to protect existing water rights in the Delta against harm by the projects was "fundamentally defective." *Racanelli,* page 116. The court stated that the State Board's primary task in its water quality role is *not* to protect *water rights,* but to protect *beneficial uses.* The State Board must establish objectives that will reasonably protect beneficial uses; this function was improperly constrained by looking only at the state and federal projects and their rights.

Second, *Racanelli* held that the State Board erred by establishing "without project" conditions as the appropriate maximum level of protection. The State Board used these criteria in order to make the projects solely responsible for the adverse effects of project conditions. The court concluded that this was wrong and that upstream non-project water users were not entitled to unlimited access to upstream waters. The State Board must consider *all* competing demands for water to arrive at a reasonable level of protection. *Racanelli,* pages 118-119.

Finally, the court held that the State Board's procedure of combining water quality and water rights functions was "unwise," because the State Board did not fully protect water quality. The Board set only those water quality objectives that could be enforced against the projects. *Racanelli,* pages 119-120. Thus, the State Board had defined the scope of its task too narrowly.

Despite its criticism of the State Board's methodology, the *Racanelli* decision firmly set forth the expansive nature of the State Board's power. It affirmed the principle that the State Board has the power to determine the proper balance between water quality interests and the effects of water diversions in order to determine whether a water use is reasonable. *Racanelli,* page 130. The court also affirmed the State Board's authority to condition the water rights of the CVP and the SWP, consistent with the public interest, as a method of implementing water quality control plans and protecting water quality. *Racanelli,* pages 125-129. It is important to note that the State Board's balancing authority is not limited merely to water uses *within* the Delta. *Racanelli* requires that "*all* competing demands for water" be considered in the balancing. *Racanelli,* page 118, emphasis in original. The court stated that a "global perspective is essential to fulfill the Board's water quality planning obligations." *Racanelli,* page 119.

After *Racanelli,* it is also apparent that the State Board has the authority to impose restrictions against water rights holders without strictly adhering to the traditional priorities of water rights law. The Bureau of Reclamation had asserted that, because its permits for the CVP had been obtained earlier, it had a higher priority than the

*In setting Delta standards,* Racanelli *requires that the balancing process include* all *competing demands for water, not merely those* within *the Delta.*

State Water Project. Thus, the Bureau argued that the State Board could not make the projects equally responsible for flows needed to maintain water quality. However, the court held that the State Board was empowered to consider the relative benefit of different uses of water and to impose conditions on water rights without respect to traditional priorities—

*Racanelli held that the State Board could impose restrictions on both the federal CVP and the SWP without regard to their respective water rights priorities.*

> The scope and priority of appropriative rights are properly defined by the Board acting within its powers to consider the relative benefits of competing interests and to impose such conditions as are necessary to protect the public interest. Here, the projects' permits were issued subject to the continuing jurisdiction of the Board to coordinate project operations. D 1485 was an exercise of that continuing jurisdiction. Accordingly, when the Board imposed Term 2—requiring equal responsibility for maintaining the water quality standards—it acted well within its authority and did not infringe upon or otherwise unlawfully impair the 'vested' appropriative rights of the U.S. Bureau, which held its permits subject to the exercise of such authority.
>
> *Racanelli,* page 133, footnote omitted.

The court also addressed the contractors' argument for water from the CVP: that the State Board had impaired their contractual rights. The court rejected this argument, finding no substantial contractual impairment. However, the court added that even if the State Board had substantially impaired the contracts, it would have been a valid exercise of the police power. *Racanelli,* page 148. Finally, the court stated that the State Board had the authority to reopen permits to protect fish and wildlife "whenever feasible," even if it had not expressly reserved jurisdiction. *Racanelli,* page 152.

## The New Bay-Delta Hearings, Beginning 1987

In 1987, pursuant to the *Racanelli* decision, the State Board began a three-phase hearing process to receive and examine evidence on beneficial uses and water quality issues for revising existing water quality objectives in the Bay-Delta Estuary. The hearings began on July 7, 1987, and consisted of more than fifty days of evidentiary hearings. These Phase I hearings culminated in the preparation of two documents: a Draft Water Quality Control Plan for Salinity for the San Francisco Bay and the Sacramento-San Joaquin Delta Estuary, and a Pollutant Policy Document (PPD).[5] These documents were released in November 1988.

*Phase I of the Bay-Delta hearings*

**PPD = Pollutant Policy Document**

[5] Pollutant Policy Document (PPD) Final Draft SWRCB, May 1990, page iii.

**Draft Plan = State Draft Water Quality Control Plan for Salinity**

The State Draft Water Quality Control Plan for Salinity ("Draft Plan") contained recommended flow and salinity objectives for the Bay-Delta Estuary as well as a program of implementation to provide reasonable protection for beneficial uses of Bay-Delta Estuary water, including export limits. Draft Plan, pages 1-4, 1-5. The plan also called for a California "water ethic." This water ethic contemplated conservation, reclamation, conjunctive use, shared responsibility (that not only the CVP and the SWP would bear the responsibility for adequate flows, but that all water users in the Bay-Delta watershed would have responsibility), physical facilities, and pollution control. Executive Summary of Draft Plan, pages 1-6, 1-7. The Draft Plan also recommended water quality objectives for beneficial use in the Estuary. Draft Plan, pages 1-8 to 1-10.

It was recognized that there would be significant water supply impacts arising from the Draft Plan. These were justified on the basis of the decline in certain aquatic species in the Delta. The Plan recommended that the amount of water exported from the Estuary in 1985 be set as a maximum export level. Draft Plan, pages 1-10, 1-11.

*Withdrawal of the Phase I Plan*

After the completion of Phase I, the State Board abruptly withdrew the Plan and revised its work plan. Water Quality Control Plan for Salinity, Revised Draft, page 1-1, June 1990. The Plan was withdrawn because of major statewide controversies over its impacts and legal underpinning.[6] Water suppliers claimed that the restrictions on exports were too severe and that the Plan predetermined water rights allocations that should have been decided in the later water rights phase of the proceedings. Environmentalists contended that the withdrawal of the Draft Plan merely demonstrated the susceptibility of the Board to the political pressure applied by water user groups.

The State Board's next effort was confined to a water quality plan only, without a determination of water rights. The Water Quality Control Plan for Salinity for the San Francisco Bay and Sacramento-San Joaquin Delta Estuary was released on May 1, 1991; and on May 31, 1991, the Sierra Club Legal Defense Fund, the Environmental Defense Fund, and 15 other environmental groups filed a lawsuit seeking to invalidate it.[7] The primary objection to the 1991 Plan was its failure to include *flow* requirements (which the State Board had scheduled for the next water rights phase) in the water quality objectives and implementation measures. The lawsuit

[6] Boronkay, "What the Bay/Delta Proceedings Reveal about the State Water Resources Control Board's Powers and Procedures," *California Water Law and Policy Reporter,* October 1990, page 7.

[7] *California Water Law Reporter,* Vol. 1, No. 11, August 1991, page 216.

alleged that populations of striped bass, Delta smelt, and winter-run Chinook salmon had declined precipitously and that the State Board had erroneously limited its work by not including fresh-water flow standards. Petition for Writ of Mandate, page 3. The central issue of this litigation has been described as follows—

*The issue—whether requirements for water flows, including releases from storage, can be imposed in a water quality plan*

> If the Board determines that certain terms or conditions should be included in the appropriate water rights permits of those diverting water from the Delta in order to protect the beneficial use of Delta waters for fishery purposes, must those terms and conditions also be included in the Delta basin plan (as water quality standards) and submitted to EPA for approval, even if those terms and conditions are flow related and are not designed to create or maintain a particular water quality constituent level in the water?[8]

This issue—whether fresh-water flow standards should be in the water quality phase of the Bay-Delta proceedings instead of the water rights phase—is significant. Because state water quality plans must be approved by the EPA, if flow objectives are required to be included in the Plan, it could effectively lead to federal control of state water allocation decisions.[9] Water rights decisions, as opposed to water quality plans, do not require EPA approval. At the time this volume went to press, the lawsuit, *Golden Gate Audubon Society, et al. v. State Water Resources Control Board*, Sacramento Superior Court No. 366984, had not gone to trial.

On September 3, 1991, the EPA sent a letter informing the State Board that the standards in the Salinity Plan were inadequate to protect fish and wildlife in the estuary. The EPA gave the State Board 90 days to revise the standards.[10] The State Board declined to do so. EPA took no immediate action, but in December 1993 published its own Draft Water Quality Standards for the Bay-Delta, claiming that it had such power in view of the state's action.

*EPA rejects the Salinity Plan.*

## D-1630

On May 8, 1992, however, the State Board posted notice of public hearings for June and July 1992 to establish "interim, near-term actions that can be taken to address the decline of public trust resources in the Bay-Delta Estuary while minimizing impacts on

*D-1630, also withdrawn*

[8] Schulz, *California Water Law and Policy Reporter,* Vol. 2, No. 1, October 1991, page 4.

[9] *California Water Law Reporter,* Vol. 1, No. 11, August 1991, p. 217.

[10] *California Water Law and Policy Reporter,* Vol. 2, No. 3, December 1991, page 41.

EBMUD's Mokelumne River aqueduct crossing the Delta

water supply reliability."[11] These proceedings were part of the water rights phase, and thus in the Board's view could properly deal with flow requirements and water allocations. The State Board conducted a 14-day hearing between June and August 1992. In December 1992, the State Board issued Draft Water Right Decision 1630 (D-1630), which also was subsequently withdrawn. D-1630 found that the public-trust resources of the Estuary were in a state of decline and that higher outflows, and modifications in the way water is diverted from the Delta, were needed to protect them. D-1630, pages 29-50. D-1630 also required compliance with the standards set forth in the 1991 Salinity Plan. D-1630, page 45.

D-1630 included several other significant features. The State Board determined that—

*Not only diverters from the Delta, but also those agencies diverting water upstream that otherwise would supply the Delta, were found to bear responsibility for Delta conditions.*

> All major water users of water from the Bay/Delta watershed share a measure of responsibility for the biological decline of the Bay/Delta Estuary; therefore, they share responsibility for mitigating the impacts of their water diversion and storage.

D-1630, page 53.

For the first time, the State Board made clear that Northern California cities such as San Francisco and Oakland (which is served by the East Bay Municipal Utility District; *see* chapter 1) were export areas that must also bear responsibility for reducing flows to the Bay-Delta Estuary. D-1630, pages 17, 53. These two urban areas divert flows upstream that otherwise would supply the Delta.

D-1630 was never finalized by the State Board. Instead, it was withdrawn at the request of California's Governor following indications from the Environmental Protection Agency that it would reject Bay-Delta standards similar to those contained in the draft decision. In addition, biological opinions issued by the National Marine Fisheries Service (NMFS) and the United States Fish and Wildlife Service (USFWS) for the winter run salmon and Delta smelt had already supplanted, as a practical matter, the water rights conditions previously imposed by the State Board. Accordingly, the Governor requested that draft D-1630 be withdrawn until the federal government was able to speak on California water issues with one voice.

**NMFS = National Marine Fisheries Service**

**USFWS = United States Fish and Wildlife Service**

---

[11] *California Water Law and Policy Reporter,* July 1992, page 205.

## State and Federal Agreement on Bay-Delta Standards

Following the State's action on D-1630, the federal government took California at its word and formed an inter-agency grouping known as the Federal Environmental Directorate or "Club Fed," comprised of EPA, NMFS, the USFWS and the Bureau of Reclamation.

*The formation of "Club Fed"*

In December 1993, Club Fed acted through the Environmental Protection Agency to issue proposed water quality standards for the Bay-Delta Estuary. On the same date, Club Fed also proposed through the USFWS a critical habitat designation for the Delta Smelt which encompassed the entire Delta. Further, again acting through the USFWS, Club Fed proposed the Sacramento splittail, a large minnow resident in the Delta, for listing as a threatened species.

The issuance of these draft proposals galvanized urban and agricultural water suppliers dependent upon Delta exports or waters that would otherwise supply the Delta. Working throughout the summer and fall of 1994, urban and agricultural water suppliers developed a joint proposal for resolving Bay-Delta issues. The urban members of the group included San Francisco and other bay area entities, as well as the Metropolitan Water District and other suppliers in Southern California.

*Formation of the "urban/ag" coalition*

Incorporating a far reaching set of standards, the "urban/ag" consensus proposal focused on the spring period (February-June), considered by biologists to be the most crucial for the protection of Delta aquatic species. The proposal was designed to substantially improve the estuarine shallow-water habitat in important areas of the estuary. In addition, it proposed export limits for the SWP and CVP's pumping plants, as well as closures during certain times for the Delta Cross-Channel. It also incorporated a series of non-outflow related measures (so-called "Category III" measures) which entailed the screening of unscreened diversions within the Delta and upstream, additional waste discharge controls and pollution prevention, controls on both legal and illegal fishing, the control of land-derived salts from agriculture operations along the San Joaquin River, and riparian, wetland and estuarine habitat restoration. In total, the joint urban/agriculture proposal recommended a reduction in Delta exports (and concomitant increases in freshwater outflows to San Francisco Bay) of more than a million acre feet in critical years and nearly 350,000 acre-feet in average years, over and above pre-existing state-imposed standards.

Pardee Dam and Reservoir on the Mokelumne River

The urban/ag consensus proposal became the basis for negotiations between the federal and state governments during the late fall of 1994. On December 15, 1994 these negotiations culminated in a detailed Statement of Principles for the Bay-Delta standards signed not only by representatives of the State and federal governments, but also by major urban, agricultural and environmental groups. A copy of this Statement of Principles is incorporated herein as appendix A.

*The December 15, 1994 accord was an agreement of historic proportions.*

Characterized correctly as an agreement of "historic" proportions, the December 15, 1994 Statement of Principles represents the first time that *all* important interest groups have concurred about the measures necessary to reasonably protect the Bay-Delta environment, while also insuring the availability of reliable supplies of water for California's urban and agricultural communities. Expanding upon the urban/ag consensus proposal, the Statement of Principles provides both water quality standards and water project operational constraints. These are designed to ensure the availability of substantially increased Delta outflows and limitations upon project exports during the crucial spring months. Additional project operational limitations are imposed during other months of the year at levels which should also protect Delta environmental resources while allowing water suppliers to recover some of the water foregone for environmental purposes during the spring. Similarly, by allowing more exports in wetter years, the agreed-upon standards permit urban and agricultural suppliers to recover water foregone in drier years. The Statement of Principles also incorporates the Category III measures recommended as part of the urban/ag consensus proposal and guarantees that $30,000,000 will be provided over the period 1995-1997 for the implementation of such measures.

California Aqueduct traversing the San Joaquin Valley

The Statement of Principles also addresses another important issue. Compliance with the "take" provisions of any future biological opinion issued under the federal Endangered Species Act is intended to result in no additional loss of water supply annually, within the limits of the water quality and operational requirements of the Principles. Further, the Principles state that the habitat protection to be provided should be sufficient to avoid the need for any additional listings during the three years that the Principles remain in effect.

To the extent that unforeseen circumstances require additional listings, the Principles provide that the protection of any such species will result in no additional water cost. If additional water is needed, the water will be provided by the federal government on a "willing seller basis" to be financed by federal funds, and *not* through additional regulatory reallocations of water within the Bay-Delta Estuary.

With regard to the provision of water from the Central Valley Project to meet the agreed-upon standards, the Principles provide that any such water shall be credited toward the CVP's obligation under section 3406(b)(2) of the Central Valley Project Improvement Act. This section calls for 800,000 acre feet of CVP yield for specified environmental purposes.

DWR's Delta Diversion and pumping plant, exporting Delta water to the San Joaquin Valley, the Central Coast, and Southern California

Finally, the Statement of Principles commits the State of California to implementation of the plan, finalizing the agreed-upon standards, and initiation of water right proceedings to implement the adopted plan. These actions are expected to occur during 1995. In the longer term, both the State of California and the federal government are expected to move forward on Delta issues pursuant to the terms of a "Framework Agreement" executed by the two entities in the summer of 1994. Among other things, the Framework Agreement commits both the state and the United States to the examination of longer term Delta alternatives, including Delta facilities, that will provide protection for Delta environmental values without jeopardizing competing urban and agricultural water uses that are also dependent upon Delta water supplies.

## The Delta Facilities Issue

The State Board in D-1630 also suggested consideration of an isolated Delta facility to remedy the adverse effects on fisheries caused by SWP and CVP diversions from the southern Delta. D-1630, page 71. State and federal fishery agencies have long advocated moving the big pumps out of the Delta. Not only can fish be lost in the pumps despite screens, but these pumps pull water through the Delta, and the suction can cause a reversal of normal Delta flow patterns. This issue continues to be significant as the Bay-Delta process moves forward in the 1990s. Both environmentalists and consumptive water users agree that the environmental water problems caused by diversions from the Delta will not be solved until new facilities are constructed or there is a massive decrease in exports from the Delta.

The debate over this issue is pivotal for the future of the Bay-Delta. In 1982, state legislation that included a peripheral canal (an isolated facility to transfer water from the Sacramento

*The peripheral canal—pro and con*

River around the Delta) was soundly defeated by referendum. This was largely due to a nine-to-one margin against the referendum in Northern California.[12] However, there are still strong proponents of an isolated facility.

Advocates of an isolated facility offer four arguments[13] in support of their position. First, it will help to alleviate the fish problems in the Bay-Delta. Under the current system, there are large pumps located in the southern end of the Delta. Fish eggs and larvae are drawn into the pumps. The pumps also cause reverse flows (where water flows upstream in channels in the southwestern Delta) when the flow of fresh water in the Delta is low. Finally, the pumping causes the flow velocity in the Delta channels to be higher than it should be in order to promote the growth of organisms that fish feed on. Moreover, fish can be transported to areas where they have increased mortality.

THM = Trihalomethane

The second argument in support of an isolated facility relates to drinking water quality. Almost 20 million Californians get some of their drinking water from the Delta, and although the sources of the water are of very high quality, the water becomes contaminated as it moves through the Delta. Contamination comes from organic materials (THM's) originating in Delta farmlands, and from bromide found in salty San Francisco Bay water. Because water quality standards are becoming more stringent, the cost of treating Delta water will continue to increase; and treatment is not a substitute for taking water from the best available source, where feasible. This contamination problem would essentially be eliminated if water were transported through a facility isolated from the Delta.

The third argument for an isolated facility relates to potential earthquake damage to the existing system. Levees in the Delta are vulnerable to severe damage from earthquakes, and levee failure could result in a failure of the existing water supply system that could take months to repair.

Finally, an isolated facility would significantly improve the opportunities for water banking and voluntary water transfers that are currently restricted by the inadequate capacity of Delta channels and by fishery problems. If exports from the Delta are limited because of State Board action, or the Endangered Species Acts, or otherwise, water transfers from north of the Delta become constrained by that same limitation.

[12] Miller, "The Peripheral Canal as a Solution to Delta Problems," *California Water Law and Policy Reporter,* February 1991, pages 87-88.
[13] Miller, pages 88-89.

Opponents of an isolated facility disagree strongly with these contentions, calling an isolated facility a "death warrant" for the Delta.[14] They argue that an isolated facility is not needed because the protection of water sources, along with conservation and some new facility construction, can better protect the economic and environmental values of the Bay-Delta, while still providing for the water needs of the rest of the state.

The primary issue here is one of trust. Opponents of an isolated facility simply do not believe that sufficient water would be released into the Delta from an isolated facility in order to maintain the Bay-Delta estuarine system. The argument is that by physically separating the Estuary's water supply and flows from the water supplied to the pumping plants, the interests of Northern and Southern California would forever be divided. An isolated facility would have the capacity to divert much of the Sacramento River around the Delta. It is argued that this would create an irresistible temptation to increase water exports, leading to an environmental disaster for the Delta. Opponents of such a facility also argue that it would cost much more than the $1.2 billion estimate made in 1982.

*The Delta facilities issue is essentially one of trust.*

It does not appear that this controversy will be resolved in the near future. Unfortunately, until the Delta is "fixed," California's water supply will suffer, as will both environmental and consumptive interests.

[14] McPeak, "The 'Repackaged' Peripheral Canal: Old Soap or New?," *California Water Law and Policy Reporter,* February 1991, pages 87-94.

# CHAPTER FIVE

# Threatened and Endangered Species[1]

## Introduction

Since its enactment in 1973, the federal Endangered Species Act (ESA) (16 U.S.C. §§ 1531-1544) has increasingly dominated the conflict between environmental and consumptive uses of water. In the early 1990s, the listing and proposed listing of water-dependent species in the Bay-Delta has essentially taken control over the operation of the State Water Project and the federal Central Valley Project.

Congress' purposes in enacting the ESA were "to provide a means whereby the ecosystems upon which endangered species and threatened species depend may be conserved" and "to provide a program for the conservation of such...species...." 16 U.S.C. § 1531(b). To further these purposes, Congress framed the primary policy underlying the ESA in strong terms: "[A]ll Federal departments and agencies shall seek to conserve endangered species and threatened species ...." 16 U.S.C. § 1531(c)(1). As discussed later in this chapter, a secondary policy holds that "Federal agencies shall cooperate with state and local agencies to resolve water resource issues in concert with conservation of endangered species." 16 U.S.C. § 1531(c)(2).

"Conservation" is the focal point of the ESA. The ESA defines "conserve" as "the use of all methods and procedures which are necessary to bring any endangered species or threatened species to the point at which the measures provided pursuant to [the Act] are no longer necessary." 16 U.S.C. § 1532(3). The United States Supreme Court has stated that the "plain intent of Congress...was

**ESA = Endangered Species Act**

*Since the early 1990s, the ESA has essentially taken control over the operations of the SWP and the federal CVP.*

---

[1] The principal author of this chapter was Janice L. Weis.

141

to halt and reverse the trend towards species extinction, whatever the cost." *Tennessee Valley Authority v. Hill* (1978) 437 U.S. 153, 57 L.Ed. 2d 117, 98 S.Ct. 2279, page 184.

The strong policies and purposes of the ESA have evolved to include not only the conservation of listed species but the preservation of their habitat as well. While habitat conservation is one of the most effective measures available to ensure the survival of a species, it may have significant impacts on the ability of water suppliers to maintain and expand water supplies to their service areas.

Although the federal ESA receives much greater publicity, the State of California also has an Endangered Species Act (Fish and Game Code §§ 2050-2098) which is very similar to the federal ESA. Both acts play an important role in water use and development in California.

This chapter provides an overview of the most important components of the federal ESA and compares it to the state ESA. This chapter will also discuss the impacts both acts may have on water rights in California.

## Overview of the Federal Endangered Species Act

### Background

Congress enacted the first federal legislation to address endangered species in 1966. The 1966 Endangered Species Act applied only to wildlife and directed the Secretary of the Interior to carry out a program to protect endangered species and to prepare a list of such species. Pub. L. No. 89-669, § 2(a), 80 Stat. 926 (1966). The ESA was amended in 1969 to grant additional authority to the Secretary of the Interior and to expand the types of wildlife covered by the ESA to include, for example, non-native wildlife. Pub. L. No. 91-135, 83 Stat. 275 (1969).

*As adopted in 1966, the ESA applied only to wildlife.*

In 1973, Congress significantly revised the ESA to expand protection to plants as well as animals, and to provide for the designation of threatened as well as endangered species. The 1973 ESA provides the basis today for the federal protection of threatened and endangered plants and animals.

*Coverage of the ESA was significantly expanded in 1973.*

There are four key provisions of the federal ESA: (1) listing species as threatened or endangered (16 U.S.C. § 1533 *et seq.*); (2) consulting with the U.S. Fish and Wildlife Service or National Marine Fisheries Service by federal agencies before undertaking federal projects (16 U.S.C. § 1536 *et seq.*); (3) prohibiting the "taking" of threatened or endangered species (16 U.S.C. § 1538); and (4) authorizing "incidental taking" of species pursuant to a permit (16 U.S.C. § 1539). Each of these provisions is discussed below.

## The Listing Process

### *Authority*

Section 4 of the ESA sets forth the provisions for listing a species as threatened or endangered. 16 U.S.C. § 1533. The Secretary of Commerce and the Secretary of the Interior share the responsibility for listing species. The Secretary of the Interior is responsible for terrestrial species, and the Secretary of Commerce is responsible for marine species. 16 U.S.C. § 1533(a)(2). The two share jurisdiction over some species such as sea turtles. 50 C.F.R. § 17.2(b). The Secretary of the Interior has delegated authority under the ESA to the United States Fish and Wildlife Service (USFWS); the Secretary of Commerce has delegated authority to the National Marine Fisheries Service (NMFS). Unless otherwise noted, the term "Secretary" as used in this chapter is intended to refer to both secretaries. These two agencies have issued joint regulations to implement the listing process under the ESA. *See generally* 50 C.F.R. Part 424. Listing a species has been held to be exempt from the National Environmental Policy Act. *Pacific Legal Foundation v. Andrus* (6th Cir. 1981) 657 F.2d 829.

> *The Secretary of the Interior is responsible for terrestrial species, the Secretary of Commerce (through NMFS) for marine species.*

> **USFWS = United States Fish and Wildlife Service**
>
> **NMFS = National Marine Fisheries Service**

Listing a species first requires a determination of whether the species meets the definition of "threatened" or "endangered" under the ESA. The ESA also provides for designation of "critical habitat" and the development of "recovery plans" for listed species.

### *Defining Threatened and Endangered Species*

The ESA defines an "endangered species" as "any species which is in danger of extinction throughout all or a significant portion of its range...." 16 U.S.C. § 1532(6). A "threatened species" is one which is "likely to become an endangered species within the foreseeable future throughout all or a significant portion of its range." 16 U.S.C. § 1532(20). The Act defines "species" as including any species or subspecies of fish, wildlife, or plant and "distinct population segment of any species of vertebrate fish or wildlife which interbreeds when mature." Together, these three definitions authorize the listing of species or subspecies throughout all of their range, a portion of their range, or only in certain geographical areas. For example, the Mojave Desert population of the desert tortoise in California and Nevada is listed, but the Sonoran Desert population in Arizona is not. 54 Fed. Reg. 32,326 (August 4, 1989); 16 U.S.C. § 1532(16). A species may be listed as endangered or threatened if its continued existence is jeopardized by one or more of the following factors—

> *The act includes not only species and subspecies but also any "distinct population segment...which interbreeds when mature."*

- The present or threatened destruction, modification or curtailment of its habitat or range
- Overuse for commercial, recreational, scientific or educational purposes
- Disease or predation
- Inadequacy of existing regulatory mechanisms
- Other natural or man-made factors affecting its continued existence. 16 U.S.C. § 1533(a)(1)

*The decision to list must be made "solely on the basis of the best scientific and commercial data available."*

The ESA directs the Secretary to make a listing decision "*solely on the basis of the best scientific and commercial data available.*" 16 U.S.C. § 1533(b)(1)(A), emphasis added. Congress added the word "solely" to the ESA in 1982, indicating an intent to restrict listing decisions to biological factors only. Pub. Law No. 97-304, § 2(a)(2), 96 Stat. 1411; see 50 C.F.R. § 424.11(c). (Secretary to make determination "solely on the basis of the best scientific and commercial" information regarding a species' status, without reference to possible economic or other impacts of such determination.) Thus, there is no mechanism in the listing process for balancing between species protection and economic impacts.

*The listing process does not consider economic impacts.*

Courts have taken this congressional directive seriously. In *Tennessee Valley Authority v. Hill* (1978) 437 U.S. 153, 57 L.Ed 2d 117, 98 S.Ct. 2279, the Tennessee Valley Authority (TVA) was ordered to stop construction and operation of the Tellico Dam when the snail darter, a fish inhabiting a small stretch of the Little Tennessee River, was listed as endangered under the federal ESA. The Supreme Court reached this conclusion despite the fact that almost $100 million had already been expended on the project, and it was 50 percent finished when the ESA became effective and 80 percent completed when the fish was officially listed as endangered. *TVA v. Hill,* page 166. The court held that the protection of endangered species had priority over the primary missions of federal agencies. (This case is also discussed later in this chapter.)

A more recent case involved the northern spotted owl, a bird that inhabits the old-growth forests of the Pacific Northwest. In *Northern Spotted Owl v. Hodel* (W.D. Wash. (1988) 716 F.Supp. 479), the court found that USFWS' initial failure to list the northern spotted owl as threatened or endangered was arbitrary and capricious. The court noted that the USFWS has a duty to assess the available technical and scientific data against the relevant listing criteria in Section 4(a)(1) of the ESA and to exercise its expert discretion in reaching a listing decision. *Hodel,* page 480. The court rejected conclusory statements by the USFWS that the owl was not endangered, noting that USFWS had ignored unrebutted, expert opinions regarding the declining status of the owl without offering credible, alternative explanations. *Hodel,* page 483. USFWS subsequently listed the owl as threatened in June 1990. 55 Fed.Reg. 26,114 (June 26, 1990).

### Designating Critical Habitat

Once a species is listed as threatened or endangered, the ESA provides for the protection of the species' ecosystem through the designation of "critical habitat." 16 U.S.C. §§ 1531(b), 1532(5)(A) and (B).

The ESA defines "critical habitat" as areas that contain "physical or biological features" which are "essential to the conservation of the species" and which "may require special management considerations or protection." 16 U.S.C. § 1532(5)(A). The ESA regulations list factors which may be considered "essential to the conservation of the species," including areas important for population growth, food and water resources, shelter, breeding and rearing sites, and habitats representative of the historic distribution of the species. 50 C.F.R. § 424.12(b).

*The ESA defines "critical habitat" as areas that contain "physical or biological features... essential to the conservation of the species" which "may require special management considerations or protection."*

In defining critical habitat, the ESA distinguishes between "occupied" and "unoccupied" areas. 16 U.S.C. § 1532(5)(A). The ESA regulations provide that habitat outside the geographical area actually occupied by a species at the time of its listing may be designated as critical "only when a designation limited to its present range would be inadequate to ensure the conservation of the species." 50 C.F.R. § 424.12(e). The ESA states that "critical habitat shall not include the entire geographical area which [can] be occupied" by the listed species, except in "circumstances determined by the Secretary." 16 U.S.C. § 1532(5)(C). There are no statutory or regulatory definitions of such circumstances.

There are two limitations on the designation of critical habitat. The Secretary is directed to designate critical habitat to the "maximum extent [1] prudent and [2] determinable." 16 U.S.C. § 1533(a)(3). Under the ESA regulations, designation of critical habitat is "not prudent" if it could be expected to increase the threat either of "taking" or "other human activity," or the designation would not be "beneficial" to the species. 50 C.F.R. § 424.12(a)(1). (The Act and regulations do not define the term "beneficial.")

The ESA regulations provide that critical habitat is not "determinable" when the "information sufficient to perform required analyses of the impacts of the designation is lacking" or when the biological needs of the species are "not sufficiently well known to permit identification of an area as critical habitat." (50 C.F.R.

§ 424.12(a)(2).) For example, in 1990, USFWS deferred designation of critical habitat for the northern spotted owl and the golden-cheeked warbler on the basis that critical habitat was not "presently determinable." 55 Fed. Reg. 26114-26192 (June 26, 1990) and 55 Fed. Reg. 53153-53159 (December 27, 1990).

*One court has held NEPA to apply to the designation of critical habitat.*

USFWS' failure to designate critical habitat for the northern spotted owl was challenged in court and USFWS was ordered to designate critical habitat. *Northern Spotted Owl v. Lujan* (W.D. Wash. 1991) 758 F.Supp. 621. In designating critical habitat, USFWS claimed it did not need to comply with the National Environmental Policy Act (NEPA). Subsequently, a court ordered USFWS to comply with NEPA in designating critical habitat. *Douglas County v. Lujan* (D.Or. 1992) 810 F.Supp. 1470.

**NEPA = National Environmental Policy Act**

Before 1978, the ESA specified that only biological factors could be used to designate critical habitat. In 1978, Congress amended the ESA to include consideration of its economic impacts. The Secretary is now directed to designate critical habitat on the basis of the "best scientific data available" and after taking into consideration any economic or other "relevant" impacts. 16 U.S.C. § 1533(b)(2). The economic analysis is required by several legal authorities.[2]

*The designation of critical habitat may include consideration of economic impacts.*

Areas may be excluded from critical habitat if the benefits of excluding a particular area outweigh the benefits of designation. If, however, failure to designate an area as critical habitat will result in the extinction of the species at issue, that area must be included, regardless of the economic or nonbiological impacts such an inclusion may cause. 16 U.S.C. § 1533(b)(2). In any proposed or final rule designating critical habitat, the Secretary must include a description and evaluation of any public or private activities which, if undertaken, either may adversely modify critical habitat or may be affected by its designation. 16 U.S.C. § 1533(b)(8).

### Procedure for Listing a Species and Designating Critical Habitat

Section 4 of the ESA sets forth detailed procedures for listing a species as threatened or endangered. The Secretary may independently list, delist, or reclassify the status of a species. 16 U.S.C. §§ 1533(a)(1), 1533(b)(1). Pursuant to a settlement agreement reached by the parties in *The Fund for Animals v. Lujan* (D.C. Dist. 1991) 794 F.Supp. 1015, the Secretary agreed to direct each region, "where biologically

---

[2]  Executive Order 12291 (46 Fed. Reg. 13193 (Feb. 17, 1981)); Regulatory Flexibility Act (5 U.S.C. §§ 601-602) and the Paperwork Reduction Act (44 U.S.C. §§ 3501-3504).

appropriate," to use a "multi-species, ecosystem" approach to their listing responsibilities under the ESA. In pursuing this approach, the Secretary is required to consider to the maximum extent feasible, the "commonality of threats" faced by different species in the same ecosystem. This agreement is expected to spark petitions to list more than one species at a time. This approach has been used in California in an attempt to list the longfin smelt and Sacramento splittail.

Alternatively, "an interested person" may petition the Secretary to list, delist, or reclassify a species. 16 U.S.C. § 1533(b)(3)(A). Species under consideration for listing are referred to as "candidate species." 50 C.F.R. § 424.02(b). However, other than being the subject of a "conference" as discussed below, candidate species do not receive any protection under the ESA. *See* 16 U.S.C. § 1533(b)(3)(C)(iii). (USFWS maintains three categories of candidate species: Category 1 includes species for which USFWS has substantial information about the species to support the biological appropriateness of proposing to list as endangered or threatened, but for which proposed rules have not yet been issued because they have been precluded by higher priority listing activity; Category 2 includes species for which USFWS has information indicating that listing is possibly warranted, but for which conclusive data on biological vulnerability and threat are not currently available; Category 3 includes species that were once considered for listing, but are not currently under such review because there is "persuasive evidence" of extinction. 54 Fed. Reg., pages 554-55.)

*Candidate species do not receive specific protection under the federal ESA.*

Upon receiving a petition to list, delist, or reclassify a species, USFWS has 90 days to make a finding as to whether the petition presents "substantial scientific or commercial information indicating that the petitioned action may be warranted." 16 U.S.C. § 1533(b)(3)(A); 50 C.F.R. § 424.14(b)(1). If the Secretary determines that the petitioned action is not warranted, he or she must make a finding to that effect. This finding is immediately subject to judicial review. § 1533(b)(3)(C)(ii).

*If the Secretary decides not to list a species, the decision is subject to judicial review, but a positive decision to list is not.*

If the Secretary finds that the petitioned action may be warranted, he or she must conduct a review of the status of the species. The ESA confers no right to judicial review of this "positive" finding. The status review includes the evaluation of the status of the species in light of the five factors enumerated in ESA Section 4(a)(1). 50 C.F.R. § 424.14(b)(3).

Although it is not authorized specifically by either the ESA or the regulations, the USFWS, in conducting its "status review" of a species, has used a status review panel. For example, during its status review of the Delta smelt, a fish which inhabits the Sacramento-San Joaquin Delta, the USFWS formed such a panel after stating that it required the assistance of experts because of the complexity of data available on the species. The panelists included fisheries experts from the Bureau of Land Management and the USFWS National Fishery Research Center. The panelists produced a "panel report" which attempted to summarize data on the Delta smelt. No court has yet ruled on the propriety of using a status review panel in light of the fact that such a panel is not authorized by the ESA or its regulations.

If the Secretary determines that the petitioned action is warranted, he or she must "promptly" publish a notice in the *Federal Register* that includes the full text of a proposed rule. (16 U.S.C. § 1533(b)(3)(B)(ii).) The Secretary must also give notice of the proposed rule to affected states, localities, or foreign countries where the concerned species are found, as well as to "appropriate scientific organizations." 16 U.S.C. § 1533(b)(5); 50 C.F.R. § 424.16(c)(1)(ii). A public comment period of at least 60 days must be allowed. 50 C.F.R. § 424.16(c)(2). In addition, a public hearing must be held if requested within 45 days of the publication of a proposed rule. 16 U.S.C. § 1533(b)(5)(E); 50 C.F.R. § 424.17. If no public hearing is requested, the informal rulemaking procedures of the Administrative Procedure Act govern. 16 U.S.C. § 1533(b)(4).

The Secretary must act on the proposed rule within one year from the date of its publication by doing one of the following through notice in the *Federal Register*: (1) promulgation of a final rule to implement a listing determination; (2) withdrawal of the proposed rule upon a finding that available evidence does not justify the action proposed by the rule; or (3) extension of the one-year period by an additional six months if the Secretary finds there is "substantial disagreement regarding the sufficiency or accuracy of the available data . . . among scientists knowledgeable about the species concerned." 16 U.S.C. §§ 1533(b)(6)(A), (B). After such an extension, the Secretary must publish a final rule or withdraw the proposed rule. 16 U.S.C. § 1533(b)(6)(B)(iii). Withdrawal of a proposed rule is subject to judicial review. 16 U.S.C. § 1533(b)(6) (B)(ii). In one case, a court delisted a species because the Secretary did not act within the 18-month period. *Idaho Farm Bureau Federation v. Babbitt* (D. Idaho 1993) 839 F.Supp. 739.

*The listing decision must include a discussion of the data on which it is based.*

In any proposed or final rule regarding a listing, the Secretary must include a discussion of the data upon which the rule is based and show the relationship of the data to the rule. 16 U.S.C. § 1533(b)(8); *Northern Spotted Owl v. Hodel* (W.D. Wash. 1988) 716 F.Supp. 479,

482. A decision not to list a species as endangered or threatened is subject to the deferential "arbitrary and capricious" judicial standard of review under the Administrative Procedure Act, 5 U.S.C. § 706(2)(A). *Hodel,* page 481. In *Endangered Species Committee of the BIA et al. v. Babbitt* (D.D.C. 1994) 852 F.Supp. 32, the court delisted the California gnatcatcher because the Secretary had refused to release the new data on which the listing was based. The ESA does not provide specifically for judicial review of a finding that a species is threatened or endangered, but does provide specifically for review of a negative finding. 16 U.S.C. § 1533(b)(3)(C)(ii).

The ESA states that a final rule designating critical habitat must be published concurrently with the final rule implementing the decision to list a species. (16 U.S.C. § 1533(b)(6)(C).) However, if the Secretary determines that it is "essential" to the conservation of the species to promptly publish a final rule listing the species before designating critical habitat, the Secretary may delay the critical habitat designation. Similarly, if the Secretary determines that critical habitat is not presently "determinable," critical habitat designation may be deferred for up to an additional year. 16 U.S.C. § 1533(b)(6)(A); 50 C.F.R. § 424.17(b)(2). Courts have emphasized that there is a statutory presumption under the ESA that critical habitat should be designated at the same time as a final listing decision except in rare circumstances and that the Secretary must justify a deferral of a critical habitat decision. *Northern Spotted Owl v. Lujan* (W.D. Wash. 1991) 758 F.Supp. 621, 629.

### Emergency Listing Procedures

Aside from the rulemaking approach to listing a species, described above, the Secretary is authorized to list a species where an emergency poses a "significant risk to the well-being of any species of fish, wildlife, or plants." 16 U.S.C. § 1533(b)(7). In such a case, the Secretary may list a species through a regulation which can take effect immediately upon publication in the *Federal Register*. 16 U.S.C. § 1533(b)(7). The Secretary must explain in detail in the *Federal Register* why the emergency action is required. In cases of domestic species, the Secretary must provide actual notice to authorities and states where the species is believed to occur. 16 U.S.C. § 1533(b)(7); 50 C.F.R. § 424.20(a).

An emergency regulation to list a species is effective only for 240 days from the date of its publication. The regulation may be revoked during this period if the Secretary determines "on the basis of the best scientific and commercial data available" that substantial

*An emergency listing may take effect immediately but is good for only 240 days.*

evidence does not exist to warrant the regulation. 16 U.S.C. § 1533 (B)(7); 50 C.F.R. § 424.20(b).

Courts have held that the Secretary has broad latitude to list species on an emergency basis. In the leading case of *City of Las Vegas v. Lujan* (D.C. Cir. 1989) 891 F.2d 927, the Secretary of the Interior listed the Mojave Desert population of the desert tortoise as an endangered species on an emergency basis. The Secretary's rationale was that desert tortoises were being threatened by a fatal respiratory disease. The State of Nevada, City of Las Vegas, and local developers challenged this emergency listing on the grounds that the data in support of the respiratory disease was inconclusive and thus violated the ESA's requirement to use the "best scientific and commercial data available."

The court, however, concluded that the ESA contemplated a "somewhat less rigorous process of investigation and explanation for emergency regulations than for normal rulemaking." *Lujan*, 891 F.2d, page 932. The court found no evidence that the Secretary had disregarded any "scientifically superior evidence" available when the emergency rule was published and held that the Secretary had thus satisfied the requirement to use the best scientific data available. *Lujan*, page 933.

Plaintiffs also contended that emergency listing of the desert tortoise was improper because listing the tortoise would not cure or alleviate its respiratory disease. The court held that the ESA does not require the Secretary to show that listing a species on an emergency basis would save it from extinction. Nor does it require the Secretary to address the emergency leading to its listing. *Lujan*, page 933.

### Recovery Plans

*The public must have an opportunity to comment on recovery plans.*

After listing a species, the Secretary is required to develop and implement "recovery plans" for the "conservation and survival" of listed species "unless he finds that such a plan will not promote the conservation of the species." 16 U.S.C. § 1533(f)(1). The public must be given notice and an opportunity to comment on proposed recovery plans. 16 U.S.C. § 1533(f)(4).

The ESA authorizes the Secretary to obtain the services of appropriate public and private agencies and institutions or "other qualified persons" in developing recovery plans. The Secretary is required to give priority, to the maximum extent practicable, to listed species which are most likely to benefit from a recovery plan, particularly those species that may be in conflict with development projects or other economic activities. 16 U.S.C. § 1533(f)(4).

The ESA sets out three components to be included in a recovery plan: (1) a description of site-specific management actions necessary for the conservation and survival of the species; (2) objective, measurable criteria which, when met, would lead to the species' eventual removal from the list of threatened or endangered species; and (3) estimates of the time and costs required to carry out the recovery plan. 16 U.S.C. § 1533(f)(1)(B).

*Required components of a recovery plan*

In *National Wildlife Federation v. National Park Service* (D. Wyo. 1987) 669 F.Supp. 384, the National Wildlife Federation argued that Section 1533(f) requires the Secretary to develop and implement recovery plans. The court disagreed, holding that the Secretary is required to initiate a recovery plan "unless he finds that such a plan will not promote the conservation of the species." *National Wildlife Federation,* page 388.

Plaintiffs also argued that since a recovery plan was already developed (in this case for the grizzly bear), the Secretary and National Park Service were required to follow it. The court cited the congressional history of the recovery plan provisions and held that the Secretary is not *required* to develop recovery plans unless he or she believes it would promote conservation. *National Wildlife Federation,* pages 388-389, emphasis added. The provision for recovery plans was added in 1978, at which time the House reported—

> Although recovery plans are implicit in the Endangered Species Act, the Act does not specifically mandate recovery plans ... The committee intends the Secretary to establish recovery teams to assist with: (1) the development of plans; (2) periodic amendment of plans; and (3) the implementation of the plans .... *Id.,* page 388, citing H.R. 1625, 95th Cong., 2d. Sess. (1978), p. 19, U.S.Code Cong. and Admin. News 1978, pp. 9453, 9469.

The court held that it would not attempt to "second guess" the Secretary's motives for not following the recovery plan and found that, confronted with newer and more sophisticated methods available to determine the effects upon the grizzly bear, the Secretary could reasonably have concluded that the implementation of such a plan should be stayed until the results of the new analysis became available.

## Consultation Provisions

Once a species is listed under the ESA, the ESA requires federal agencies, in consultation with the Secretary, to avoid undertaking actions that are likely to jeopardize the continued existence of listed

*Federal agencies are required to avoid actions that are likely to jeopardize the existence of a listed species or adversely impact critical habitat.*

species or result in the destruction or adverse modification of critical habitat. Section 7(a)(2); 16 U.S.C. § 1536(a)(2). Section 7(a)(12) also imposes an affirmative obligation on federal agencies to undertake actions to "conserve" listed species. This provision is gaining attention but is not as widely used as Section 7(a)(2).

Section 7(a)(2) of the ESA requires all federal agencies to—

> insure that any action authorized, funded, or carried out by such agency . . . is not likely to jeopardize the continued existence of any endangered species or threatened species or result in the destruction or adverse modification of habitat of such species which is determined by the Secretary, . . . to be critical . . . . 16 U.S.C. § 1536(a)(2).

The ESA regulations define "action" as—

> All activities or programs of any kind authorized, funded, or carried out, in whole or in part, by federal agencies . . . . Examples include, but are not limited to (a) actions intended to conserve listed species or their habitat; (b) the promulgation of regulations; (c) the granting of licenses, contracts, leases, easements, right-of-way, permits, or grants in aid; or (d) actions directly or indirectly causing modifications to the land, water, or air. 50 C.F.R. § 402.02.

The regulations provide further that federal agency actions subject to Section 7(a)(2) are only those actions authorized, funded, or carried out "in the United States or upon the high seas." 50 C.F.R. §§ 402.01, 402.02. Moreover, Section 7 applies only to actions in which there is "discretionary federal involvement or control." 50 C.F.R. § 402.03. Despite these limitations, it is difficult to conceive of a federal agency action not subject to Section 7.

To ensure that federal actions will not "jeopardize" listed species, Section 7(a)(2) requires the "action agency" to consult with the appropriate Secretary regarding potential effects of the agency's proposed action on listed species. (The action agency is the federal agency that proposes to authorize, fund, or carry out the action in question. 16 U.S.C. § 1536(a)(2).) For species under the jurisdiction of the Secretary of the Interior, USFWS is the consulting agency. For species under the jurisdiction of the Secretary of Commerce, NMFS is the consulting agency. These latter agencies are referred to as the "consulting agencies."

*For species under the jurisdiction of the Secretary of the Interior, USFWS is the consulting agency.*

### Consultation Process

Under the consultation provisions, the action agency is first required to determine the scope of its "action area." This is defined as "all areas to be affected directly or indirectly by the Federal action and not merely the immediate area involved in the action." 50 C.F.R. § 402.02. The definition of the action area is critical to determining what the impact of the action will be on the listed species.

After the action area has been defined, the action agency must then request information from the consulting agency on whether any listed species or species proposed to be listed exist in the action area. 16 U.S.C. § 1536(c)(1). If the consulting agency indicates, based on the best scientific and commercial data available, that such species may be present, the action agency must prepare a "biological assessment." *Id.* Such an assessment contains information about the relevant species, designated and proposed critical habitat that may be present in the action area, and an evaluation of the potential effects of the action on the species and its habitat. 50 C.F.R. § 402.02.

A biological assessment is required only if the proposed action involves a "major construction activity," defined as—

*If the proposed action is a major construction activity, a biological assessment is required, and one may be prepared for any action.*

> A construction project (or other undertaking having similar physical impact) which is a major federal action significantly affecting the quality of the human environment, as referred to in the National Environmental Policy Act (citations omitted). 50 C.F.R. §§ 402.12(b), 402.02.

In such cases, the action agency may not enter into any contract for construction or begin construction before the biological assessment is finished. 50 C.F.R. § 402.12(b)(2). An action agency *may* prepare a biological assessment for actions other than major construction.

When preparation of a biological assessment is not required, the action agency may choose to consult informally to determine whether its proposed action is likely to adversely affect listed species or critical habitat. 50 C.F.R. § 402.13. Informal consultation is used to determine whether formal consultation or a conference is required. If the action agency and consulting agency agree that the proposed action is not likely to adversely affect listed species, then no further consultation is required. 50 C.F.R. § 402.13.

Formal *consultation* is required if a proposed action is likely to adversely affect *listed* species or *designated* critical habitat. 50 C.F.R. § 402.14. A *conference* is required if a proposed action is likely to jeopardize a species *proposed* for listing or is likely to result in the destruction or adverse modification of *proposed* critical habitat. 50 C.F.R. § 402.10.

If formal consultation is required, the consulting agency prepares a "biological opinion" which identifies the potential effects of the proposed action on listed species or critical habitat. If the consulting agency finds that the proposed action is *not* likely to jeopardize the continued existence of a listed species or to destroy or adversely modify critical habitat, the consulting agency issues a "no jeopardy" biological opinion. 50 C.F.R. § 402.14(h)(3).

"Jeopardize the continued existence of" is defined as:

> engag[ing] in an action that reasonably would be expected . . . to reduce appreciably the likelihood of *both* the survival *and* recovery of a listed species in the wild by reducing the reproduction, numbers, or distribution of that species. 50 C.F.R. § 402.02, emphasis added.

"Destruction or adverse modification" of critical habitat is defined as—

> a direct or indirect alteration that appreciably diminishes the value of critical habitat for both the survival and recovery of a listed species. Such alterations include, but are not limited to, alterations adversely modifying any of those physical or biological features that were the basis for determining the habitat to be critical. 50 C.F.R. § 402.02.

Thus, a jeopardy finding must be based on adverse impacts to both the recovery and survival of a species.

If the consulting agency finds that the proposed action *is* likely to jeopardize listed species or adversely modify critical habitat, the consulting agency issues a "jeopardy" biological opinion. 50 C.F.R. § 402.02. The consulting agency is required to include "reasonable and prudent alternatives" to the proposed action which would avoid the adverse impacts, if any. 16 U.S.C. § 1536(b)(3); 50 C.F.R. § 402.14(h)(3). One court has held that the preparation of a biological opinion is a "major federal action" requiring NEPA review. *Westlands Water District v. U.S.* (E.D.Cal. 1994) 850 F.Supp. 1388, 1422. The same court held that a claim could be made that a balancing should occur when choosing reasonable and prudent alternatives which consider economic effects. *Westlands,* page 1426.

The action agency may accept or reject, in whole or in part, the advice of a consulting agency contained in a biological opinion. 50 C.F.R. § 402.15(b). However, action agencies may deviate from the recommendations in the consulting agency's biological opinion without violating the ESA only if the action agency has taken reasonable and prudent alternative steps to ensure the continued existence of the listed species. *Tribal Village of Akutan v. Hodel* (9th Cir. 1988) 859 F.2d 651, 660. The ESA also requires both the action and consulting agency to use the "best scientific and commercial data available" when carrying out their respective obligations under Section 7(a). 16 U.S.C. § 1536(a)(2).

Generally, formal consultation must be finished within 90 days of the date it is initiated. 16 U.S.C. § 1536(b)(1)(A). If a permit or license application is involved, the consulting and action agency may extend the consultation period from 90 to 150 days. If no permit or license application is involved, the agencies may agree to extend the consultation for any period of time that is mutually agreeable. 16 U.S.C. § 1536(b)(1)(A). An action agency can obtain early consultation if a federal permit or license application is involved. This allows for resolution of potential conflicts between actions and listed species early in the planning stages of a project. Early consultation is optional on the part of the prospective permit or license applicant. 50 C.F.R. § 402.11.

*An action agency can obtain early consultation if a federal permit or license application is involved.*

Congress wanted agency decision-making to remain flexible during the consultation stage. Thus, the Section 7 consultation provisions include a provision that prohibits action agencies from making any "irreversible or irretrievable" commitment of resources to the proposed action that has the effect of foreclosing the development of "reasonable and prudent" alternatives to the action. 16 U.S.C. § 1536(d).

### Conference Provisions

As noted above, Section 7 also requires action agencies to "confer" on proposed actions that may affect species proposed for listing or critical habitat proposed for designation.

The conference process may be either formal or informal. An informal conference is comprised of discussions between the action and consulting agencies. The consulting agency generally issues a "conference report" which contains recommendations for minimizing or avoiding adverse effects. 50 C.F.R. § 402.10(c). These recommendations are advisory only. The Section 7(a)(2) limitations on federal agency action do not apply until a species is actually listed or critical habitat finally designated. 50 C.F.R. 402.10(c).

An action agency may request a "formal" conference after which the consulting agency issues a "conference opinion" (similar to a biological opinion). The advantage of requesting a formal conference for a species proposed to be listed is that if the species is listed or critical habitat is designated later, the action agency can request the consulting agency to adopt the conference opinion as its biological opinion if no new significant information has arisen in the meantime. 50 C.F.R. § 402.10(d).

### Consultation Exemption Process

The leading case regarding Section 7 consultation is *Tennessee Valley Authority v. Hill* (1978) 437 U.S. 153, 57 L.Ed. 2d 17, 98 S.Ct. 2279. As discussed above, after almost $100 million had been spent on construction of the Tellico Dam on the Little Tennessee River, the snail darter was listed as endangered, and the stretch of the Little Tennessee River in which the dam was located was designated as critical habitat.

*Appeal to the "God Squad"*

Shortly after this case was decided, Congress established the "Endangered Species Committee" (also known as the "God Committee" or "God Squad"), which can allow projects to proceed even if they jeopardize the continued existence of an endangered species. 16 U.S.C. § 1536(e). The Endangered Species Committee consists of seven members: the Secretary of the Interior who acts as the chair, the Administrator of the National Oceanic and Atmospheric Administration, the Secretary of the Army, Secretary of Agriculture, the Chairman of the Council of Economic Advisors, the Administrator of the Environmental Protection Agency and an individual from the affected state, appointed by the President. 16 U.S.C. § 1536(e).

The Endangered Species Committee can allow a project to proceed even if it will jeopardize the continued existence of a species if it finds—

- There are no reasonable and prudent alternatives to the agency action
- The benefits of the action "clearly outweigh" the benefits of alternative courses of action consistent with conserving the species or its critical habitat, and such action is in the public interest
- The action is of regional or national significance
- Neither the agency concerned nor the exemption applicant made any "irreversible or irretrievable" commitment of resources prohibited by Section 7(d). 16 U.S.C. § 1536(h)(1)(A)

If the committee grants an exemption, it must establish reasonable mitigation and enhancement measures to minimize the adverse affects of a proposed action. 16 U.S.C. § 1536(h)(1)(B). An exemption decision by the Committee is not subject to NEPA, provided that an environmental impact statement which discusses the impacts upon listed species or their critical habitat has been previously prepared with respect to any agency action exempted by the committee. 16 U.S.C. § 1536(K).

The four findings must be made by not less than five of the committee's members and must be based on a report by the Secretary as well as any testimony and evidence it may receive. 16 U.S.C. § 1536(h)(1). A federal agency, governor of the affected state, or permit or license applicant may apply to the Secretary for an exemption. The Secretary must make certain findings and must prepare a report for the Endangered Species Committee. 16 U.S.C. § 1536(g)(2)(B).

Since the exemption process was established in 1978, the Endangered Species Committee has considered only three applications. It granted an exemption in 1979 for the Grayrocks Dam and Reservoir project in Wyoming, which had been enjoined by court order because it would jeopardize the downstream habitat of the whooping crane. *Nebraska v. Rural Electrification Administration* (1978) 12 Envt'l. Rep. Cas. (BNA) 1156 (D. Neb. Oct. 2, 1978).

In voting unanimously to grant the exemption, the committee found that there were no reasonable alternatives to the project, that its benefits clearly outweighed any alternate courses of action, and that the project was in the public interest. The Endangered Species Committee ordered that certain mitigation and enhancement provisions be implemented before the exemption would be granted. These provisions included establishing an irrevocable trust fund for the maintenance of the whooping crane's critical habitat and controlling water withdrawals and releases from the dam throughout the year. By granting this exemption, the Endangered Species Committee permitted the building of the dam and reservoir on the Laramie River in Wyoming. On the same day, the committee voted unanimously to deny an exemption for the snail darter in the Tellico Dam case. The committee found that the project benefits did not clearly outweigh a proposed alternative course of action (removing part of the dam and developing the Little Tennessee River Valley).[3]

In 1991, then Secretary of the Interior Lujan called the Endangered Species Committee to convene and review the designation of old-growth forests in the Pacific Northwest as critical habitat for the northern spotted owl. The owl was listed as threatened by USFWS in 1990. 55 Fed. Reg. 26114 (June 26, 1990). This listing was opposed by the Pacific Northwest timber industry.

On May 15, 1992, the committee granted an exemption for timber sales and harvest in certain areas of the spotted owl's habitat. The Portland Audubon Society appealed this decision to the Ninth Circuit. In *Portland Audubon Society v. The Endangered Species*

---

[3] Endangered Species Committee Decision on Grayrocks Dam and Reservoir Application for Exemption (February 7, 1979) cited in Note, "The Exemption Process under the Endangered Species Act: How the 'God Squad' Works and Why," 66 *Notre Dame L. Rev.* 825, 846 (1991).

*Committee* (9th Cir. 1993) 984 F.2d 1534, the Ninth Circuit held that communications between Bush Administration representatives and members of the committee violated the Administrative Procedure Act (APA), which prohibits *ex parte* communications between "interested parties" and members of a judicial or quasi-judicial federal entity. The Ninth Circuit rejected arguments that the APA did not apply the committee, holding that since the committee is required by the ESA to make factual findings, hold a hearing, and make its decision on the record, it acts as a quasi-judicial body. *Portland Audubon,* page 1541.

The court also rejected the committee's argument that the President and his staff were not "interested parties" within the purview of the APA. The court held that the President's position "at the center of the Executive Branch renders him *ex officio,* an 'interested person' for purposes" of the APA. *Id.,* page 1545.

The committee also asserted that the APA's ban on *ex parte* communications does not apply to the committee and the White House staff since the committee itself is comprised of administration cabinet members. The court rejected this argument, holding that the cabinet members' roles on the committee were separate from their roles in the executive branch. *Id.,* pages 1545-1546.

Finally, the committee argued that including presidential communications within the APA's ban would violate the separation of powers doctrine, since it would be an impermissible attempt by Congress to interfere with the functions of the executive branch. The Ninth Circuit disagreed, stating that this argument would "effectively destroy the integrity" of all federal agency adjudications. *Id.,* page 1547.

## Taking Provisions

### *Prohibitions Against Take*

One of the strictest protections of the ESA is the prohibition in Section 9 against the "taking" of a listed species by "any person." § 1538(a)(1). The taking prohibitions do not apply to candidate species. The ESA defines "any person" to include not only private persons and entities but also federal, state and local governmental entities. 16 U.S.C. § 1532(13).

The ESA defines the term "take" as "harass, harm, pursue, hunt, shoot, wound, kill, trap, capture, or collect, or attempt to engage in any such conduct." 16 U.S.C. § 1532(19). The legislative history of this section indicates that it was drafted in the "broadest possible manner" to include every conceivable way in which wildlife could be taken. Senate Report No. 93-307, 93rd Cong., 1st Sess. 2. The term "harm" is defined further in the ESA regulations as—

*The prohibition against "taking" a listed species includes any kind of harm and was drafted in the "broadest possible manner."*

An act which actually kills or injures wildlife. Such act may include significant habitat modification or degradation where it actually kills or injures wildlife by significantly impairing essential behavioral patterns, including breeding, feeding, or sheltering. 50 C.F.R. § 17.3.

Section 9 provides a broad array of enforcement mechanisms. Any person who knowingly violates the taking provisions is subject to a civil penalty of not more than $25,000 for each violation. 16 U.S.C. § 1540(a)(1). Deliberate violations can also be punishable by criminal fines of not more than $50,000 or imprisonment for not more than one year in jail, or both. 16 U.S.C. § 1540(a)(1). In addition, the federal government may bring a civil suit or any person may bring a citizen's suit to enforce Section 9. 16 U.S.C. §§ 1540(e)(6), (g).

*Any person who knowingly violates the taking provisions is subject to a civil penalty of not more than $25,000 for each violation. Deliberate violations can also be punishable by criminal fines of not more than $50,000 or imprisonment for not more than one year in jail, or both.*

Both the Fifth and Ninth Circuits have held that Section 9 prohibits not only actions that kill a member of a listed species directly, but also actions that modify a species' habitat. In *Palila v. Hawaii Department of Land and Natural Resources* (D. Haw. 1979) 471 F.Supp. 985, 995, aff'd, (9th Cir. 1981) 639 F.2d 495 (*Palila I*), the court found that a Section 9 taking of the Hawaiian Palila bird had occurred when defendant's state game management program for sheep and goats had adversely affected the Palila habitat.

After the decision in *Palila I*, the USFWS made a minor amendment to the definition of "harm" in the ESA regulations to state that only those actions that result in the "actual" killing or injuring of wildlife violate Section 9. The introduction to the final rule emphasized that Section 9 was still intended to apply to significant habitat modifications that injure or kill wildlife and was still intended to focus on individual members of a listed species. 46 Fed. Reg. 57,749 (June 2, 1981); final definition is found at 50 C.F.R. § 17.3.

The State of Hawaii asserted that this redefinition should change the holding in *Palila I*. The court disagreed and in *Palila II* (D. Hawaii 1986) 649 F.Supp. 1070, aff'd (9th Cir. 1988) 852 F.2d 1106, found a second Section 9 taking when defendants allowed mouflon sheep to destroy Palila habitat. The court stated—

A finding of 'harm' does not require death to individual members of the species; nor does it require a finding that habitat degradation is presently driving the species further toward extinction. Habitat destruction that prevents the recovery of a species by affecting essential behavioral patterns causes actual injury to the species and effects a taking under section 9 of the Act. *Palila II*, 649 F. Supp., page 1075.

The *Palila* cases are also notable for the fact that the court applied Section 9's prohibitions against a non-federal entity.

In *Sierra Club v. Lyng* (E.D. Tex. 1988) 694 F.Supp. 1260, the Sierra Club alleged that timber management practices by the U.S. Forest Service in eastern Texas were adversely impacting the habitat of the endangered red-cockaded woodpecker and were responsible for serious declines in the woodpecker population. The district court agreed and found that such practices, including even-age management for harvesting timber, would cause the extinction of the woodpecker if no changes were made. The district court relied upon the holding in *Palila II* that proof of "harm" to a species does not require proof of actual death to a member of a species, and held that the decline in the woodpecker population was sufficient evidence that the Forest Service's practices had "harmed" the woodpecker in violation of Section 9. *Lyng,* pages 1266-1268. The court was particularly influenced by the fact that the Forest Service admitted it had failed to implement the terms of its own wildlife management handbook and, among other things, allowed clearcutting within 200 feet of trees with woodpecker cavities.

The Fifth Circuit affirmed this holding and stated that because the purpose of the wildlife management handbook was intended to preserve the diminishing woodpecker population, it was not "unreasonable to conclude that a failure to follow the handbook would result in a 'taking'" of the bird. *Sierra Club v. Yeutter* (5th Cir. 1991) 926 F.2d 429, 437. In *Sweet Home Chapter v. Babbitt* (D.C. Cir. 1994) 17 F.3d 1463, the court held the opposite, that taking the habitat was not harmful. This created a split in the courts that will be reviewed by the United States Supreme Court in 1995.

### Incidental Take

*The "incidental" taking of a listed species may be allowed under a Section 10(a) permit.*

There is some flexibility in Section 9 because the ESA authorizes the "incidental" taking of listed species if a permit is obtained under Section 10(a) of the ESA. 16 U.S.C. § 1539. In order to qualify for an incidental taking permit, the taking must be "incidental to, and not the purpose of, the carrying out of an otherwise lawful activity." 16 U.S.C. § 1539(a)(1)(b).

To obtain a Section 10(a) permit, a proposed permittee must submit a "habitat conservation plan" to the Secretary which specifies the following: (1) the impacts which are likely to result from the taking; (2) the steps the applicant will take to mitigate and minimize the impact; (3) the funding that will be available to implement such steps; (4) the alternative actions to the taking which the applicant has considered; (5) the reasons why alternatives are not being adopted; and (6) such other measures as the Secretary may require. 16 U.S.C. § 1539(a)(2)(A).

The Secretary is authorized to issue an incidental taking permit only if he or she finds that the applicant, to the maximum extent practicable, has minimized and mitigated the impacts of the taking, that adequate funding for the plan will be provided and that the taking will not appreciably reduce the likelihood of the survival and recovery of the species in the wild. 16 U.S.C. § 1539(a)(2)(B).

The process for applying for and issuing an incidental taking permit is set forth in 50 Code of Federal Regulations Part 17, subparts C and D. The action is treated as a federal action and triggers the requirements of the National Environmental Policy Act. 42 U.S.C. §§ 4321-4370a. Habitat conservation plans typically take more than one year to prepare and must include substantial information regarding the species and measures to be undertaken to protect the species.

*Habitat conservation plans*

The first habitat conservation plan (HCP) prepared and approved by USFWS was for the San Bruno Mountain Butterfly in California. HCPs have also been prepared, or are in the process of being prepared, in the Palm Springs area for the fringe-toed lizard, in Florida for endangered woodrats and cotton mice, and in the Las Vegas area for the desert tortoise.

**HCP = Habitat Conservation Plan**

One of the most recently prepared HCPs was for the federally endangered Stephens' Kangaroo Rat, which resides in California's Riverside County. The species, listed in 1988, brought much of the development activity in Riverside County to a standstill. In response, Riverside County and several cities in Riverside County prepared an HCP and obtained a joint Section 10(a) permit. The agencies decided to prepare a short-term HCP before preparing a long-term HCP. The purpose of the short-term HCP is to protect potential habitat reserve sites from development encroachment while developing a long-term HCP.

*The "K" rat solution*

The terms of the short-term HCP allow the development of up to 4,500 acres of the approximate 22,000 acres of remaining occupied habitat for the species. The loss of habitat is to be mitigated by the acquisition of an equivalent or greater amount of occupied habitat. Funding for the evaluation and acquisition of these permanent reserve areas is provided in part by the imposition of a mitigation fee on new development within the historic range of the species. The HCP also provides for the identification of several areas in Riverside County which currently contain occupied habitat that would be suitable for reserves and for the initiation of detailed technical studies to evaluate the suitability of potential reserve sites.

The HCP also authorized the formation of a joint powers authority to oversee the development and implementation of the reserve program. The permittees have since formed a joint powers authority known as the Riverside County Habitat Conservation Agency. The long-term HCP, which is being drafted currently, will be based on similar concepts.

## California Endangered Species Act

### General

CESA = California
Endangered Species Act

*The California Endangered Species Act generally parallels the federal ESA.*

The State of California has its own Endangered Species Act legislation. Fish and Game Code §§ 2050, *et seq.* The California ESA (CESA) was first enacted in 1970, and substantial amendments were made to the Act in 1984. CESA generally parallels the main provisions of the federal ESA. At the time of this publication, there was only one published case interpreting CESA's provisions. *Department of Fish and Game v. Anderson-Cottonwood Irrig. Dist.* (1992) 8 Cal.App.4th 1554.

The definitions of threatened and endangered species under CESA are similar to those under the federal ESA, except that the term "endangered species" is defined under the CESA as a species which is "in *serious* danger of becoming extinct throughout all, or a significant portion, of its range." Fish and Game Code § 2062, emphasis added. Under the federal ESA, an endangered species is one which is "in danger of extinction throughout all or a significant portion of its range." 16 U.S.C. § 1532(6). The language in CESA suggests that a higher standard must be met. CESA contains the same major provisions as the federal ESA, outlined briefly in the following sections.

*A listing under the state ESA may be more difficult to establish.*

### Listing

The procedure for listing a species as threatened or endangered under CESA generally parallels that under the federal ESA and is found at Sections 2070-2079 of the Fish and Game Code. A species is listed as threatened or endangered by a petition process. Fish and Game Code §§ 2070 *et seq.* CESA requires the Fish and Game Commission ("Commission") to adopt regulations for the processing of such petitions (Fish and Game Code § 2071) and regulations that provide criteria for determining whether a species subject to such a petition is threatened or endangered. Fish and Game Code § 2071.5. These regulations set forth the required contents for a petition (Cal. Code of Regulations, tit. 14, § 670.1(a)) and provide that a species shall be listed as threatened or endangered if the Commission determines that "its continued existence is in serious danger or is threatened" by one or more of the following factors—

- Present or threatened modification or destruction of its habitat
- Overexploitation
- Predation
- Competition
- Disease
- Other natural occurrences or human-related activities. Cal. Code Regs., tit. 14, § 670.1(b)

These criteria generally follow those specified under the federal ESA, except that the federal ESA provides more detail in its criteria and includes "inadequacy of existing regulatory mechanisms" as a factor. 16 U.S.C. § 1533(a)(1).

Petitions may come from interested persons or from the Department of Fish and Game (Fish and Game Code §§ 2071, 2072.7) and must include, among other things, scientific information regarding the species' population trend, range, distribution, abundance, history, factors affecting the ability of the species to survive and reproduce, the degree and immediacy of threat, the impact of existing management efforts, suggestions for future management and sources of information. The petition must also include information regarding the habitat necessary for the species' survival, a detailed distribution map and any other factors the petitioner deems relevant. Fish and Game Code § 2072.3. The petition must be submitted on an authorized petition form, provided by the Commission. Cal. Code Regs., tit. 14, § 670.1(a).

The Commission must refer a petition to the Department of Fish and Game (DFG) within 10 days and must provide notice in the California Regulatory Notice Register of its receipt of a petition. Fish and Game Code §§ 2073, 2073.3. The Commission must also notify interested persons by mail of the receipt of petitions. Fish and Game Code § 2073.3(b).

**DFG = Department of Fish and Game**

DFG must evaluate the petition and within 90 days provide a report to the Commission on the petition's adequacy. Fish and Game Code § 2073.5. In its report, DFG must recommend: (1) that the petition should be rejected for lack of information that the action is warranted; or (2) that the petition should be accepted and considered because there is sufficient information to indicate the petitioned action may be warranted. Fish and Game Code § 2073.5.

The Commission must consider the petition, DFG's report, and comments received "at its next available meeting" (Fish and Game Code §§ 2074, 2074.2) and must find either: (1) that the petition is inadequate for failure to provide sufficient information that the listing is warranted; or (2) that the petition contains sufficient information. In the latter case, the Commission must provide public notice that the species is a "candidate species." Fish and Game Code § 2074.2. The Commission must make the petition available for review and provide notice of its meetings to interested persons. Fish and Game Code § 2074.

If the petition is accepted, the Commission must make "all reasonable attempts" to notify interested and affected parties and to solicit data and comments from as many persons as practicable. Fish and Game Code § 2074.4. DFG must "promptly" begin review of the status of the species and provide a written report within 12 months indicating whether the petitioned action is warranted, identifying habitat essential to the species, and recommending management activities and other measures for the recovery of the species. Fish and Game Code § 2074.6. (The terms "critical habitat" and "recovery plans" are not used specifically in CESA as they are in the federal ESA.) Neither the Commission nor the DFG is required to undertake an independent assessment of the species. Fish and Game Code § 2074.8.

The Commission then meets for final consideration of the petition at its next available meeting, where it must find either: (1) that the petitioned action is not warranted; or (2) that the petitioned action is warranted, thereby resulting in a notice of rulemaking to add the species to (or remove it from) the list of threatened or endangered species. Fish and Game Code § 2075.5. Judicial review of these findings must be made under Code of Civil Procedure Section 1094.5. Fish and Game Code § 2076.

Like the federal ESA, CESA provides for emergency listing of species if the Commission finds that "there is any emergency posing a significant threat to the continued existence of the species." Fish and Game Code § 2076.5. The Commission must notify affected or interested parties of the adoption of such an emergency regulation. Fish and Game Code § 2076.5. Unlike the federal ESA, CESA does not specify a time limit for an emergency listing.

To provide access to information and notice of pending actions to list or delist a species, the Commission must distribute its agendas to persons who have so requested in writing. Notifications of actions to list or delist species must be published in the California Regulatory Notice Register. The Commission is authorized to impose a fee on persons who request such notices. Fish and Game Code § 2078.

### Taking

CESA contains taking prohibitions which are not as clearly defined as those under the federal ESA. Fish and Game Code §§ 2080-2085. Section 2080 of CESA prohibits the "take" of listed species "except as otherwise provided in this chapter." Section 2085 applies the take prohibitions to candidate species, unlike the federal Act. Section 2086 of the Fish and Game Code defines "take" as "hunt, pursue, catch, capture, or kill, or attempt to hunt, pursue, catch, capture, or kill." (The broader definitions of taking in the federal ESA, federal ESA guidelines, and federal case law were discussed earlier in this chapter.) No courts have interpreted CESA's taking provisions to include harm to habitat, as federal courts have interpreted the federal ESA.

*Unlike the federal act, the state ESA applies the "take" prohibitions to candidate species.*

The one published opinion discussing CESA's taking provisions is *Department of Fish and Game v. Anderson-Cottonwood Irrig. Dist.* (1992) 8 Cal.App.4th 1554. In that case, the court held that Section 2080's prohibitions against take do not apply only to hunting or fishing activities, but to activities such as operation of pump diversions. The court held that the term "take" as used in CESA applied to the killing of species and held the irrigation district liable for taking endangered winter-run chinook salmon because its pump diversion killed the species. *Anderson-Cottonwood,* pages 1560-1563.

*The "take" provisions have been applied to the impact of agricultural pump diversions on winter-run salmon.*

Limited takings are allowed under CESA. Section 2081 provides that DFG, through permits or memoranda of understanding, may authorize "individuals, public agencies, universities, zoological gardens, and scientific or educational institutions, to import, export, take, or possess any endangered, threatened, or candidate species for scientific, educational, or management purposes." Section 2084 provides that the Commission may authorize, subject to terms and conditions it prescribes, the taking of any candidate species or the taking of an endangered, threatened, or candidate species of fish for sport.

The Natural Community Conservation Planning Act (NCCP Act) was added to CESA in 1991. Fish and Game Code §§ 2800-2840. These provisions provide for voluntary cooperation among DFG, landowners, and other interested parties to develop natural community conservation "plans" which provide for early coordination of efforts to protect listed species or species that are not yet listed. The dual goals of the NCCP Act are to preserve species and their habitats (ideally before they become threatened or endangered), while allowing reasonable and appropriate development to occur on affected lands.

**NCCP Act = The Natural Community Conservation Planning Act**

*The 1991 Natural Community Conservation Planning Act is a vehicle for comprehensive planning on a cooperative basis.*

The NCCP process is intended to involve affected landowners earlier in planning for the conservation of species than the general listing process, to provide greater certainty to landowners and other parties about the limits that may be imposed upon them by CESA, and to provide a method for addressing the needs of many species at one time rather than one species at a time. Having a plan in place may also allow earlier "take" of the species than other provisions of CESA. Section 2835 of the Fish and Game Code provides that DFG may permit the taking of a species whose conservation and management is provided for in a DFG-approved natural communities conservation plan. These plans may also forestall the need to list species under CESA.

*The coastal sage scrub—the first implementation of the NCCP*

The first attempt to implement these principles occurred in Orange, Riverside, and San Diego counties in efforts to protect the coastal sage scrub, which provides habitat for many species, including the California gnatcatcher. Many landowners and local agencies have entered into voluntary agreements with DFG which include a commitment not to convert sage scrub to other uses pending a determination of the amount of habitat needed for the species.

Another recent development in preservation of habitat is the newly enacted Habitat Maintenance Funding Act. Senate Bill 445 was signed by the governor in October 1993 and adds sections 2900 and 2901 to the Fish and Game Code and section 50060 *et seq.* to the Government Code. Like the NCCP process described above, the Habitat Maintenance Funding Act is not restricted to listed species. Rather, this new act provides authority for local agencies to establish an assessment district pursuant to Government Code section 50060 *et seq.* for the "improvement or maintenance of natural habitat." Fish and Game Code § 2901(a). Such assessments can be used only where there is a DFG-approved plan for the conservation of natural habitat. Fish and Game Code § 2901(b).

"Incidental takings" are discussed in the consultation provisions of CESA outlined below.

## Consultation

**CEQA = California Environmental Quality Act**

A "lead agency" is defined under the California Environmental Quality Act (CEQA) (Pub. Resources § 21000 *et seq.*; Fish and Game Code § 2065) as the public agency which has principal responsibility for carrying out or approving a project that may have a significant effect on the environment. Pub. Resources Code § 21067. State lead agencies are required to consult with DFG to ensure that any action it carries out is "not likely to jeopardize the continued existence of any endangered or threatened species." Local lead agencies have the option to consult with the DFG. Fish and Game Code § 2090. Consultation is triggered when a "project," as defined by the California Environmental Quality Act (Pub. Resources Code § 21000 *et seq.*), is anticipated. Fish and Game Code §§ 2064, 2065, 2090.

DFG must issue a written finding based on its determination of whether the proposed project would jeopardize the continued existence of an endangered or threatened species or result in the adverse modification or destruction of its habitat. Fish and Game Code § 2091. The written finding must also include DFG's determination of whether the proposed project would result in a taking of a listed species "incidental to the proposed project." Fish and Game Code § 2091. CESA's consultation provisions do not apply to candidate species. Fish and Game Code § 2096. However, a lead agency or project proponent may request informal consultation with DFG for any project that may affect a candidate species. Fish and Game Code § 2096. CESA provides that it is the intent of the legislature to "facilitate resolution of potential conflicts between proposed projects and candidate species on the basis of information available *at that time*" and not to require alteration of project schedules pending final determination of the status of candidate species. Fish and Game Code § 2096.

If jeopardy is found, DFG must specify to the lead agency "reasonable and prudent alternatives" consistent with conserving the species which would prevent the jeopardy. Fish and Game Code § 2091. If a taking incidental to the project is found, DFG must specify "reasonable and prudent measures" to minimize the adverse impacts of the incidental taking. Fish and Game Code § 2091. A taking that is in compliance with those alternatives or measures is not prohibited. Fish and Game Code § 2096. Thus, "incidental takings" are allowed under CESA in these limited circumstances. Unlike the federal ESA, no special permit is required for such incidental takings, and compliance with measures to mitigate a proposed project's impacts is used instead of a "habitat conservation plan."

*A taking in compliance with DFG's "reasonable and prudent alternatives" does not require a special "incidental takings" permit.*

Notwithstanding CEQA's requirements that an agency must not approve a project with significant environmental impacts unless it makes certain findings, CESA states that a state lead agency must require "reasonable and prudent alternatives" consistent with conserving the species which would prevent jeopardy. Fish and Game Code § 2092(a). If specific economic, social or "other conditions" make the alternatives infeasible, the lead agency may approve a project when jeopardy is found (unless it will result in the extinction of a listed species under Fish and Game Code § 2092(c)), if the state lead agency requires reasonable mitigation and enhancement measures to minimize the project's adverse impacts on the listed species; *and* finds *all* of the following—

*A project may be approved even though jeopardy is found as long as it will not result in the extinction of a listed species.*

- The benefits of the project as proposed "clearly outweigh" the benefits of the project were it to be carried out with the reasonable and prudent alternatives

- An irreversible or irretrievable commitment of resources to the project, made after initiation of consultation, which has "the effect of foreclosing the opportunity for formulation and implementing reasonable and prudent alternatives which prevent jeopardy," has not been made. Fish and Game Code § 2092(a) and (b)

A project may not be approved if it will result in the extinction of a listed species. Fish and Game Code § 2092(c).

If a project may affect species that are listed under both the federal and state ESA, DFG is required to participate in the federal consultation "to the greatest extent practicable." Fish and Game Code § 2095.

## Impacts of ESA on Water Supplies

*The exercise of water rights under state law may be considered a "taking," prohibited under federal law.*

Because of the strong policies and provisions of endangered species legislation, both federal and state, the implementation of these laws sometimes conflicts with the exercise of water rights. The federal ESA has had the most impact in this area and, unlike California courts, federal courts have issued several published opinions on this issue. In particular, based on the broad definition of "taking" in the federal ESA and its interpretation in *Palila II*, the exercise of water rights under state law could be considered a taking. For example, if an endangered species which exists downstream of a water diversion depends on a certain flow level for its existence, use of that water by an upstream diverter could, in some instances, be considered a "taking" if it resulted in significant habitat modification. The taking prohibitions exempt no one; public and private entities alike are subject to their broad reach.

In 1982, an effort was made to substantially weaken the federal ESA's potential to impact water rights. An amendment was proposed that would have added a provision to the federal ESA similar to Section 101(g) of the federal Clean Water Act. Section 101(g) states in part—

It is the policy of Congress that the authority of each State to allocate quantities of water within its jurisdiction shall not be superseded, abrogated or otherwise impaired by this chapter.... [N]othing in this chapter shall be construed to supersede or abrogate the rights to quantities of water which have been established by any State. Federal agencies shall co-operate with State and local agencies to develop comprehensive solutions to prevent, reduce and eliminate pollution in concert with programs for managing water resources. 33 U.S.C. § 1251(g).

However, the effort to add similar language to the federal ESA failed.[4] Instead, Congress added as one of the policies of the federal ESA that: "Federal agencies shall cooperate with State and local agencies to resolve water resource issues in concert with conservation of endangered species." 16 U.S.C. § 1531(c)(2). Such broad language has left to the courts the job of resolving water rights issues "in concert with" the conservation of listed species. As discussed below, endangered species have generally prevailed.

In *Carson-Truckee Water Conservancy District v. Clark* (9th Cir. 1984) 741 F.2d 257, the Ninth Circuit held that the Secretary of the Interior had the discretion under the federal ESA to devote the entire supply of the Stampede Dam and Reservoir, which impounds water from a Truckee River tributary in California, to endangered fish species in Pyramid Lake in Nevada. This action was upheld by the court even though the purpose of the dam was to provide water for agricultural uses in Nevada.

In *Riverside Irrigation District v. Andrews* (10th Cir. 1985) 758 F.2d 508, the Riverside Irrigation District and Public Service Company of Colorado planned to build a dam and reservoir on Wildcat Creek in Colorado to store water for irrigation and for cooling a coal-fired power plant. The irrigation district obtained a water right under state law for this project and also applied for a Section 404 "dredge and fill" permit under the federal Clean Water Act.

The Army Corps of Engineers refused to issue the Section 404 permit in part because of concerns that the project could impact downstream whooping crane habitat. A USFWS biological opinion had concluded that the reservoir would jeopardize continued existence of the whooping crane and adversely modify its critical habitat. *Andrews,* pages 511-512.

Colorado argued that the Corps could base its decision only on the impacts of the deposit of dredge and fill material during construction of the dam. However, the Tenth Circuit held that the Corps could properly consider all direct and indirect effects of the project in assessing whether to issue a Section 404 permit, and held that the Corps acted within its authority in denying the permit. The court also characterized Section 101(g) of the federal Clean Water Act as a "policy statement" only. *Id.,* page 513.

The winter-run chinook salmon, listed as endangered under the CESA and listed as threatened under the federal ESA, has posed

---

[4] Tarlock, "The Endangered Species Act and Western Water Rights," 20 *Land and Water L. Rev.* 1 (1985).

*Diversions by the Glenn-Colusa Irrigation District were held to constitute a "taking" of fingerling salmon.*

problems in court for at least one water supplier in California. The winter-run salmon migrates from the Pacific Ocean up the Sacramento River to spawn between January and June. The National Marine Fisheries Service brought an action in federal court to enjoin the Glenn-Colusa Irrigation District from "taking" fingerling salmon in the course of pumping water from the Sacramento River at its Hamilton City pumping station. *United States v. Glenn-Colusa Irrigation District*, (E.Dist. CA. 1992) 788 F.Supp. 1126. It was estimated that the district's pumping operation killed approximately 800,000 to 9,100,000 juvenile salmon annually prior to 1972, when DFG installed a screen at the district's pump. *U.S. v. Glenn-Colusa Irrig.*, page 1129. However, even with the screen in place, 400,000 to 10,000,000 juveniles were still lost annually. *U.S. v. Glenn-Colusa Irrigation*, page 1130.

In late 1989, the district applied to the Army Corps of Engineers for a permit to dredge its diversion channel. Pursuant to the federal ESA, the Army Corps consulted with the USFWS. USFWS determined that issuance of the permit was likely to jeopardize the winter-run salmon in violation of the ESA. *U.S. v. Glenn-Colusa Irrigation*, pages 1130-1132. In its biological opinion, USFWS indicated that harm could be avoided if the district installed a new, more effective fish screen. USFWS also concluded that if this new screen were installed,

Salmon Fish Ladder on the American River near Folsom Dam

the district would be eligible for an incidental taking permit. In December 1990, USFWS notified the district that without an incidental taking permit it would be liable for unauthorized takings of the fish. (*U.S. v. Glenn-Colusa Irrigation*, page 1131. The district never applied for a taking permit, and the federal government filed for an injunction.

In reviewing the matter, the district court declined the district's invitation to consider the "social utility" of ordering it to cease taking the winter-run salmon, noting that a weighing of competing considerations is precluded by the federal ESA. The district also asserted that CESA's definition of "taking" should apply, rather than the federal definition, since Congress intended to integrate the state and federal laws protecting endangered species. The court, however, noted that "taking" is defined similarly in both laws. To the extent that California state law is less protective than the federal law, the court held it to be preempted. Moreover, the court noted that under either state or federal law, it was clear that the district was "taking" salmon through the operation of its pumps. *U.S. v. Glenn-Colusa Irrigation*, page 1134.

The district also asserted that state water rights should prevail over the ESA, citing the policy of the federal ESA to "cooperate with states . . . to resolve water resource issues regarding the conservation of endangered species." (*Id.*, page 1134, citing § 1531(c)(2).) The court stated—

> This provision does not require, however, that state water rights should prevail over the restrictions set forth in the [federal] Act. Such an interpretation would render the Act a nullity. The Act provides no exemption from compliance to persons possessing state water rights, and thus the District's state water rights do not provide it with a special privilege to ignore the Endangered Species Act. Moreover, enforcement of the Act does not affect the District's water rights but only the manner in which it exercises those rights. *U.S. v. Glenn-Colusa Irrigation,* page 1134.

The court concluded that the district was taking winter-run salmon in violation of the federal ESA and that neither state nor federal law exempted it from the federal ESA. The court enjoined the district from pumping water from its Hamilton City facility during the winter-run salmon's peak downstream migration season of July 15 through November 30 of each year. *U.S. v. Glenn-Colusa,* page 1135.

The court opined that "there [was] no unfairness" in this injunction since the district had failed to contest the design of the original fish screen to DFG and had not applied for an incidental taking permit. *U.S. v. Glenn Colusa Irrigation,* page 1135.

In another case involving water suppliers in California, the Delta smelt, a fish that inhabits the Sacramento-San Joaquin Delta, was listed as threatened under the federal ESA. 58 Fed.Reg. 12854, March 5, 1993. The California Fish and Game Commission rejected an earlier petition to list the Delta smelt on the basis that there was inadequate data available to support a listing. The consequences of the federal listing could be enormous for the millions of people in California who depend on the Delta for all or part of their water supplies. Most of the area of the Delta used by California's major water suppliers has been proposed to be designated as critical habitat. Moreover, listing the smelt subjects these suppliers to the takings provisions of the federal ESA under the same theories used in the *Glenn-Colusa* case.

The impacts of listed species on water supplies are not limited to fish species. In Texas, a federal district court held that the flow of underground

*The district also asserted that state water rights should prevail over the ESA.*

Tiny Delta Smelt: a threatened species under the Federal ESA. Ruler measures in centimeters, not inches

water from the Edwards Aquifer to two springs must be maintained to protect various species of animals and plants that depend on the springs for their habitat. This aquifer is the sole source of drinking water for the City of San Antonio. *Sierra Club v. Lujan* (W.D. Tex. 1993) 36 ERC 1533.

Similarly, the sole source of domestic and irrigation water to property owners within the San Luis Rey Municipal Water District in California may be significantly curtailed to maintain the San Luis Rey River as part of the critical habitat for the Least Bell's Vireo, a bird federally classified as endangered. *See* 57 Fed. Reg. 34893 (Aug. 7, 1992).

These cases make it clear that courts will continue to take the policies of the ESA seriously, even in the face of a severely limited water supply. It is also clear that a water supplier is not protected from the ESA by virtue of holding legally obtained state water rights. The issue of whether such endangered species regulations constitute a taking of water rights in violation of the Fifth Amendment to the U.S. Constitution has not been resolved. Essentially, there are only three ways to avoid the stringent requirements of the ESA: (1) to apply to the Endangered Species Committee; (2) to apply for a taking permit; or (3) to develop reasonable and prudent alternatives to avoid a negative biological opinion from the USFWS. None of these alternatives is easy to accomplish.

*A water supplier is not protected from the stringent requirements of the ESA by virtue of holding state water rights.*

# CHAPTER SIX

# Two Traditional Approaches to Water Allocation Conflicts

## Introduction

Chapter 3 reviewed three significant methods which courts have used to reallocate California's water resources in the last 30 years: (1) the public trust doctrine; (2) the law of reasonable use as set forth in Article X, Section 2, of the California Constitution; and (3) Sections 5937 and 5946 of the Fish and Game Code. The application of these doctrines has made significant inroads into what were considered vested property rights.

This chapter discusses two more traditional methods for allocating waters among competing consumptive uses—equitable apportionment and the physical solution. In *EDF v. EBMUD* (1990) Alameda Co. Superior Ct. No. 425955, a physical solution was used to accommodate not only consumptive but also environmental uses. Equitable apportionment has also been suggested as a way to accommodate consumptive and environmental water uses.[1]

## Equitable Apportionment

Equitable apportionment has long been used in western water disputes to allocate water resources. Under this apportionment method, the strict rules of priority are largely disregarded in favor of an allocation that will be fair to all water users. This doctrine has been considered in several groundwater cases in California. *See City of Pasadena v. Alhambra, et al.* (1949) 33 Cal.2d 908; *Tehachapi-Cummings*

*Equitable apportionment in California*

[1]  Dunning, "State Equitable Apportionment of Western Water Resources," 66 *Nebraska Law Review* 76 (1987).

*County Water District v. Armstrong* (1975) 49 Cal.App.3d 992; *City of Los Angeles v. San Fernando* (1975) 14 Cal.3d 199. The courts in these cases have differed over the factors to be taken into account in an equitable apportionment situation. In *Pasadena v. Alhambra* (discussed in chapter 2), the court used the doctrine of "mutual prescription" to reach an equitable apportionment. In that case, the court concluded that applying rules of strict priority would lead to—

*In the* Pasadena *case, mutual prescription was used to reach an equitable apportionment.*

> ...an unequal sharing of the burden of curtailing the overdraft.... Such a result does not appear to be justified where all the parties have been producing water from the underground basin for many years, and none of them have acted to protect the supply or prevent invasion of their rights until this proceeding was instituted. Moreover, it seems probable that the solution adopted by the trial court will promote the best interests of the public, *because a pro tanto reduction of the amount of water devoted to each present use would normally be less disruptive than total elimination of some of the uses.* (Pasadena v. Alhambra, pages 932-933, emphasis added.)

Los Angeles v. San Fernando *partially overruled mutual prescription, but supported equitable apportionment.*

In 1975, the mutual prescription doctrine was partially overruled by the California Supreme Court in the case of *Los Angeles v. San Fernando*. The primary reason for this result may have been that the doctrine focused on past pumping, rewarding pumpers on the basis of their highest pumping levels. Thus, it provided the greatest benefit to the pumpers who had been contributing the most to the overdraft. In the words of the court in *Los Angeles v. San Fernando*, it caused a "race to the pumphouse" by groundwater pumpers. *San Fernando,* page 267. However, *Los Angeles v. San Fernando* did endorse the equitable apportionment idea expressed by the court in *Pasadena*.

*Mechanical allocations of water based on formulas or strict priorities do not necessarily produce an equitable result.*

Although the court in *San Fernando* concluded that mutual prescription allowed a fair result on the facts presented in the *Pasadena* case, it noted that mechanical allocations based on formulas such as mutual prescription do not necessarily lead to the most equitable apportionment of water and may produce just as unfair a result as a strict priority system. *San Fernando,* pages 256, 265. The implication of the court's statement is that a court should apply the rules that will produce the most equitable result in a given situation. These can be the rules of prior appropriation, riparian law, or mutual prescription (except against public agencies), or the discretionary approach used by federal courts in intrastate water controversies.[2]

---

[2] Dunning, page 103.

Insofar as *Los Angeles v. San Fernando* suggests a future soften-
ing of priorities, it is extremely significant. However, there is language
in the decision which seems to limit how far courts may depart from
the rules of priority. In rejecting the doctrine of mutual prescription,
the court noted that a truly equitable apportionment would take into
account many more factors. *San Fernando,* page 265. In a footnote,
the court then quoted from the Supreme Court's opinion in *Nebraska
v. Wyoming* (1945) 325 U.S. 589—

> But if an allocation between appropriation States is to be just and
> equitable, strict adherence to the priority rule may not be possible.
> For example, the economy of a region may have been established
> on the basis of junior appropriations. So far as possible those es-
> tablished uses should be protected though strict application of
> the priority rule might jeopardize them. Apportionment calls for
> the exercise of an informed judgment on a consideration of many
> factors. *Priority of appropriation is the guiding principle.* But phys-
> ical and climactic conditions, the consumptive use of water in the
> several sections of the river, the character and rate of return flows,
> the extent of established uses, the availability of storage water, the
> practical effect of wasteful uses on downstream areas, the damage
> to upstream areas as compared to the benefits to downstream areas
> if a limitation is imposed on the former—these are all relevant
> factors. They are merely an illustrative, not an exhaustive catalog.
> They indicate the nature of the problem of apportionment and the
> delicate adjustments of interests which must be made. (*Nebraska v.
> Wyoming,* page 618, emphasis added.)

*Factors to be considered in making an equitable apportionment*

*Priority of appropriation remains the guid-ing principle.*

While only a footnote, the *San Fernando* court seems to
endorse the concept that priorities remain the starting point for any
allocation of water.

Factors that may be considered in adopting an equitable
apportionment are also outlined in *Tehachapi-Cummings Water
District v. Armstrong* (1975) 49 Cal.App.3d 992—

> By analogy to riparian rights, where there is insufficient water for
> the current reasonable needs of all the overlying owners, many fac-
> tors are to be considered in determining each owner's proportion-
> ate share: the amount of water available, the extent of ownership
> in the basin, the nature of the projected use—if for agriculture, the
> area sought to be irrigated, the character of the soil, the practica-
> bility of irrigation, i.e., the expense thereof, the comparative profit
> of the different crops which could be made of the water on the
> land—all these many and other considerations must enter into the
> solution of the problem. *Tehachapi,* pages 1001-1002.

Excessive reliance on equitable apportionment, however, leads to more uncertainty in water rights. Water users can never be certain of the rules or the outcome until a case is tried in court. The doctrine does not easily lend itself to needed predictability. Although certainty may be diminished, the doctrine calls into play the full powers of equity to produce, in individual cases, results that are fair and in the public interest.[3]

## The Physical Solution

*The doctrine of physical solution is a "common sense approach to water rights litigation."*

The doctrine of physical solution is a "common sense approach to water rights litigation."[4] A physical solution resolves competing claims to water by cooperatively satisfying the reasonable needs of each user. Unlike an equitable apportionment, a physical solution is not aimed at a reduction in water rights. Rather, it seeks to satisfy the basic rights or needs of the users through manipulation of the water supply or through other practical measures. The "substantial enjoyment" of a prior right must be protected. *Peabody v. Vallejo* (1935) 2 Cal.2d 351, 383-84. The concept has a long judicial history, having originally developed because California courts were reluctant to enjoin water use in situations where a less drastic remedy was available. The traditional remedy for water rights infringement is a prohibitive injunction ordering the wrongful, subordinate water use halted. *See City of Lodi v. East Bay Municipal Utility District* (1936) 7 Cal.2d 316, 337. However, this equitable remedy was often too harsh, and as early as 1904 has been limited to those rare cases where "no other relief is adequate." *See Montecito Valley Co. v. Santa Barbara* (1904) 144 Cal. 578, 592. As the Supreme Court stated—

> It would be a manifest hardship and injustice to deprive the defendant by injunction of the right to take any of the water when only a small part of that which it does take is subject to the claim of plaintiff....*Montecito Valley Co.*, 144 Cal., page 592.

The 1928 amendment to the California Constitution, now Article X, Section 2, added a second doctrinal basis for the imposition of a physical solution. Furthermore, it elevated the concept to a favored status and created a duty incumbent upon every trier of fact—

---

3   The Governor's Commission characterized "relative uncertainty" as "the distinctive attribute" of water rights law in California. The Commission made a number of recommendations toward gaining greater certainty in water rights. Final Report, Governor's Commission to Review California Water Rights Law, December 1978, pages 16 *et seq.*

4   Rogers and Nichols, *Water for California* (1967) § 404, page 548.

Since the adoption of the 1928 constitutional amendment, it is not only within the power but it is also the duty of the trial court to admit evidence relating to possible physical solutions, and if none is satisfactory to it to suggest on its own motion such physical solution. *City of Lodi v. East Bay Municipal Utility District* (1936) 7 Cal.2d 316, 341.

*Courts have a duty to consider physical solutions, even on their own motion.*

The doctrine of physical solution is a practical way of carrying out the mandate of Article X, Section 2, that the water resources of the state be put to use "to the fullest extent of which they are capable." Under the doctrine, as one text states, "[s]olution of water rights problems by use of all available information and expertise is attempted in order that the best possible use is made of the waters in their apportionment among contending parties."[5]

*A physical solution is a practical way to implement the constitutional mandate that water resources be put to use "to the fullest extent of which they are capable."*

Physical solutions are enforceable by courts and are not dependent upon the consent of the parties. (*City of Lodi v. East Bay Municipal Utility Dist.* (1936) 7 Cal.2d 316, 341; *Tulare Irrigation District v. Lindsay-Strathmore Irrigation Dist.* (1935) 3 Cal.2d 489, 547.) The physical solution must, however, take into account the priorities of water rights, and may not be applied in such a way that vested rights are eliminated. *Peabody v. Vallejo* (1935) 2 Cal.2d 351; *Rancho Santa Margarita v. Vail* (1938) 11 Cal.2d 501.

Physical solutions have been employed in a variety of situations. As shown by the cases discussed below, the California courts have recognized physical solutions based on the provision of substitute surface water supplies, replacement of waters previously available without pumping from an artesian well, canal lining to prevent seepage losses, protection of groundwater against saltwater intrusion and, most importantly, regulation of diversion and reservoir release schedules so as to protect prior and paramount water rights.

### California Physical Solution Cases

In *Tulare Irrigation District v. Lindsay-Strathmore Irrigation District* (1935) 3 Cal.2d 489, a large number of individual landowners and other entities held water rights that were prior and paramount to the appropriation proposed by Lindsay-Strathmore, which sought to export groundwater to lands outside the watershed. Plaintiffs filed the action to enjoin Lindsay-Strathmore from pumping groundwater. The injunction was granted by the trial court. The Supreme Court, however, applied what is now Article X, Section 2, to reverse the judgment insofar as certain riparian and overlying owners were concerned. It ordered the trial court to take evidence to determine the quantity of

[5] Rogers and Nichols, pages 547-548.

water necessary for the reasonable beneficial uses of such owners, and to issue a judgment protecting that quantity for them. The Supreme Court then offered the trial court the following guidance on adopting a physical solution—

*Water rights disputes are generally cases in equity, and courts should use their broad equitable powers "to do substantial justice."*

Moreover, the trial court should not lose sight of the fact that this is an equity case. The equity courts possess broad powers and should exercise them so as to do substantial justice. Heretofore, the equity courts, in water cases, apparently have not seen fit to work out physical solutions of the problems presented, unless such solutions have been suggested by the parties. But it should be kept in mind that the equity court is not bound or limited by the suggestions or offers made by the parties to this, or any similar, action, [sic] For purposes of illustration, if the trial court, on the retrial, comes to the conclusion, based upon proper evidence, that a substantial saving can be effected at a reasonable cost, by repairing or changing some of the ditches, as above mentioned, it undoubtedly has the power regardless of whether the parties have suggested the particular physical solution or not, to make its injunctive order subject to conditions which it may suggest and to apportion the cost thereof as justice may require, keeping in mind the fact that respondents have prior rights and cannot be required lawfully to incur any material expense in order to accommodate appellant. Other physical solutions, such as the possible impounding of some of the water during periods, if any, when it is not needed by respondents, whereby some water can be made available to appellant without injury to respondents may suggest themselves. *Tulare v. Lindsay-Strathmore,* page 574.

*A physical solution must protect the "substantial enjoyment" of a prior right.*

*City of Lodi v. East Bay Municipal Utility District* (1936) 7 Cal.2d 316 involved the East Bay Municipal Utility District's (EBMUD's) Pardee Dam on the Mokelumne River. The City of Lodi was located downstream, and the wells supplying it were fed by the Mokelumne River. The City of Lodi brought the action to determine the priority of its rights, and to enjoin EBMUD from storing or diverting any water from the Mokelumne River. The trial court issued a decree that required EBMUD to make large releases so that the groundwater table below the City of Lodi would not be lowered.

**EBMUD = East Bay Municipal Utility District**

The Supreme Court examined this decree under the requirements of Article X, Section 2, and found that the very large releases required of EBMUD were a wasteful and inefficient way of maintaining the city's groundwater supply. The court wrote that Article X, Section 2, required the trial court, "before issuing a decree entailing such waste of water, to ascertain whether there exists a physical solution of the problem presented that will avoid the waste, ..." *Lodi v. EBMUD*, page 339.

The quote below from *Lodi*, although lengthy, provides an excellent example of how a court may approach a physical solution—

The court possesses the power to enforce such solution regardless of whether the parties agree. If the trial court desires competent expert evidence on this or any other problem connected with the case, it possesses the power to refer the matter to the division of water rights of the board of public works, or to appoint it as an expert. (*Peabody v. City of Vallejo, supra*, page 373; *Tulare Irr. Dist. v. Lindsay-Strathmore Irr. Dist., supra*, page 575)

• • •

With the foregoing considerations and principles in mind we now turn to a discussion of how they should be applied to the present case. We have here a city whose prior right is 3,600 acre-feet annually. The city is at present securing this quantity by wells sunk into the underground water table supplied from the Mokelumne [River]. The city's method of diversion appears to be reasonable, and the use to which the water is put is a reasonable beneficial one.... There is adequate water available to supply the city's right and to supply the District's ultimate needs, except in the very driest years. In this connection certain other factors should be mentioned. The evidence shows that prior to judgment the city's wells, instead of being lowered by the defendant District's operations had in fact slightly risen.... the fact that there is no immediate danger to the City of Lodi's water right is an element to be considered in working out a proper solution.

• • •

However, whatever the reasons may be, the record conclusively establishes the fact that the plaintiff's water supply had not been materially diminished between the time the District commenced operations and the time judgment was entered herein. One of the expert witnesses called by the plaintiff conceded that its wells could go down at least twenty-five feet below their present levels without danger or substantial injury to the plaintiff. Assuming a lowering of one foot a year by the District's operations, as found by the trial court, it is apparent that the plaintiff's water supply is in no immediate danger. What, then, should the trial court have done or now do in such circumstances? Under the present law of the state, in accomplishing the necessary and beneficent purpose

*A court has the power to enforce a physical solution, "regardless of whether the parties agree."*

A physical solution should "prevent an unreasonable waste of the waters of the stream."

A court should retain continuing jurisdiction to modify a physical solution decree as may be required.

of the 1928 constitutional amendment, the trial court should attempt to cause its decree to protect fully the prior appropriator's rights, and at the same time should so frame its decree as to prevent an unreasonable waste of the waters of the stream. A consideration of the facts in this case and as above outlined leads to the inevitable conclusion that the decree entered herein would result in an unjustifiable and unreasonable waste which should be avoided if a practical physical solution may be found. The question then is, what solution is available under the facts here presented?

In our opinion the cause should be sent back to the trial court to permit it to take evidence as to the levels, to which plaintiff's wells may be lowered without substantial danger to the city's water supply. In fixing this danger level an adequate safety factor in favor of the city should be allowed .... The decree should then be reframed to provide that the duty rests upon the District to maintain the levels of the plaintiff's wells above the danger level so fixed by the trial court; that in the event the levels of the wells reach the danger points, the duty be cast upon the District to supply water to the city, or to raise the levels of the wells above the danger mark; and if the District does not comply with this order within a reasonable time, then the injunction decree already framed, or upon a proper showing as modified by the court under its continuing jurisdiction, shall go into effect. The trial court should by its judgment preserve its continuing jurisdiction, to change or modify its orders and decree as occasion may require.

Such a decree would adequately meet the requirements of the Constitution by preventing an unreasonable waste of the waters of the stream and at the same time would adequately protect the prior rights of the City of Lodi. It would afford to the city a continuance of its water supply, the same, for all practical purposes, as if natural conditions were required to persist. If its wells go down to the danger level, it would immediately obtain water from the District at the latter's expense, or the injunction decree by means of which the underground levels will be artificially maintained would go into effect. It would accord to the District the right and place upon it the duty of working out a physical solution unhampered by a rigid decree which, with changing conditions and new methods of conservation constantly being developed, may not only operate inequitably but might actually encourage waste. It would place upon the District the duty at its expense to maintain the underground water levels, and if the District fails to do so, or fails to supply water directly to the City of Lodi, the decree provides for compulsory releases so as to maintain natural conditions. Such a decree would say to the District: You should maintain the water levels so as not to cause substantial damage to the city, and you may do this in any way best suited to your needs, or if you do not maintain those levels you should supplement the city's supply to the extent of the deficiency caused by your operations by the furnishing of water by artificial means and at your expense. If you do not do these things you are subject to an injunction compelling releases to maintain natural conditions. Such a decree would undoubtedly prevent a multiplicity of suits. It would fix the rights of the prior appropriator and would determine the effect of the subject subsequent appropriator's diversions. Since there is no immediate danger to the prior appropriator, it would fix the danger levels of the prior appropriator's wells and when that level is reached, upon a showing to that effect, it would require the subsequent appropriator either by direct delivery of water or by compulsory releases to supply the prior appropriator's needs.

Such a decree would permit the full use of all available waters, guarantee to the prior appropriator full protection, and would do this without unduly restraining the operations of the subsequent appropriator. *Lodi v. EBMUD,* pages 341-345.

*The decree in* Lodi v. EBMUD *permitted "the full use" of all available waters, guaranteed the prior appropriator "full protection," without "unduly restraining" the operations of the subsequent appropriator.*

In *Reclamation District No. 833 v. Quigley* (1937) 8 Cal.2d 183, the trial court enjoined the defendant from interfering with or impounding any of the water flowing in Lateral A (a part of the reclamation works of the plaintiff). The court relied upon the holding in *Lindsay-Strathmore* and stated that the trial court should have endeavored to determine the most feasible physical solution.

In *Meridian Ltd. v. San Francisco* (1939) 13 Cal.2d 424, the court protected a riparian from pollution and allowed storage through the physical solution process. The court noted that generally jurisdiction must be retained to determine whether the physical solution is effective, and to order adjustments that might be necessary. *Meridian,* pages 452-453.

In *Montecito Valley Water Co. v. City of Santa Barbara* (1904) 144 Cal. 578, plaintiff held rights to water from a creek which he sold for beneficial purposes to the residents of a nearby city. Defendants built tunnels contiguous to the creek. Plaintiff brought suit, contending that the effect of these tunnels was to withdraw water which had flowed naturally into the creek, and that these tunnels permanently impaired and reduced his supply. Plaintiff sought an injunction and monetary compensation for the value of the water. *Montecito Valley Water*, pages 583-584. In directing the trial court to fashion a physical solution, the Supreme Court held that plaintiff was entitled to monetary compensation for the unlawful diversion of his water. The court also directed the trial court to prevent continuing injury to the plaintiff by either a mandatory injunction requiring the restoration of the given amount of water or by "other equitable manner." *Montecito Valley Water*, page 602. The court also held that the trial court should make further provision to protect the respective rights of the parties in the event that an extension of the tunnel were to threaten plaintiff's rights in the future. The court noted that a prohibitory injunction could be proper in this instance, but should only be granted if any and all other forms of relief are found inadequate. *Montecito Valley Water*, page 602.

In *Peabody v. City of Vallejo* (1935) 2 Cal.2d 351, the plaintiffs, downstream riparian landowners, brought suit to enjoin the City of Vallejo, an appropriator, from storing the waters of a creek. Plaintiffs alleged that they needed all the water from the creek for irrigation and other beneficial purposes. *Peabody*, page 358. In discussing remedies, plaintiffs suggested that in lieu of damages the trial court should prescribe a physical solution and direct the city to provide and maintain the solution permanently at its own expense. Plaintiffs noted that the court could enforce such requirements by a prohibitory or mandatory injunction. *Peabody*, page 380. The Supreme Court agreed and noted that, if the trial court found such a physical solution appropriate, "it should by its judgment preserve its continuing jurisdiction to change or modify its orders and decree as occasion may require." *Peabody*, page 380. The court stated that—

> . . . if a physical solution be ascertainable, the court has the power to make and should make reasonable regulations for the use of the water by the respective parties, provided they be adequate to protect the one having the paramount right in the substantial enjoyment thereof and to prevent its ultimate destruction, and in this connection the court has the power to and should reserve unto itself the right to change and modify its orders and decree as occasion may demand, either on its own motion or on motion of any party. *Peabody*, pages 383-384.

In *Rancho Santa Margarita v. Vail* (1938) 11 Cal.2d 501, appellants and respondent sought a determination of their respective rights in a river which flowed over both of their ranches. Appellants

(Vail) had been diverting water upstream for irrigation for many years, and had constructed a series of pumping plants which allegedly threatened to divert 60 to 85 percent of the river water. Rancho Santa Margarita, the downstream owner, brought suit claiming that it was entitled to six-sevenths of the water of the stream and sought an injunction to prohibit diversions by appellants beyond one-seventh of the total flow. Vail claimed that it had the right to five-sevenths of the total flow of the river. *Rancho Santa Margarita,* page 517. The trial court held that Rancho Santa Margarita was reasonably entitled to three-quarters of the flow of the mainstream, and Vail to one-quarter. *Rancho Santa Margarita,* page 508.

In reviewing this decision, the Supreme Court noted that in considering whether an injunction should be granted in such a case, "it is the duty of the trial court to ascertain whether there is a physical solution of the problem that will avoid waste and which will not unreasonably or adversely affect the rights of the parties." *Rancho Santa Margarita,* page 559. The court also added: "No injunction should be granted if its effect will be to waste water that can be used." *Rancho Santa Margarita,* page 559. In citing what is now Article X, Section 2, of the California Constitution, the court stated—

> Under this section it has been held that it is not only within the power, but it is the duty of the trial court, to work out, if possible, a physical solution, and if none is suggested by the parties to work out one independently of the parties. In this connection, if the trial court needs or desires expert assistance or evidence on this, or any other phase of the case, it possesses the statutory power either to refer matter to the division of water rights, or to appoint it as an expert. *Rancho Santa Margarita,* page 559.

The Supreme Court made specific suggestions to the trial court to aid it in fashioning a physical solution. The court observed that it might be possible for Vail to divert and store winter waters which were previously being wasted, perhaps supplemented by a small portion of the summer flow. In this manner, Vail could secure all the water it reasonably needed. The court also suggested that releases from the reservoirs could be regulated in the summer months, making surface flow available to respondent. On the other hand, the court observed that there might also be reservoir and storage sites on Rancho Santa Margarita's property where winter water could be conserved and then released in the summer months. The court also suggested the installation of pumping plants upstream from the reservoir to provide drinking places for respondent's cattle. *Rancho*

*A physical solution may involve the storage and use of waters previously wasted to the ocean.*

*Santa Margarita,* page 560. In making these suggestions, the court stated: "With the small quantity of water available in this stream in the summer months, the trial court should thoroughly investigate the possibility of some physical solution, before granting an injunction that may be ruinous to either or both parties." *Rancho Santa Margarita,* page 560.

With regard to the costs of a physical solution, the court held—

[T]he lower owner cannot be expected or required to endure an unreasonable inconvenience or to incur an unreasonable expense in order to make more water available for the use of the upper riparian. If on the new trial it shall develop that the only feasible physical solution will involve the expenditure of large sums of money by respondent, and that the sum required, when all the facts, including the necessities and uses of the parties, are considered, is unreasonable, the trial court has full power to make its injunctive order conditional so as to require appellants to bear a portion of the expense. In other words the trial court, if the facts warrant it, can grant an injunction in favor of respondent unless appellants agree to bear a fair proportion of the expense necessary to construct the required improvements on respondent's ranch. This would appear to be a fair, just and equitable rule. If appellants, as upstream owners, desire to use more than their fair share of the available flow, . . . appellants should be required, . . . to bear their reasonable share of expense in making it available. *Rancho Santa Margarita,* pages 561-562.

In *Hillside Water Co. v. City of Los Angeles* (1938) 10 Cal.2d 677, plaintiff Hillside Water Company brought suit seeking to enjoin the defendants, City of Los Angeles and its Board of Water and Power Commissioners, from "flowing, pumping, or otherwise exporting any of the waters" from any of the defendants' water wells. *Hillside Water Co.,* page 679. Plaintiff alleged that defendants' withdrawals and diversions deprived it of waters necessary for its use. A city, two school districts, a lumber company and 14 individuals intervened, seeking the same relief sought by the plaintiff. The trial court found that the pumping and diversion operations of the defendants had caused the level of water under plaintiff's and intervenors' lands to be lowered to the extent that it had been impossible to properly irrigate the lands. The trial court further noted that the supply of water underlying these lands would be completely exhausted if defendants were to continue their pumping operations. *Hillside Water Co.,* page 683. Thus, the trial court's injunctive order required the underground water table to be maintained in its natural state, uninfluenced by the pumping operations of the defendants. *Hillside Water Co.,* page 685.

In reviewing this decision, the Supreme Court stated that the trial court's order, in effect, would prevent the beneficial use of water beneath 98 percent of the area in order that the water table beneath 2 percent of the area be maintained in its natural condition. *Hillside Water Co.,* page 685. The court held that a physical solution might be more appropriate because the Constitution requires that these waters be put to beneficial use to the fullest extent possible. However, the court held that a physical solution should be applied only to the schools, since the other plaintiffs could be adequately compensated with damages. *Hillside Water Co.,* page 686. The court stated—

> The Bishop Union Grammar School has been supplied with water for drinking and garden purposes from an artesian well the pressure of which receded during the pumping operations of the defendants. Obviously it is within the power of the defendants to insure an adequate supply of water to this school and the court should safeguard that right by its judgment without the necessity of a prohibitive injunction, with the consequence above indicated, except in aid of the enforcement of the physical solution applied. (*Hillside Water Co.,* pages 688-689.)

In *Allen v. California Water and Telephone Co.* (1946) 29 Cal.2d 466, plaintiffs, owners of land overlying a portion of an underground basin, brought suit against a defendant who also owned land and wells in the same valley. Plaintiffs alleged that their paramount right to waters of the basin would be adversely impacted by defendant's construction of a large pipeline which would convey water from the basin to points outside of the watershed. Moreover, it was alleged that after defendants removed a large quantity of water there would not be sufficient water left in the basin for their use. *Allen,* pages 471-472. The trial court held that defendant was not entitled to take any water from the basin for exportation, except when such water was not reasonably required by those with paramount rights. The court held that in the latter situation the defendant could only export fixed amounts for each year from 1942 to 1944, and after 1944 could not divert or export any water whatsoever from the basin unless it was water which would otherwise "waste into the ocean." *Allen,* pages 474-475. Defendant appealed, alleging that there was surplus water for exportation and stressing the necessity for a physical solution. *Allen,* pages 474-475.

In lieu of a complete injunction against exports, the decree may include payment for deepening and improving wells.

The Supreme Court observed that the defendant had presented a feasible physical solution to the trial court. Furthermore, defendant had agreed to pay for any deepening of plaintiffs' wells or any replacement of equipment necessitated by its taking water from the basin. The Supreme Court found the trial court's order too restrictive, since there were findings that at certain times surplus water was present due to seepage and return waters from irrigation. Thus, the Supreme Court observed that defendant could pump more water than would normally be allowed under the trial court's injunction. The court held that the trial court should retain jurisdiction to consider the effect of this added source of water, and its dependability, in working out a physical solution. *Allen,* page 488. In so doing, the Supreme Court held that the trial court would be "carrying out the policy inherent in the water law of this state to utilize all water available." *Allen,* page 448. The Supreme Court further observed that even though this additional source of water might be an undependable source, "this water should not remain unused so long as it is available. In order to provide for the full utilization of this water, the trial court has the power to consider this source of supply so long as it is available." *Allen,* page 488.

## Trial Court Physical Solutions

*The doctrine of physical solution applied to a stream system adjudication involving thousands of parties.*

**Orange County Water District v. City of Chino, et al., *1969 Orange County Superior Court No. 117628.*** Over the past few decades, the doctrine of physical solution has been employed in the settlement of several major groundwater adjudications. Each of the cases described herein was ultimately settled, at least among the major parties, so the judgment was not appealed. These cases demonstrate the complex but practical types of solutions reached under the physical solution doctrine. In each, the trial court remained involved through continuing jurisdiction.

In 1963, the Orange County Water District brought suit against all upstream pumpers and diverters taking water from the Santa Ana River water system. Approximately 2,500 defendants were served, including all the major cities, water districts, water companies, and individual pumpers or diverters within Riverside and San Bernardino counties. Ultimately, cross-complaints were filed against those claiming water rights within Orange County, raising the total number of parties in the litigation to over 4,000. Basically, the action sought a general adjudication of all water rights within the Santa Ana River system, including groundwater and surface rights. The area included in the adjudication was from the base of the San

Bernardino mountains to the Pacific Ocean, a distance of some 75 miles. Total annual production of water from within the system was approximately 600,000 acre-feet.

After six years of intermittent court proceedings and negotiations, a settlement was reached in the form of a physical solution. Under the settlement, all defendants were dismissed except plaintiff Orange County Water District and three upstream water districts whose boundaries embraced the remainder of the watershed. These three upstream districts guaranteed a certain flow of water in the Santa Ana River, measured at Prado Dam, the point where the river entered Orange County. This guaranteed flow represented Orange County's total share of the natural river supply. The guarantee to Orange County was underwritten by a complex series of agreements and judgments among the upstream districts that allocated their respective responsibilities.

*A guarantee of the downstream area's total share of the natural river system supply*

The judgment was entered in 1969 and included the appointment of a Watermaster Committee to administer it. The judgment was not appealed, and it has served to keep the peace on the Santa Ana River since that time. Annual reports to the court are made by the Watermaster Committee.

This application of the doctrine of physical solution represented an expansion of earlier judicial authority, but the complexity of the action demanded a practical and innovative approach. Following is an excerpt from the judgment, which describes the need for a physical solution and its advantages in this case—

a. *Complaint.* The complaint herein was filed on October 18, 1963, seeking an adjudication of water rights against substantially all water users in the area tributary to Prado Dam in the Santa Ana River Watershed.

b. *Cross-Complaints.* Thirteen cross-complaints were subsequently filed in the period of February 22 to March 22, 1968, by which said adjudication of rights was extended to substantially all water users within the Santa Ana River Watershed downstream from Prado Dam.

c. *Physical and Legal Complexities.* The physical and legal complexities of the case as framed by the complaint and cross-complaints are unprecedented. In excess of 4,000 individual parties have been served and the water supply and water rights of an entire stream system extending over 2,000 square miles and into four counties have been brought into issue. Every type and nature of water rights known to California law, excepting only

Pueblo rights, is in issue in the case. Engineering studies by the parties jointly and severally leading toward adjudication of these rights or, in the alternative, to a physical solution, have required the expenditure of over four years' time and many hundreds of thousands of dollars.

*In an action involving more than 4,000 parties, with every kind of right and priority, in a stream system including river flows and connected groundwater basins extending over 2,000 square miles, an inter-basin allocation of rights and obligations substituted for a determination of individual rights.*

d. *Need for Physical Solution.* It is apparent to the parties and to the court that development of a physical solution based upon a formula for inter-basin allocation of obligations and rights is in the best interests of all the parties and is in furtherance of the water policy of the State. For purposes of such a physical solution, it is neither necessary nor helpful to define individual rights of all claimants within the watershed. Nontributary supplemental sources of water are or will be available to the parties in quantities sufficient to assure implementation of a solution involving inter-basin allocation of the natural water supply of the Santa Ana River system. Sufficient information and data of a general nature are known to formulate a reasonable and just allocation as between the major hydrologic sub-areas within the watershed, and such a physical solution will allow the public agencies and water users within each such major hydrologic sub-area to proceed with orderly water resource planning and development.

e. *Parties.* Orange County Water District, Chino Basin Municipal Water District, Western Municipal Water District of Riverside County and San Bernardino Valley Municipal Water District are public districts overlying, in the aggregate, substantially all of the major areas of water use within the watershed. Said districts have the statutory power and financial resources to implement a physical solution. Accordingly, dismissals have been entered as to all defendants and cross-defendants other than said four public districts.

f. *Cooperation by Dismissed Parties.* As a condition of dismissal of said defendants and cross-defendants, certain of said parties have stipulated to cooperate and support the inter-basin water quality and water management objectives of the physical solution and this Judgment.

**Chino Basin Municipal Water District v. City of Chino, et al., 1978, San Bernardino Superior Court No. 164327.** This case represents perhaps the most far-reaching application of the doctrine of physical solution. Like the judgment in the previous case, it was imposed by stipulation, and development of the physical solution was aided by special legislation. Water Code §§ 72140 *et seq.* This litigation involved a general adjudication of the water rights of the

Chino Basin, a large basin involving many hundreds of pumpers. After several years of negotiations, judgment was entered on January 27, 1978, and was not appealed.

The unique feature of this judgment was that pumpers were divided into three groups, or "pools." These pools consisted of (1) agricultural pumpers, largely dairy farmers; (2) certain overlying industrial pumpers; and (3) appropriative pumpers serving water for municipal use. The agricultural pool was assigned a gross share of the total Basin supply, and since agricultural pumping was gradually declining, no replenishment charges were imposed. On the other hand, since the water in the Basin was overdrafted, industrial and city pumpers were assigned specific rights and required to pay replenishment assessments to the extent that these rights were exceeded. The funds raised by such assessments are used to purchase supplemental water to maintain the Basin in a stable condition and to finance other water management activities such as water quality improvements. Each of these three pools has a separate management structure. A representative of each of the pools reports to the Watermaster, which is the plaintiff Chino Basin Municipal Water District. The judgment has further detailed provisions for the transfer of water rights, for the storage of water underground, and for the allocation of the agricultural rights as that pumping gradually diminishes.

Spreading Grounds along Santa Ana River for recharge of groundwater basins

*Using the doctrine of physical solution to divide agricultural pumpers, overlying industrial pumpers, and appropriators into three separate "pools," each group was treated differently.*

**Western Municipal Water District of Riverside County, et al. v. East San Bernardino County Water District, et al.,** *Riverside Superior Court No. 78426.* This case further illustrates the imposition by the court of a physical solution to a water rights conflict. The judgment in this case was also entered by stipulation as part of the settlement of the Orange County Water District litigation. The judgment acknowledges that a "decree of physical solution" has been entered in the Orange County suit, whereby the San Bernardino Valley Municipal Water District and Western Municipal Water District of Riverside County assumed responsibility for the deliveries of certain flows to Orange County. The judgment imposes an additional physical solution in the upper portion of the watershed in order to implement the entire watershed program.

In this case, the San Bernardino and Western Districts agreed that if pumping within their respective areas exceeded certain limits, thereby diminishing the guaranteed downstream flows to Orange

*Water districts guarantee replenishment water if total pumping exceeds certain amounts.*

County, each district would provide replenishment water supplies. Such water would be purchased either from the State Water Project or from the Metropolitan Water District of Southern California.

Furthermore, the court retained jurisdiction to adjust the pumping limits, since the natural safe yield of the local supply might change over time. Once again, a Watermaster Committee was established to keep track of all local pumping and to make annual reports to the court, which has been done regularly since 1969.

## CHAPTER SEVEN

# The Interaction of Federal Law and State Water Law

## Introduction

Federalism is a cornerstone of the United States Constitution. By allowing both federal and state governments to govern the same territory, the Constitution solved the problem of combining an independent local government with an effective central government. The Tenth Amendment to the Constitution reserved for the states all powers not delegated to the federal government or prohibited by the Constitution. Because of this policy, states have generally made their own laws relating to the distribution of water. Thus, California has historically been responsible for its own water planning, development, and management, and has been free to choose whether it would have an appropriative, riparian, or combined system of water rights.

From time to time conflicts have erupted between California and federal law, conflicts most easily understood in the context of the historical development of water use in the state. Legislation in the early years clearly supported state control, but in the 1950s and 1960s several court decisions imposed federal law on California water policy and law. The Supreme Court's 1978 decision in *California v. United States* 438 U.S. 645 [57 L.Ed.2d 1018] sharply reversed this trend, once again shifting California water use to state control. However, in the 1980s the swing of the pendulum began moving back toward federal management. The change was mainly seen in the San Joaquin-San Francisco Estuary (Bay-Delta), which provides domestic water to 20 million Californians and supplies irrigation

*From time to time, conflicts have erupted between the application of California or federal law over water resource management.*

191

to the fertile Sacramento and San Joaquin Valleys. Efforts at federal control stemmed from the Endangered Species Act, the claim of the federal EPA regarding flows that must be retained in the Bay-Delta for environmental purposes, and the federally supported San Francisco Estuary Project which developed a management plan for the Bay-Delta calling for major outflows of fresh water to San Francisco Bay. All of these federal efforts, some of which have already been implemented, cut into the supply of water available for urban, farm, and other uses under state law.

*Recently, the applications of federal environmental laws have cut into the supply of water available for farms and cities.*

### The Mining Act of 1866 and the Desert Land Act of 1877

The United States acquired the rivers, lakes, and streams of California from Mexico under the 1848 Treaty of Guadalupe Hidalgo. When California was admitted to the Union two years later, no specific provisions were made for the unappropriated waters of California's streams and rivers. As the population of the West increased, it became apparent that some governmental action was needed. However, the passage of the Homestead Act in 1862 only created further uncertainty. Did settlers who acquired public land rights under the Homestead Act, and thus became successors to the rights of the United States, have rights superior to those of the miners who had previously been using water?[1]

The Mining Act of 1866, which allowed public lands to be explored for minerals, addressed these issues, specifically recognizing local laws relating to the priority of rights to water—

> Whenever, by priority of possession, rights to the use of water for mining, agricultural, manufacturing, or other purposes, have vested and accrued, and the same are recognized and acknowledged by the local customs, laws, and the decisions of courts, the possessors and owners of such vested rights shall be maintained and protected in the same; . . . but whenever any person, in the construction of any ditch or canal, injures or damages the possession of any settler on the public domain, the party committing such injury or damage shall be liable to the party injured for such injury or damage. *United States v. Rio Grande Dam and Irrigation Company* (1898) 174 U.S. 690, 704 [43 L.Ed. 1136, 1142].

The scope of this language was somewhat tempered in the *Rio Grande* decision. *Rio Grande,* page 705. The Rio Grande Dam

---

[1] Walston, "Reborn Federalism in Western Water Law: The New Melones Dam Decision," 1979, 30 *The Hastings L.J.* 1645, 1653 (hereinafter "Reborn Federalism").

and Irrigation Company had successfully argued at the lower court level that it should be allowed to construct a dam across the Rio Grande River and appropriate its waters for irrigation. *Rio Grande,* page 695. It was alleged that the goal of the company was to control all the waters of the river and to create the largest artificial lake in the world. The company wanted the court to interpret the Mining Act to prohibit federal control over navigable streams. The court refused to do this, finding that the Mining Act protected only those water rights that had "vested and accrued" under local law—

> This legislation [the Mining Act] must be interpreted in the light of existing facts—that all through this mining region in the west were streams not navigable, whose waters could safely be appropriated for mining and agricultural industries, without serious interference with the navigability of the rivers into which those waters flow. And in reference to all these cases of purely local interest the obvious purpose of Congress was to give its assent, so far as the public lands were concerned, to any system, although in contravention to the common-law rule, which permitted the appropriation of those waters for legitimate industries. To hold that Congress, by these acts, meant to confer upon any state the right to appropriate all the waters of the tributary streams which unite into a navigable watercourse, and so destroy the navigability of that watercourse in derogation of the interests of all the people of the United States, is a construction which cannot be tolerated. *Rio Grande,* page 706.

Thus the court reaffirmed the federal government's powers to control navigable waters pursuant to the commerce clause. *See* Art. I, Section 8, of the United States Constitution; *Gibbons v. Ogden* (1824) 22 U.S. (1824) (9 Wheat.) 1, 189-193. In light of these statements, the holding in *Rio Grande* is less than an overwhelming endorsement of a state's sovereignty over its waters. Nonetheless, it is clear that the federal government recognized local customs and that, where appropriate, it would uphold them.

The next major piece of legislation encouraging the settlement of public lands in the western United States was the Desert Land Act of 1877. This legislation also contained provisions affecting water use which were interpreted in the case of *California Oregon Power Company v. Beaver Portland Cement Company* (1935) 295 U.S. 142 [79 L.Ed. 1356]. The facts of the case demonstrate the conflict between the riparian and appropriative systems. California Oregon Power owned property along the Rogue River in Oregon and brought the court action to prevent Beaver Portland Cement from interfering with the flow of river water in a manner that would decrease the flow through the power company's property. The power company based its claim on the common-law rights of a riparian proprietor, having acquired its lands from a predecessor-in-interest who had received the lands and patent from the United States under the 1862 Homestead Act. The question before the court was whether the Homestead Act patent carried with it the common-law rights that attach to riparian ownership. The court evaluated the water rights significance of the patent in light of the language of the Desert Land Act, which stated—

> ... all surplus water over and above such actual appropriation and use, together with the water of all lakes, rivers and other sources of water supply upon the public lands and not navigable, shall remain and be held free for the appropriation and use of the public for irrigation, mining and manufacturing purposes subject to existing rights. Chap. 107, 19 Stat., at L. 377, U.S.C. title 43, § 321. *California Oregon Power,* page 79 L.Ed. 1360.

The Supreme Court interpreted this language to mean that the Desert Land Act had severed all waters of the public domain from the land. *California Oregon Power,* pages 155-156. In other words, a patent issued by the United States carried with it no water rights, and the patent holder had to appropriate water pursuant to local customs or laws. Thus, as a result of this holding, non-navigable waters were severed and reserved for the use of the public, who had to follow the laws of the states or territories.

From the tone of the court's opinion, the majority seemed to feel that the court had little choice. To hold that the patent carried with it a riparian right would have greatly undermined the prior appropriation system in the West. The court stated several times in its opinion that the riparian doctrine was simply not suitable for water distribution on arid lands. *California Oregon Power,* pages 157-158.

*Federal patents carried no water rights with them; patent holders were required to establish water rights pursuant to state law.*

### The Reclamation Act of 1902

The Reclamation Act of 1902 marked a watershed in federal-state water relations. As Justice William Rehnquist was to write some 65 years later in *California v. United States* (1978) 438 U.S. 645, Western water distribution was such a significant issue at the turn of the century that President Theodore Roosevelt addressed it in his first message to Congress after assuming the presidency—

> The pioneer settlers on the arid public domain chose their homes along streams from which they could themselves divert the water

to reclaim their holdings. Such opportunities are practically gone. There remain, however, vast areas of public land which can be made available for homestead settlement, but only by reservoirs and main-line canals impracticable for private enterprise. These irrigation works should be built by the National Government. The lands reclaimed by them should be reserved by the Government for actual settlers, and the cost of construction should so far as possible be repaid by the land reclaimed. *The distribution of the water, the division of the streams among irrigators, should be left to the settlers themselves in conformity with State laws and without interference with those laws or with vested rights. California v. United States,* pages 1031-1032, footnote 18, emphasis added.

*President Theodore Roosevelt: "The distribution of the water... should be left to the settlers themselves in conformity with state laws."*

With this policy in mind, Congress adopted the Reclamation Act of 1902. Section 8 of the Act provided that—

Nothing in this Act shall be construed as affecting or intended to affect or to in any way interfere with the laws of any State or Territory relating to the control, appropriation, use, or distribution of water used in irrigation, or any vested right acquired thereunder.... 43 U.S.C. 383.

*Section 8 of the Reclamation Act of 1902 provides that nothing in the Act shall "in any way interfere with the laws of any state... relating to the control, appropriation, use, or distribution of water used in irrigation."*

Shortly after the passage of the 1902 Act, the Supreme Court recognized the policy of Section 8—

It [a state] may determine for itself whether the common-law rule in respect to riparian rights or that doctrine which obtains in the arid regions of the West of the appropriation of waters for the purposes of irrigation shall control. Congress cannot enforce either rule upon any state. *Kansas v. Colorado* (1907) 206 U.S. 46, 94 [51 L.Ed. 956, 973].

President Theodore Roosevelt and John Muir at Glacier Point, Yosemite in 1903

The Supreme Court upheld this interpretation of the language of Section 8 in *Nebraska v. Wyoming* (1935) 295 U.S. 40 [79 L.Ed. 1289]—

Reservoirs of large capacity have accordingly been constructed and operated by the United States, but solely under and subject to the irrigation and appropriation laws of Wyoming.... All of the acts of the Reclamation Bureau in operating the reservoirs so as to impound and release waters of the river are subject to the authority of Wyoming;... *Nebraska,* page 42.

This seemingly simple distribution of federal and state authority worked well for many years after the passage of the 1902 Act. However, in the late 1950s several decisions seemed to reverse the earlier direction and to enlarge federal authority over state water.

Federal Central Valley Project canal,
north of Kettleman City

*Beginning in 1958, several federal court decisions increased federal authority over state water.*

The first of these, *Ivanhoe Irrigation District v. McCracken* (1958) 357 U.S. 275 [2 L.Ed. 2d 1313], involved a direct conflict between federal and state authority over water use. Pursuant to Section 5 of the 1902 Act, contracts between the United States and local water districts limited water usage to 160 acres or less in single ownership. *Ivanhoe,* page 285. The California Supreme Court found that these contracts violated California law and, on this basis, refused to confirm them. The two local irrigation districts appealed to the United States Supreme Court.

The United States Supreme Court overruled the California decision. The court found that, although Section 8 favored state law, it did not control the provisions of Section 5. Therefore, state law could not invalidate the federal 160-acre limitation. The court went on to say that Section 8 only required the United States to comply with state law when the United States, in the construction and *operation* of a reclamation project, needed to *acquire* water rights. Noting the difference between the *acquisition* of water rights and the *operation* of federal projects, the court stated that Section 5 was a congressional limitation on the operation of reclamation projects, and that Section 8 did not compel the United States to deliver water under conditions imposed by California. *Ivanhoe,* pages 291-292.

Five years later, another case arose involving the application of Section 8. In *City of Fresno v. State of California* (1963) 372 U.S. 627 [10 L.Ed. 2d 28], Fresno contended that Section 8 required compliance with California statutes relating to preferential rights for counties and watersheds of origin and to the priority of domestic over irrigation uses. The court rejected this argument, holding that Section 8 does not allow state law to prevent the United States from exercising the power of eminent domain to acquire water rights. Based on *Ivanhoe,* the court found that in an eminent domain case, Section 8 allows state law to define the property interests for which compensation must be paid. *Fresno,* page 630.

The language of this decision went beyond the dictum in *Ivanhoe.* While the court in *Ivanhoe* held that Section 8 only applied to the acquisition (not the delivery) of water, the *Fresno* court held that Section 8 did not apply even when the United States acquired water, at least by condemnation.[2]

[2]  *See Reborn Federalism,* page 1668.

This trend continued in the landmark decision of *Arizona v. California* (1963) 373 U.S. 546 [10 L.Ed 2d 542], in which the Supreme Court held that the Secretary of the Interior was not bound by state laws in allocating Colorado River water to Arizona and California. *Arizona v. California,* pages 586-587. The court rejected the argument that a state could condition deliveries from the Boulder Canyon Project. These state claims were based on Section 18 of the Boulder Canyon Project Act, which reads much like Section 8 of the Reclamation Act—

**BCPA = Boulder Canyon Project Act**

> Nothing herein shall be construed as interfering with such rights as the States had on December 21, 1978, have either to the waters within their borders or to adopt such policies and enact such laws as they deem necessary with respect to the appropriation, control, and use of waters within their borders.... 43 U.S.C. § 617q.

The court held—

> Since § 8 of the Reclamation Act did not subject the Secretary to state law in disposing of water in that case, we cannot, consistently with *Ivanhoe,* hold that the Secretary must be bound by state law in disposing of water under the Project Act. *Arizona v. California,* pages 586-587.

The court stated that Section 18 simply preserved the rights the states had at the time the BCPA was passed. Although the states had some jurisdiction over the river before the adoption of the BCPA, any inconsistent state laws were voided when the federal government exercised its authority to regulate and develop the River. *Arizona v. California,* page 587. The court read Section 18 to conflict with the Secretary's contractual power under Section 5—

> As in *Ivanhoe,* where the general provision preserving state law was held not to override a specific provision stating the terms for disposition of the water, here we hold that the general saving language of § 18 cannot bind the Secretary by state law and thereby nullify the contract power expressly conferred upon him by § 5. (Footnote omitted.) Section 18 plainly allows the States to do things not inconsistent with the Project Act or with federal control of the river, for example, regulation of the use of tributary water and protection of present perfected rights. (Footnote omitted.) What other things the States are free to do can be decided when the occasion arises. But where the Secretary's contracts, as here, carry out a congressional plan for the complete distribution of waters to users, state law has no place. (Footnote omitted.) *Arizona v. California,* pages 587-588.

*Arizona v. California allocated Colorado River water pursuant to the Secretary of the Interior's contracts. The court held that such contracts carried out Congress' plan "for the complete distribution of water to users," and under the circumstances "state law has no place."*

These three opinions seemed to limit the impact of Section 8 and to give the federal government much greater authority in controlling water allocation. Indeed, after these three decisions, there was a serious question as to whether state supremacy with respect to the acquisition of water would continue.[3] Fifteen years later, however, state supremacy was clearly reestablished.

### California v. United States

*1978—The pendulum swings back toward state control over the water rights of federal projects.*

*California v. United States* (1978) 438 U.S. 645 arose as a result of the United States' attempt to impound 2.4 million acre-feet of water from the Stanislaus River behind the New Melones Dam. This project was part of the Central Valley Project, the largest project authorized by Congress under the provisions of the Reclamation Act of 1902. *California v. United States,* page 651. In reviewing the Bureau of Reclamation's application for a permit, the State Water Resources Control Board of California determined that water could be allocated to the federal government only pursuant to state law. Applying California law, the State Board attached 25 conditions to its approval of the Bureau's permit to use the water impounded by the dam. The most important condition prohibited full impoundment until the Bureau was able to show firm commitments for use of the water, or at least a specific plan. Without a plan for beneficial use, the State Board concluded that the Bureau had not met California's statutory requirements for appropriation. *California v. United States,* pages 652-653.

The federal government argued that it could impound unappropriated water for a federal reclamation project without complying with state law. *California v. United States,* page 673. The District Court held that as a matter of comity the federal government had to apply for an appropriation permit, but that California had to issue the permit if unappropriated water was available. *United States v. California* E.D. Cal. (1975) 403 F.Supp. 874. The Ninth Circuit Court of Appeals affirmed on the basis that Section 8 of the Reclamation Act prevented California from conditioning its allocation of water to a federal reclamation project. The United States Supreme Court reviewed the case to determine whether Section 8 of the Reclamation Act of 1902 required the United States to comply with state law and apply for the permit.

In its decisions in *Ivanhoe, Fresno,* and *Arizona,* the Supreme Court focused on the narrow issues before it. *California v. United States* marked the Supreme Court's first comprehensive pronouncement of

---

[3]  Rogers and Nichols, *Water for California,* 1967, page 409.

the relationship between the powers of federal and state governments in reclamation law. In reaching its conclusion, the court literally started at the beginning—

> [T]he afternoon of July 23, 1847, was the true date of the beginning of modern irrigation. It was on that afternoon that the first band of Mormon pioneers built a small dam across City Creek near the present site of the Mormon Temple and diverted sufficient water to saturate some 5 acres of exceedingly dry land. Before the day was over they had planted potatoes to preserve the seed. *California v. United States,* pages 648-649.

The opinion discusses in detail the history of the relationship between the United States government and individual states regarding water usage. Through that relationship "runs the consistent thread of purposeful and continued deference to state water law by Congress." *California v. United States,* page 653. Tracing the adoption of the Homestead Act of 1862, the Mining Act of 1866, and the Desert Land Act of 1877, as well as reclamation legislation adopted in the late 1880s and early 1890s, the court concluded that the prevailing legal climate was that "with limited exceptions not relevant to reclamation, authority over intrastate waterways lies with the States." *California,* page 662.

According to the court, this division of federal and state authority worked well for nearly fifty years. *California v. United States,* page 670. Although this harmony was disrupted in the late 1950s by the *Ivanhoe* and *City of Fresno* cases, the court stated that California did "not ask us to overrule these holdings, nor are we presently inclined to do so. (Footnote omitted.)" *California v. United States,* page 672. Instead, the court interpreted California's request to be that it "may impose any condition on the 'control, appropriation, use, or distribution of water' through a federal reclamation project that is *not inconsistent with clear congressional directives regarding the project.*" *California v. United States,* page 672, emphasis added.

This placed the court in a difficult position, because, as discussed earlier, the dicta in *Ivanhoe* and *City of Fresno* were contrary to that position. The opinion, however, distinguished all three cases—

> While we are not convinced that the above language [in *Ivanhoe, City of Fresno,* and *Arizona*] is diametrically inconsistent with the position of petitioners (footnote omitted), or that it squarely supports the United States, it undoubtedly goes further than was necessary to decide the cases presented to the Court. Ivanhoe and

*California may impose such conditions on the control, appropriation, use, and distribution of water through a federal reclamation project that are not "inconsistent with clear congressional directives regarding the project."*

City of Fresno involved conflicts between § 8, requiring the Secretary to follow state law as to water rights, and other provisions of Reclamation Acts that placed specific limitations on how the water was to be distributed. *Here the United States contends that it may ignore state law even if no explicit congressional directive conflicts with the conditions imposed by the California State Water Control Board.* (Footnote omitted.)

In *Arizona v. California*, the States had asked the Court to rule that state law would control in the distribution of water from the Boulder Canyon Project, a massive multistate reclamation project on the Colorado River. (Footnote omitted.) After reviewing the legislative history of the Boulder Canyon Project Act, 43 USC §§ 617 *et seq.* [43 USCS §§ 617 *et seq.*], the Court concluded that because of the unique size and multistate scope of the Project, Congress did not intend the States to interfere with the Secretary's power to determine with whom and on what terms water contracts would be made. (Footnote omitted.) While the Court in rejecting the States' claim repeated the language from *Ivanhoe* and *City of Fresno* as to the scope of § 8, there was no need for it to reaffirm such language except as it related to the singular legislative history of the Boulder Canyon Project Act.

*California v. United States disavows certain dicta in earlier federal decisions.*

But because there is at least tension between the above-quoted dictum and what we conceive to be the correct reading of § 8 of the Reclamation Act of 1902, *we disavow the dictum to the extent that it would prevent petitioners from imposing conditions on the permit granted to the United States which are not inconsistent with congressional provisions authorizing the project in question.* Section 8 cannot be read to require the Secretary to comply with state law only when it becomes necessary to purchase or condemn vested water rights. That section does, of course, provide for the protection of vested water rights, but it also requires the Secretary to comply with state law in the 'control, appropriation, use, or distribution of water.' Nor, as the United States contends, does § 8 merely require the Secretary of the Interior to file a notice with the State of his intent to appropriate but to thereafter ignore the substantive provisions of state law. The legislative history of the Reclamation Act of 1902 makes it abundantly clear that Congress intended to defer to the substance, as well as the form, of state water law. The Government's interpretation would trivialize the broad language and purpose of § 8. *California v. United States,* pages 673-675, emphasis added.

The court added that, until the "unnecessarily broad" *Ivanhoe* language, there had been no question that the uniform practice of the Bureau had been to comply with state law that did not conflict with a clear congressional directive. *California v. United States,* page 676.

The court left unanswered the question of whether federal law preempts state law if state law conflicts with federal *policy*, although the federal law itself is silent on the issue. The United States argued that, even if the 1902 Act intended for the Secretary of the Interior to comply with state law, subsequent legislative enactments had subjected reclamation projects to federal policies that did not leave room for state regulation. The court rejected this argument, noting that more recent legislation, such as the Flood Control Act of 1944, explicitly continued Congress' deference to state law. *California v. United States,* page 678.

## Section 8 in the 1980s

After its decision in *California v. United States*, the Supreme Court directed the lower court to reconsider the issues involved. In *United States v. California State Water Resources Control Board* (1982) 694 F.2d 1171, the Ninth Circuit upheld the conditions imposed by the State Board on the Bureau. Some of the 25 conditions the State Board imposed were: (1) that water storage for the project be deferred until the Bureau developed a specific plan for consumptive water uses, (2) that the Bureau provide a preference for water uses for counties of origin, and (3) that the Bureau be required to meet downstream water quality needs.

*Twenty-five conditions imposed by the State Board on the federal New Melones Dam project were upheld by the federal appellate court.*

In considering the first condition, the court reasoned that, until it developed a plan to use the water, the Bureau could not demonstrate that the water would be put to beneficial use. Therefore, it could not appropriate the water pursuant to California law. The court held that Congress did not intend to override the state's laws relating to beneficial use, and therefore this condition did not conflict with congressional directives. The court upheld the second and third requirements because neither was inconsistent with congressional directives, although the court ruled that the state could not actually operate a federal project, since the intent of Congress was for federal agencies to operate them. *United States v. California,* page 1182.

The opinion is unclear as to which conditions relate to water allocation and use (within a state's power) and which relate to project operation (beyond a state's power). However, the court's statement that Section 8 requires that state law should apply unless there is contrary congressional *intent* (not necessarily a clear statement) indicates that courts will look to the substantive effect of state law on a project, not its procedural effect on the Bureau's operational power. This view is supported by the court's statement that California could not impose conditions inconsistent with the project's goals. *United States v. California,* page 1182.

The next Section 8 case was *South Delta Water Agency v. United States* (1985) 767 F.2d 531, involving the Bureau's operation of the Central Valley Project. The South Delta Water Agency alleged that the Bureau was operating the Central Valley Project in a manner that violated the agency's prior water rights. The issue was whether state law applied to the Central Valley Project under Section 8 of the Reclamation Act of 1902.

Citing *California v. United States,* the Ninth Circuit held that, contrary to the contention of the United States, the federal government must acquire water rights in accordance with state law. *South Delta v. U.S.,* page 536. The court also noted that the Rivers and Harbors Act of 1937, which reauthorized the Central Valley Project, provided that reclamation law would govern the Central Valley Project. The court required the United States to comply with state law in both its operations of the Central Valley Project *and* its acquisition of water rights for the Project. *South Delta v. U.S.,* pages 537-538.

*The courts have required the United States to comply with state law in both the operation and acquisition of water rights for the CVP.*

The court rejected the United States' contention that Water Code Section 11460(a), which mandates a preference for Central Valley Project water for watersheds of origin, did not apply. The court acknowledged the dicta in *City of Fresno* that Section 8 did not require the federal government to comply with California statutes relating to watersheds of origin, and that, even if Section 11460 did apply to the defendants in that case, their operations of Friant Dam did not violate the Act. However, the court relied on *California v. United States* and its holding that Section 8 of the Reclamation Act of 1902 required the United States to comply with state law in the absence of clear congressional directives. *South Delta v. U.S.,* page 538. Since the court in *California v. United States* dismissed as dictum the statement in *City of Fresno* that Section 8 did not require federal defendants to comply with state law, the Ninth Circuit rejected the United States' argument. The court also determined that the United States must bear the burden of proof in demonstrating that compliance with state law would violate congressional directives. *South Delta v. U.S.,* page 539.

A year later, the case of *United States v. State Water Resources Control Board* (1986) 182 Cal.App.3d 82 (the *Racanelli* decision) provided an opportunity for California's courts to address the competing roles of California and the federal government in water resource allocation.

The federal-state issue arose because the Bureau argued that the State Water Resources Control Board did not have the authority to regulate a federal facility, and thus could not impose conditions for salinity control on the Central Valley Project. The California Court of Appeal disagreed with this conclusion on the basis that, when it was authorized for federal financing, the Central Valley Project was made expressly subject to reclamation laws. *U.S. v. SWRCB*, page 134. The court then relied on *California v. United States* and *South Delta Water Agency v. U.S.* for the proposition that the Bureau's operation of the Central Valley Project was subject to state law with respect to the acquisition of water rights. *U.S. v. SWRCB*, page 134.

The Bureau argued that one of the main congressional purposes of the Central Valley Project was to provide water for export for irrigation and domestic uses, and that salinity control in the Delta was an incidental benefit. Since Congress never intended water quality or salinity control to have priority over the primary uses, the Bureau contended that the Board could not impose conditions for salinity control on the Central Valley Project. *U.S. v. SWRCB*, page 135.

The court rejected this argument on the grounds that one of the primary purposes in the congressional authorization of the Central Valley Project construction was "river regulation." The court interpreted this to include salinity control. *U.S. v. SWRCB*, page 135.

*The* Racanelli *decision upheld the right of the State Board to impose conditions for salinity control in the Delta on the federal CVP.*

The *Racanelli* decision increased California's control over federal projects and broadened the state's authority to govern water quality as well as water quantity regulation. Coupled with the decisions in *United States v. California* and *South Delta Water Agency*, the *Racanelli* decision strengthened California's authority to regulate federal projects in the absence of a conflict with clear congressional directives. Similarly, *NRDC v. Patterson* (1992) 791 F.Supp. 1425 found that at least some state laws relating to fish and wildlife protection are applicable to the operation of federal reclamation projects.

## The Federal Energy Regulatory Commission and States Rights

Hydroelectric licensing under the Federal Power Act (FPA) has been an area of longstanding controversy involving the control of federal and state water. Adopted by Congress in 1920, the FPA comprehensively regulates the use of the nation's water resources for hydroelectric power. Pursuant to its provisions, licenses are issued that are "best adapted to a comprehensive plan for improving or developing a waterway..." 16 U.S.C. § 803(a).

**FPA = Federal Power Act**

Although it provides that a federal agency, now the Federal Energy Regulatory Commission (FERC), will regulate the electricity generation, the FPA contains "savings clauses" to assure that states have the authority to manage and regulate water. Thus, during the 1920s and 1930s the FPA was interpreted as requiring permit applicants to fully comply with state water law as a prerequisite to obtaining a license for hydropower.[4]

Section 9(b) of the FPA requires license applicants to supply FERC with—

(b) Satisfactory evidence that the applicant has complied with the requirements of the laws of the State or States within which the proposed project is to be located with respect to bed and banks and to the appropriation, diversion, and use of water for power purposes and with respect to the right to engage in the business of developing, transmitting, and distributing power, and in any other business necessary to effect the purposes of a license under this chapter. 16 U.S.C. § 802(b).

Section 27 of the Act states—

Nothing contained in this chapter shall be construed as affecting or intending to affect or in any way to interfere with the laws of the respective States relating to the control, appropriation, use, or distribution of water used in irrigation or for municipal or other uses, or any vested right acquired therein. 16 U.S.C. § 821.

Since the language in Section 27 is very similar to that in Section 8 of the Reclamation Act of 1902, it would seem logical for the Supreme Court to have interpreted it similarly, requiring federal licensees to comply with state law. However, this was not the case.

In the case of *First Iowa Hydro-Electric Cooperative v. Federal Power Commission* (1946) 328 U.S. 152 [90 L.Ed 1143], the United States Supreme Court held that the FPC could license a hydropower project even though the licensee was in violation of Iowa law which prohibited the dewatering of a river and required the licensee to obtain a state permit to construct a dam. The court stated that Section 9(b) did not require the FPC to demand that its applicants supply satisfactory evidence of compliance with state law. The court

*Hydroelectric licensing under the Federal Power Act is an exception to the rule of state control over water.*

---

[4] Bell and Johnson, "State Water Laws and Federal Water Uses: The History of Conflict, The Prospects for Accommodation," 1991, 21 *Envtl.L.* 1, 30; Walston, "California v. Federal Energy Regulatory Commission: New Roadblock to State Water Rights Administration," 1991, 21 *Envtl.L.* 89, 104, fn. 57.

also stated that requiring the licensee to obtain a state permit before being able to obtain a federal license would give the state veto power over a federal project. *First Iowa,* page 164. The court ruled that Section 27 preempted all state laws except those relating to control, appropriation, use, or distribution of water for irrigation or municipal use. Thus, an applicant did not need a state permit as a condition for a license. *First Iowa,* pages 175-176.

After *California v. United States* interpreted Section 8 of the Reclamation Act of 1902 to give states the authority to condition reclamation project operations, states were hopeful that the Supreme Court might overrule *First Iowa.* When the Supreme Court reviewed its decision in *First Iowa* in *California v. FERC* (1990) 495 U.S. 490 [109 L.Ed. 2d 474], other states intervened as *amici curiae* (friends of the court).

The lawsuit arose out of the operation of the Rock Creek Hydroelectric Project, which is located near the confluence of the south fork of the American River and one of the river's tributaries, Rock Creek. In 1983, FERC issued a license, pursuant to its authority under the FPA, authorizing the operation of the Rock Creek project. FERC issued the licenses after considering the project's economic feasibility and environmental consequences and set minimum instream flows of 11 cfs (cubic feet per second) from May through September and 15 cfs for the rest of the year.

The following year, the licensee applied for state water permits. The State Board issued a permit that conformed to the minimum flow requirements set by FERC but reserved the right to set different permanent minimum flow rates. Three years later, as the State Board was considering setting higher flow rates, the licensee petitioned for a declaration that FERC had exclusive jurisdiction to set minimum flows. FERC determined that it had exclusive jurisdiction, setting the stage for the lawsuit.

In its opinion, the court stated that the FPA expresses a strong congressional intent for FERC to have a major role in the development and licensing of hydroelectric power. However, the court admitted that, if this were a case of first impression, the argument based on FPA language would present a close question. The court stated that California's minimum stream flow requirement could be considered a law not preempted by Section 27 of the FPA, because FERC licensing could be viewed as interfering with California law relating to the protection of fish. *California v. FERC,* page 497.

However, the court found that because of *First Iowa* the preemptive effect of the FPA was not a matter of first impression.

*In 1990, the Supreme Court ruled that FERC, not the states, had exclusive jurisdiction to set minimum stream flow standards for hydroelectric projects under the FPA.*

The court stated that both *First Iowa* and the statutory scheme of the FPA indicated that Congress intended to provide FERC with broad authority to issue licenses. The court concluded that it would not overrule *First Iowa* and cause the restructuring of a "highly complex and long-enduring regulatory regime." *California v. FERC*, page 500.

The court's ruling did not affect its holding in *California v. United States* (1978) 438 U.S. 645 or *United States v. State Water Resources Control Board* (1986) 182 Cal.App.3d 82. Rather, it upheld the principle that federal laws override inconsistent state laws. Specifically, under the FPA a federal licensee need not comply with state laws that conflict with the FPA's objectives. *U.S. v. SWRCB*, page 505.

The opinion dismissed *California v. United States* by stating that Section 27 of the FPA was different than Section 8 of the Reclamation Act of 1902. The Supreme Court also indicated that it intended for its holding to be narrow, applying only to water use under the FPA. Therefore, this decision should probably be considered as a narrow *stare decisis* (relying on previous cases) decision in which the court was following precedent. As a result of the *FERC* decision, it seems that the FPA may completely preempt any state laws governing hydropower licensing or the use of water for hydropower generation.

A project license is a federal authorization to use the waters of a project's water source. The position that it is essentially a federal water right was bolstered by the subsequent decision in *California v. FERC* (1992) 966 F.2d 1541, which upheld FERC's authority to consider minimum flows for fish and wildlife when issuing licenses.

### Federal Reserved Rights

Another area in which federal law and state water resource management have clashed is that of the "federal reserved water rights" doctrine. The doctrine creates a "federal right" to surface water under federal law. This right is based on the theory that, when the federal government "withdraws" (removes) land from the public domain and reserves it for a specific federal purpose, the government reserves sufficient unappropriated water for the purposes of the reserved land.

*The "Winters Doctrine"—when Congress creates an Indian or other federal reservation, it reserves water for the land.*

The doctrine originally developed in the case of *Winters v. United States* (1908) 207 U.S. 564 [52 L.Ed 340]. In *Winters*, the court held that, when it created the Fort Belknap Reservation for the Assiniboine and Gros Ventre Indian tribes, Congress must have intended to reserve water for land that would otherwise be worthless.

In that case, the United States brought suit on behalf of the Indian tribes to enjoin the upstream diversion of water from Milk River. The upstream diverters contended that they had a prior right under state appropriation law to take water from the Milk River, since they had diverted water before any water was taken by the United States or the tribes. The Supreme Court rejected this argument, reasoning that the reservation the Indians now occupied was originally part of a much larger tract which they had a right to occupy and use. *Winters v. U.S.*, page 576. Reflecting the thinking of the time (1908), the court stated that this larger tract of land "was adequate for the habits and wants of a nomadic and uncivilized people. [But] it was the policy of the government, it was the desire of the Indians, to change those habits and to become a pastoral and civilized people." *Winters v. U.S,* page 576.

The court held that the Indians did not give up the waters that made the land valuable and that their water right was superior to the non-Indian appropriations acquired after the creation of the reservation but before Indian use. In other words, the priority of the right begins at the creation of the reservation, not at the time of actual use. *Arizona v. California* (1963) 373 U.S. 546 extended federal reserved rights to non-Indian reservations. That case followed the *Winters* decision and stated that the principle underlying the reservation of water rights for Indian reservations was "equally applicable" to other federal reservations. *Arizona v. Calif.,* pages 598-601.

*The priority of rights under the* Winters *doctrine dates back to the creation of the reservation, not the time of actual water use.*

The next reserved rights case was *Cappaert v. United States* (1976) 426 U.S. 128 [48 L.Ed. 2d 523]. *Cappaert* presented the issue of the extent of the water right reservation for Devil's Hole National Monument. The Cappaerts owned a large ranch near Devil's Hole which they used for cattle raising, as well as for growing Bermuda grass, alfalfa, wheat, and barley. The Cappaerts' groundwater pumping on their ranch, located about 2½ miles from Devil's Hole, caused a decline in the summer water level of the pool in Devil's Hole. This decreasing water level threatened the survival of a unique species of fish, the Devil's Hole Pupfish.

The court articulated the test for determining whether the government intended to reserve a water right—

> This Court has long held that when the Federal Government with-draws its land from the public domain and reserves it for a federal purpose, the Government, by implication, reserves appurtenant water then unappropriated to the extent needed to accomplish the purpose of the reservation. In so doing the United States acquires a reserved right in unappropriated water which vests on the date

of the reservation and is superior to the rights of future appropriators. Reservation of water rights is empowered by the Commerce Clause, Art. I, § 8, which permits federal regulation of navigable streams, and the Property Clause, Art. IV, § 3, which permits federal regulation of federal lands. The doctrine applies to Indian reservations and other federal enclaves, encompassing water rights in navigable and nonnavigable streams. . . .

In determining whether there is a federally reserved water right implicit in a federal reservation of public land, the issue is whether the Government intended to reserve unappropriated and thus available water. Intent is inferred if the previously unappropriated waters are necessary to accomplish the purposes for which the reservation was created. *Cappaert v. U.S.*, pages 138-139, citations omitted.

The court found that the purpose of reserving the Devil's Hole monument was to preserve the pool. Therefore, the pool had to be preserved, consistent with the intention expressed in the reservation (as set forth in the Proclamation) to the extent necessary to preserve its scientific value as the natural habitat of the species. *Cappaert,* pages 141-142.

*The "Pupfish" case sidestepped the issue of whether the reserved rights doctrine applies to groundwater.*

By finding that water in the pool was surface water, the court sidestepped the issue of whether the reserved rights doctrine applies to groundwater. *Cappaert* did not prove to be a significant expansion of federal control over state waters. In *United States v. New Mexico* (1978) 438 U.S. 696 [57 L.Ed 2d 1052], the Supreme Court revisited the issue of federally reserved rights. The issue in that case was the quantity of water that the United States had reserved out of the Rio Mimbres River in setting aside the Gila National Forest in 1899. The court started with the assumption that, based on the *Winters, Arizona v. California,* and *Cappaert* decisions, it was apparent that the United States had the authority to reserve unappropriated water for use on appurtenant lands withdrawn from the public domain for specific federal purposes. However, expanding on the holding in *Cappaert,* it said that the recognition of congressional authority to reserve water left open the quantity of water reserved and the purposes for which it may be used. *U.S. v. New Mexico,* page 699.

*The federal government may reserve only the amount of water necessary to fulfill the purposes of the reservation.*

The federal government may reserve only the amount of water necessary to fulfill the purposes of the reservation. The court limited this holding by stating that the purposes of the reservation must be completely frustrated without the use of the water from the reserved rights. *U.S. v. New Mexico,* page 700. The reasoning behind this strict examination is that the reservation is implied, not expressed; also, Congress has historically shown deference to state jurisdiction over water allocation. *U.S. v. New Mexico,* page 701.

In *United States v. New Mexico*, the river involved, the Rio Mimbres River, was fully appropriated. Thus, allocation of water to federally reserved water rights required a gallon-for-gallon reduction in the amount of water available to other appropriators. *United States v. New Mexico,* page 705. Perhaps based on this fact, and certainly based on its narrow interpretation of the reserved rights doctrine, the court determined that Congress had not intended to reserve minimum instream flows for purposes of aesthetics, recreation, and fish preservation. The court stated that water for these secondary purposes must be obtained under state law. *United States v. New Mexico,* page 716.

In an extensive review of the legislative history relating to national forests, the court concluded that water for national forest lands had been reserved primarily to preserve forest growth and to use for other purposes after it left forest boundaries. *United States v. New Mexico,* pages 712-713. By limiting itself to the purposes expressed in the legislative history, much of which dated from the late 1800s, the court drastically limited the extent of federally reserved water rights. Because environmental concerns were not prevalent in the years when many forest reservations took place, it now seems unlikely that the reserved rights doctrine will provide the environmental protection expected by some in the wake of the *Cappaert* decision.

*Because environmental concerns were not prevalent when many forest reservations were made, the reserved rights doctrine is unlikely to provide the basis for significant environmental protection.*

## Federal Riparian Water Rights

For many years, it was assumed that the federal government had no riparian water rights on federal reserved lands because the United States did not "own" land in the manner that would allow it to claim riparian rights. However, the California Supreme Court issued a decision in 1988 which surprised the California water world, although its practical effect may turn out to be limited. This decision, *In re Water of Hallett Creek Stream System v. United States* (1988) 44 Cal.3d 448, held that the federal government did possess riparian rights on federal reserved lands. *Hallett Creek,* page 472.

*Hallett Creek* arose when a private water user petitioned the State Board for a determination of the water rights of various claimants on Hallett Creek in Lassen County. The United States claimed reserved and riparian water rights for use in the Plumas National Forest, a claim which arose as a result of the *U.S. v. New Mexico* decision. *Hallett Creek,* pages 454-455. *Cappaert* and *U.S. v.*

*New Mexico* firmly established that the United States implicitly reserves enough water to accomplish the "primary" purpose or purposes of a reservation. However, *U.S. v. New Mexico* stated that for secondary purposes the federal government must seek water under state law. Although in New Mexico the only method of acquiring water under state law is through appropriation, California has a dual system of appropriative and riparian rights. Thus, the United States claimed a riparian right to use the waters of Hallett Creek for wildlife enhancement purposes on national forest land.

The State Board vigorously argued that the United States had voluntarily relinquished all proprietary claims to Western waters, except for reserved water rights, by virtue of the Mining Act of 1866, the Desert Land Act of 1877, and other similar laws. The Mining Act of 1866, by expressly recognizing rights to use water on public lands that had previously been recognized by state law, was a federal confirmation of the validity of water appropriations recognized by state and local law. *Hallett Creek,* page 463. The Desert Land Act of 1877 made the prior appropriation doctrine generally applicable to the waters of the western United States and limited the settlers of these lands to water rights which they had actually appropriated and used. It declared all surplus waters free for appropriation and required that these waters be allocated through the prior appropriation method established under state law. *Hallett Creek,* pages 467-468.

The starting point of the dispute between the State Board and the United States was *Lux v. Haggin* (1886) 69 Cal. 255, the decision that adopted the dual water rights system in California. *Hallett Creek,* page 464. In that decision, the court reasoned that the United States retained title to the public lands and waters of the West, although sovereignty passed to states as they were admitted to the Union. Thus, according to the court in *Hallett Creek*, states had the power to determine the rights attaching to federal lands, and California's recognition of riparian rights gave the federal government state law riparian rights as the owner of public lands. *Hallett Creek,* page 464. The court examined *California Oregon Power Company v. Beaver-Portland Cement Company* (1935) 295 U.S. 142, discussed earlier, and concluded that although the Desert Land Act severed the waters of the public domain from the soil so that a federal patentee had rights to the land but not the water, *California-Oregon Power* did not hold that the United States had relinquished water rights in the land it retained. If the federal government retained the land, it retained the water rights. Therefore, riparian rights exist in reserved federal lands just as they do in private lands, although they are subordinated to the rights of

*The United States has riparian rights arising from its ownership of land.*

subsequent appropriators recognized under state and local law. *Hallett Creek,* pages 467-468.

The potential impact of the court's decision was severely restricted, however, by language near the end of the opinion. The State Board had argued that such a decision would have an extremely disruptive effect on California water law, but the court responded that this was not the case because the State Board had great power to regulate riparian rights. Citing *In re Waters of Long Valley Creek* (1979) 25 Cal.3d 339, the court stated that, pursuant to the trial court's decree, the United States must apply to the State Board before it exercises a riparian right so that the State Board may decide if the proposed use should be permitted. *Hallett Creek,* page 472.

In taking this approach, the California Supreme Court essentially gave its blessing to redefining riparian rights in a manner convenient to the State Board. Thus, the practical effect of the decision is quite limited and the disruption feared by the State Board unlikely.[5]

*The practical impact of the* Hallett Creek *case is likely to be limited.*

## The Endangered Species Act

The federal Endangered Species Act has had a significant impact on California's water supply. The winter run salmon is listed as an "endangered" species and the Delta smelt is listed as "threatened." In February 1993, the pumps of both the Central Valley Project and the State Water Project were shut down because of restrictions designed to protect the salmon. This federal mandate overrode the State Board's pumping limitations that would have allowed pumping at that time. The ESA is discussed in greater detail in chapter 5.

## Water Quality Regulation

An area of current conflict between federal and state regulation of water planning, policy, and allocation is that of water quality regulation. Since the passage of the 1972 amendments to the Water Pollution Control Act (also known as the Clean Water Act), the federal government has taken an ever-increasing role in the regulation of water quality. At times this regulation has threatened to intrude into the state's traditional province of exclusive control over the allocation of its water resources.

*The 1972 federal Clean Water Act is a source of conflict between federal and state regulation.*

The federal Clean Water Act was adopted in 1972. Several provisions of the Clean Water Act provide a basis for federal regulatory control over the processes of water allocation and planning:

[5] Freyfogle, "Context and Accommodation in Modern Property Law," 1989, 41 *Stan.L.Rev.* 1529, 1534.

(1) Section 208 requires water pollution from non-point sources to be managed through area-wide waste treatment management plans, (2) Section 303 requires states to adopt water quality standards, (3) Section 402 prohibits the discharge of a pollutant from a point source without a permit, and (4) Section 404 limits the discharge of dredged or fill material into navigable waters. The passage of the Clean Water Act was in large part due to the federal perception that states were not adequately protecting water quality. It is probably safe to say that this perception still exists.

The tension that the Clean Water Act created in federal-state water relations can be seen in several cases that have arisen in the past two decades. *Environmental Defense Fund, Inc. v. Costle* (1981) 657 F.2d 275 is perhaps the most comprehensive discussion of the provisions of Section 208. *Costle* is of particular interest to Californians because it involved salinity control efforts on the Colorado River. Salinity is a serious problem on the Colorado River. The record before the court indicated that damages to the river from salinity were approximately $53 million annually and that by the year 2000 these damages would reach $124 million annually. Estimates of the present value of salinity damage through the year 2000 ranged from $1 billion to $1.5 billion. *Costle,* page 280.

As a part of the water quality control standards for salinity that were adopted by Colorado River Basin, each state adopted an implementation plan. These plans were approved by the Environmental Protection Agency. The Environmental Defense Fund, however, claimed that the approved implementation plans were inadequate and ineffective. The district court supported the EPA's approval of the plans as satisfying the required statutory test "to protect the public health or welfare, enhance the quality of water and serve the purposes of this Act." *Costle,* page 290. The appellate court also upheld the district court's decision. *Costle,* page 290.

The EDF asserted that the plan overstated stream flow levels. *Costle,* page 290. It also claimed that the plan understated new water depletions and therefore underestimated expected salinity increases. But the court agreed with the district court that—

**EDF = Environmental Defense Fund**

*The Environmental Defense Fund's challenge to the states' plan for salinity control of the Colorado River, approved by EPA, was rejected.*

[EDF's] challenge to the states' plan of implementation amounts to a plea that there is a 'better' way to control salinity than that followed by the states and approved by EPA. It is not the function of the court, however, to establish a preference between conflicting approaches to salinity control in the Colorado River. The court may not substitute its judgment for that of EPA so long as the agency's actions met 'minimum standards of rationality,' as they have here (citation omitted). *Costle,* page 292.

In upholding the EPA's approval, the court was highly deferential to the EPA's interpretation of the Clean Water Act. *Costle,* page 292. The dispute in this case is illustrative of those that frequently arise in water quality cases. Environmentalists often seek more stringent controls than those promulgated by the states or desired by (consumptive) water users. Although *Costle* upheld the state standards, it is evident that a primary factor in its decision was EPA's finding that the standards were sufficient. It seems likely that, if the EPA had disapproved the standards, the court would have sided with the EPA. Therefore, *Costle* should not be seen so much as a victory for state water quality authority, but as a case of judicial deference to an administrative agency.

*Homestake Mining Company v. EPA* (1979) 477 F.Supp. 1279 upholds a state's authority to govern water quality under the Clean Water Act, as long as the water quality standards set are at least as stringent as those of the federal government. In *Homestake Mining,* the plaintiff contended that the EPA's approval of South Dakota's water quality standards, which were stricter than those mandated by the federal Clean Water Act, was invalid. Although South Dakota law did not allow South Dakota's Board of Environmental Protection to consider economic or social factors in establishing water quality standards, the plaintiff argued that Section 303(c)(2) of the Clean Water Act required that the Board consider economic and social factors.[6] In rejecting the plaintiff's argument, the court cited *Weyerhaeuser Company v. Costle* (1978) 590 F.2d 1011—

> In contrast, Congress did not mandate any particular structure or weight for the many consideration factors. Rather, it left EPA with discretion to decide how to account for the consideration factors, and how much weight to give each factor.... More particularly, we do not believe that EPA is required to use any specific structure

*The states and EPA have discretion over the weight to be given to the various factors required to be considered in setting water quality standards.*

---

6  Section 303(c)(2) states: "Whenever the State revises or adopts a new standard, such revised or new standard shall be submitted to the Administrator. Such revised or new water quality standard shall consist of the designated uses of the navigable waters involved in the water quality criteria for such waters based upon such uses. Such standards shall be such as to protect the public health or welfare, enhance the quality of water and serve the purposes of this chapter. Such standards shall be established taking into consideration their use and value for public water supplies, propagation of fish and wildlife, recreational purposes, and agricultural, industrial, and other purposes, and also taking into consideration their use and value for navigation." 33 U.S.C. § 1313(c)(2).

such as a balancing test in assessing the consideration factors, nor do we believe that EPA is required to give each consideration factor any specific weight. *Weyerhaeuser,* page 1045.

Nothing in these statutes requires a state to give equal weight to all listed factors. Instead, the amount of weight given each individual factor is within the state's discretion. *Homestake Mining,* page 1283. It is within a state's power to achieve better water quality, even if doing so results in economic and social dislocations caused by plant closings. *Homestake Mining,* page 1284. Of course, a state may not set standards more lenient than the federal standards. Therefore, within the parameters of the federal standards, the State Board must rely on California law in determining factors to consider when setting water quality standards.

*A state may establish standards to achieve better water quality than that required by federal law.*

*National Wildlife Federation v. Gorsuch* (1982) 693 F.2d 156 is a pivotal case in the federal-state, water quantity-quality debate. The issue in *Gorsuch* was whether water quality changes resulting from operation of a dam constituted the "discharge of a pollutant" as that term is defined in the Clean Water Act. 33 U.S.C. § 1362(12). The dam-induced water quality changes at issue were (1) low dissolved oxygen, (2) dissolved minerals and nutrients, (3) water temperature changes, (4) sediment release, and (5) super-saturation.

**NWF = National Wildlife Federation**

The National Wildlife Federation (NWF) argued that these changes constituted the discharge of a pollutant under the Clean Water Act, and thus required the EPA to regulate dams under the Section 402 permit program. The EPA argued for a more narrow reading under which dams would not require discharge permits but instead would be regulated under the area-wide planning process of Section 208. The EPA maintained that a pollutant introduced from a point source must be introduced into the water from the outside world. The EPA contended that merely passing water through a dam from one body of navigable water into another (from the reservoir into the downstream river) was not pollution and therefore not a point-source discharge. The NWF argued that any adverse change in the quality of reservoir water from its natural state involves a "pollutant" and that releasing polluted water through a dam into a downstream river constitutes the addition of a pollutant from a point source.

As in *Costle,* the court's decision gave great deference to the EPA's construction of the Clean Water Act. *Gorsuch,* page 166. However, the court was careful to note that, if EPA's interpretation was not consistent with the language of the Clean Water Act, as interpreted in light of the legislative history, or if it frustrated the policy that Congress sought to implement, no amount of deference could protect it. *Gorsuch,* page 171.

The court noted that the five dam-induced changes listed above were not within the statutory list of pollutants in Section 502(6). 33 U.S.C. § 1362(6). Rather, the court found that these dam-induced changes were water conditions, not substances added to the water. *Gorsuch,* page 171. Therefore, they were not subject to regulation by the federal government under the National Pollutant Discharge Elimination System program of Section 402 but rather were subject to state control under the Section 208 process.

At issue in the *Gorsuch* case was how water quality protection responsibilities would be divided. Under NWF's argument, the federal role would have been significantly increased because of the broadening of the NPDES permit program. This would have given the federal government *de facto* water quantity regulation, since it would have been regulating the amount of water allowed to flow through dams and thus the amount of water available to downstream users.

The court refused this argument, in large part because of the historic state supremacy in water allocation and regulation. The court cited the legislative history of the Clean Water Act to this effect—

> In 1972, the Congress made a clear and precise distinction between point sources, which would be subject to direct Federal regulation, and nonpoint sources, control of which was *specifically reserved* to State and local governments through the section 208 process. . . .

The Senate Report also expresses a positive intent to leave certain pollution problems to the states, at least for the time being—

> Section 208. . . may not be adequate. It may be that the States will be reluctant to develop [adequate] control measures. . . and it may be that some time in the future a Federal presence can be justified and afforded.

> But for the moment, it is both necessary and appropriate to make a distinction as to the kinds of activities that are to be regulated by the Federal Government and the kinds of activities which are to be subject to some measure of local control.

*Id.,* page 10, 1977 Leg.Hist. 644, 1977 U.S. Code Cong. & Ad. News, page 4336. *Gorsuch,* page 176; emphasis in original.

The court stated that Congress did not intend the Clean Water Act to interfere any more than necessary with state water management. *Costle, Homestake Mining,* and *Gorsuch* are all decisions that upheld the authority of individual states to regulate water quality, and, at least in the *Gorsuch* case, water quantity. These decisions, coupled with the legislative history discussed below, would seem to strengthen California's authority to regulate water quality and to maintain its control of water quantity.

## Section 101(g): The Wallop Amendment

The Wallop Amendment, named for Malcolm Wallop, the Wyoming Senator who sponsored it, states—

*The Wallop Amendment, included in the policy section of the Clean Water Act, states that the Act shall not be used to control "rights to quantities of water" established by the states.*

> It is the policy of Congress that the authority of each State to allocate quantities of water within its jurisdiction shall not be superseded, abrogated or otherwise impaired by this...[Act]. It is the further policy of Congress that nothing in this chapter shall be construed to supersede or abrogate rights to quantities of water which have been established by any State. Federal agencies shall co-operate with State and local agencies to develop comprehensive solutions to prevent, reduce and eliminate pollution in concert with programs for managing water resources. § 101(g), 33 U.S.C. § 1251(g).

The Wallop Amendment is an impediment to the EPA's ability to interfere with the State Board's planning process, although how serious a hindrance remains the subject of debate. Proponents of federal control argue that the legislative history of the Wallop Amendment indicates that legitimate water quality concerns allow regulation to impact existing water rights. Furthermore, the EPA has interpreted the Wallop Amendment to be a policy statement that does not prevent the EPA from taking actions affecting water usage.[7] Lajuana Wilcher, the former assistant administrator of EPA for water, has repeatedly expressed this opinion—

> Water quality and water quantity are not separate elements. Yet for a while, we seemingly forgot about the connection between the two. When many of today's western water policies were developed, they served the needs of a developing and expanding frontier nation....

> Water and depletion signaled progress and growth. Food could be grown, livestock raised and civilization anchored. Yet development had its costs. The first costs were human health effects— typhoid, cholera. But humans and human health are not the only parts of the ecosystem affected by water quality and water quantity. We are all aware of the interest across the nation when ducks

[7] Lilly, "EPA's Emerging Role in Water Allocation Decisions," 1991, 36 *Rocky Mt.Min.L.Inst.,* pages 22-1, 22-26.

at Kesterson Refuge in California were poisoned by high selenium levels, and when Mono Lake water levels dropped so low that coyotes could walk across sections and devour California seagulls.

In aquatic ecosystems, the regulation, timing, volume, withdrawal and return of water flows are often critical factors determining the condition of aquatic habitats, particularly in arid, low flow areas. The National Fisheries Survey (Volume 1, 1982) indicated that water quantity problems adversely affect fish communities in 68% of the nation's streams. As population and economic growth result in increased water diversions and consequent reductions in flows, maintenance of water quality and aquatic ecosystems has become more difficult....

Some of you probably are saying 'What's wrong with this picture? What's EPA doing affecting our water quantity?!' Some of you right now may be mentally reciting Section 101(g) of the CWA, the 'Wallop amendment.' [The Wallop Amendment is recited here.] Sounds like pretty strong stuff. Seems to preclude any federal action affecting a State's water quality allocation. But then listen to the goals and other requirements that the CWA prescribes for EPA:

> *Section 101(a)*—the objective of the CWA is to '...restore and maintain the physical, chemical and biological integrity of the Nation's waters.'

> *Section 101(a)(2)*—establishes a goal to '...provide for the protection of and propagation of fish, shellfish, and wildlife and provide for recreation in and on the water....'

> *Section 303(c)(2)(A)*—requires States to adopt water quality standards to '...protect the public health and welfare, enhance the quality of water and serve the purposes of this Act.' EPA reviews and approves these standards.

So how does all of that relate to Section 101(g)? Although EPA is well aware of State water allocation rights, the exact limitations imposed by Section 101(g) are not as clear as some would like to believe. Speech of Lajuana S. Wilcher at University of Colorado School of Law, June 7, 1991.

*EPA on the Wallop Amendment: The limitations "are not as clear as some would like to believe."*

No court has chosen to define the full impact of the Wallop Amendment. The *Gorsuch* court's interpretation of Section 101(g) is the most lengthy judicial interpretation of this provision and is therefore set forth at some length—

In light of its intent to minimize federal control over state decisions on water *quantity,* Congress might also, if confronted with the issue, have decided to leave control of dams insofar as they affect water *quality* to the states. Such a policy would reduce federal/state friction and would permit states to develop integrated water management plans that address both quality and quantity. *See* H.R.Rep., *supra* note 52, page 96, 1972 Leg.Hist. 783 (In some states, 'water resource development agencies are responsible for allocation of stream flow and are required to give full consideration to the effects on water quality'; those states 'should continue to exercise the primary responsibility in both of these areas and thus provide a balanced management control system.') *Gorsuch,* page 179, emphasis in original.

The court continued—

*The* Gorsuch *opinion discussing the legislative history of the Wallop Amendment*

Section 101(g) was not intended to take precedence over 'legitimate and necessary water quality considerations.' 123 Cong.Rec. 39, 212 (1977), *1977 Leg. Hist.* 532 (statement of Sen. Wallop, the sponsor of the amendment that added § 101(g)). However, with respect to one area where quality and quantity are in conflict—salt-water intrusion caused by water diversion for drinking or irrigation—Congress explicitly declined to require the states to control water quality. Section 208(b)(2)(F)-(H), 33 U.S.C. § 1288(b)(2)(F)-(H) requires state area-wide waste management plans to set forth 'procedures and methods...to control to the extent feasible' agricultural, silvicultural, mine-related, and construction-related nonpoint sources. In contrast, § 208(b)(2)(I) requires the state plan merely to 'set forth procedures and methods to control [salt water] intrusion to the extent feasible *where such procedures and methods are otherwise a part of the waste treatment management plan.'* (Emphasis added.) The italicized clause, not present in earlier versions of the bill, *see, e.g.,* S. 2770, 92d Cong., 1st Sess. § 209(b)(2)(I) (1971), *1972 Leg. Hist.* 1597-98, was intended to prevent water quality goals from interfering with state water allocation plans. See the House debate, in which Representative Waldie comments: 'I have to conclude that this was a major weakening of this bill and that it was done at the request of someone who does not desire to have salt water intrusion...controlled in the bill'; and Representative Johnson explains that the change reflects the concern of the California State Water Resources Control Board that it 'was losing control of its water resources programs.' 117 Cong.Rec. 10,256 (1971), *1972 Leg.Hist.* 484-485. *Gorsuch,* page 179, fn. 67, emphasis in original.

Representative Johnson stated that one of the purposes of the amendment was to affirm the State Board's control over its water resources planning, clarifying that the Board still has a great deal of latitude. However, the *Gorsuch* court's holding relied heavily on the EPA's interpretation of the terms of the Clean Water Act. As in *Costle* and *Homestake*, the court was able to defer to an EPA interpretation that upheld state authority. In light of the EPA's current interpretation of Section 101(g), it seems quite likely that the courts will eventually be presented with a case where deferring to the EPA's interpretation will mean taking authority away from the states. The possibility that a court will still defer to the EPA and limit state authority is enhanced by decisions in two cases in which the EPA was not involved: *Riverside Irrigation District v. Andrews* (1985) 758 F.2d 508 and *United States v. Akers* (1986) 785 F.2d 814.

## The *Riverside Irrigation District* and *Akers* Decisions

Senator Wallop stated that the purpose of his amendment was to protect state water rights creation and administration from "[f]ederal land use planning" while allowing "[l]egitimate water quality measures" that may have "some effect on the method of water usage." 123 Cong.Rec. 39, 211-212 (1977). Senator Wallop understood that Sections 208, 402, and 404 of the Clean Water Act might "incidentally affect the use of water under an individual water right," but emphasized that the amendment affirmed state jurisdiction over "priority of usage," which was to remain "inviolate"—

> Water quality and interstate movement is an acceptable Federal role and influence. But the States' historic rights to allocate quantity, and establish priority of usage, remains inviolate because of this amendment. The Water Pollution Control Act was designed to protect the quality of water and to protect critical wetlands in concert with the various States. In short, a responsible Federal role. 123 Cong.Rec. 39, 212 (1977).

Senator Wallop was concerned that the Clean Water Act might be used by the federal government to control state water allocation—

> The conferees accepted an amendment which will reassure the State that it is the policy of Congress that the Clean Water Act will not be used for the purpose of interfering with State water right systems. 123 Cong.Rec. 39, 211 (1977).

However, Senator Wallop stated that Congress did not intend to "prohibit those incidental effects" that could occur in connection with "the use of water under an individual water right." 123 Cong.Rec. 39, 212 (1977). Proponents of federal regulation argue that as long as its primary aim is to protect water quality, a regulation

*Senator Wallop intended his amendment to prevent the Act from "interfering with state water right systems," but not to preclude "incidental effects" on an "individual water right."*

may affect an individual water right. The issue is: when does a regulation become more than an "incidental effect"? Unfortunately, the legislative history is not helpful—

> This amendment does seek to clarify the policy of Congress concerning the proper role of Federal water quality legislation in relation to State water law. It should be clear. Legitimate water quality measures authorized by this act may at times have some effect on the method of water usage. Water quality standards and their upgrading are legitimate and necessary under this act. The requirements of section 402 and 404 permits may incidentally affect individual water rights. Management practices developed through State or local 208 planning units may also incidentally affect the use of water under an individual water right. 123 Cong. Rec., 39, 212 (1977).

*Cases have upheld the Corps of Engineers' permit authority under Section 404 against claims of interference with state water rights.*

The *Andrews* and *Akers* cases shed some light on this issue. In *Riverside Irrigation District v. Andrews* (1985) 758 F.2d 508, the Corps of Engineers denied the plaintiffs a Section 404 permit to deposit dredge material for construction of a dam and reservoir. The Corps based its decision on the potential downstream impact on an endangered species, the whooping crane, which would result from increased consumptive use of water. The plaintiffs argued that the Corps exceeded its authority by considering the effect of depletions caused by the consumptive use of water stored in the reservoir. In addition to a number of other arguments, the plaintiffs argued that the Corps' permit denial would impair the state's right to allocate water within its jurisdiction, a violation of Section 101(g) of the Clean Water Act.

Without deciding whether a denial of the permit constituted an impairment of the state's authority to allocate water, the court determined that the Corps acted within its authority. The court wrote that, since the statute and regulations expressly required the Corps to consider changes in water quantity in granting nationwide permits and since Section 101(g) was only a general policy statement, the clear and specific grant of jurisdiction was not nullified. Thus, the Corps did not exceed its authority in denying the permit. In addressing the scope of the Wallop Amendment, the court wrote—

> A fair reading of the statute as a whole makes clear that, where both the state's interest in allocating water and the federal government's interest in protecting the environment are implicated, Congress intended an accommodation. Such accommodations are best reached in the individual permit process. *Riverside Irrigation v. Andrews,* page 513.

*Andrews* demonstrates that certain actions within the Corps' jurisdiction, such as the issuance of nationwide permits, can impair an individual's use of state-allocated water. It is important to note that the nationwide permit process is free from most of the normal Section 404 permit requirements, and this may have been a factor in the court's decision. Furthermore, the District Court's citation of Senator Wallop's statement that Section 101(g) was not intended to interfere with existing law is a strong indication that the Section 404 permitting process is not impacted by its provisions. *Riverside Irrigation District v. Andrews* (1983) 568 F.Supp. 583, 589.

Even strong advocates of state water law authority concede that *Andrews* was properly decided because the Corps of Engineers has authority over site-specific permit applications. However, they argue, the provisions of Section 101(g) were not really tested in that case, because none of its three sentences were analyzed.[8]

Perhaps the lesson of *Andrews* is that Section 101(g) is a general policy statement that does not nullify a clear grant of jurisdiction and that the accommodation between the state's interest in allocating water and the federal government's interest in protecting the environment to which the court referred is best left to the individual permit process. *See Andrews,* page 513.

*United States v. Akers* (1986) 785 F.2d 814 also involved the Section 404 permitting process. Akers planned to convert a wetland area to upland farming but did not apply for a Section 404 permit. *United States v. Akers,* pages 816-817. The District Court enjoined him from filling the wetlands on his property without complying with the Section 404 permitting process. Akers argued that the District Court had interpreted the Wallop Amendment too narrowly, "rendering his state-allocated water rights 'virtually meaningless.'" *United States v. Akers,* pages 820-821. The court rejected this argument with the statement that any incidental effect on Akers' water right was justified, because protecting wetlands is the type of legitimate purpose for which the Clean Water Act was intended.

### *PUD No. 1 v. Washington*

The most recent decision discussing water quality and water quantity regulation is in *PUD No. 1 v. Washington Department of Ecology* (1994) 511 U.S. ___ [128 L. Ed. 2d 716]. A city and utility district challenged minimum stream flows imposed by the state pursuant to the provisions of the Clean Water Act. The Supreme Court upheld the

---

[8]  Hobbs and Raley, "Water Rights Protection in Water Quality Law," 1989, 60 Univ. of *Colo. L.Rev.,* page 871.

state's imposition of the flow requirement. In its decision the court addressed the Clean Water Act's regulation of water quantity.

Petitioners also assert more generally that the Clean Water Act is only concerned with water 'quality,' and does not allow the regulation of water 'quantity.' This is an artificial distinction. In many cases, water quantity is closely related to water quality; a sufficient lowering of the water quantity in a body of water could destroy all of its designated uses, be it for drinking water, recreation, navigation or, as here, as a fishery. In any event, there is recognition in the Clean Water Act itself that reduced stream flow, i.e., diminishment of water quality, can constitute water pollution. First, the Act's definition of pollution as 'the man-made or man induced alternation of the chemical, physical, biological, and radiological integrity of water' encompasses the effects of reduced water quality. 33 U.S.C. @ 1361(19); This broad conception of pollution—one which expressly evinces Congress' concern with the physical and biological integrity of water—refutes petitioners' assertion that the Act draws a sharp distinction between the regulation of water 'quantity' and water 'quality'. . . .

Petitioners assert that two other provisions of the Clean Water Act, §§ 101(g) and 510 (2), 33 U.S.C. §§ 1251(g) and 1370(2), exclude the regulation of water quality from the coverage of the Act. Section 101(g) provides 'that the authority of each State to allocate quantities of water within its jurisdiction shall not be superseded, abrogated or otherwise impaired by this chapter.' 33 U.S.C. § 1251(g). Similarly, § 510(2) provides that nothing in the Act shall 'be construed as impairing or in any manner affecting any right or jurisdiction of the States with respect to the waters ...of such States.' 33 U.S.C. § 1370. In petitioners' view, these provisions exclude 'water quality issues from direct regulation under the federally controlled water quality standards authorized in § 303.' (Citation omitted.)

This language gives the States authority to allocate water rights; we therefore find it peculiar that petitioners argue that it prevents the State from regulating stream flow. In any event, we read these provisions more narrowly than petitioners. Sections 101(g) and 510(2) preserve the authority of each State to allocate water quantity as between users; they do not limit the scope of water pollution controls that may be imposed on users who have obtained, pursuant to state law, a water allocation. Pages 732-733.

Although this language has yet to be interpreted, it certainly raises questions about the future significance of Section 101(g).

## CHAPTER EIGHT
# Water Transfers[1]

## Introduction

In California the concept of "water transfers" (also referred to as "water marketing" or "water brokering") is considered a partial solution to the shortage of water. The underlying tenet is that market forces in a free market will reallocate water. Usually the transfer would be from agricultural to urban uses and could substitute, to some extent, for additional diversions from streams and rivers. Purchasing water rights for environmental uses could also occur.

*Transfers as a partial solution to water shortages*

While these ideas have been in existence for decades, "free market" water transfers have not been widely used because of significant legal, social, environmental, and institutional barriers. California's history has also contributed to the slow development of transfers, which are often negatively associated with controversial actions taken by the City of Los Angeles in the early 1900s to obtain water from the Owens Valley. Los Angeles acquired water rights by purchasing thousands of acres of Owens Valley land, and many blame Los Angeles for devastating the Valley's economy and environment.[2]

*The Owens Valley legacy still affects the concept of water transfers.*

Transfers have also been hampered by the fact that current laws provide local agencies (and not the transferor) with an opportunity to prevent or veto the transaction. Local community opposition brought to bear upon such local agencies can be tremendous.

While formidable, these barriers are not necessarily insurmountable. In fact, transfers are becoming more widely accepted.

---

[1] The principal author of this chapter was Janice L. Weis.
[2] Reisner, *Cadillac Desert,* 1986, pages 100-107.

A 1978 report issued by the Rand Corporation urged water users to make water available for free market transfers and to allow private parties to participate.[3] While these suggestions were initially met with heavy resistance from those fearful of losing their water rights, the combination of droughts and escalating economic and environmental costs of developing new water supplies has forced water users all over California to take a closer look at reallocating existing supplies through transfers. Even so, agricultural users remain concerned that using their water to meet growing urban demands will undercut the need to develop new supplies for both farms and cities.

This chapter outlines the most significant laws governing water transfers in California, discusses some of the existing limitations, and provides a few examples of transfers that have occurred. The vast majority of these transfers have been short-term and have involved a transfer of water, rather than a transfer of water rights.

## Statutory Framework for Transfers

### Early Legislation

The Water Commission Act of 1913, without specifically mentioning water transfers, established a permit system for obtaining and a procedure for changing appropriative surface water rights, known as "post-1914 appropriative rights."[4] Water Code §§ 1700-1706.

Section 1701 of the Water Code provides that a post-1914 appropriator may change the point of diversion, place of use, or purpose of use from that specified in the appropriator's application permit or license, subject to approval by the State Water Resources Control Board. The State Board may grant this request only if it finds that the change will not initiate a new right or injure any other appropriator or lawful water user. Water Code § 1702.

Permission of the State Board is not required to change the point of diversion, place of use, or purpose of use of a "pre-1914" appropriative right, but these changes may not injure other water users. Water Code § 1706.

---

[3]  Phelps, Moore and Graubaurd, *Efficient Water Use in California: Water Rights, Water Districts and Water Transfers,* Rand Corporation Report R-2386-CSA/RF, November 1978.

[4]  As discussed in chapter 2, an appropriative surface water right is the right to divert surface water for use on land that does not abut the surface stream. Since 1914, a person wishing to appropriate surface water has been required to apply for a permit from the State Water Resources Control Board. Water Code §§ 1225, 1052; *see Temescal Water Co. v. Department of Public Works* (1955) 44 Cal.2d 90, 95.

## General Policy Statements

While employing these early provisions to change the place and purpose of use, few appropriators used them to transfer water to other users, perhaps fearing a permanent loss of their water rights.[5] To encourage transfers, the legislature enacted several statutes during the 1980s which contain policy statements rather than procedural guidance. In 1980, the legislature found that "the growing water needs of the state require the use of water in an efficient manner and that the efficient use of water requires certainty in the definition of property rights to the use of water and transferability of such rights." Water Code § 109(a). It declared that it is the policy of the state to "facilitate the voluntary transfer of water and water rights where consistent with the public welfare of the place of export and the place of import." Water Code § 109(a).

*Few transfers to other users occurred under early legislation.*

*In the 1980s, the legislature enacted a number of statutes encouraging water transfers.*

In 1982, the legislature ordered the Department of Water Resources (DWR), the State Board, and all other "appropriate" state agencies "to encourage voluntary transfers of water and water rights, including, but not limited to, providing technical assistance" to transferors. Water Code § 109(b).

**DWR = Department of Water Resources**

In 1986, the legislature enacted the Costa-Isenberg Water Transfer Act. Water Code §§ 470, 475-484. It declared that "voluntary water transfers between water users can result in a more efficient use of water, benefiting both the buyer and the seller"; that "transfers of surplus water on an intermittent basis can help alleviate water shortages, save capital outlay development costs, and conserve water and energy"; and that the public interest requires water conservation and "the coordinated assistance of state agencies for voluntary water transfers to allow more intensive use of developed water resources in a manner that fully protects the interests of other entities which have rights to, or rely on, the water covered by a proposed transfer." Water Code § 475.

The 1986 legislation also increased involvement by DWR in water transfers. For example, Water Code Section 480 requires DWR to establish a program "to facilitate the voluntary exchange or transfer of water and implement the various state laws that pertain to water transfers." Sections 481 through 483 authorize DWR to: (1) create and maintain a list of entities seeking to enter into water transfer arrangements; (2) prepare a water transfer guide containing specified information; and (3) consult and coordinate its activities with other state agencies.

*It is the policy of California to "facilitate the voluntary transfer of water and water rights where consistent with the public welfare of the place of export and the place of import."*

[5]  Gray, "A Primer on California Water Transfer Law," 1989, 31 *Ariz.L.Rev.* pages 745, 768-769.

As the agency responsible for the State Water Project, DWR is also required to negotiate with the federal Bureau of Reclamation (the agency which operates the Central Valley Project) "to contract for interim rights to stored water from the federal Central Valley Project (CVP) for use in the State Water Resources Development System by state water supply contractors." Water Code § 10008. The legislature also directed DWR to "discuss" with the Bureau of Reclamation the possibility of permitting federal water contractors to transfer water to "any public entity which supplies water for domestic use, irrigation use, or environmental protection ... during times of shortage." Water Code § 10009.

In 1986, the legislature also provided for the use of public conveyance facilities for transfers, passing the "Katz bill," named after its author, Assemblyman Richard Katz. §§ 1810-1814. Water Code Section 1810 requires DWR and all other public agencies that operate water conveyance facilities to make available to *bona fide transferors* unused capacity in the conveyance facilities for the transfer of water. A *"bona fide transferor"* is defined as a person or public agency "with a contract for sale of water which may be conditioned upon the acquisition of conveyance facility capacity to convey the water that is the subject of the contract." Water Code § 1811(a). The transferor must pay "fair compensation" for use of the aqueduct, and the transfer must meet certain conditions, including preventing injury to legal water users and fish and wildlife. Water Code § 1810. As discussed in more detail below, DWR has used these statutes to allow the Bureau of Reclamation to move CVP water through the California Aqueduct to CVP contractors and other users in the Central Valley.

*Unused capacity in conveyance facilities must be made available for transfers at "fair compensation."*

In 1992, Congress enacted the Central Valley Project Improvement Act (CVPIA), which in part facilitates the transfer of federal water from the CVP. This Act is discussed further later in this chapter.

## Types of Surface Water Statutory Transfers

***Short-Term Transfers.*** Short-term transfers are those that last for a year or less. There are several specific types:

***Temporary urgency changes.*** Water Code Section 1435 allows a permittee or licensee (a post-1914 appropriator) with "an urgent need" to change a point of diversion, place of use, or purpose of use to petition the State Board for a temporary change "without complying with other procedures or provisions of this division ...." Water Code § 1435(a). "Urgent need" is the existence of circumstances from which the State Board may determine that a temporary change "is necessary to further the constitutional policy that the water resources of the state be put to beneficial use to the fullest extent of which they are capable and that waste of water be prevented . . . . " Water Code § 1435(c).

The State Board must make four findings before granting a temporary urgency change: (1) the permittee or licensee has an urgent need to make the proposed change; (2) the proposed change will not injure any other legal user of water; (3) the proposed change will not result in unreasonable effect on fish, wildlife, or other instream beneficial uses; and (4) the change is in the public interest. Water Code § 1435(b).

A temporary urgency change can be granted for no more than 180 days. Water Code § 1440. The State Board can renew the time period for an additional 180 days and has the power at all times to modify or revoke the temporary change order. Water Code §§ 1440, 1441. Unlike the temporary changes discussed below, the Water Code does not specifically exempt temporary urgency changes from review under the California Environmental Quality Act (CEQA).[6] Pub. Resources Code §§ 21000, *et seq.* Adherence to the requirements of CEQA can delay the implementation of transfers because it requires the preparation of environmental documents and allows for public comment. In addition, unlike temporary changes, the State Board must post or publish notice of requests for temporary urgency changes, allowing any interested person to object. Water Code § 1438(b), (d). The State Board must consider any such objections and may decide to hold a hearing. Water Code § 1438(e).

*Temporary changes.* The Water Code also allows "temporary changes" of post-1914 appropriative rights. Water Code §§ 1725-1732. A temporary change is "any change of point of diversion, place of use, or purpose of use involving a transfer or exchange of water or water rights for a period of one year or less." Water Code § 1728. These changes are limited by two factors: (1) they must include only the amount of water that the transferor would have consumptively used or stored during the period of the transfer; and (2) they must not injure any legal user of the water or unreasonably affect fish, wildlife, or other instream beneficial uses. Water Code § 1725.

To obtain a temporary change, a water user must provide written notice to the State Board and the Department of Fish and Game describing the amount of water consumptively used, the amount of

*There are shortcut procedures for temporary urgency changes, but approval is limited to 180 days unless renewed.*

*These changes are not specifically exempt from CEQA. The time required to comply with CEQA may render the emergency moot.*

**CEQA = California Environmental Quality Act**

---

[6] Depending on the facts surrounding the particular transfer, the exemptions set forth under CEQA itself, such as the emergency exemption, may apply. (Pub. Resources Code § 21080(b)(4); State CEQA Guidelines § 15269.)

water proposed for the transfer, the parties involved in the transfer, and "any other information" the State Board may require by rule. Water Code § 1726.

The State Board can approve a temporary change without conducting a public hearing if it finds the proposed change: (1) will not injure any legal user of water; and (2) will not unreasonably affect fish, wildlife, or other instream beneficial uses. Water Code § 1727(a). If it cannot make these findings within 60 days of receiving notice of the proposed change, the State Board must conduct a public hearing. Water Code § 1727(c). When the temporary change period expires, the right to the water automatically reverts to the original holder of the right. Water Code § 1731. Temporary changes are technically exempt from CEQA, although the State Board may still require substantial environmental analysis. Water Code § 1729.

*One year temporary changes are exempt from CEQA, but the State Board still requires analysis of impacts on fish and wildlife.*

***Long-Term Transfers.*** Water Code Sections 1735 through 1737 govern long-term transfers of post-1914 appropriative water. A long-term transfer is one which lasts for more than a year. Water Code § 1735. Under Section 1735, the State Board is authorized to consider a petition for a long-term transfer of water or water rights "involving a change of point of diversion, place of use, or purpose of use." It may approve such a petition, after providing notice and opportunity for a hearing, including an opportunity for review by the Department of Fish and Game, "where the change would not result in substantial injury to any legal user of water and would not unreasonably affect fish, wildlife, or other instream beneficial uses."[7] Water Code § 1736.

There are no maximum time limits for a long-term transfer. As with a temporary change, once the long-term transfer has expired, all rights revert automatically to the original holder of the right.[8] Water Code § 1737. Long-term transfers are not exempt from CEQA.

*The vast majority of transfers have involved the transfer of water, not water rights, and have been short-term.*

As noted below, the vast majority of water transfers in California have involved the transfer of water, not water rights, and have been short-term rather than long-term.

[7] Legislation introduced during the 1992 legislative session proposed to delete this requirement and substitute that a long-term transfer cannot unreasonably affect the environment or the overall economy of the county or local community from which the water is being transferred. Assembly Bill 52, Katz. This change is purportedly intended to respond to concerns about the third-party impacts of transfers, discussed later in this chapter. This legislation has not yet been adopted.

[8] As one noted commentator has stated, although the long-term transfer provisions overlap with Sections 380-386 discussed below, the legislature failed to explain how or whether the new law should be integrated with these long-term transfer provisions. Gray, "A Primer on California Water Transfer Law," 1989, 31 *Ariz.L.Rev.*, pages 745, 779.)

***Examples of Short- and Long-Term Transfers.*** The Yuba County
Water Agency (YCWA) has taken advantage of the surplus water
transfer provisions of Sections 380 through 387 (discussed below)
and the short-term provisions set forth above. According to one
study, because YCWA's storage facilities exceeded its customers'
demands, YCWA was the largest transferor of water during the
1980s and the principal source of temporary water for agencies in
the San Francisco Bay Area during the 1987 drought.[9]

In 1987, the State Board approved, pursuant to Water Code
Section 1727 (providing for temporary changes of appropriative
rights), the transfer of 83,100 acre feet of water from YCWA to DWR
between July and September of 1987 for rediversion and use south
of the Delta. This water permitted an equal amount of water to be
retained by DWR in its reservoir in Oroville to provide carryover
storage in anticipation of the continuing drought.[10]

In 1988, the State Board approved the transfer of 122,000 acre
feet to DWR pursuant to Water Code Sections 1735 *et seq.* (providing
for long-term transfers) and 1435 *et seq.* (providing for temporary
urgency changes) for use by the State Water Project to meet Delta
outflow requirements. Staff Report, page 30. Similar transfers were
approved by the State Board in 1989, 1990, and 1991. Staff Report,
pages 30, 37. YCWA also transferred some of its unused water to the
1991 Drought Water Bank, discussed below.[11]

State Board hearings during 1992 regarding YCWA's water
rights addressed, among other issues, whether YCWA had "exercised
reasonable diligence in perfecting its water rights permits on the
Yuba River" and questioned whether the State Board should reduce
its rights under its permits. Staff Report, page 3. Because of these
inquiries, YCWA decided not to transfer any more water. Thus, while
many of YCWA's past transfers were successful, the State Board's
inquiries may have had a chilling effect on future transfers.

There are few examples of long-term transfers. During the
1980s, the State Board received only one application for a long-term
transfer. This was a request by the Bureau of Reclamation under
Section 1735 for a long-term exchange of water between the Arvin-
Edison Water Storage District and the Metropolitan Water District.

**YCWA = Yuba County Water Agency**

*Transfer of surplus water from Yuba
County has been the major drought source
of supply for DWR and San Francisco.
Yuba County's water rights were then
questioned.*

[9] Gray, "Water Transfers in California: 1981-1989," Executive Summary,
page 3, published in *The Water Transfer Process as a Management
Option for Meeting Changing Water Demands,* chapter 2, 1990.
[10] State Water Resources Control Board, Division of Water Rights, Staff
Report, Lower Yuba River, August 1991, page 30, hereafter "Staff Report."
[11] "Unresolved Issues in Water Marketing," May/June 1992, *Western Water,*
page 7, hereafter *Western Water.*

## Transfers of Conserved and Surplus Water

*State law permits the transfer of conserved or surplus water. Local agencies with jurisdiction can veto these transactions.*

***Legal Standards.*** The legislature has also enacted statutes facilitating the transfers of conserved and surplus water. Water Code §§ 380-387 and §§ 1010-1011. These statutes, however, also provide examples of instances in which a local agency has the opportunity to block or veto transfers.

Sections 380 through 387 of the Water Code empower local agencies to sell water and to serve as "brokers" between individual users within their service area and potential buyers. Section 382(a) provides that "[n]otwithstanding any other provision of law, every local or regional public agency authorized by law to serve water to persons or entities within the service area of the agency may sell, lease, exchange, or otherwise transfer" for use outside the agency either or both of the following: (1) water that is surplus to the needs of the agency's water users; and (2) water, the use of which is voluntarily foregone during the period of the transfer by the agency's water user." The legislature intended this section to preempt other laws containing "more stringent limitations on the authority of a particular public agency to serve water for use outside the agency, to the extent those other laws are inconsistent" with Section 382. Water Code § 381.

The legislature defined "surplus water" in three ways for purposes of these provisions. Section 383(a) allows the local agency to transfer water that it finds will be "in excess of the needs of water users within the agency for the duration of the transfer." Section 383(b) defines surplus water as that "which any water user agrees with the agency, upon mutually satisfactory terms, to forego use [of] for the duration of the transfer." Section 383(c) authorizes an individual water user within an agency to negotiate a transfer for itself that is surplus to the user's needs. This section provides that "the water user and the agency [may] agree, upon mutually satisfactory terms, that the water user will forego use for the period of time specified in the agreement" with the transferee, and directs "that the agency shall act as agent for the water user to effect the transfer." Transfers cannot exceed seven years, unless the agency and transferee agree to a longer period. Water Code § 387.

Other conditions must also be met before surplus water can be transferred. The water agency with jurisdiction over the area to which the water will be transferred must approve the agreement. Water Code § 385. Also, transfers must comply with all other provisions of the Water Code that govern transfers, including those regarding changes in point of diversion, place of use, and purpose of use.

Water Code § 384. Such transfers are also subject to Section 386, which says that the State Board can approve water transfers "only if it finds that the change can be made without injuring any legal user of the water and without unreasonably affecting fish, wildlife, or other instream beneficial uses and does not unreasonably affect the overall economy of the area from which the water is being transferred." Water Code § 386.

Transferring "surplus" water under these provisions raises legal questions. Under the California Constitution, every water user has a right only to the amount of water which can be put to reasonable and beneficial use. Cal. Const., art. X, § 2. Water not put to such use is subject to forfeiture. The legislature recognized that users willing to transfer water "surplus" to their needs may be concerned about forfeiture. Sections 1010, 1011, and 1244 of the Water Code address this concern by allowing a water user to reduce water demands by conserving water or by substituting reclaimed wastewater without losing the rights to the water saved and made available for transfer.

*There is a legal question about the right to transfer water not needed by the owner of the water right.*

Section 1244 states that "[t]he sale, lease, exchange, or transfer of water or water rights...shall not constitute evidence of waste or unreasonable use, unreasonable method of use or unreasonable method of diversion...." Section 1011(a) provides that "[w]hen any person entitled to the use of water under an appropriative right fails to use all or any part of the water because of...conservation efforts, any cessation or reduction in the use of such ...water shall be deemed equivalent to a reasonable beneficial use of water to the extent of such cessation or reduction in use." Section 1010 states: "[C]essation of, or reduction in, the use of water under any existing right...as the result of the use of reclaimed water...to a degree which unreasonably affects the water for other beneficial uses and is deemed equivalent to, and for purposes of maintaining any right shall be construed to constitute, a reasonable beneficial use of water to the extent and in the amount that the reclaimed, desalinated, or polluted water is being used...."

***Example.*** An agreement between the Metropolitan Water District of Southern California (MWD) and the Imperial Irrigation District (IID) was based, in part, on some of the statutes discussed above. This agreement is not a sale of water rights, but rather a "water salvage" arrangement, which involves saving water that was previously being wasted and making it available for use by others.[12]

**MWD = Metropolitan Water District of Southern California**

**IID = Imperial Irrigation District**

[12] "A Guide to Water Transfers in California," Draft Report by the Department of Water Resources, June 1989.

## Projects Authorized by MWD-IID Water Conservation Agreement

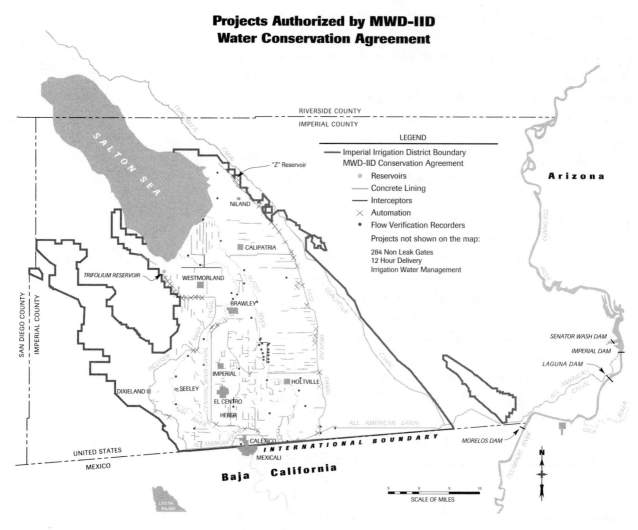

**LEGEND**

— Imperial Irrigation District Boundary
MWD-IID Conservation Agreement
- Reservoirs
— Concrete Lining
— Interceptors
✕ Automation
• Flow Verification Recorders
Projects not shown on the map:
284 Non Leak Gates
12 Hour Delivery
Irrigation Water Management

The MWD/IID transfer itself was not subject to the State Board's approval because it involved water from the Colorado River, which is subject to federal control. However, the State Board played an important role in this transfer through its duty to investigate allegedly wasteful uses of water.

In 1983 and 1984, the State Board investigated claims that IID's use of water was wasteful. The claims were based on, among other things, IID's lack of storage facilities, the lack of a tailwater recovery system, and the resulting flooding of the Salton Sea. In June 1984, the State Board found that IID's failure to implement additional water conservation measures was unreasonable and a misuse of water under Article X, Section 2, of the California Constitution, which requires that water resources "be put to beneficial use to the fullest extent of which they are capable." State Board Decision 1600 (June 21, 1984). Among other things, IID was ordered to prepare a comprehensive water conservation plan. The State Board's decision was upheld by California courts. *Imperial Irrigation District v. State Water Resources Control Board* (1986) 186 Cal.App.3d 1160.

At the same time, MWD was seeking long-term water supplies to compensate for the fact that the Central Arizona Project began taking water in late 1985, thereby jeopardizing MWD's entitlement to Colorado River water. MWD and IID began to investigate the possibility of MWD's financing conservation measures for IID, in return for which MWD would receive the salvaged water. In 1988, the State Board ordered IID to conserve at least 100,000 acre feet per year by 1994. State Board Order 88-20 (September 7, 1988). Shortly thereafter, IID agreed to transfer 100,000 acre feet per year to MWD for a minimum of 35 years in exchange for MWD's $92 million funding of delivery of irrigation system improvements and other conservation measures.[13]

*The MWD-IID agreement transfers 100,000 acre-feet annually of conserved water for 35 years at a cost of $92 million.*

One of the most difficult issues that arose during the negotiations between MWD and IID was whether to characterize the agreement as a water "sale" or a water "salvage" agreement. IID asserted that it was selling the water pursuant to Water Code Section 1011, which, as noted above, allows the sale, lease, or exchange of conserved water. MWD, however, refused to take the position that it was buying the water, asserting instead that under the Colorado River priority system, it had the right to any water not put to beneficial use by IID. The final agreement finessed the issue and characterized the arrangement as a conservation agreement, not a sale of water.

MWD's rights to Colorado River water are also junior to those of the Palo Verde Irrigation District and the Coachella Valley Water District. MWD needed the consent of both of these agencies in order to receive any of IID's conserved water. The Coachella Valley Water District challenged the IID/MWD agreement in court, claiming, among other things, that the agreement would impair its water rights and that IID had no right to transfer water outside of its district. The lawsuit was later settled pursuant to an agreement which guarantees Coachella water in times of shortage. Palo Verde Irrigation District also approved the IID/MWD agreement in December 1989.[14]

---

[13] McMorrow and Schwarz, "The Imperial Irrigation District/Metropolitan Water District Water Transfer: A Case Study," in Reisner and Bates, *Overtapped Oasis: Reform or Revolution for Western Water,* 1990, pages 149, 156-163

[14] "Water Officials Express Relief at Historic Pact," *Imperial Valley Press,* December 20, 1989.

## Transfers of Stored/Conserved Water

Assembly Bill 2897 (Cortese) added Sections 1745 through 1745.11 to the Water Code in January 1993. These sections apply to both surface water and groundwater and are intended to be in addition to, and not a limitation on, the authority of public agencies to transfer water under other provisions. Water Code § 1745.08.

Under these provisions, a water supplier (defined as including public agencies and private companies that supply or store water) may transfer water to a state drought water bank or to any other water supplier or user inside or outside the service area of the supplier. Water Code § 1745.04. The type of water that can be transferred under these provisions is water stored by the water supplier or water made available from—

*The Water Code now allows the transfer of groundwater as well as surface water and water made available by a user who contracts to reduce water usage.*

- Conservation or alternate water supply measures taken by individual water users or by the water supplier
- Water made available by a user who has contracted with a supplier to reduce its water use.

Water Code § 1745.05.

According to these provisions, water can be transferred whether or not it is "surplus" to the needs of the supplier's service area. Water Code § 1745.06. A water user who transfers surface water cannot replace that water with groundwater unless such use is consistent with an applicable groundwater management plan or is approved by the water supplier from whose service area the water is to be transferred. The supplier must also determine that the transfer will not create or contribute to overdraft. Water Code § 1745.10.

## Conjunctive Use of Surface and Groundwater

*"Conjunctive use": The use and underground storage of surface water when it is available; an increase in groundwater pumping when surface supplies are short.*

***Legal Authority.*** The "conjunctive use" of surface water and groundwater involves the storage of surface water underground for use later in times of need. This procedure has also been referred to as "imported groundwater banking."[15]

Section 1011.5 of the Water Code specifically authorizes the conjunctive use of surface water and groundwater. It sets forth a state policy to encourage conjunctive use of surface water and groundwater supplies and to make surface water available for other beneficial uses. Water Code § 1011.5(a). Section 1011.5 provides that water, the use of which has been "ceased or reduced" as the result of conjunctive use of surface water and groundwater which involves substitution of an alternate supply, may be "sold, leased,

[15] Kletzing, "Imported Groundwater Banking: The Kern Water Bank—A Case Study," 1988, 19 *Pac. L.J.*, pages 1225-26.

## Table 8-1
## Main Types of Statutory Water Transfers

| Type of Transfer | Temporary Urgency Change | Temporary Change | Long-Term Transfer | Conserved/ Surplus Water | Stored/ Conserved Water |
|---|---|---|---|---|---|
| *Water Code Section* | 1435 | 1725 | 1735 | 382 | 1745 |
| Required Findings (Include) | | | | | |
| 1. Urgent need | X | | | | |
| 2. No injury to other water rights | X | X | X | X | |
| 3. No unreasonable effect on fish wildlife, instream uses | X | X | X | X | |
| 4. Change is in public interest | X | | | | |
| 5. Involves only water consumptively used or stored | | | X | | |
| 6. Water must be "surplus" under § 383 | X | | X | X | |
| 7. No unreasonable effect on economy of area of transfer | | | | X | |
| 8. Water agency in area to which water will be transferred must approve | | | | X | |
| 9. Water is stored or conserved under § 1745.05 | | | | | X |
| 10. Cannot replace surface water with groundwater unless consistent with plan or approved by supplier | | | | | X |
| 11. No unreasonable economic impact | | | | X | |
| 12. Will not create/contribute to overdraft | | | | | X |
| *Duration* | 180 days | one year or less | over one year | 7 years | no limit |
| Water code exempts from CEQA | | | X | | |
| *Comments* | | | | | |
| 1. Application/petition must be filed with Board | X | | X | | |
| 2. Permittee notifies Board of change | | X | | | |
| 3. Board provides notice and opportunity for hearing; reviews objections by interested parties | X (Hearing optional) | | | X | |
| 4. No Board hearing unless needed to make required findings | | | X | | |

exchanged, or otherwise transferred" pursuant to any provision of law relating to water transfers. Water Code § 1011.5(d). "Substitution of an alternate supply" is defined as "replacement of water diverted under an appropriative right by the substitution of an equivalent amount of groundwater." Water Code § 1011.5(e).

Several sources provide authority for DWR, the operator of the State Water Project, to carry out imported groundwater banking. In *Niles Sand and Gravel Co. v. Alameda County Water Dist.* (1974) 37

Cal.App.3d 924, the court upheld the right of the Alameda County Water District, a State Water Project contractor, to store imported groundwater even though it would injure an overlying user. The court based its holding in part on the police power granted the district by the legislature. Water Code Section 11258 provides similar police power to DWR. This section states: "The [SWP] shall include facilities south of the...Delta for utilizing groundwater storage space, determined by the director to be feasible for the purpose of providing yield for the [SWP]." In *City of Los Angeles v. City of San Fernando* (1975) 14 Cal.3d 199, the California Supreme Court affirmed the rights of public agencies to store imported water in natural underground basins and to protect and recover stored water for later use.

**SWP = State Water Project**

Other statutes provide for protection of groundwater rights while the holder of those rights ceases or reduces the use of groundwater to use a nontributary alternate source of water or to allow the replenishment of the groundwater. Water Code §§ 1005.1, 1005.2, 1005.4. "Nontributary source" is defined as including water transferred from another watershed or water conserved in the same watershed by a water conservation plan without which the water would have been wasted. Water Code §§ 1005.1, 1005.2. Water users seeking the protection of these statutes must file statements with the State Board. Water Code §§ 1005.1, 1005.2, 1005.4. San Luis Obispo, Santa Barbara, Ventura, Los Angeles, Orange, San Diego, Imperial, Riverside, and San Bernardino counties are subject to special filing requirements. Water Code § 1005.2.

*DWR's Kern Water Bank utilizes underground storage of surface deliveries from the SWP.*

**Examples.** The Kern Water Bank is an attempt by the SWP to conduct a substantial groundwater banking program. The proposed "bank" would use the aquifer underlying the lower Kern River Valley at the extreme southern end of the San Joaquin Valley. The basin is to be recharged with water diverted from the Sacramento-San Joaquin Delta through the California Aqueduct. Water would be withdrawn in dry years to satisfy part of SWP contract entitlement of the Kern County Water Agency, one of the SWP's largest contractors. The bank is intended to add 150,000 acre feet to the SWP's yield.[16] A limited amount of water is being pumped on a trial basis.

Transfers of groundwater also have occurred or been proposed. The City of Los Angeles extracts Owens Valley groundwater in Inyo County and uses it in Los Angeles. Mono County landowners have proposed pumping groundwater from Mono County to Southern California via the Los Angeles Aqueduct. In 1991, the Drought Water

[16] Kletzing, page 1226.

Bank purchased more than 250,000 acre feet of groundwater for transfer from Northern California, via State Water Project and Delta facilities, to coastal and Central Valley cities and farms.

## Other Types of Transfers in California

Most of the transfers in California have not been based on the statutes set forth above. The vast majority of transfers that have taken place have been within the Central Valley Project or State Water Project. The large service areas of these projects allow contractors or users to transfer water without changing the water rights held by the state or federal governments.

*Most transfers have not been pursuant to statutory provisions to transfer water rights, but rather among users within the CVP without changing the federal rights.*

### Transfers of Central Valley Project and State Water Project Water

**Transfers between CVP Contractors.** A large portion of California's water comes from the CVP, which is operated by the United States Bureau of Reclamation (Bureau). Pursuant to the Reclamation Act of 1902, 43 U.S.C. § 371.600(e), the Bureau built many large water projects throughout the West and holds state-granted appropriative water rights for the operation of these projects, including the CVP.[17] The CVP is a system of dams, aqueducts, and canals providing irrigation water to farmers in California's Central Valley from the Sacramento and San Joaquin rivers and their tributaries. (For a detailed discussion of the CVP, *see* chapter 1.)

CVP contractors or users have engaged in transfers among themselves on an informal basis for years. Between 1981 and 1989, there were more than 1,200 transfers, primarily to provide for changing water needs due to changes in cropping patterns and weather.[18] The most common method for transferring CVP water has been by agreement between individual farmers. Because such transfers do not require a change in the Bureau's water rights permits for the CVP, they are not subject to the State Board's jurisdiction.

*CVP transfers*

Although the parties submit their transfer proposals to the Bureau and request its approval, the Bureau generally does not evaluate the proposals. Rather, the Bureau routinely approves these transfers subject to certain conditions, including the availability of surplus water and consistency with the transferor's contract with

---

[17] O'Brien, "Water Marketing in California," 1988, 19 *Pac. L.J.*, pages 1165, 1181.

[18] Thompson, "Institutional Perspectives on Water Policy and Markets," 1993, 81 *Cal.L.Rev.*, pages 671, 719, citing Gray, "Water Transfers in California: 1981-1989" (Gray Study), published in MacDonnell, *The Water Transfer Process as a Management Option for Meeting Changing Water Demands*, 1990, chapter 2, page 22.

the Bureau and with federal reclamation law. Such transfers must be for the current water-delivery year only.

Aside from transfers between individual contractors, two groups of contractors have set up permanent "pooling" systems. The Sacramento River Contractors Association entered into a pooling agreement in 1974, and the Tehama-Colusa Canal Authority set up one in 1981. The pools establish "banks" where participants can "deposit" water when they have excess and withdraw water when they need it.

In addition to the above arrangements, the Bureau itself has "transferred" water within its service area by "wheeling" water through the California Aqueduct, owned and operated by the California Department of Water Resources. These were not true transfers of water because the Bureau retained the right to use the water. As part of a "Coordinated Operating Agreement" signed by the two entities in 1986, DWR agreed to make excess capacity in the aqueduct available to the Bureau to transfer water from the Delta to the users in the San Joaquin Valley. The agreement allows the Bureau to "wheel" water through the Aqueduct by diverting water from the Delta through DWR's pumping plant at Clifton Court Forebay. The Bureau's transfer of water through the California Aqueduct is subject to approval by the State Board because it requires a change in the Bureau's point of diversion under its state water rights permits.

The Bureau submitted ten applications for temporary urgency changes to the State Board for such transfers between 1985 and 1989. All were approved by the State Board. With one exception, the purpose of each of the transfers was to provide for environmental needs (for example, to assist salmon spawning and migration, to provide greater flows in the Delta, to supply water to wildlife refuges in the San Joaquin Delta).

**Transfers outside the CVP Service Area.** Prior to 1992, transfers of CVP water to areas outside the CVP service area were not allowed, and water districts had the power to block extrajurisdictional transfers of CVP water. On October 30, 1992, President Bush signed into law a significant piece of legislation governing transfers of water from the CVP, known as the Central Valley Project Improvement Act. (P.L. 102-575, 106 Stat. 4706.) The CVPIA lists as one of its many purposes—

> to increase water-related benefits provided by the [CVP] to the State of California through expanded use of voluntary water transfers and improved water conservation. CVPIA § 3402(e).

The Act's provisions regarding water transfers are found in Section 3405. Section 3405(a) provides that all individuals or districts who receive CVP water are entitled to transfer all or part of that water to "any other California water user or water agency, State or Federal agency, Indian Tribe or private non-profit organization for [CVP] purposes or any purpose recognized as beneficial under appiicable State law." As long as the transfer meets certain enumerated conditions, the exact terms of such transfers are to be mutually agreed upon by the transferor and transferee. CVPIA § 3405(a). Therefore, a farmer who receives CVP water (but who does not necessarily hold the water contract or the water right himself) can transfer the water he would have received to a non-CVP individual or entity such as a city.

*The CVPIA allows transfers outside the CVP service area.*

*Not only water districts but also individual farmers may transfer water received from the federal CVP.*

The Act mandates that all transfers of CVP water be subject to review and approval by the Secretary of the Interior. Transfers involving more than 20 percent of CVP water subject to a long-term contract within any contracting district or agency are also subject to review and approval by that district or agency. CVPIA § 3405(a)(1). Decisions on water transfers subject to review by a district/agency or by the Secretary must be rendered within 90 days of their receipt of a written transfer proposal from the transferee or transferor. CVPIA § 3405(a)(2)(A). Transfers must be approved if they meet the terms and conditions specified in the Act. CVPIA § 3405(a)(2)(A). If a transfer is disapproved, the district/agency or Secretary must specify, in writing, why the transfer does not comply with the Act and what alternatives, if any, could be included to make the transfer comply. CVPIA § 3405(a)(2)(B). A transfer is deemed approved if the district/agency or Secretary fails to act on a proposed transfer within 90 days. CVPIA § 3405(a)(2)(D).

*Under certain conditions, approval of the local water district, as well as of the Secretary of the Interior, is required for a transfer.*

The Act sets forth several conditions that CVP transfers must meet (§ 3405(a)(1)(A)-(M)), summarized below.

*Transfer conditions*

- Transfers are limited to water actually delivered to a CVP contractor, on average, over a three-year period, and to water consumptively used or irretrievably lost to beneficial use during the period in question.

- All water transferred to a non-CVP agricultural user must be repaid at the greater of the full cost or cost of service rates. Water transferred for municipal and industrial purposes is to be paid at the greater of the cost-of-service or municipal and industrial rates.

- All transfers must be between willing buyers and willing sellers under mutually agreed-upon terms and conditions.

- Transfers must be consistent with State law, including provisions of the California Environmental Quality Act.

- All transfers are deemed "beneficial uses" of water by the transferors as that term is used in Section 8 of the 1902 Reclamation Act.

- All transfers for use outside the CVP service area are subject to a right of first refusal by entities within the CVP service area as long as the right of first refusal is exercised within 90 days and the entity exercising the right compensates the transferee for the total costs associated with the development and negotiation of the transfer.

- No transfer confers supplemental or additional benefits on CVP water contractors as provided in Section 203 of Pub. L. 97-293. 43 U.S.C. § 390(cc).

- Transfers cannot be approved if they violate the provisions of this or other federal law or will have significant adverse effect on the Secretary's ability to deliver water pursuant to CVP contractual obligations or fish and wildlife obligations under the Act because of limitations in conveyance or pumping capacity.

- Transfers cannot be approved if they will have significant long-term adverse impacts on groundwater conditions in the transferor's service area.

- Transfers cannot be approved if they will unreasonably impact the water supply, operations, or financial conditions of the transferor's contracting district or agency or its water users.

- Transfers cannot be approved if they will significantly reduce the quantity or quality of water currently used for fish and wildlife purposes, unless the Secretary determines, pursuant to findings, that such adverse effects would be more than offset by the benefits of the proposed transfer. In making such a determination, the Secretary must develop and implement alternatives and mitigation measures to provide fish and wildlife benefits substantially equivalent to those lost as a consequence of the transfer.

- Transfers between CVP contractors within counties, watersheds, or other areas of origin, as those terms are utilized under California law, are deemed to meet the conditions set forth in the first point above.

This Act is expected to significantly improve the process for transfers of CVP water by providing that both the supplying district and individual user have the right to sell water. It also allows sales of water outside the CVP service area for the first time and allows

CVP conveyance facilities to be used for transfers of water from agricultural to municipal and industrial users. However, some of the requirements, especially those protecting fish and wildlife and groundwater conditions, may substantially limit the actual quantity of water available for transfer, especially for transfers outside the CVP service area.

The Bureau has issued interim guidelines for implementing transfers under the CVPIA. The interim guidelines (February 19, 1993 version) include conditions for transfers that parallel and interpret the conditions set forth in the Act. In addition, these guidelines provide, among other things, that a transferee can subsequently transfer water during the period of the initial transfer. The transferee is then treated as a transferor for purposes of meeting the conditions in the Act and interim guidelines. All long-term transfers will be reviewed annually by the Bureau to ensure that no changes in CVP operations or environmental conditions have occurred. All transfers of CVP water outside the place of use specified in the CVP's state permits must be approved by the State Water Resources Control Board. Bureau Interim Guidelines, page 5.

The interim guidelines also make clear that it is the transferor's responsibility to comply with all transfer criteria as well as all state and federal laws including CEQA, the National Environmental Policy Act (NEPA), and the state and federal Endangered Species Acts. Bureau Interim Guidelines, page 5. A claim that implementation of the CVPIA was subject to NEPA was rejected. *Westlands Water District et al. v. United States*, 9th Cir. Dec. 22, 1994, 94 Daily Journal D.A.R. 17892.

**NEPA = The National Environmental Policy Act**

In September 1993, MWD approved in concept the first agricultural-to-urban water transfer under the Central Valley Project Improvement Act. Under the proposed agreement, MWD would pay $6.25 million to Areias Dairy Farms of Los Banos for up to 35,000 acre feet of water over a 15-year period. Another $375,000 would be paid into the environmental restoration fund established under the Act.[19]

*The MWD-Areias Dairy Farms agreement represents the first effort to transfer water outside the CVP service area.*

**Transfers of SWP Water.** In contrast to the CVP contractors, only a few transfers between SWP contractors have occurred. The Castaic Lake Water Agency has purchased 8,500 acres of land within the Devil's Den Water District. Castaic plans to retire this land and transfer the water previously used on the land through the California

---

[19] *California Water Law and Policy Reporter*, November 1993, page 26.

Aqueduct to its service area sometime in 1997. This is an example of "water ranching" or "farming" where an entity purchases land to obtain the accompanying water rights.[20]

The Kern County Water Agency and Kings County Water Agency, both SWP contractors, have water transfer programs for their member agencies. Transfers that have occurred under these programs have been between agricultural users or from municipal users to agricultural users.

### Transfers of Colorado River Water

*MWD's land fallowing agreement with the Palo Verde Irrigation District*

**PVID = Palo Verde Irrigation District**

In addition to the Metropolitan Water District/Imperial Irrigation District transfer of Colorado River water referred to above, MWD has reached a Colorado River water transfer agreement with the Palo Verde Irrigation District (PVID). Pursuant to this agreement, up to 22,000 acres within PVID's service area would be fallowed over a two-year period. MWD would compensate the landowners and lessees of the land and receive up to 20,000 acre feet of water.

*MWD's Colorado River-SWP exchange with the Coachella Valley Water District and the Desert Water Agency*

**CVWD = Coachella Valley Water District**

**DWA = Desert Water Agency**

The Coachella Valley Water District (CVWD) and the Desert Water Agency (DWA), both SWP contractors, have also entered into "exchange" agreements with MWD. Under these agreements, CVWD and DWA exchange their SWP entitlements for an equal amount of MWD's Colorado River water. From the point of view of the two desert agencies, the exchange was made because they are not connected to the SWP system. Their delivery point is near San Bernardino at the Devil's Canyon Afterbay, some 50 miles away from the Coachella Valley. However, MWD's Colorado River Aqueduct runs through the service areas of both CVWD and DWA, and water is immediately available. Under the exchange, Colorado River water is released by MWD into the Whitewater River channel and then delivered to large spreading grounds, where it percolates underground and recharges the wells of the two local agencies. MWD then takes the SWP entitlements from its own delivery points on the California Aqueduct.

The arrangement is also beneficial to MWD. Not only does it receive water of better quality, but it also can take Colorado River water whenever any surplus is available and bank it underground in the Coachella Valley. In essence, it can pre-pay its obligations to CVWD and DWA. At times, MWD has placed in excess of 400,000 acre feet in storage under these agreements, which were originally made in 1967 and were amended in 1983 to extend their terms until 2035.

[20] *A Guide to Water Transfers in California*, page 2.

## Transfers of Delta Water

One area in California that has the potential to provide for significant water transfers is the Sacramento-San Joaquin Delta. However, currently there are no facilities which would allow for efficient transfers of water from north of the Delta to areas where it is needed south of the Delta. Such facilities continue to be controversial since the defeat in 1982 by the electorate of the Peripheral Canal, a proposed 42-mile canal that would have taken water from the Sacramento River and transported it around the Delta.

*Transfers from areas upstream of the Delta, and across the Delta for export south, are constrained by current Delta standards.*

Some advocates of Delta transfers are still in favor of an isolated transfer facility, while others favor widening existing channels and continuing to use "through Delta" transfers.[21] Transfers through the Delta continue to be discussed by urban, environmental, and agricultural interests. Environmentalists want to link any Delta transfer facilities to some type of limit on exports. Agricultural water users want long-term water marketing to be tied to construction of future facilities to increase the capacity of the State Water Project. Urban water users believe that an isolated channel is needed to protect fishery resources by reducing or eliminating pumping from the Delta and to ensure high-quality domestic water. These could be the purposes of an isolated channel, along with the accommodation of water transfers, rather than an increase in the export and use of natural flow.

*A Delta facility could be designed primarily to accommodate water transfers rather than increases in exports of the natural flows.*

## Emergency Drought Water Banks

One type of transfer mechanism that developed and gained attention during the prolonged California drought during the 1980s and early 1990s was the "water bank," intended to encourage those with available water to "deposit" it in a "bank," so those who needed water could "withdraw" it.

*The 1991 Drought Water Bank was extraordinarily successful; all types of transfers were involved.*

As a result of the continuing drought in California, Governor Wilson signed Executive Order No. W-3-91 in 1991, which established a "drought action team" comprised of state and federal officials. In February 1991, the drought action team prepared a report for the governor which included a number of recommendations. One of those recommendations was that the state develop an "Emergency Drought Water Bank." The purpose of the Drought Water Bank would be to develop water to meet four critical needs: (1) carryover storage for 1992; (2) protection of fish and wildlife and their habitats; (3) municipal and industrial uses; and (4) agricultural uses. DWR was given the responsibility for operating the Drought Water Bank.

[21] *Western Water,* page 6.

## Table 8-2
## Water Distribution for the 1991 Drought Water Bank
### in 1,000s of acre-feet

| Item | Jan | Feb | Mar | Apr | May | Jun | Jul | Aug | Sep | Oct | Nov | Dec | Total |
|---|---|---|---|---|---|---|---|---|---|---|---|---|---|
| **Water Supply** | | | | | | | | | | | | | |
| *Delta Fallowing* | 0 | 0 | 0 | 29 | 42 | 55 | 82 | 55 | 15 | 7 | 0 | 0 | 285 |
| *Ground Water Exchange* | | | | | | | | | | | | | |
| Sacramento River | 0 | 0 | 0 | 7 | 15 | 17 | 26 | 17 | 18 | 4 | 0 | 0 | 104 |
| Feather River | 0 | 0 | 0 | 28 | 21 | 14 | 23 | 8 | 2 | 4 | 0 | 0 | 100 |
| Yuba River | 0 | 0 | 0 | 0 | 0 | 0 | 29 | 53 | 0 | 0 | 0 | 0 | 82 |
| *Non-Delta Fallowing* | | | | | | | | | | | | | |
| Above Shasta reservoir | 0 | 0 | 0 | 0 | 2 | 1 | 2 | 2 | 0 | 0 | 0 | 0 | 7 |
| Below Shasta reservoir | 0 | 0 | 0 | 1 | 11 | 9 | 10 | 7 | -2 | 1 | 0 | 0 | 37 |
| *Storage Releases* | | | | | | | | | | | | | |
| Yuba County Water Agency | 0 | 0 | 0 | 0 | 0 | 0 | 0 | 0 | 84 | 15 | 0 | 0 | 99 |
| Browns Valley I.D. | 0 | 0 | 0 | 0 | 0 | 0 | 5 | 0 | 0 | 0 | 0 | 0 | 5 |
| Oroville-Wyndotte I.D. | 0 | 0 | 0 | 0 | 0 | 0 | 0 | 0 | 0 | 0 | 10 | 0 | 10 |
| Little Holland | 0 | 0 | 0 | 0 | 0 | 0 | 0 | 0 | 0 | 1 | 1 | 0 | 2 |
| Wilson & McCall Inc. | 0 | 0 | 0 | 0 | 1 | 0 | 0 | 0 | 0 | 0 | 0 | 0 | 1 |
| TOTAL WATER SUPPLY | 0 | 0 | 0 | 65 | 92 | 96 | 172 | 147 | 117 | 32 | 11 | 0 | 732 |
| **Water Disposal** | | | | | | | | | | | | | |
| *Delta Exports* | | | | | | | | | | | | | |
| H.O. Banks Pumping Plant | 0 | 0 | 0 | 2 | 6 | 9 | 40 | 80 | 116 | 133 | 14 | 0 | 400 |
| *Carriage Water* | 0 | 0 | 0 | 0 | 1 | 1 | 7 | 13 | 19 | 22 | 2 | 0 | 65 |
| TOTAL WATER DISPOSAL | 0 | 0 | 0 | 2 | 7 | 10 | 47 | 96 | 135 | 155 | 16 | 0 | 465 |
| **SWP/CVP Storage Change** | 0 | 0 | 0 | 63 | 85 | 86 | 125 | 54 | -18 | -123 | -5 | 0 | 267 |

Several factors allowed the 1991 Drought Water Bank to function efficiently. Two key pieces of emergency legislation were passed in 1991 which helped speed the bank's implementation. AB 9X gave water suppliers explicit authority to enter into contracts with the water bank or with other water suppliers for transfer of water outside the water supplier's service area. AB 10X declared that no temporary transfer of water under any provision of law for drought relief in 1991 or 1992 would affect any water right.

In addition, the 1991 water bank was set up so that DWR was able to work with potential buyers as a group (represented by a water purchase committee), rather than working with numerous parties negotiating separate transfers. Farmers and water districts

## Table 8-3
## Water Distribution for the 1992 Drought Water Bank
### in 1,000s of acre-feet

| Item | Jan | Feb | Mar | Apr | May | Jun | Jul | Aug | Sep | Oct | Nov | Dec | Total |
|---|---|---|---|---|---|---|---|---|---|---|---|---|---|
| **Water Supply** | | | | | | | | | | | | | |
| *Ground Water Exchange* | | | | | | | | | | | | | |
| Sacramento River | 0 | 0 | 0 | 0 | 0 | 9 | 14 | 14 | 14 | 3 | 0 | 0 | 54 |
| Feather River | 0 | 0 | 0 | 0 | 0 | 1 | 12 | 14 | 13 | 10 | 0 | 0 | 50 |
| Delta (East Contra Costa) | 0 | 0 | 0 | 0 | 0 | 0 | 0 | 1 | 1 | | | | 2 |
| *Storage Releases* | | | | | | | | | | | | | |
| Browns Valley I.D. | 0 | 0 | 0 | 0 | 0 | 0 | 0 | 2 | 3 | 0 | 0 | 0 | 5 |
| Oroville-Wyndotte I.D | 0 | 0 | 0 | 0 | 0 | 0 | 0 | 0 | 0 | 0 | 10 | 0 | 10 |
| Placer County Water Agency | 0 | 0 | 0 | 0 | 0 | 0 | 0 | 0 | 6 | 4 | 0 | 0 | 10 |
| Oakdale I.D./ So. San Joaquin I.D. | 0 | 0 | 0 | 0 | 0 | 0 | 0 | 15 | 14 | 21 | 0 | 0 | 50 |
| Merced I.D. | 0 | 0 | 0 | 0 | 0 | 0 | 0 | 0 | 0 | 7 | 5 | 0 | 12 |
| TOTAL WATER SUPPLY | 0 | 0 | 0 | 0 | 0 | 10 | 26 | 46 | 51 | 45 | 15 | 0 | 193 |
| **Water Disposal** | | | | | | | | | | | | | |
| *Delta Exports* | | | | | | | | | | | | | |
| H.O. Banks Pumping Plant | 0 | 0 | 0 | 0 | 0 | 0 | 0 | 28 | 28 | 13 | 0 | 0 | 69 |
| Tracy Pumping Plant | 0 | 0 | 0 | 0 | 0 | 0 | 32 | 20 | 4 | 5 | 4 | 0 | 65 |
| Contra Costa Canal Pumping Plant | 0 | 0 | 0 | 0 | 0 | 0 | 0 | 0 | 2 | 8 | 0 | 0 | 10 |
| *Carriage Water* | 0 | 0 | 0 | 0 | 0 | 0 | 6 | 10 | 9 | 7 | 1 | 0 | 33 |
| TOTAL WATER DISPOSAL | 0 | 0 | 0 | 0 | 0 | 0 | 38 | 58 | 43 | 34 | 5 | 0 | 178 |
| **SWP/CVP Storage Change** | 0 | 0 | 0 | 0 | 0 | 10 | -12 | -12 | 8 | 11 | 10 | 0 | 15 |

*15 TAF allocated t0 DFG but not scheduled for delivery, therefore, not exported (pumped) from the Delta

were the sellers of water; municipal and other agricultural users purchased water. DWR and the Bureau of Reclamation also worked together to operate their reservoirs to hold the purchased water until sufficient canal and pumping capacity was available to move it to the buyers.[22] Through the 1991 water bank, DWR purchased about 820,000 acre feet of water for $125 per acre foot from farmers who agreed to fallow their land, from farmers who gave up their surface diversions and shifted to groundwater, and from water districts that sold stored water in surface reservoirs. About 400,000

*In 1991, through the Bank, DWR purchased more than 800,000 acre-feet for $125 per acre-foot and sold about half to cities and farmers for $175 per acre-foot; the balance was stored to protect against the possible continuation of the drought.*

[22] Potter and Sergent, "Water Transfers and the Drought: Were They Good for You?" April 1992, *California Water Law and Policy Reporter,* page 123.

acre feet were sold to urban and agricultural buyers for $175 an acre foot (excluding transportation costs). Much of the remaining water was used to maintain Delta salinity standards. The State Water Project also purchased water for carryover storage and waterfowl and fisheries resources.

According to most commentators, the 1991 Drought Water Bank was highly successful in meeting the state's water needs for 1991, but it did have some problems. Many farmers who sold their water to the water bank fallowed their land. Yolo County officials claimed that such actions caused the loss of 450 jobs. However, DWR rejected this claim, in part because it did not believe there was reliable information to link the number of unemployed farm workers to fallowed land.

A preliminary study of the 1991 water bank revealed that half the water for the bank came from fallowing approximately 170,000 acres of land, and most third-party effects stemmed from this fallowing. Despite these effects, observers asserted that the benefits to cities and other buyers outweighed income lost to rural communities by about $92 million.[23]

Since the drought continued, another bank was created in March 1992. Demands were substantially lower than in 1991 because the reduction in SWP deliveries was less, and local conservation efforts in 1992 were successful. There were 20 sellers and 16 buyers in the 1992 bank (compared to 350 sellers and 13 buyers in 1991). Water was purchased mostly from groundwater and from some surface supplies, not from fallowing as in 1991. About 193,000 acre feet were purchased.[24]

## Constraints on Transfers

### Type of Right as Constraint

***Appropriative Rights.*** As noted above, post-1914 appropriators may change their point of diversion, place of use, or purpose of use, but only upon permission from the State Board.[25] Before such permission is granted, the person seeking the change must establish that the change "will not operate to the injury of any legal user of the

---

23 *Western Water,* pages 8-9.

24 Potter, "Water Transfers in 1993: Relationships between Federal, State, Local, and Individual Water Systems" (unpublished report), presented at March 19, 1993 Continuing Legal Education seminar, San Francisco.

25 Pre-1914 appropriators are neither required nor permitted to request Board permission to change the purpose of use. A pre-1914 appropriator may change the purpose of use "without such permission and also without whatever protection such permission might afford him." Code Commission Note following Water Code § 1700.

water involved." Water Code § 1702. Under this "no-injury rule," senior appropriators may not change their water uses if it will harm junior water users. The "no-injury" rule also limits changes to pre-1914 appropriative rights. Water Code § 1706.

Appropriators with junior rights often depend upon the return flow from senior users for their water supply. If a senior user transfers his or her use to another user in a different place, these return flows will no longer be available to the junior user in the original place of use. Thus, the no-injury rule may prevent water transfers in some instances if the transfer undertaken by a senior user will adversely affect any junior users on that particular water system. *See,* for example, *Scott v. Fruit Growers Supply Co.* (1927) 202 Cal. 47, 55. Some transferors have attempted to overcome this limitation by transferring only that portion of water previously consumed by their use, leaving the portion attributed to return flow in the stream.

Transfers of pre-1914 appropriative rights face special problems because pre-1914 rights, while quantified by use, are not measured or limited by a permit or license from the State Board. Therefore, the quantified amounts are subject to proof of beneficial use over many years, and transferring a specified amount of water can be difficult.

**Riparian Rights.** While the holder of an appropriative right may use and divert water away from the watercourse, a riparian water right is limited to reasonable and beneficial use of water on the land which abuts the water course, taking into account the riparian rights of others. *Anaheim Union Water Co. v. Fuller* (1907) 150 Cal. 327. Riparian uses of water do not require a permit from the State Board for their exercise and are not lost by nonuse. Thus, as with pre-1914 rights which do not require a permit, riparian rights are not easily quantifiable. These characteristics can hamper transfers of riparian rights. However, such transfers may be possible if others who share the water source agree to the transfer, or if the legislature should specifically intervene. Moreover, where riparian or overlying rights have been quantified in an adjudication, transfer of such decreed rights may be permitted.

### Groundwater

**Limits on non-overlying use.** Just as a riparian right is limited to use on land adjoining the watercourse, an overlying right to use percolating groundwater is limited to reasonable, beneficial use on the land overlying the groundwater basin. *Peabody v. Vallejo* (1935) 2 Cal.2d 351, 372. Like a riparian right, groundwater rights are correlative, that is, shared among all users of a common basin. Overlying rights are neither gained by use nor lost by disuse but are considered part and parcel of the land. *Burr v. Maclay Rancho Water Company* (1911) 160 Cal. 268, 281-282.

If groundwater is transferred to land which does not overlie the basin, California law considers this to be an appropriation of water. *Katz v. Walkinshaw* (1903) 141 Cal. 116, 135-136. Overlying rights extend only to the quantity of water necessary for beneficial use on the overlying land, and appropriators may take only what is surplus to overlying rights. *Katz*, page 136. As discussed in chapter 2, the acquisition of an appropriative right occurs on a "first in time, first in right" basis. Those who begin to pump groundwater and transfer it for appropriative use first would have a higher priority right than those who put the groundwater to a later-in-time appropriative use. This, however, becomes important only in situations where a basin does not have surplus water available for all appropriations. *See Pasadena v. Alhambra* (1949) 33 Cal.2d 908.

Under California law, the rights of overlying users are paramount and superior to the rights of those who use groundwater outside the basin. *See Corona Foothill Lemon Co. v. Lillibridge* (1937) 8 Cal.2d 522, 529-531. Thus, a transfer of groundwater outside the basin is deemed to be inferior (with regard to priority) to an overlying right and to the rights of prior appropriators. *Katz*, page 136. Again, priorities are only important in basins which are used by many pumpers and which are overdrafted. Groundwater may generally be transferred outside the basin if other overlying users do not object.

As with pre-1914 and riparian rights, overlying rights are not easily quantifiable, which makes determining the amount of water available for transfer difficult. In basins which have been "adjudicated" (that is, the amount of water each overlying user may extract has been determined by a court), transfers may be easier.

*Local ordinances have been enacted to prevent the transfer of groundwater.*

***Groundwater management statutes and ordinances.*** As a further complication to transferring groundwater, some state laws and county ordinances that purport to manage groundwater were actually enacted to prevent the export of groundwater. These legal restrictions can be powerful barriers to transfers of groundwater, since the pressure on politicians brought by local residents to restrict out-of-county exports can be tremendous.

In Monterey County, for example, the Monterey Peninsula Water Management District may require groundwater producers, both overlying users and exporters, to reduce groundwater extractions. Water Code App. §§ 118-365. The Monterey County Water Resources

Agency is also authorized "to develop and distribute water to persons in exchange for ceasing or reducing groundwater extractions, and to prevent groundwater extractions which are determined to be harmful to the groundwater basin." Water Code App. §§ 52-9(o) This language may be broad enough to allow the agency to limit or prohibit groundwater extractions for export.

State law also limits groundwater exports within Sierra and Plumas counties by providing that no groundwater shall be exported from the Sierra Valley and Long Valley groundwater basins unless the exporter has obtained a permit from the managing district. The district establishes the quantity of water which may be exported and the conditions of export. Water Code App. §§ 119-706. Similar groundwater management exists in other counties pursuant to state law.[26]

Counties have also adopted their own ordinances to regulate groundwater exports. Imperial County enacted an ordinance designed to prevent export of groundwater to Mexico. Imperial County Ordinance No. 432 (Nov. 21, 1972) adding §§ 56200 *et seq.* to Imperial County Codified Ordinances. Butte and Glenn counties enacted ordinances during the 1977 drought that require permits to be obtained, after hearing, for groundwater exports. Ord. No. 1859 (Aug. 23, 1977), adding §§ 33-1 *et seq.* to Butte County Code; Ord. No. 672 (Sept. 6, 1977), adding §§ 20.04.010 *et seq.* to Glenn County Code. An ordinance adopted by Inyo County contains detailed procedures for obtaining a permit to pump groundwater, but it was intended to limit or prevent exports of groundwater by the City of Los Angeles. Inyo County Code §§ 7.01.010 *et seq.* (added by referendum in 1980). Other counties have enacted similar ordinances. For example, Sacramento Ord. No. 410, § 2 (Feb. 26, 1980), adding section 15.08.095 to the Sacramento County Code; Nevada Ord. No. 1365 (Jan. 27, 1986), adding sections L-X 6.1 *et seq.* to the Nevada County Land Use and Development Code; Tehama Ord. No. 1552 (Feb. 4, 1992), adding Chapter 9.40 to the Tehama County Code. In general, these ordinances all set up some type of permit scheme pursuant to which an intended exporter must submit specified hydrogeological

---

[26] For example, Water Code App. §§ 123-411, 125-411, and 126-411, establishing programs in Colusa, Sutter, and Placer counties to establish priorities for use of groundwater with exports receiving the lowest priority; §§ 124-101 *et seq.* establishing the Pajaro Valley Water Management Agency, operative in Santa Cruz and Monterey Counties, which has the power to regulate groundwater extractions (§§ 124-711, 712); §§ 128-201 and 129-101 establishing the Mono County Tri-Valley Groundwater Management District and Honey Lake Valley Groundwater Basin (in Lassen County), respectively, and requiring exporters to obtain permits.

data to an administrative body in order to assure that certain problems (such as overdraft) do not occur.

The validity of statutes and ordinances of this kind is questionable. They may conflict with Article 10, Section 2, of the California Constitution which requires that water resources of the state be put to reasonable use to the maximum extent possible. The Sierra/ Plumas Counties law may violate the interstate commerce clause, since this law was designed to protect those counties from pumping by the state of Nevada.[27] In fact, both the Inyo and Nevada County ordinances were struck down in unpublished trial court opinions on the ground that they were preempted by state law. Inyo County settled the suit brought by the city of Los Angeles against its ordinance by agreeing, among other things, not to enforce its ordinance against the city. The validity of the Tehama County ordinance, however, was upheld by the Court of Appeal. *Baldwin v. County of Tehama,* (1994) 31 Cal.App.4th 166.

***Groundwater management plans.*** In 1992, Assembly Bill 3030 added sections 10750 through 10755.4 to the Water Code. These provisions allow local agencies that provide water service and whose service areas include a groundwater basin,[28] or a portion of a groundwater basin, to adopt a groundwater management plan. Water Code § 10753. Adjudicated and low-yield basins are excluded. Water Code §§ 10753(a); 10750.2(b).

This legislation does not specifically authorize groundwater export limitations. However, agencies may attempt to limit or control exports in the development of their "groundwater management plans." The components of such plans include mitigation for overdraft and monitoring well levels. Water Code § 10753.7. Agencies are somewhat limited in their enforcement abilities by Section 10753.8(c), which provides that limitations in extractions are authorized only if the agency has determined "through study and investigation" that groundwater replenishment programs or alternative sources of supply are "insufficient or infeasible" to lessen the demand for groundwater. Water Code § 10753.8(c).

## Area of Origin Protections

*Area of origin protections are more technical and limited in scope than most people believe.*

California has adopted certain "area of origin" statutes that are designed, in part, to provide to local areas protection from the export of water. However, these statutes are more technical and limited in scope than people generally believe. Indeed there have been

[27] Kletzing, pages 1225, 1261-1262.

[28] "Groundwater basin" is defined as basins identified in DWR Bulletin No. 118, September 1975. Water Code § 10752(b).

few, if any, direct applications enforcing these statutes. As a practical matter, the protection they provide is very narrow.

The concept of area of origin protections first arose when the California legislature in 1927 adopted the Feigenbaum Act, which authorized the state to file for unappropriated water in its development of the State Water Project. 1927 Stat. Ch. 286, §§ 1-2, pages 508-510 (codified as amended at Water Code §§ 10500-10507). When these provisions were enacted, counties from which the water would be taken expressed concern about the effects of the loss of water from their areas. In 1931, the legislature amended the Feigenbaum Act to protect counties from which the water originated. Water Code § 10505 now provides: "No priority under this part shall be released nor assignment made of any application that will, in the judgment of the [State Board], deprive the county in which the water covered by the application originates of any such water necessary for the development of the county."

This "county of origin" law applies only to DWR's appropriations for the State Water Project. Counties of origin are not protected as to waters of streams upon which there are no state filings. Water Code § 10505; *see also* Rogers and Nichols, *Water for California* (1967), page 116.

*The "county of origin" law applies only to DWR appropriations for the SWP.*

Areas of origin were also purported to be protected when the Central Valley Project Improvement Act[29] was adopted in 1993. 1933 Stat. Ch. 1042 (codified as amended in Water Code §§ 11100-11198). This Act contains what is known as the "Watershed Protection Act," which provides that the watershed of origin or areas "immediately adjacent thereto which can conveniently be supplied with water therefrom," are given a paramount right to the use of the water. Water Code § 11460. At the state level, this provision is limited only to DWR. Water Code § 11461. As construed, if a dam and reservoir were constructed to serve the area of origin, the water rights for that project would be prior to those of DWR. The local area also has a right to be served by DWR's project, but only upon appropriate payment.[30]

*The Watershed Protection Act*

Area of origin protection was also granted specifically to the Sacramento-San Joaquin Delta in 1959 when the California legislature adopted the Delta Protection Act. Water Code §§ 12200-12227. This Act incorporates by reference the county of origin and watershed protection statutes above and declares as a policy of the state

*The Delta Protection Act*

---

[29] The Central Valley Project Improvement Act was later incorporated by reference into the Burns-Porter Act of 1959. Water Code § 12931.

[30] For a complete analysis of the "county of origin" law and "Watershed Protection Act," see 25 Ops. Cal.Atty.Gen. 8 (1955) and 29 Ops.Cal.Atty Gen. 136 (1957).

"that no person, corporation or public or private agency or the State or the United States should divert water from the channels of the Sacramento-San Joaquin Delta to which the users within said Delta are entitled." Water Code §§ 12201, 12203. The word "entitled" seems to limit protection from this statute to rights that such users would have in any event under their existing water rights.[31]

*Other "protected" areas*

In 1984, the legislature adopted statutes for "protected areas." Water Code §§ 1215-1222. Pursuant to these statutes, water users in designated "protected areas" are given the right to obtain a water right which would have priority over the rights of an exporter. In addition, the statutes give such water users the right to purchase water made available by the construction of any "works by a water supplier exporting or intending to export water for use outside the protected area." Water Code §§ 1216, 1217(a). The statutes apply only to applications to appropriate water filed after January 1, 1985. The applications for California's major projects like the CVP and SWP were, of course, filed long before then. The "protected areas" include all lands within the following river systems: Sacramento River; Mokelumne River; Calaveras River; San Joaquin River; Mono Lake; the combined Truckee, Walker, and Carson rivers; and the combined river systems which lead to the ocean from and including the Russian River system north to the California-Oregon border. Water Code § 1215.5. The counties overlying the combined Sacramento and Delta-Central Sierra basin are authorized to undertake groundwater management plans to determine the circumstances when export pumping will be permitted. Water Code § 1220.

Because they raise many uncertainties, these statutes have the potential to impact water transfers. Aside from the "protected areas" specified above, the statutes are not specific about which geographic areas are covered by area-of-origin protections, providing generally for areas "immediately adjacent" to the watershed or area of origin, "or an area immediately adjacent thereto which can conveniently be supplied with water therefrom." How much protection is granted by the area of origin statutes is unclear as well.[32] The "protected area" provisions also raise ambiguities. For example, do they bar pumping for export for use on land in another county that is within the same "protected area" as the county of origin? The elements of a "groundwater management plan" are also unspecified.

[31] In fact, the concept of "entitlement" was substituted in the Act for the concept of "need." (Cf. § 12204 as introduced in 1959 by SB 1327 to current version.)
[32] O'Brien, pages 1165, 1179.

## Economic and Social Impacts of Transfers

The transfer of water from agricultural areas to urban areas can impact the communities that depend on farming for their economic base. Third-party effects can include loss of income and jobs to agricultural suppliers, farm workers, and other farm-dependent entities, and can even extend to non-agricultural businesses. For example, if agricultural production is reduced because the associated water has been transferred to other areas, some commentators argue that the remaining agriculture may not support local businesses such as packinghouses and seed, machinery, and fertilizer distributors. The community as a whole may become less prosperous and other essential businesses, such as banks, may be adversely affected.[33]

*The farmer who sells water may profit, but what about the impact on the community?*

The Kern County Water Agency opposed attempts by at least one of its member agencies, the Berrenda Mesa Water District (BMWD), to market part of its State Water Project supply. Concern over third-party effects was stated as one of the reasons for the opposition. BMWD receives its water through the Kern County Water Agency from the State Water Project. BMWD foreclosed on the land of some of its customers when they were unable to pay for water service and proposed to market the water released by these lands.

**BMWD = Berrenda Mesa Water District**

The Kern County Water Agency argued, among other things, that its assessment of all taxpayers in Kern County of about 15 percent of the cost of delivering water to districts where agriculture predominates should prevent transfers of water out of the county. The assessment is based on the theory that all of Kern County has an interest in seeing water remain in the county to preserve its present agricultural base and to provide for future urban use. Underlying all of the Kern County Water Agency Agreements was the simple fact that the county as a whole is short of water, and the County leadership did not want to see any water leave this area. The proposed transfer was also opposed by other SWP contractors, who argued that they had the first claim on any surplus SWP supplies. In the end, BMWD was unable to sell the unneeded water because of the rules governing transfers of SWP water.

One of the current debates over water transfers is how to address these third-party effects. Legislation has been proposed that would limit how much land in an irrigation district could be fallowed due to water transfers, but it has not passed. AB 2090, Katz. Other proponents of water transfers have supported the idea of providing

[33] "Water Transfers in the West: Efficiency, Equity, and the Environment" (A National Research Council Publication), 1992, pages 226-228.

assistance to diversify rural economies, and offering job retraining for displaced farm workers.[34]

*One study concludes that transfers will primarily involve low-value crops and will have minimal impacts on rural communities.*

However, proponents of water transfers have questioned the extent of the impacts of water transfers on rural communities. According to a study prepared by the Bay Area Economic Forum and Metropolitan Water District, voluntary water marketing would have minimal impacts on rural communities because the transfers would primarily affect low-value crops.[35]

### Environmental Impacts of Transfers

Another concern over water transfers relates to the impact of such transfers on the environment. In many areas, fish, wildlife, and vegetation depend on a certain amount of water for their existence. Water transfers can take water away from these important resources.

At least two proposals to allocate additional water to rivers, wetlands, and other fish and wildlife uses have also been put forward. Some environmentalists have proposed taxing water transfers to provide the state with funds to purchase water elsewhere to use for environmental purposes. Alternatively, environmentalists have proposed that the state impose a general tax on California residents and use those funds to purchase water for such instream uses. Such taxes could, however, adversely impact water transfers by making them less attractive financially.[36]

The "public trust doctrine" also plays a role in the environmental effects of water transfers. *See* chapter 3, *supra*, for a discussion of the public trust doctrine. The California Supreme Court, in *National Audubon Society v. Superior Court* (1983) 33 Cal.3d 419, held that the public trust imposed a continuing duty to assure some level of protection of environmental needs. The public trust doctrine has been used to limit appropriations by the Los Angeles Department of Water and Power in the Mono Lake Basin. It might also be used to prevent or modify transfers from one basin to another to maintain certain water levels within a watershed of origin. The ramifications of the public trust doctrine have not been fully elaborated by the courts or the State Board. This uncertainty could hamper proposed transfers unless clearer rules and procedures to address environmental impacts are developed.[37]

---

[34] *Western Water,* page 7.
[35] *Focus,* a publication of the Metropolitan Water District, Issue 3, 1993, page 3.
[36] *Western Water,* page 7.
[37] "Water Transfers in the West," page 229.

## CHAPTER NINE
## Water Conservation[1]

### The Legal Authority to Limit the Use of Water

California Constitution Article X, Section 2, sets the benchmark against which the use of all water in California is measured. Article X, Section 2, states—

> It is hereby declared that because of the conditions prevailing in this State the general welfare requires that the water resources of the State be put to beneficial use to the fullest extent of which they are capable, and that the waste or unreasonable use or unreasonable method of use of water be prevented, and that the conservation of such waters is to be exercised with the view to the reasonable and beneficial use thereof in the interest of the people and for the public welfare. The right to water or to the use or flow of water in or from any natural stream or water course in this state is and shall be limited to such water as shall be reasonably required for the beneficial use to be served, and such right does not and shall not extend to the waste or unreasonable use or unreasonable method of use or unreasonable method of diversion of water. . . . This section shall be self-executing, and the Legislature may also enact laws in the furtherance of the policy in this section contained.

Although it is unlikely that the water problems now facing California were foreseen in 1928 when the predecessor to Article X, Section 2, was adopted, the electorate nonetheless recognized that

*The Constitution requires that "conservation" of the waters of the state be exercised with a view toward "the reasonable and beneficial use thereof in the interest of the people and for the public welfare."*

1   Initial research for this chapter was done by Kevin K. Randolph.

California needed to protect and conserve its scarce water resources. Despite the investment of billions of dollars in water storage and distribution facilities, the 1987-1992 drought demonstrated that California remains susceptible to the impacts of a sustained drought. Even in normal rainfall periods, California's ability to meet future water demands without additional development has now become questionable. A growing population, water-intensive agriculture, and the needs of the environment all place increased demands upon California's developed water supply. California's population now exceeds the projections made in the 1980's, and growth continues despite the recent economic recession.

With the political and legal constraints that have blocked additional water development in recent times, conservation has come to play an increasingly important role in the management of the state's water resources. Virtually all water purveyors have some type of conservation program in place. The legislature has provided water purveyors the legal authority to ration and allocate supplies in times of shortage. This chapter treats the authority of water suppliers to impose conservation measures when faced with shortages and the legal challenges that have been raised. It also discusses programs that have been developed to use water more efficiently.

*Conservation has come to play an increasingly important role in the management of the state's water resources.*

## Water Shortage Emergencies

***Water Code, Section 350.*** Chapter 3 of Division 1 of the Water Code, commencing with Section 350, authorizes local water suppliers to declare a water shortage emergency and to take appropriate steps to meet that emergency, including the denial of applications for new or additional service connections for its duration. One of the useful attributes of the statutory scheme is a provision that makes the chapter applicable to *any* distributor of a public water supply, whether publicly or privately owned, including mutual water companies. § 350.

*Powers of a local water supplier during a water shortage emergency*

During "emergency conditions," water suppliers can exercise the powers granted to them by Sections 350-359 of the Water Code. Section 350 provides—

> The governing body of a distributor of a public water supply, whether publicly or privately owned and including a mutual water company, may declare a water shortage emergency condition to prevail within the area served by such distributor whenever it finds and determines that the ordinary demands and requirements of water consumers cannot be satisfied without depleting the water supply of the distributor to the extent that there would be insufficient water for human consumption, sanitation, and fire protection.

Section 351 provides that, except in the event of a breakage or failure of a dam, pump, pipeline, or conduit causing an immediate emergency, the declaration of an emergency pursuant to Section 350 shall be made only after a public hearing. The public hearing allows consumers an opportunity to protest the declaration and to present their respective needs to the governing body. Once an emergency has been properly declared, a supplier is given wide discretion in deciding how to respond.

*A declaration of local emergency generally requires a public hearing.*

A water supplier may adopt such regulations and restrictions on the delivery and consumption of water "as will in the sound discretion of such governing body conserve the water supply for the greatest public benefit with particular regard to domestic use, sanitation, and fire protection." § 353. Section 356 provides that the regulations and rules adopted pursuant to Section 353 may include the right to deny applications for new or additional service connections. It also declares that the supplier may discontinue service to existing consumers who willfully violate conservation regulations and restrictions. Section 355 provides that the emergency regulations and restrictions shall remain in force during the period of the emergency and until the supply of water has been replenished or augmented.

*Emergency measures may include a moratorium on new connections.*

Frequently, it has been the imposition of a moratorium on new connections that has led to litigation about the rights of consumers to receive water service. Developers and consumers have argued that moratoria violate equal protection guarantees by treating applicants for new water service differently from existing consumers. It has also been argued (based on inverse condemnation theories) that property owners have been unconstitutionally deprived of the right to develop their property. Almost universally, these challenges have been unsuccessful.

*Swanson v. Marin Municipal Water District* (1976) 56 Cal.App. 3d 512 involved the first significant challenge to a public water supplier's moratorium based on an emergency water shortage declared pursuant to Section 350. In *Swanson*, the court rejected a property owner's claim that the water district was obligated to provide him a new service connection notwithstanding the existence of a new connection moratorium pursuant to Section 356.[2]

The *Swanson* decision provides guidance to those water suppliers enacting a new connection moratorium. First, the court held that

---

[2] Section 356 provides: "The regulations and restrictions may include the right to deny applications for new or additional service connections, and provision for their enforcement by discontinuing service to consumers willfully violating the regulations and restrictions."

Section 358[3] limits a reviewing court's analysis to a determination of whether the supplier's actions were fraudulent, arbitrary, or capricious. Second, the *Swanson* court noted that Section 355 "clearly envisions that when an undepleted supply cannot be augmented to meet increasing demand, a water shortage emergency may be declared to prevail within the service area." *Swanson,* page 520. Thus, water suppliers which enact water conservation ordinances pursuant to Section 356 need not wait until their reservoirs are empty. Water suppliers can invoke the powers granted to them under Sections 350 *et seq.* when their own forecasting predicts a water shortage. For example, in *Swanson*, at the time of declaring the emergency, the Marin Municipal Water District had more than 53,000 acre feet of water in storage, at least a two-year supply. Nonetheless, the district's forecasting indicated a significant likelihood that the district would encounter emergency shortage conditions at some point beyond that two-year window. Accordingly, the court found that the district was authorized to declare a water-shortage emergency.

One question confronting water suppliers that enact moratoria and other conservation measures is the extent of their obligation to augment their water supply. In important *dicta*, the *Swanson* court noted—

*The local water supplier has a continuing obligation to make every reasonable effort to augment its supply.*

> Nevertheless, we do foresee a continuing obligation on the part of District to exert every reasonable effort to augment its available water supply in order to meet increasing demands. Clearly, the Legislature anticipated the need for such a requirement when it limited the duration of such restriction to the period of the emergency and 'until the supply of water available for distribution within such area has been replenished or augmented.' (§ 355.) *Swanson,* page 524.

The *Swanson* court noted a duty on the part of a water supplier that has declared an emergency shortage to augment its supply but provided no further guidance on the critical question of the *extent* of the duties. That guidance came 15 years later in the case of *Building Industry Association of Northern California (BIA) v. Marin Municipal Water District* (1991) 235 Cal.App.3d 1641. The *BIA* court took up

**BIA = Building Industry Association of Northern California**

---

[3] Section 358 states: "Nothing in this chapter shall be construed to prohibit or prevent review by any court of competent jurisdiction of any finding or determination by a governing board of the existence of an emergency or of regulations or restrictions adopted by such board, pursuant to this chapter, on the ground that any such action is fraudulent, arbitrary or capricious."

the unanswered question from *Swanson* and held that, although *Swanson* imposes a duty to increase its water supply on a supplier that imposes a moratorium, the decision as to how and when to fulfill that obligation is left to the "reasonable discretion" of the supplier. The *BIA* court assured water suppliers that the courts will not substitute their discretion for the suppliers' discretion, so long as it is reasonably exercised. The *BIA* court also held that a supplier has no obligation to reallocate supplies from existing nondomestic users to serve potential domestic users.

*Hollister Park Investment Co. v. Goleta County Water Dist.* (1978) 82 Cal.App.3d 290 also provides significant assistance to those water suppliers enacting conservation measures under Sections 350 *et seq.* In *Hollister Park*, the court rejected an inverse condemnation claim based on the landowner's inability to develop his property due to a declared water shortage emergency and connection moratorium. The court reaffirmed the rule in *Swanson* that a potential water user has no compensable property interest in future water service and denied the landowner's claim. *Hollister Park,* page 294.

Water suppliers, other than cities and counties, cannot use water shortage emergencies as a pretext to implement a "no- or limited-growth" land use policy. Both the *Swanson* and *Hollister Park* courts made it clear that, although they will not generally inquire into the motives behind a supplier's water shortage emergency declaration, they will invalidate a moratorium or other conservation measure if they find evidence that the conservation measures are really being used to effectuate a no-growth or limited-growth policy. Land use decisions are within the legislative purview of cities and counties, not special districts such as municipal water districts. This issue is discussed in further detail below.

*A water district may not use a water shortage as a pretext to implement a "no-growth" policy.*

An interesting twist on the application of Sections 350 *et seq.* was presented in *Gilbert v. State of California* (1990) 218 Cal.App.3d 234. The court rejected an attempt to compel the California Department of Health Services to require the Bolinas Community Public Utility District to find ways to augment its water supply so that the district's new connection moratorium could be lifted. The court declared that it was up to the water supplier, not the state, to initiate the changes that would eliminate the need for a moratorium. The *Gilbert* court also reaffirmed the *Swanson* and *Hollister Park* principle that a water supplier could not be held liable in inverse condemnation for failing to provide new water connections. *Gilbert,* page 250; *see also Bank of America National Trust & Savings Association v. Summerland County Water District* (9th Cir. 1985) 767 F.2d 544.

The state courts have been uniform in their rejection of inverse condemnation claims based on water connection moratoria. However, the federal Ninth Circuit Court of Appeals has taken a different view and has held, in some instances, that a water connection moratorium may render a supplier liable in inverse condemnation. In *Lockary v. Kayfetz* (9th Cir. 1990) 917 F.2d 1150, the court affirmed the California rule that there is no protectable property interest in potential water use. However, the *Lockary* court considered the claimant's "development interest" separately from its interest in receiving water service. Under the appropriate circumstances, such as a supplier's moratorium that denies a property owner all economically viable use of his or her land, a supplier may be liable in inverse condemnation for the value of the lost use of the land. *Lockary,* pages 1154-55, 1157.

Unfortunately, *Lockary* involved a question of law and did not provide any factual basis against which a water supplier can evaluate its conduct to determine whether it may be exposing itself to inverse condemnation liability. Inverse condemnation claims are determined on an *ad hoc* basis, and resolution of the issue depends upon the court's answer to the amorphous question of whether the regulation has gone "too far."

The *Lockary* court may have been sympathetic to the plaintiff's claim in part because the court doubted whether a water shortage existed. The court noted that the district had granted additional water hookups for secondary units and had voluntarily relinquished rights to certain water sources after enacting the moratorium. Although not explicitly stating so, the Ninth Circuit apparently had the same concerns as the *Swanson* and *Hollister Park* courts, that the moratorium was a pretext to control land use. The message conveyed by these decisions is that courts will grant wide latitude to a water supplier dealing with a water shortage, so long as the supplier is not using the shortage as a pretext to control land use and development.

***Municipal Water Districts and County Water Districts.*** The enabling statutes of municipal and county water districts also contain specific provisions for the imposition of conservation measures. Water Code Section 71640 states that municipal water districts may restrict water services—

> [D]uring any emergency caused by drought, or other threatened or existing water shortage, and may prohibit the wastage of district water or the use of district water during such periods. . . . A district may also prohibit use of district water during such periods for specific uses which it finds to be non-essential.

Section 71640 provides an alternate basis for a municipal water district to enact water conservation measures during periods of threatened or existing water shortages. Like Sections 350 *et seq.*, Section 71640 does not require that a municipal water district wait until there is an existing, actual water shortage to enact water conservation measures and to implement prohibitions on non-essential uses of water. Violation of a water conservation ordinance adopted pursuant to Section 71641 is a misdemeanor, punishable by imprisonment for up to 30 days, a fine not exceeding $600, or both.

Section 71640 was cited by the court in *Swanson v. Marin Municipal Water District* (1976) 56 Cal.App.3d 512 as an alternate basis for upholding the new connection moratorium at issue in that case. The court noted that a municipal water district may impose restrictions on the use of water during either a threatened or existing emergency and that a district may prohibit nonessential uses of water. The *Swanson* court held that Section 71640 was not limited in its application to existing water users and could be used as the basis to justify a new connection moratorium. *Swanson*, page 521. Section 31026 of the Water Code provides nearly identical authority for county water districts.

***"Will Serve" Letters.*** Before local land use authorities will grant development or other permits, the developer is usually required to present evidence that a water supply has been secured for the project. This assurance often takes the form of a "will serve" letter from the local water supplier. When a water supplier, after having issued a will serve letter but before beginning water delivery, imposes a new connection moratorium, a question arises as to whether the will serve letter is a contractual commitment such that the water supplier must provide water service regardless of the moratorium.

In its most common form, a will serve letter is not a contractual offer but a representation that the proposed development area is within the serving district, and any resulting agreement to serve is not a contract. If the developer meets certain conditions specified by the water district, service is available to supply the property. In some instances, however, a will serve letter will be construed as a contract. The courts employ a case-by-case approach to resolving the "notice" versus "contract" issue.

If the will serve letter is intended to be a valid contract, it is essential that the parties to the contract and the subject matter of the contract be specified, and that a specific price and definite terms be set. There also must be a valid offer which manifests an intent to

*In its most common form, a "will serve" letter is not a contract.*

be bound, an acceptance of the terms of the offer, and adequate legal consideration. A will serve letter will not be construed by a court as an offer to contract unless it clearly manifests an intent to be bound. *See Winnaman v. Cambria Community Services District* (1989) 208 Cal.App.3d 49; *Santiago County Water District v. County of Orange* (1981) 118 Cal.App.3d 818.

*A "will serve" letter should specify that it is subject to the availability of water.*

To avoid being interpreted as a binding commitment, the will serve letter should specify that it is subject to the availability of water to service the development. In that event, there is no manifest intent on the part of the water supplier to be bound unless an adequate supply of water exists at the time of request for connection. Conversely, when seeking a binding commitment on the part of the water supplier, the developer should insist upon an unconditional obligation on the part of the supplier to provide water service at the time it is requested.

Even in situations where a will serve letter is construed as a contractual commitment, contractual principles, including the defense of impracticability, apply. Although there are several elements to an impracticability defense, it is essential that an event which makes performance impracticable occurs after the contract is formed. Events recognized by the courts as rendering performance impractical include acts of God and *force majeure* (acts beyond the control of the parties that could not be avoided with due care).

*One trial court ruled that a developer did not have a vested right to water service, despite the presence of a will serve agreement.*

Although not yet addressed by any appellate court, a serious drought is probably an event which would make performance of a water service contract (created by a will serve letter) impracticable. A trial court in Riverside County found that a developer had no vested right to water service, despite the presence of a will serve agreement, in the face of a new connection moratorium enacted as a result of a declared water emergency under Water Code Section 350.

### Restriction of New Hook-ups in the Absence of a Declared Emergency

Because they possess limited powers, water districts may not refuse to extend service to new users in order to control growth. In *Swanson* the court stated—

> Politically, the power to 'cut off one's water' by the simple expedient of imposing a moratorium such as the one here involved is a potent weapon in effecting a no-growth policy within a community. Since [the] District has neither the power nor the authority to initiate or implement such a policy, the imposition of any restriction on the use of its water supply for that purpose would be invalid. *Swanson,* page 524.

In short, a water district may enact new service moratoria and other conservation measures as a result of an existing or threatened water shortage, but it may not do so as a tool to implement a land use (limited-growth) policy. However, the case of *Wilson v. Hidden Valley Municipal Water District* (1967) 256 Cal.App.2d 271 presents an interesting exception.

In *Hidden Valley*, the trial court found that the district had been formed for the sole purposes of preserving the agricultural nature of the community and preventing the development which would occur if an adjoining municipal water district were able to provide water service to the area. *Hidden Valley, supra*, page 275. A landowner within the district wanted to develop his lands but could do so only if furnished water by either the adjoining district or The Metropolitan Water District of Southern California.

In order to receive service, the landowner sought to detach his lands from the district. When the district refused to allow the exclusion, the landowner sued. On appeal, the court held that the district could properly refuse to allow the detachment as a means to prevent unwanted development. Although an exception to the general rule against water supply decisions being used as a surrogate no-growth policy, the *Hidden Valley* case seems to have limited application due to its unique facts.

In contrast to water districts, it appears that cities and counties *may* refuse to provide additional connections in pursuit of a growth control policy. A municipality's ability to control land use and growth is part of its general police powers expressed in California Constitution Article XI, Section 7. In *Construction Industries Assn. v. City of Petaluma* 522 F.2d 897 (9th Cir. 1975), the court discussed the scope of a city's power to zone and control growth. In that case, certain landowners disputed the validity of the City of Petaluma's growth control measure, which included limiting the issuance of new residential building permits to 500 per year. *Petaluma*, page 901. The court rejected the plaintiffs' claim that the plan was arbitrary and unreasonable, holding—

*In contrast to water districts which lack land use authority, cities and counties may limit new connections in pursuit of a growth control policy.*

> We must determine further whether the *exclusion* bears any rational relationship to *a legitimate state interest*. If it does not, then the zoning regulation is invalid. If, on the other hand, a legitimate state interest is furthered by the zoning regulation, we must defer to the legislative act . . . . It is well settled that zoning regulations 'must find their justification in some aspect of the police power, asserted for the public welfare.' *Petaluma*, page 906.

The court then explored the scope of the city's police power and concluded that the city had a right to restrict uncontrolled growth to preserve the town's rural and family environment and to regulate growth "at an orderly and deliberate pace." *Petaluma,* pages 906-909. Other courts have ruled that the prevention of the negative effects of widespread urbanization is a valid and legitimate state interest when restricting land use. *See Village of Belle Terre v. Borass* (1974) 416 U.S. 1; *Twain Harte Associates Ltd. v. County of Tuolumne* (1990) 217 Cal.App.3d 71.

Although no cases have explicitly addressed the issue, analogous case law suggests that cities may control growth by refusing to provide additional water connections. In *Dateline Builders, Inc. v. City of Santa Rosa* (1983) 146 Cal.App.3d 520, a developer sued the city for declaratory relief and damages for the city's refusal to permit the builder to connect its housing development beyond the city's boundaries with the city's existing sewer trunk line. The city maintained that the development violated its growth plans by contributing to urban sprawl. *Dateline,* page 530. The court stated that a city may restrict the extension of utility services to control growth—

> Neither common law nor constitutional law inhibits the broad grant of power to local government officials to refuse to extend utility service so long as they do not act for personal gain nor in a wholly arbitrary or discriminatory manner. *Dateline,* page 530.

The court held that the refusal to extend utility services bore a rational relation to the legitimate government interest of "grow[ing] at an orderly pace and in a compact manner." *Dateline,* page 528.

Although the primary issue in *Dateline* was whether the city could deny utility services outside of its boundaries in order to control land use there, the court's approval should also apply with equal force within city limits. By permitting the city to deny sewer connections to control growth, *Dateline* suggests that restricting the availability of new water connections is a valid method of growth management.

Some older California case law also indicates that a water supplier may restrict supplies in the absence of emergency conditions. In *Lukrawka v. Spring Valley Water Company* (1915) 169 Cal. 318, residents of San Francisco demanded that a public water utility extend its lines to them. In explaining the parameters of a public utility's duty to provide services to additional customers, the court stated—

> [T]he right of an inhabitant of the municipality... to compel the service to them . . . is not an absolute and unqualified right.... The duty which the water company has undertaken is of a public nature

and to meet a public necessity for the supplying of water to the community. The obligation of the company is not to supply each or any number of inhabitants of the municipality on demand as an absolute right on their part but it has only assumed and become charged with the public duty of furnishing it where there is a reasonable demand for it and a reasonable extension of the service can be made to meet the demand. *Lukrawka,* pages 332-333.

Factors to be considered in determining reasonableness include, among others, the supply of water, the rights of existing customers, and the necessities of the region. *Lukrawka,* pages 333-334.

Similar concepts appear in *Butte County Water Users Assn. v. Railroad Commission* (1921) 185 Cal. 218, in which the plaintiff sought to enjoin a public utility from extending its services to new users. The court stated—

> [A] water company supplying water for irrigation has not the power to take on new customers without limit. Its power to supply water is, of course, limited by the amount of its supply, and when the demands of its consumers upon it have reached this limit, it has no right to take on new customers to the necessary injury of those it has. *Butte County,* page 230.

The court also noted that determining whether supply considerations justify restrictions must be done on a case-by-case basis. "The matter is one of judgment, a judgment which...should be exercised conservatively, but a matter of judgment nevertheless." *Butte County,* page 230. These cases imply that water suppliers can refuse to provide additional connections when to do so would impose some degree of burden on current users. However, it is unclear whether rationing or mandatory conservation measures would constitute a sufficiently severe burden to allow the water supplier to refuse new extensions of service under these common law doctrines.

## Legal Authority for Water Conservation

Following the severe 1976-77 drought, the legislature enacted Chapter 3.5 of Division 1 of the Water Code (beginning with Section 375) entitled "Water Conservation Programs." Policy provisions of the 1993 amendments to the statute declare that water conservation "is an important component of California's water policy for the future," and that all reasonable efforts to conserve water "should continue to be a high priority of California's water policy." Stats. 1993 Ch. 313. Section 375 enables any public entity which supplies

*The legislature has declared conservation to be "an important component of California's water policy for the future."*

water at either retail or wholesale to adopt a water conservation program to reduce the quantity of water used. The public entity may specifically require (except for agricultural uses) the installation of water-saving devices, such as low flow showerheads or water-saving toilets. Since the 1993 amendment, water conservation may also be encouraged through "rate structure design," that is, higher unit charges for higher usage.

The legislature has also required, since January 1, 1992, that meters be installed as a condition of *new* service of potable water. Water Code § 110. Most of the major urban areas were at the time of this legislation already fully metered. However, certain cities, such as Sacramento, were largely unmetered and still provide water on an inexpensive flat-rate basis, no matter how much water is used.

Water Code Section 1009 also authorizes water conservation programs. It provides that any public or private supplier of water for municipal uses may undertake a water conservation program and may require as a condition of new service that reasonable water saving devices and water reclamation devices be installed. Unlike Section 375, this statute applies to both public and private suppliers of water but is limited in its application to water supplied for municipal uses. Moreover, Section 1009 permits the requiring of water saving devices only as a condition of new service. Provisions similar to Section 1009 can also be found in individual enabling acts. *See,* for example, Water Code Sections 31035 and 71610.5 governing county and municipal water districts.

## Water Conservation Planning

**The Urban Water Management Planning Act.** In 1983, the legislature enacted Water Code Sections 10610 *et seq.*, entitled the "Urban Water Management Planning Act." The act is limited in its application to any publicly or privately owned water supplier providing water for municipal purposes to more than 3,000 customers, or supplying more than 3,000 acre feet of water annually. Both retail and wholesale water suppliers are included. As part of the policy provisions of the act, the legislature has declared that the conservation and efficient use of urban water supplies "are of statewide concern," and "shall be a guiding criterion in public decisions." §§ 10610.2, 10610.4. The legislature also found that "the planning for that use and implementation of those plans can best be accomplished at the local level." § 10610.2.

The act calls for the preparation of an urban water management plan which describes and evaluates the reasonable, practical, and efficient uses of the entity's supplies, including reclamation and conservation activities. The first plans were required in 1985, and more than 95 percent of the affected agencies submitted plans.[4] Although the statute provides that the components of the plan may vary according to individual community needs and characteristics, at a minimum the plan must address measures for residential, commercial, governmental, and industrial water management. The plan must also include a strategy and timetable for implementation. § 10615.

The plan must meet a number of specific requirements set forth in Section 10631, must be updated at least once every five years, and must be filed with the Department of Water Resources. § 10621. Required elements in the plan include—

*Required elements of an urban water management plan*

- An estimate of not only projected potable water use, but also of reclaimed water use
- A description of alternative conservation measures, including, but not limited to, consumer education, metering, water saving fixtures and appliances, pool covers, lawn and garden irrigation techniques, and low water use landscaping, together with an evaluation of their costs and environmental impacts
- An urban water shortage contingency plan that includes an estimate of the minimum water supply available at the end of 12, 24, and 36 months, assuming the worst case water supply shortages, and the action to be undertaken in response to such shortages
- Consumption limits in the most restrictive stage; for example, percentage reductions in water allotments, per capita allocations, and increasing block rate schedule for high usage of water with incentives for conservation, or restrictions on specific uses
- Planning and implementation steps related to such matters as water use audits, leak detection and repair, increase in the use of reclaimed water, dual water systems in new construction permitting the use of reclaimed water for flushing toilets, landscaping, golf courses, and irrigation, and the elimination of once-through cooling systems and non-recirculating water systems

The plan must be adopted at a public hearing after notice. Its preparation is exempt from CEQA, as is the implementation of the water shortage contingency portion of the plan. § 10652. Any other "project" for the implementation of the plan, including expanded or additional water supplies, remains subject to CEQA. § 10652.

[4]  *California Water Plan Update,* Department of Water Resources Bulletin, 160-93, volume 1, page 44, October 1994.

Installation of drip irrigation system for eucalyptus tree

**Agricultural Conservation.** Whether agriculture has the capacity to conserve significant amounts of water remains controversial. Environmentalists and some urban users contend that farmers can save water, while farmers respond that water comprises a significant cost of production and is not wasted. Studies with data from the 1980's demonstrate that agricultural water use is more efficient than is usually perceived.[5] Moreover, the cost of some proposed conservation measures may make growing certain crops financially impossible, which is significant since California's agriculture is a $20 billion a year industry and produces nearly one half of the nation's fruits, nuts, and vegetables.

Agriculture's applied water decreased over 4 million acre feet annually during the 1980s. This was due in part to the lack of available water during the 1987-92 drought, but also to changes in agricultural practices and increased emphasis on conservation, as well as the urbanization of some irrigated land. The amount of irrigated agricultural acreage reached its peak in 1981 at 9.7 million acres and since has declined slightly.

In 1986, the legislature made a timid move into this political thicket with the enactment of the Agricultural Water Management Planning Act. Water Code § 10800, *et seq.* This act was in some ways the counterpart of the Urban Water Management Planning Act adopted three years earlier. However, the Agricultural Act was repealed as of January 1, 1993 by the terms of Water Code Section 10855. In its place, the legislature has now enacted the Agricultural Water Supplier's Efficient Water Management Practices Act. Water Code §§ 10900 *et seq.* This legislation steps away from required plans and contains findings that agriculture is a vital industry in California which has already implemented many improvements to water use efficiency, but that the implementation of additional water management practices could further improve efficiency in many areas. § 10901.

The Act defines "efficient water management practices" (EWMPs) as "reasonable and economically justifiable programs to improve the delivery and use of water used for agricultural purposes." § 10902(b). "Water conservation" is defined as the reduction of water irretrievably lost to saline sinks, moisture-deficient soils, water surface evaporation, or noncrop evapotranspiration. Percolation from unlined canals or runoff from furrow irrigation may not constitute "waste" as some

---

[5]    *See,* for example, *California Water Plan Update,* volume 1, pages 164-165, 173-177.

generally perceive but rather may recharge the groundwater basin and be part of the downstream farmers' supply.

The Act establishes an advisory committee comprised of representatives of agriculture, the Department of Food and Agriculture, the University of California, public interest groups, and other interested parties. Water Code § 10903. The function of the committee is to review the effectiveness of EWMPs, both potential and those already in effect. The committee is now developing consensus on a list of EWMPs and their implementation.

The Act contains no mandatory provisions, but it appears that the Drought Water Bank will not be open to any area if the local water supplier is not implementing EWMPs according to the schedule agreed upon or as determined by DWR.[6] A draft list of EWMPs includes: improvement of water measurement and accounting; irrigation efficiency studies; providing farmers with normal year and real time irrigation scheduling and evapotranspiration information; monitoring water quality, soil moisture, soil salinity, groundwater elevations, and drainage water quality; lining or piping of canals and ditches; construction of tailwater reuse systems, regulatory reservoirs, and recharge basins; and "where appropriate" to facilitate alternative land uses.

Strawberries being irrigated by drip irrigation in San Diego County

## Water Use and Conservation Measures

Per capita water use in California increased steadily from the turn of the century until the 1970s.[7] The figures can be somewhat misleading, however, because they are computed by simply dividing the total amount of water used by the population. The growth thus includes the consumption by industry, commerce, and government, as well as residential use. Some water use cannot be reduced without cutting into industrial productivity and causing job loss.[8] Since the 1976-77 drought, industrial use has already been reduced significantly, largely through capital improvements to facilitate conservation and recycling. In 1980, applied industrial water amounted to 14 percent of total urban use. In 1990, this had dropped to 9 percent. Such savings, once achieved, cannot be counted on again to help meet future droughts.

*Per capita water use increased steadily from the turn of the century until the 1970s. That trend has now leveled off.*

---

[6]  1993 *Draft EIR on State Drought Water Bank,* pages 183-184.

[7]  *California Water Plan Update,* volume 1, pages 149-150.

[8]  Water is essential in the manufacturing processes of some surprising industries: aerospace, film processing, asphalt roofing materials, petroleum refining, electronics, food processing, beverages, metal fabrication, intravenous solutions, and not least, the processing of algin products from ocean kelp which are then used in many foods and pharmaceutical items.

Furrow irrigation in San Joaquin Valley

Average residential use in California, which is greatly affected by climate and the amount of single-family housing and landscaping requirements in any particular area, is now about 120 gallons per day. The San Francisco area, enjoying favorable climactic conditions, averages 104 gpd, while Southern California averages 124 gpd. Despite perceptions in the northern part of the state, the reductions in total per capita water use in Los Angeles and San Diego during the 1988-90 drought years were comparable to those in the East Bay, San Francisco, and San Jose.

It is difficult to isolate the statewide reductions in per capita water use due to conservation. While per capita water use has leveled off, and while conservation has surely been a major reason, other factors such as the trend toward multifamily housing also contribute. Conversely, population growth in warmer inland areas and higher household incomes act to offset conservation gains. Nonetheless, the Department of Water Resources estimates that urban applied water has been reduced by about 435,000 acre feet annually since 1980 by virtue of ongoing conservation programs. Net urban water demand is now about 6.8 million acre feet annually, and demands for the year 2020 are estimated at 11 million acre feet. It is clear that these requirements cannot be met, as some suggest, by conservation alone.[9]

### The 1992 Urban Water Conservation MOU

In 1992, more than 100 water agencies and 50 public interest and environmental groups signed a Memorandum of Understanding Regarding Urban Water Conservation in California. *See* Appendix B. This MOU arose out of the Bay-Delta hearing proceedings and was the result of a three-year negotiating effort by water interests, environmentalists, and state agencies. The MOU identifies 16 Best Management Practices (BMPs) for urban water use and commits the signatories to certain implementation efforts over the period 1991 to 2001. These include interior and exterior water audits and incentive programs, new and retrofit plumbing, leak detection and repair, metering and commodity rates for all new connections, landscape conservation requirements, and programs of public information and school education.

The MOU also established the California Urban Water Conservation Council to monitor progress under the MOU, and to research the feasibility of other potential BMPs. It is estimated that reductions

*DWR estimates that urban water use has been reduced by about 435,000 acre-feet annually by conservation measures.*

*It is clear, however, that future urban demands cannot be met by conservation alone.*

*In 1992, more than 100 water agencies and 50 public interest and environmental groups signed an MOU on urban water conservation.*

**BMPs = Best Management Practices**

[9] *California Water Plan Update,* volume 1, pages 153, 156.

in use due to full implementation of these BMPs will range between 7 and 10 percent of forecasted per capita use.[10]

## The Water Conservation in Landscaping Act

Pursuant to legislative direction in the Water Conservation in Landscaping Act, Government Code Sections 65595 *et seq.*, the State Department of Water Resources has prepared a model local water-efficient landscape ordinance for areas having similar climactic, geological, or topographical conditions. Government Code Section 65595 provides that if a local agency (defined as a city or county) has not adopted its own water-efficient landscape ordinance, or has not adopted findings based upon local climactic, geological, or topographical conditions which state that a water-efficient landscape ordinance is unnecessary, the model ordinance developed by the department shall automatically take effect and must be enforced by the local agency. By January 31, 1993, each local agency was required to file with the Department a copy of its water-efficient landscape ordinance. § 65599.

Demonstration garden of drought-tolerant plants in Riverside

## The 1988 MWD-IID Agreement

A unique agreement reached between The Metropolitan Water District of Southern California and the Imperial Irrigation District represents a form of incentive conservation. Metropolitan and Imperial both have rights to water from the Colorado River. Imperial has a higher priority to the Colorado River supply than Metropolitan, but its conveyance facilities and unlined canals are older and involve large losses. Faced with a State Board order (WR 88-20) requiring conservation of 100,000 acre feet annually, Imperial finally reached an agreement with MWD. Under the agreement, MWD will pay a total cost of about $222 million to finance both construction and operation costs within Imperial that are designed to conserve approximately 106,000 acre feet of water annually. In return, MWD will receive the water saved, diverted from the Colorado River through its own aqueduct system. This mutually beneficial approach may serve as a model for other projects throughout the state.

## Mandatory Conservation Ordinances

While some communities during the 1987-1992 drought relied upon public education and voluntary conservation, many water suppliers adopted ordinances legally restricting water use. One common technique is the establishment of a reduced percentage allocation of the customer's prior historical use. Charges for use over the allotted

*Drought ordinances—mandatory conservation*

[10] *California Water Plan Update,* volume 1, page 54.

Working soil to increase water use efficiency

amounts are then set at rates designed to discourage excess use. While simple to administer, this approach penalizes those who have been careful in their past usage of water and rewards the previously profligate. A variation of this approach is to determine a specific amount of water deemed reasonable for a specific connection, such as a residence. Any excess use is then subject to much higher charges, and perhaps ultimately prohibited. However, this solution also has inequities. It may not take into account the size of the family or property, or different landscaping requirements. These ordinances usually provide for variances, but that safeguard is generally not sufficient to prevent community discontent when water usage is restricted.

Drought ordinances also typically prohibit certain kinds of water uses: for example, using water to hose down sidewalks and driveways, to wash cars, or for construction grading and dust control. Landscape watering may be limited to certain hours and days of the week, or prohibited under severe conditions. And, of course, a moratorium may be imposed upon any new connections. Because reasonable savings can be achieved most easily in the residential sector, and because of the potential economic impacts of curtailing water deliveries to industry and business, special rules are generally tailored for nonresidential uses.

**EBMUD = East Bay Municipal Utility District**

*EBMUD's ordinance—a comprehensive approach*

One of the long-time leaders in water conservation has been the East Bay Municipal Utility District (EBMUD) which serves over a million people in Alameda and Contra Costa Counties. In May 1988, during the recent drought, EBMUD began its conservation program, and by August had achieved a 30 percent reduction in use. The program centered around rate schedule changes but included public education, water audits, waste water patrols, and expansion of its water reclamation facilities. A copy of EBMUD's conservation ordinance may be found in Appendix C.

However, EBMUD's drought management program came under strong attack in 1991 from customers "residing in the hot climate areas east of the Berkeley–Oakland hills." *Brydon v. EBMUD* (1994) 24 Cal.App.4th 178, 182, 199, 200. These customers argued that adequate conservation had been achieved without the necessity of imposing a steeply inclining block rate structure and, moreover, that the system was discriminatory in that customers in the inland area used less than 50 percent of the water provided to all residential customers yet paid under a predecessor ordinance over 75 percent of the drought surcharges. The court, however, upheld the basic allocation of 250 gallons per day for each single residential connection having up to four persons in the household, with a drought surcharge on excess use. The court approved the use of the inclining block rate schedule to control consumption, rejecting the argument that the rate structure constituted a "special tax" prohibited by Article XIIIA of the California Constitution. None of the plaintiffs' statistical arguments was found sufficient to overcome the presumption that the rates were "reasonable, fair, and lawful." *Brydon,* pages 199-200.

*The court upheld the basic allocation of 250 gallons per day for a single-family residence with up to four persons in the household.*

## Application of CEQA

The implementation of certain conservation measures may impose a duty upon the water supplier to conduct an environmental analysis pursuant to CEQA. For some conservation statutes, the legislature has directed how CEQA applies. For example, Water Code Sections 10652 and 10851 (which pertain to conservation plans adopted pursuant to the Urban Water Management Planning Act and the Agricultural Water Management Planning Act) exempt adoption of the plans required by those Acts from any CEQA analysis. However, in other instances the legislature has provided no specific direction as to whether CEQA applies to water conservation measures.

In *Marin Municipal Water District v. KG Land California Corporation* (1991) 235 Cal.App.3d 1652, the appellate court upheld an environmental impact report prepared by the Marin Municipal Water District to support its decision to enact a water moratorium of indefinite duration. Initially, the appellate court questioned whether an EIR was required at all for a new connection moratorium, since the moratorium would maintain the status quo rather than foster development. *KG Land,* page 1661, fn. 4. In any event, because the district saw fit to prepare an EIR, the court considered the question of its adequacy.

The court reaffirmed the principle that the primary focus of an EIR must be on adverse physical changes to the environment, and that the economic and social changes occasioned by a moratorium need be considered only when they occur in conjunction with physical changes. *KG Land,* pages 1662-1663. The court also approved the district's discussion of feasible alternatives, which was limited to a no-project alternative and a form of mandatory conservation. *KG Land,* pages 1665-1666. The court upheld the district's decision that the moratorium was the environmentally superior alternative. *KG Land,* pages 1666, 1669.

Orange County Water District's Green Acres Treatment Plant supplying 5500 acre feet of reclaimed water per year for parks and urban landscaping

CEQA, of course, by its own terms does not apply to actions necessary to prevent or mitigate an "emergency." Public Resources Code § 21080. An emergency is defined in CEQA as a "sudden, unexpected occurrence, involving a clear and imminent danger, demanding immediate action to prevent or mitigate loss of, or damage to, life, health, property or essential public services." Public Resources Code § 21060.3. Listed as potential emergencies are fire, flood, earthquake, riot, accident, and sabotage. A drought is not specifically listed, but under certain conditions might well meet the general requirements of an emergency.

## Water Reclamation

### Recycled Municipal Wastewater

*A 1991 study estimated that 380,000 acre-feet of municipal wastewater was being reused, most of it in Southern California.*

*The state's goal is to recycle 700,000 acre-feet by the year 2000 and one million by 2010.*

The "Water Recycling Act of 1991" establishes a statewide goal of recycling 700,000 acre feet of water annually by the year 2000 and one million acre feet by 2010. Water Code §§ 13575 *et seq.* Approximately 380,000 acre feet of municipal wastewater are being recycled. A little less than one-half of this amount was recycled for groundwater recharge. In descending order, the balance went to agricultural irrigation, landscape irrigation, industrial, and environmental uses.[11] Most of the reclamation occurred in Southern California and in the Tulare Lake region.

Reuse of reclaimed water varies with the degree of treatment provided. Primary treatment involves sewage solids removal, generally through sedimentation but not biological oxidation. Reuse is limited to surface irrigation of orchards and some crops. Secondary treatment adds further removal of organic materials through biological processes, and the reclaimed water can be used for groundwater recharge and a much broader array of irrigation applications. Tertiary treatment adds chemical flocculation, sedimentation, and filtration. Disinfection in varying degrees is part of all the treatment processes. Tertiary treated water has the widest range of uses, including those involving some body contact such as irrigation of golf courses, parks, and recreational lakes.

Diagram of Talbert Barrier: Injection of reclaimed water into Orange County groundwater basin to prevent seawater intrusion

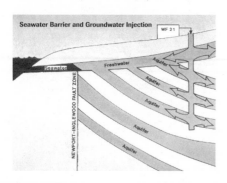

Seawater Barrier and Groundwater Injection

About 2 million acre feet of wastewater is discharged annually into the ocean from California's coastal cities. Most of this wastewater receives secondary treatment and would be the primary source of increased future reclamation. However, large capital and operating expenses are necessary in order to recycle this water.

[11] *California Water Plan Update,* page 70.

Most uses of wastewater require that tertiary, not only secondary, treatment be provided at the sewage treatment plant. Moreover, separate distribution systems must be constructed to deliver reclaimed wastewater to areas of potential reuse, since reclaimed water cannot be put into potable water pipelines. Generally the reuse areas are distant from the plant, and the wastewater must also be pumped from coastal to higher elevations. However, cost is not the only constraint to the reclamation of municipal wastewater.

Use of tertiary treated reclaimed water for community park irrigation

The California Department of Health Services enforces strict requirements on the use of wastewater, even for groundwater recharge. For example, the amount of wastewater permitted to be percolated underground for replenishment purposes in the San Gabriel and San Fernando Valleys is limited not by the lack of facilities or supply, but by the health department for public health reasons. Uses of reclaimed wastewater for crops and for recreational uses involving bodily contact (for example, parks, school yards) are also tightly controlled by the Department of Health Services. Specific treatment standards are set for various kinds of crops, depending on whether the crop is consumed by humans or will be used as fodder for animals.[12]

*Health considerations limit water reclamation to some extent.*

The legislature has prohibited the use of potable domestic supplies to irrigate cemeteries, golf courses, parks, highway landscaping, or for industrial use *if* suitable reclaimed water is available as determined by the State Board. Water Code §§ 13551, 13552.6. The State Board, after notice and hearing, must find that the reclaimed water supply is of adequate quality and is available at reasonable cost, and the Department of Health Services must agree that such use will not be detrimental to public health. § 13550. Local agencies may also require the use of reclaimed water for residential landscaping, subject to the same findings by the State Board. § 13552.4.

San Diego now has plans to mix reclaimed water into a domestic water supply reservoir. The Department of Health Services has given preliminary approval to a project that would pipe "repurified" water into the San Vicente Reservoir where it would mix with water from the Colorado River and the State Water Project. The repurified water would receive conventional tertiary treatment and then be put through an even more advanced treatment system using microfiltration,

*San Diego now has plans to mix "repurified" reclaimed water into a domestic water supply reservoir.*

[12] *See* Table 3-4, *California Water Plan Update,* pages 72-73.

Orange County Water District's Water Factory 21 which supplies reclaimed water for seawater intrusion barrier

*Desalination is still expensive and energy-intensive.*

*MWD is undertaking a major pilot project.*

reverse osmosis, ozone disinfection, and ion exchange. The water would be stored in the reservoir for about a year, and then further disinfected through normal drinking water processes before being delivered for domestic use. Costs of the project are estimated at $924 an acre-foot, or about twice the cost of buying imported water. If all goes well, the project is expected to be on line by 2000.

### Desalination

The reclamation of brackish water, and seawater itself, also provide potential sources of future water supplies. Cost is the principal limitation. Technology is available to produce large quantities of water of suitable purity. The cost of desalination varies with the salinity and quality of the water being reclaimed. Seawater, for example, contains about 35,000 mg/L of total dissolved solids, and desalting costs have been estimated between $1200 and $3000 per acre foot.[13] Brackish water, on the other hand, may cost only on the order of $500 per acre foot. Brine disposal from the desalination process represents another significant problem, and another cost unless the plant can discharge directly into the ocean. The City of Santa Barbara recently completed a desalination plant capable of producing 7500 acre feet a year at a cost of about $2000 per acre foot. In 1992, however, the plant was placed on indefinite standby when the city was able to secure additional fresh water supplies at substantially less cost.

At the present time, The Metropolitan Water District of Southern California has appropriated about $5 million toward a pilot desalination project located on the coast at Huntington Beach. A small test plant is being constructed to produce about 2,000 gallons of freshwater daily. The plant will run for one year and will help in the design of a full-scale demonstration facility that will desalt 5,000 acre feet a year. The process will boil seawater, turning it into steam which is then collected and cooled into freshwater. Heat from an adjoining power plant will be used in the process. If the demonstration plant is successful, MWD expects to construct a plant producing between 50,000 and 100,000 acre feet annually.

### Graywater

The use of "graywater" to provide for residential landscape irrigation is another conservation measure urged by some people. Graywater is defined to mean household wastewater which has not been contaminated by toilet discharge or by any infections or contaminated bodily wastes. Water Code § 14876. It includes wastewater from

---

[13] *Draft EIR on State Drought Water Bank,* page 185.

bathtubs, showers, washbasins, washing machines, and laundry tubs, but does not include water from kitchen sinks or dishwashers. Obviously, there are many questions regarding the health risks of graywater systems. The Department of Water Resources, in consultation with the Department of Health Services, was directed by July 1993 to adopt standards for the installation of graywater systems in residential buildings. However, cities and counties may require more stringent criteria, or may prohibit graywater systems altogether. Water Code § 14877.3.

## CHAPTER TEN

# The Law of the Colorado River

## Introduction

The Colorado River is the second longest river in the continental United States. Its characteristics were eloquently summarized by Justice Black in his opinion in *Arizona v. California* (1963) 373 U.S. 546—

*The Colorado River is the second longest river in the continental U.S. and drains an area almost 900 miles long and 300 to 500 miles in width.*

> The Colorado River itself rises in the mountains of Colorado and flows generally in a southwesterly direction for about 1,300 miles through Colorado, Utah, and Arizona and along the Arizona-Nevada and Arizona-California boundaries, after which it passes into Mexico and empties into the Mexican waters of the Gulf of California. On its way to the sea it receives tributary waters from Wyoming, Colorado, Utah, Nevada, New Mexico, and Arizona. The river and its tributaries flow in a natural basin almost surrounded by large mountain ranges and drain 242,000 square miles, an area about 900 miles long from north to south and 300 to 500 miles wide from east to west—practically one-twelfth the area of the continental United States excluding Alaska. Much of this large basin is so arid that it is, as it always has been, largely dependent upon managed use of the waters of the Colorado River System to make it productive and inhabitable. *Arizona*, page 552.

The Colorado River Basin is divided into two regions, the upper and lower basins. This division came about as a result of a proposal by Herbert Hoover, the federal representative at the Colorado River Compact negotiations. This proposal was developed because the states in what became the upper basin were concerned that the lower basin states would put Colorado River water to beneficial use before the upper basin and thus develop a priority—

> The major legal dispute lies between the upper and lower basin. Indeed all the problems very naturally divided themselves into two parts—that is into the two basins of the river separated by the canyon. The character of agriculture, industry, and the engineering problems in the two basins are of widely different nature, and it became the natural and logical thing to divide the Colorado River into two parts at the canyon, and to assign to each part a certain portion of the flow of the river permanently, and to develop the two basins as two separate principalities.[1]

*The Upper Basin consists of the area upstream of Lee Ferry; the Upper Basin states are Utah, Colorado, and Wyoming. The Lower Basin states are Nevada, Arizona, New Mexico, and California.*

The Upper Basin consists of the Colorado River and its tributaries north of Lee Ferry, Arizona, and encompasses the states of Utah, Colorado, and Wyoming. The river and its tributaries drain approximately 110,000 square miles within the upper basin. The three primary tributary rivers of the Colorado River in the upper basin are the Green, Gunnison, and San Juan rivers. The lower basin consists principally of two rivers, the Colorado River and the Gila River, and encompasses portions of Nevada, Arizona, New Mexico, and California. Most of the water supply of the lower basin comes from the waters of the upper basin.

The waters of the Colorado River are governed by various treaties, acts of Congress, compacts, agreements, and contracts, which collectively are known as the "Law of the River." This chapter will summarize the Law of the River as it affects California and will give the reader an understanding of how and why the waters of the Colorado River are allocated as they are.

## The Colorado River Compact

Between 1918 and 1920, an organization called the League of the Southwest held several meetings at which the governors of Arizona, California, Nevada, New Mexico, Oklahoma (Wyoming was later substituted for Oklahoma), Texas, and Utah were represented. One topic at these meetings was the development of the waters of the Colorado River by the Reclamation Service (which later became the Bureau of Reclamation). The upper basin states feared that the lower basin states would use the Colorado River's waters sooner. Under the doctrine of prior appropriation, this would allow the lower basin

[1] Wilbur and Ely, *The Hoover Dam Documents* (1948) page 22, citing "Transactions of the Commonwealth Club of California," volume 17, number 11, page 451.

states to develop a priority. The upper basin states believed they had only two ways to protect themselves: (1) a Supreme Court lawsuit based on the doctrine of equitable apportionment (to avoid prior appropriation); or (2) an interstate compact that was not based on the doctrine of prior appropriation.[2]

Colorado River flowing through the Grand Canyon

In 1920, the League of the Southwest adopted a resolution that the states whose territory was included within the drainage of the Colorado River should enter a compact to settle the rights of the use of the water of the Colorado River. This resolution also suggested that each state legislature appoint a commissioner to represent that state in negotiations and agreement on a compact. In that same year, the legislatures of the seven states authorized the appointment of commissioners and negotiation of a compact, and in 1921 Congress authorized the negotiation of the Colorado River Compact. Negotiations on the compact began in January 1922 under the direction of the federal representative to the Colorado River Commission, Herbert Hoover. The primary goal of the Colorado River Compact was to provide storage needed for flood protection in the lower basin, and to allow junior appropriators in the upper basin to divert water. The compact is perhaps the most important element of the Law of the River, and its key provisions are discussed briefly below.

Interstate water disputes historically have been settled on the basis of the doctrine of equitable apportionment. The origin of the doctrine dates back to *Kansas v. Colorado* (1907) 206 U.S. 46.[3] That case set forth the basis for equitable apportionment—

> One cardinal rule, underlying all the relations of the states to each other, is that of equality of right. Each state stands on the same level with all the rest. It can impose its own legislation on one of the others, and is bound to yield its own views to none. Yet, whenever ... the action of one state reaches, through the agency of natural laws, into the territory of another state, the question of the extent and the limitations of the rights of the two states becomes a matter of justiciable dispute between them, and this court is called upon to settle that dispute in such a way as will recognize the equal rights of both and at the same time establish justice between them. *Kansas v. Colorado* (1907) 206 U.S. 46, 97-98.

---

2  Wilbur and Ely, pages 17-19.
3  Sax and Abrams, *Legal Control of Water Resources*, 1986, page 698.

In *Wyoming v. Colorado* (1922) 259 U.S. 419, the court's decree protected the priorities of the individual state law appropriators, regardless of state lines. *Wyoming,* page 468. The impact of this decision was described by the Colorado River Commissioner for the State of Colorado—

> The upper state has but one alternative, that of using every means to retard development in the lower state until the uses within the upper state have reached their maximum. The states may avoid this unfortunate situation by determining their respective rights by interstate compact before further development in either state, thus permitting freedom of development in the lower state without injury to future growth in the upper.[4]

After the decision in *Wyoming v. Colorado*, the upper basin states believed it was imperative to enter into a compact.

The compact was signed on November 22, 1924, and its provisions are described below. The compact was the first one ever to be approved by Congress, and the first time the federal government had ever subjected the exercise of federal powers to the terms of an interstate compact. Article I outlines the purposes of the compact—

> The major purposes of this compact are to provide for the equitable division and apportionment of the use of the waters of the Colorado River System; to establish the relative importance of different beneficial uses of water; to promote interstate comity; to remove causes of present and future controversies; and to secure the expeditious agricultural and industrial development of the Colorado River Basin, the storage of its waters, and the protection of life and property from floods. To these ends the Colorado River Basin is divided into two Basins, and an apportionment of the use of part of the water of the Colorado River System is made to each of them with the provision that further equitable apportionments may be made.[5]

Article II is the definitional section. Article II (a) defines the "Colorado River System" to include the portion of the river and its tributaries in the United States. Article II (b) defines the "Colorado River Basin" to include all of the drainage area of the Colorado River System and all other territory in the United States where the waters of the Colorado River System are beneficially applied. Article II (f) defines the "upper basin" to include the portions of Arizona, Colorado, New Mexico, Utah, and Wyoming from which waters naturally

*The 1924 interstate compact divided the Colorado River System between the Upper and Lower Basins. Arizona refused to approve the Compact until 1944.*

---

[4]  Wilbur and Ely, pages A18, 22, 30.
[5]  Wilbur and Ely, page A18.

drain into the Colorado River System above Lee Ferry, Arizona. The upper basin also includes all parts of these states located outside the Colorado River System drainage which are beneficially served by waters diverted from the system above Lee Ferry. According to Article II (g), the "Lower Basin" consists of the portions of Arizona, California, Nevada, New Mexico, and Utah from which waters drain into the Colorado River System below Lee Ferry. The lower basin also includes all parts of those states located outside the Colorado River System drainage which are beneficially served by waters diverted from the system below Lee Ferry.

Lake Powell located in the Upper Basin of the Colorado River

Article III apportions the waters of the Colorado River. Article III(a) allocates in perpetuity to both the upper basin and the lower basin the right to a beneficial consumptive use of 7.5 million acre-feet of water each year. Additionally, Article III(b) gives the lower basin the right to increase its beneficial consumptive use by up to 1 million acre-feet per year. Article III(d) requires the upper basin to release 75 million acre-feet of water during each ten-year period at Lee Ferry, Arizona. Water to satisfy the requirements of a Mexican water treaty would come from the surplus waters, and if no surplus waters existed, the two basins would have their rights equally reduced. Article III(c). In 1944, the United States and Mexico negotiated a water treaty concerning the Colorado River. The treaty obligated the United States to deliver to Mexico 1.5 million acre-feet of water per year and up to 1.7 million acre-feet of water in surplus years.[6]

*The Compact apportions 7.5 million acre-feet of consumptive use per year to both the Upper Basin and the Lower Basin, and gives the Lower Basin the right to increase its use by up to 1 million acre-feet annually.*

As we look at the situation today, it is important to note that the compact apportioned not only the mainstream supply, but also tributary flows. Herbert Hoover, in his analysis of the compact, stated that the term "Colorado River System" covered the entire river and its tributaries.[7] On this basis, it is also clear that the parties believed the supply was large enough to satisfy the apportionments and still have some surplus. Indeed, from 1906 to 1921 the average natural flow of the river was 18.1 million acre-feet. However, natural flows from 1906-1990 were only 15.2 million acre-feet.[8] Hoover himself estimated the undivided surplus of annual flow

*The Upper Basin is required to release 75 million acre-feet over each 10-year period at Lee Ferry.*

6  Wilbur and Ely, pages 25-26, A851-A852.
7  *The Hoover Dam Documents,* pages A33-A36.
8  Smith and Vaughn, "Deconstructing the Colorado River: Part I, Water Strategist," 1994, 7 *Water Strategist,* page 4.

*The Compact appears to have overestimated the long-term supply now available.*

to be approximately 5 million acre-feet. Of course, later developments also excluded tributary flows from the allocation process, and it appears that in the long run it will be shortages, not surpluses, that cause a problem.

Article VIII of the compact states that "present perfected rights" are not impaired by the compact. Remarkably, this phrase was not defined in the compact. It refers to rights which have vested by being put to beneficial use prior to the Boulder Canyon Project Act according to the law of the state.

Article XI required all seven states and Congress to ratify the Colorado River compact for it to become effective, but Arizona refused to give its approval until 1944.[9]

## Federal Legislation Leading to the Boulder Canyon Project Act

In 1904, the Mexican government approved the delivery of Colorado River water diverted from Mexico and carried through the Alamo Canal, located in Mexico, to the United States. Almost immediately there were problems with levee breaks and with Mexican laws that impeded levee and canal maintenance.[10] This situation spurred calls for a canal located entirely within the United States to divert and deliver Colorado River water, but it quickly became clear that this proposal would never come to fruition without federal legislation. The first Kettner Bill (H.R. No. 6044, 66th Cong., 1st Sess. (1919)) authorized the construction of such an All-American Canal. Although hearings were held on the bill, it did not come to a vote. The second Kettner Bill (H.R. No. 11553, 66th Cong., 2d Sess. (1920)) included provisions for storage reservoirs and an All-American Canal. This bill was never enacted either.[11]

The Kinkaid Act, approved on May 18, 1920, authorized a study of the Imperial Valley to determine the feasibility of irrigation in the area. The resulting study became known as the Fall-Davis Report, which was submitted to Congress on February 28, 1922. It recommended the construction of the All-American Canal and a storage reservoir at or near Boulder Canyon. Two months later, the first Swing-Johnson bill (H.R. No. 11449, 67th Cong., 2d Sess. (1922)), authorizing construction of the All-American Canal and a dam at or near Boulder Canyon, was introduced to carry out the recommendations of the Fall-Davis Report. Hearings were held on the bill, but it was not voted on. The second Swing-Johnson bill (H.R. No. 2903,

---

[9] Wilbur and Ely, pages A21-A24.
[10] Wilbur and Ely, pages 115-116.
[11] Wilbur and Ely, pages 14-16.

68th Cong., 1st Sess. (1923)) contained provisions similar to those in the first Swing-Johnson bill, and it met the same fate.[12]

These bills generated a great deal of controversy. Arizona's unrelenting opposition to the compact meant that it could not be ratified. The upper basin states feared that if Congress passed river control legislation before the compact was ratified, California would be free to take as much water as it wanted. The upper basin states wanted Congress to allow the compact to become effective with the approval of six states and to require California to limit itself to a specific amount of water. Ultimately, this solution prevailed.[13]

The third Swing-Johnson bill (H.R. No. 6251, 69th Cong., 1st Sess. (1925)), containing essentially the same provisions as the second Swing-Johnson bill, was submitted to the Secretary of the Interior and was redrafted and reintroduced on February 27, 1926. This bill was favorably reported out of committee but was prevented from passing by a filibuster in the Senate. The fourth Swing-Johnson bill was then introduced in the House of Representatives on December 5, 1927, and in the Senate on December 6, 1927. It finally passed Congress on December 18, 1928, and was signed by President Coolidge on December 21, 1928. Because certain precedent conditions set forth in Section 4 had to be fulfilled, the Act did not immediately become law. On June 25, 1929, however, President Hoover issued a proclamation declaring the Boulder Canyon Project Act effective.[14]

*It took four Swing-Johnson bills, over the period of 1922 to 1928, to secure passage of the Boulder Canyon Project Act, since Arizona would not sign the Compact.*

## The Boulder Canyon Project Act

The Boulder Canyon Project Act (BCPA) sought to balance the interests of the lower basin in the construction of the All-American Canal and a storage reservoir, with those in the upper basin securing an interstate agreement to protect against a lower basin water grab. The goals of the lower basin states were satisfied in the purposes of the BCPA, which were set forth in Section 1 as being for—

**BCPA = The Boulder Canyon Project Act**

> ...controlling the floods, improving navigation and regulating the flow of the Colorado River, providing for storage and for the delivery of the stored waters thereof for reclamation of public lands and other beneficial uses exclusively within the United States, and for the generation of electrical energy as a means of making the project herein authorized a self-supporting and financially solvent undertaking, the Secretary of the Interior, subject to the terms

[12] Wilbur and Ely, pages 15, 38-39.
[13] Hundley, *The Great Thirst*, 1992, page 217.
[14] Wilbur and Ely, pages 40-42.

of the Colorado River compact hereinafter mentioned, is hereby authorized to construct, operate, and maintain a dam and incidental works in the main stream of the Colorado River at Black Canyon or Boulder Canyon adequate to create a storage reservoir of a capacity of not less than twenty million acre feet of water and a main canal and appurtenant structures located entirely within the United States connecting the Laguna Dam, or other suitable diversion dam, which the Secretary of the Interior is hereby authorized to construct if deemed necessary or advisable by him upon engineering or economic considerations, with the Imperial and Coachella Valleys in California....[15]

Section 6 set forth the priorities of the purposes set forth in Section 1—

First, for river regulation, improvement of navigation, and flood control; second, for irrigation and domestic uses and satisfaction of present perfected rights in pursuance of Article VIII of said Colorado River compact; and third, for power.[16]

*The BCPA became effective with the approval of six out of the seven Compact states if California would limit its use to 4.4 million acre-feet plus half the surplus; California did so in 1929. Only Arizona refused to ratify the Compact.*

Pursuant to Section 4(a), the BCPA became effective only if all seven basin states approved the Colorado River compact. However, since it seemed unlikely that Arizona would ratify the compact, Section 4(a) also allowed the compact to become effective with the approval of the six states, if California enacted a statute limiting its use of water to 4.4 million acre-feet of Article III(a) water and not more than half of any excess or surplus waters not apportioned by the compact.[17] Because Arizona would not ratify the compact, California enacted the California Limitation Act to comply with Section 4(a)(2) of the BCPA—

[T]he State of California...agrees irrevocably and unconditionally with the United States and for the benefit of the states of Arizona, Colorado, Nevada, New Mexico, Utah, and Wyoming as an express covenant and in consideration of the passage of the said 'Boulder Canyon Project Act' that the aggregate annual consumptive use (diversions less returns to the river) of water of and from the Colorado river for use in the State of California including all uses under contracts made under the provisions of said 'Boulder Canyon Project Act', and all water necessary for the supply of any rights which may now exist, shall not exceed four million four

[15] Wilbur and Ely, page A213.
[16] Wilbur and Ely, page A219.
[17] Wilbur and Ely, pages A215-A216.

hundred thousand acre-feet of the waters apportioned to the lower basin states by paragraph 'a' of article three of the said Colorado river compact, plus not more than one-half of any excess or surplus waters unapportioned by said compact, such uses always to be subject to the terms of said compact. Act of March 4, 1929; Ch. 16, 48th Sess.; Statutes and Amendments to the Codes, 1929, pages 38-39.[18]

Section 5 of the Act gave the Secretary of the Interior the power to contract for the storage and delivery of Colorado River water. Section 8 subjected the construction, management, and operation of the dam, reservoirs, canals, and other works to the provisions of the compact. Section 13(b) made any water rights of the United States subject to the provisions of the compact.[19]

## The Seven Party Agreement

Neither the Boulder Canyon Project Act nor the Colorado River compact allocated the Colorado River water to users within the individual states. Therefore, the next step in utilizing California's Colorado River entitlement was to allocate the water among California water users. By 1928, plans were under consideration to use 6 million acre-feet of the Colorado River each year on 1.5 million acres. The two primary competing interests were the Los Angeles and San Diego areas versus the regions' agricultural interests. On February 21, 1930, the cities and agricultural interests entered into a preliminary agreement allocating 3.85 million acre-feet of water each year to agriculture and 550,000 acre-feet of water to the Metropolitan Water District of Southern California. This agreement accounted for 4.4 million acre-feet of water. The next 550,000 acre-feet of water per year was allocated to the Metropolitan Water District, and all water available in the river for California use above 4.95 million acre-feet per year was allocated to agriculture. This preliminary agreement did not allocate priorities internally within each group.

When the Secretary of the Interior attempted to negotiate a contract for the All-American Canal with the Imperial Irrigation District, it became clear that a more precise intrastate allocation of water was needed. Although the agricultural allocation included the Imperial Irrigation District, the Coachella Valley Water District, and the Palo Verde Irrigation District, there was no method to apportion the water among them. Furthermore, a dispute had arisen between the Metropolitan Water District and the agricultural interests involving

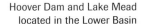

*The Seven Party Agreement allocated the California share among California water users.*

Hoover Dam and Lake Mead located in the Lower Basin

18. Wilbur and Ely, pages A231-A232.
19 Wilbur and Ely, pages A217, A220, A233.

the priority of use of the 4.4 million acre-feet of water. In November 1930, the Secretary of the Interior requested that California make a recommendation as to the allocation and priorities of parties to be given water contracts.

Consensus on priorities and allocation, the Seven Party Agreement, was reached on August 18, 1931.[20] Article I of this agreement apportioned the Colorado River water available to California as follows—

*Priorities and allocations under the Seven Party Agreement*

Section 1. A first priority to Palo Verde Irrigation District for beneficial use exclusively upon lands in said district as it now exists and upon lands between said district and the Colorado River, aggregating (within and without said district) a gross area of 104,500 acres, such waters as may be required by said lands.

Section 2. A second priority to Yuma project of the United States Bureau of Reclamation for beneficial use upon not exceeding a gross area of 25,000 acres of land located in said project in California, such waters as may be required by said lands.

Section 3. A third priority (a) to Imperial Irrigation District and other lands under or that will be served from the All-American Canal in Imperial and Coachella Valleys, and (b) to Palo Verde Irrigation District for use exclusively on 16,000 acres in that area known as the "Lower Palo Verde Mesa," adjacent to Palo Verde Irrigation District for beneficial consumptive use, 3,850,000 acre feet of water per annum less the beneficial consumptive use under the priorities designated in sections 1 and 2 above. The rights designated (a) and (b) in this section are equal in priority. The total beneficial consumptive use under priorities stated in sections 1, 2, and 3 of this article shall not exceed 3,850,000 acre feet of water per annum.

Section 4. A fourth priority to the Metropolitan Water District of Southern California and/or the City of Los Angeles, for beneficial consumptive use, by themselves and/or others, on the coastal plain of Southern California, 550,000 acre feet of water per annum.

Section 5. A fifth priority (a) to the Metropolitan Water District of Southern California and/or the City of Los Angeles, for beneficial consumptive use, by themselves and/or others, on the coastal plain of southern California, 550,000 acre feet of water per annum and (b) to the City of San Diego and/or County of San Diego, for beneficial consumptive use, 112,000 acre feet of water per annum. The rights designated (a) and (b) in this section are equal in priority.

[20] Wilbur and Ely, pages 106-107.

Section 6. A sixth priority (a) to Imperial Irrigation District and other lands under or that will be served from the All-American Canal in Imperial and Coachella Valleys, and (b) to Palo Verde Irrigation District for use exclusively on 16,000 acres in that area known as the 'Lower Palo Verde Mesa,' adjacent to Palo Verde Irrigation District, for beneficial consumptive use, 300,000 acre feet of water per annum. The rights designated (a) and (b) in this section are equal in priority.

Section 7. A seventh priority of all remaining water available for use within California, for agricultural use in the Colorado River Basin in California, as said basin is designated on map No. 23000 of the Department of the Interior, Bureau of Reclamation.[21]

These priorities, summarized in Table 10-1, remain in use today, although agreements in 1946 and 1947 between MWD, the United States, and the City of San Diego provided for the consolidation of the MWD and San Diego water allocations as a result of the decision to include San Diego in the MWD. No contract was entered into between the United States and the City of Los Angeles because the contract between the United States and MWD comprehends the rights recognized jointly, but not cumulatively, in Los Angeles and MWD in the Seven Party Agreement.[22]

Arizona refused to ratify the Colorado River compact until 1944 because it feared that California would take all of the Colorado River water. This long-simmering dispute between the two states ultimately resulted in the 1964 Supreme Court opinion given in *Arizona v. California* (1963) 373 U.S. 546.

### Arizona v. California

The dispute between Arizona and California over the use of Colorado River water extends at least as far back as the negotiations over the Colorado River compact. The completion of the compact did nothing to diminish this animosity. In 1930, Arizona sued the Secretary of the Interior and the other six lower basin states to prevent the construction of Hoover Dam and the All-American Canal, to enjoin contracts for delivery of stored water, and to have the Boulder Canyon Project Act and the Colorado River compact declared unconstitutional. The United States Supreme Court found that the compact and the Boulder Canyon Project Act were constitutional and that the Secretary could construct Hoover Dam. *Arizona v. California* (1931) 283 U.S. 423.

*Arizona's effort to have the BCPA and the Compact declared unconstitutional failed.*

---

[21] Wilbur and Ely, pages A480-A481.
[22] Wilbur and Ely, pages 109-110.

In 1934, Arizona filed another lawsuit to perpetuate the testimony of the negotiators of the Colorado River compact for use in a future action. The defendants were the other six states, several California public agencies, and the Secretary of the Interior. The United States Supreme Court denied Arizona's claim. *Arizona v. California* (1934) 292 U.S. 341.

*Arizona threatened military force to block the construction of Parker Dam.*

In 1935, the United States sued Arizona to enjoin its interference with the construction of Parker Dam. Arizona had threatened to use military force and had physically prevented continuance of the construction. The court denied the injunction on the ground that the United States could not show that the Secretary was authorized to construct the dam. *United States v. Arizona* (1935) 295 U.S. 174. Later in 1935, Congress specifically authorized the construction of Parker Dam. 49 Stat. 1039. In 1935, Arizona also filed suit against California, Colorado, Nevada, New Mexico, Utah, and Wyoming for

## Table 10-1
## Seven Party Agreement Priorities

| Priority | Description | Acre Feet Annually |
|---|---|---|
| 1 | Palo Verde Irrigation District gross area of 104,500 acres | Priorities 1, 2, and 3 shall not exceed 3,850,000 |
| 2 | Yuma Project Reservation Division—not exceeding a gross area of 25,000 acres | " |
| 3(a) | Imperial Irrigation District and lands in Imperial and Coachella Valleys to be served by All-American Canal | " |
| 3(b) | Palo Verde Irrigation District—on 16,000 acres of mesa lands | " |
| 4 | Metropolitan Water District, and/or City of Los Angeles, and/or others on the coastal plain | 550,000 |
| 5(a) | Metropolitan Water District, and/or City of Los Angeles, and/or others on the coastal plain | 550,000 |
| 5(b) | City and/or county of San Diego | 112,000 |
| | (5 (a) and 5(b) are equal in priority) | |
| 6(a) | Imperial irrigation District and other lands in Imperial and Coachella Valleys served from All-American Canal | 300,000 |
| 6(b) | Palo Verde Irrigation District—on 16,000 acres of mesa lands | 300,000 |
| | (6(a) and 6(b) are equal in priority) | |
| | TOTAL | 5,362,000 |

Nathanson, *Updating the Hoover Dam Documents,* page 30.

a judicial apportionment of the unappropriated water of the Colorado River. The Supreme Court denied the petition on the basis that the United States was required to be a party. *Arizona v. California* (1936) 298 U.S. 558.[23]

In 1944, Arizona entered into a contract with the Bureau of Reclamation for an investigation of the best means of utilizing Colorado River water in Arizona. This investigation was the beginning of the plan for the Central Arizona Project. In 1948, the Secretary of the Interior sent the Bureau's report to Congress. The report concluded that the proposed Central Arizona Project could transport water from the Colorado River to an area in Central Arizona. Congress considered the Central Arizona Project for several years, finally concluding in 1951 that it should be "postponed until such time as use of the water in the Lower Colorado River Basin is either adjudicated or binding or mutual agreement as to the use of the waters is reached by the States of the Lower Colorado River Basin."[24] Arizona had no intention of waiting any longer than necessary for the water to be adjudicated.

On August 13, 1952, Arizona filed a motion in the United States Supreme Court to bring a lawsuit against California and seven public agencies in California. The public agencies were the Palo Verde Irrigation District, the Imperial Irrigation District, Coachella Valley Water District, The Metropolitan Water District of Southern California, the City of Los Angeles, the City of San Diego, and the County of San Diego. This motion was granted in January 1953. Subsequently, both the United States and Nevada intervened in the lawsuit. Trial began in June 1956 and continued until August 1958. The matter was submitted for consideration in July 1959, and in December 1960 the Special Master issued his report. The Supreme Court issued its opinion on June 3, 1963, and issued a decree on March 9, 1964.[25]

*In 1953, Arizona brought suit in the U.S. Supreme Court against California and seven public agencies in the state.*

The central issue in the case concerned the amount of water each state could legally divert from the Colorado River. 373 U.S. 551. Arizona claimed that the apportionment of Colorado River waters in the BCPA included only the mainstream waters of the River. California, seeking more water for itself and with its eye on Arizona's Gila River, contended that the apportionment included all tributary waters of the Colorado River. 373 U.S. 563.

*The central issue concerned the amount of water that each state could divert from the Colorado River.*

[23] Wilbur and Ely, pages 146-150.

[24] 1968 U.S. Code, *Congressional and Administrative News,* volume 3, page 3678.

[25] Nathanson, *Updating the Hoover Dam Documents,* 1978, pages 127-128, 143.

The Special Master concluded that the Colorado River compact, the law of prior appropriation, and the doctrine of equitable apportionment (the doctrine the Supreme Court uses to resolve interstate water claims in the absence of a compact or statutory apportionment) did not control in the case. 373 U.S. 562. The Supreme Court agreed with this interpretation, and wrote that, although the doctrine of equitable apportionment was generally applicable in interstate water disputes, it did not control in this situation because Congress had made a statutory apportionment. 373 U.S. 565.

*The Supreme Court held that in passing the BCPA Congress had enacted its own apportionment of the Lower Basin Waters.*

The court held that Congress, in enacting the Boulder Canyon Project Act, had created its own comprehensive scheme for apportioning the waters of the lower basin between California, Arizona, and Nevada. 373 U.S. 565. The court held that Section 4(a) of the Act limited California to "water of and from the Colorado River," not from the "Colorado River system," and that the legislative history demonstrated that in the BCPA Congress only meant to refer to mainstream waters. 373 U.S. 568. The court's determination that Congress had left tributary waters to the individual states was a blow to the hopes of California, which had argued that the water apportioned by Congress also included tributary waters. 373 U.S. 567.

*Congress' apportionment—*
*4.4 million acre-feet to California; 2.8 million acre-feet to Arizona; 300,000 acre-feet to Nevada; and any surplus to be divided equally between California and Arizona.*

The congressional apportionment divided the first 7.5 million acre-feet of mainstream waters as follows: (1) 4.4 million acre-feet to California; (2) 2.8 million acre-feet to Arizona; and (3) 300,000 acre-feet to Nevada. Arizona and California would split equally any surplus. Although the states could have agreed on a compact to incorporate these terms, by granting the Secretary of the Interior the power to make contracts for the delivery of water and by preventing any person from receiving water without a contract, Congress had already accomplished this. 373 U.S. 565.

The court concluded that three factors indicated that Congress intended to apportion the mainstream waters among Arizona, California, and Nevada: (1) the legislative history of the BCPA; (2) the provisions of the BCPA itself, which in Sections 4(a) and 8(b) set forth several methods to accomplish the apportionment; and (3) the fact that, if the states did not agree on an apportionment, the Secretary had the power to carry out the provisions of the BCPA by making contracts to apportion water among the states, and by allocating water among the individual users within each state. 373 U.S. 578-579.

The court also faced a significant issue involving the contract-making power of the Secretary of the Interior. Could the Secretary contract with any users he or she might choose, or was the Secretary bound by the provisions of state law? Sections 14 and 18 of the BCPA provide as follows—

> [Section 14.] This Act shall be deemed a supplement to the reclamation law, which said reclamation law shall govern the construction, operation, and management of the works herein authorized, except as otherwise herein provided.

> [Section 18.] Nothing herein shall be construed as interfering with such rights as the States now have either to the waters within their borders or to adopt such policies and enact such laws as they may deem necessary with respect to the appropriation, control, and use of waters within their borders, except as modified by the Colorado River compact or other interstate agreement.[26]

The effect of Section 14 is to incorporate into the BCPA the non-conflicting provisions of the Reclamation Act of 1902, one of which is Section 8 of that Act—

> That nothing in this Act shall be construed as affecting or intended to affect or to in any way interfere with the laws of any State or Territory relating to the control, appropriation, use, or distribution of water used in irrigation, or any vested right acquired thereunder, and the Secretary of the Interior, in carrying out the provisions of this Act, shall proceed in conformity with such laws . . . . 43 U.S.C. § 383.

Although federal law clearly governs interstate apportionments of water, it has been suggested that nothing in the statutory scheme would prevent the application of state law once the BCPA water entered a state's boundaries.[27] However, the court interpreted the statutory scheme differently. It relied on Section 1 of the BCPA, which authorized the Secretary to construct and operate the facilities of the BCPA, as well as the language of Sections 5 and 8(b) of the BCPA. Section 5 grants the power to contract to the Secretary—

> That the Secretary of the Interior is hereby authorized, under such general regulations as he may prescribe, to contract for the storage of water in said reservoir and for the delivery thereof at such points on the river and on said canal as may be agreed upon, for irrigation and domestic uses, and generation of electrical energy and delivery at the switchboard to States, municipal corporations, political subdivisions, and private corporations of electrical energy

Hayfield Pumping Plant along MWD's Colorado River Aqueduct, east of Indio

---

[26] Wilbur and Ely, pages A224-A225.
[27] Meyers, "The Colorado River," 1966, 19 *Stanford L.Rev.,* page 59.

generated at said dam, upon charges that will provide revenue which, in addition to other revenue accruing under the reclamation law and under this Act, will in his judgment cover all expenses of operation and maintenance incurred by the United States on account of works constructed under this Act and the payments to the United States under subdivision (b) of section 4. Contracts respecting water for irrigation and domestic uses shall be for permanent service and shall conform to paragraph (a) of section 4 of this Act. No person shall have or be entitled to have the use for any purpose of the water stored as aforesaid except by contract made as herein stated.[28]

Section 8(b) allowed the lower basin states to negotiate a compact allocating the waters of the river. However, if the compact was approved after January 1, 1929, it was to be subject to any contracts entered into by the Secretary. 373 U.S. 580.

*Subject to certain limitations, the Supreme Court ruled that the Secretary had the power to enter into delivery contracts within a state with whichever users he chose.*

Based on these provisions, the court concluded that the Secretary had the power to enter into contracts with whichever users he chose, regardless of priority, so long as the Secretary followed the limitations on his power set out in the BCPA: (1) allocating water in the order set forth in Section 6 of the BCPA; (2) making revenue provisions to ensure the recovery of the expenses of the project; (3) complying with the provisions of the Colorado River compact; (4) not contracting so as to interfere with the allocation between the upper and lower basins; and (5) satisfying present perfected rights. 373 U.S. 584. The court viewed the Secretary's general authority to enter contracts as being sufficient to override state law in the absence of a specific declaration to the contrary in the BCPA. 373 U.S. 580-581. The opinion did discuss Section 8 of the Reclamation Act but concluded that the Secretary was not bound by state law in disposing of water under the BCPA. 373 U.S. 587. The opinion also upheld the reserved rights doctrine articulated in *Winters v. United States* (1908) 207 U.S. 564.

*Water was reserved to meet present and future needs of the Native American reservations.*

In regard to Native American water rights, the court held that the United States had reserved an amount of Colorado River water for the Native American reservations sufficient to satisfy their present and future needs. The amount of water reserved was enough to irrigate all of the practicable irrigable acreage on the reservations. These water rights became effective at the time of the reservation, and since this predated the BCPA, they were classified as "present perfected rights." 373 U.S. 600.

---

[28] Wilbur and Ely, page A217.

The term "present perfected rights" was not defined until the decree of the Supreme Court in *Arizona v. California* (1964) 376 U.S 340—

> (G) 'Perfected right' means a water right acquired in accordance with state law, which right has been exercised by the actual diversion of a specific quantity of water that has been applied to a defined area of land or to definite municipal or industrial works, and in addition shall include water rights created by the reservation of mainstream water for the use of federal establishments under federal law whether or not the water has been applied to beneficial use;
>
> (H) 'Present perfected rights' means perfected rights, as here defined, existing as of June 25, 1929, the effective date of the Boulder Canyon Project Act. . . . 376 U.S. 341.

*"Present perfected rights" were defined as those existing as of June 25, 1929, the effective date of the BCPA.*

Article VI of the decree also provided for the determination of present perfected rights—

> Within two years from the date of this decree, the States of Arizona, California, and Nevada shall furnish to this Court and to the Secretary of the Interior a list of the present perfected rights, with their claimed priority dates, in waters of the mainstream within each State, respectively, in terms of consumptive use, except those relating to federal establishments. Any named party to this proceeding may present its claim of present perfected rights or its opposition to the claims of others. The Secretary of the Interior shall supply similar information, within a similar period of time, with respect to the claims of the United States to present perfected rights within each State. If the parties and the Secretary of the Interior are unable at that time to agree on the present perfected rights to the use of mainstream water in each State, and their priority dates, any party may apply to the Court for the determination of such rights by the Court.[29]

The significance of present perfected rights is found in Article II(B)(3) of the decree. In any year in which there is less than 7.5 million acre-feet of mainstream water available for consumptive use in Arizona, California, and Nevada, the Secretary of the Interior first must satisfy present perfected rights in the order of their priority dates.

*Present perfected rights have a priority if there is less than 7.5 million acre-feet of mainstream water available for use in Arizona, California, and Nevada.*

As a result of the decree in *Arizona v. California*, the Bureau of Reclamation, authorized to carry out the provisions of Article VI of the decree, required the parties to prepare a draft stipulation of present

[29] Nathanson, page IX-33.

MWD's diversion facilities from Colorado River

perfected rights. After years of meetings and arguments on this issue, Arizona, Nevada, and California in 1977 moved the Supreme Court under Article VI of the decree to determine present perfected rights. In 1979, the Supreme Court issued a supplemental decree determining present perfected rights. *Arizona v. California* 439 U.S. 419. In California, present perfected rights were quantified for federal establishments, water districts and projects, and miscellaneous water users. The federal establishments were the Chemehuevi, Yuma, Colorado River, and Fort Mojave Indian reservations, in amounts ranging from 11,340 acre-feet to 51,616 acre-feet. The amounts allocated to water districts and projects were as follows—

*Some present perfected rights within California*

*The Palo Verde Irrigation District* in annual quantities not to exceed (i) 219,780 acre-feet of diversions from the mainstream or (ii) the quantity of mainstream water necessary to supply the consumptive use required for irrigation of 33,604 acres and for the satisfaction of related uses, whichever of (i) or (ii) is less, with a priority date of 1877.

*The Imperial Irrigation District* in annual quantities not to exceed (i) 2,600,000 acre-feet of diversions from the mainstream or (ii) the quantity of mainstream water necessary to supply the consumptive use required for irrigation of 424,145 acres and for the satisfaction of related uses, whichever of (i) or (ii) is less, with a priority date of 1901.

*The Reservation Division, Yuma Project, California* (non-Indian portion) in annual quantities not to exceed (i) 38,270 acre-feet of diversions from the mainstream or (ii) the quantity of mainstream water necessary to supply the consumptive use required for irrigation of 6,294 acres and for the satisfaction of related uses, whichever of (i) or (ii) is less, with a priority date of July 8, 1905. *Arizona v. California* (1979) 439 U.S. 419, 428-429.

*Subsequent proceedings and legislation affecting Native American rights*

In December 1978, prior to the issuance of this decree, the United States filed an order for modification of the 1964 decree on behalf of five Indian reservations. The court rejected the tribes' request to increase their water rights to serve lands that initially had been omitted from calculations because the United States did not claim them. *Arizona v. California* (1983) 460 U.S. 605. The court also refused to increase water rights for irrigable acreage in new lands determined to be in the reservation boundaries because these boundaries had not been "finally determined" under the definition of the 1964 decree. The court did agree that the tribes' water rights should be increased in consideration of irrigable acreage in the lands adjudicated to be within reservation boundaries because these boundaries had been "finally determined" under the definition of the 1964 decree. 460 U.S. 636.

Since this decree, there have been several Settlement Acts that quantified Native American claims. In 1988, Congress enacted the Colorado Ute Settlement Act, which quantified the water rights of the Southern Ute Tribe and Ute Mountain Ute Indian Tribe. 100 Stat. 585. In 1992, Congress enacted H.R. 522, the Jicarilla Apache Tribe Water Rights Settlement Act, and also H.R. 429, which resolved long-standing water rights claims of the Northern Ute Tribe.

## The Mexican Water Treaty

In 1944, the United States signed a treaty with Mexico concerning the Colorado River. The treaty requires the United States to deliver 1.5 million acre-feet of water per year to Mexico and up to 1.7 million acre-feet of water in years when a surplus exists.

*Mexico has a right to 1.5 million acre-feet of Colorado River water; salinity is the main problem.*

Pursuant to the terms of the Colorado River compact, this treaty obligation is to be met first out of surplus waters. If there is no surplus, both the upper and lower basins must bear equal responsibility. Colorado River compact, Article III(c).

Salinity is a major problem in the delivery of water to Mexico, although the Mexican water treaty did not specifically mention the quality of water to be delivered at the Mexican border.[30] Salinity control efforts by states and the federal government date back to the early 1960s. *EDF v. Costle* (1981) 657 F.2d 275, 280. Salinity regulations proposed by the EPA were the subject of the lawsuit in *EDF v. Costle* and are described in detail in that decision. *Costle,* pages 280-281.

In 1972 and 1973, the United States entered into an additional agreement with Mexico to deliver water to Mexico with a salinity not to exceed that of the water arriving at Imperial Dam by more than 115 milligrams per liter. Construction of the Yuma desalting plant was one measure undertaken to deal with the salinity issue, as was the enaction of the Colorado River Basin Salinity Control Act of 1974.[31]

---

[30] Nathanson, pages 217-222.
[31] Abbott, "California Colorado River Issues," 198, 19 *Pacific L.J.,* pages 1431-1432.

## Water Rights of the Imperial Irrigation District

The Imperial Irrigation District has been involved in litigation on a number of key water rights issues. The dispute involving the Imperial Irrigation District and the State Water Resources Control Board over waste and conservation is discussed briefly in chapters 3 and 8. However, one case, *Bryant v. Yellen* (1980) 447 U.S. 352, should be mentioned here. The *Bryant* case involved the present perfected rights of Imperial, and the issue was whether the use of Colorado River water delivered under contract with the Secretary of the Interior was subject to the 160-acre limitation of reclamation law. In 1933, the Secretary of the Interior stated that the 160-acre limitation did not apply. *Bryant,* pages 193-194. However, in 1964, the Department of the Interior took the view that the limitation should apply to all Imperial Valley lands in private ownership. This later position was rejected by the court, which held that the 160-acre limitation did not apply to Imperial Valley lands that were under irrigation in 1929. Section 6 of the BCPA, which required the satisfaction of present perfected rights, was held to override the acreage limitation. Thus, Imperial's present perfected rights could be satisfied without regard to the 160-acre issue. *Bryant,* pages 364, 368, 370.

## The Colorado River Today

### The Central Arizona Project

**CAP = Central Arizona Project**

*Legislation authorizing the Central Arizona Project subordinates the delivery of Arizona's 2.8 million acre-feet entitlement to California's 4.4 million acre-feet.*

In 1968, Congress authorized the Colorado River Basin Project Act. 43 U.S.C. §§ 1501-1556. This authorization included the Central Arizona Project (CAP), which Arizona had been seeking since prior to initiating the *Arizona v. California* litigation. Section 301(b) of the Act subordinates deliveries of CAP water to the deliveries of 4.4 million acre-feet in California, as well as to users in Arizona and Nevada who hold present perfected rights or had diversion works as of the date of the Act. Of Arizona's 2.8 million acre-foot entitlement, approximately 1.5 million acre-feet is available to the CAP.[32] As it becomes more evident that the long-term supply of the Colorado River has been over-estimated, and with the increase in demands, Arizona has become increasingly concerned about this subordination requirement. As the affected states negotiate possible changes in the present allocation of Colorado River water, Arizona seeks relief from this provision.

[32] Brophy, "The Effect of the Central Arizona Project on the Allocation of Colorado River Water Supplies," February 10-11, 1994, *Proceedings of the 12th Annual ABA Water Conference,* pages 4-6.

California has consistently taken more than its 4.4 million acre-foot entitlement by using the water that the CAP has not been taking. From 1987 to 1992, California's use averaged nearly 5 million acre-feet.[33] In 1993, California used approximately 4.8 million acre-feet. In the early 1990s, the CAP was nearing completion and fears arose in California that Arizona would soon begin taking its full share of the Colorado River. On October 1, 1993, the Secretary of the Interior declared the CAP substantially complete.[34] However, CAP use remains considerably under its full share of Colorado River water. In 1987-1992, Arizona's use averaged 2 million acre-feet, or 800,000 acre-feet less than its entitlement.[35] Moreover, in 1992, it became clear that Arizona's agricultural CAP subcontractors were in serious financial distress.[36] Currently it appears unlikely that the subcontractors will be able to afford CAP water, and the future of Arizona's use and its Colorado River entitlement are uncertain. In the meantime, Nevada is growing rapidly and seeking additional water, and California seeks to maintain, if not increase, the share it has been using.

Central Arizona Project canal wending its way to Tucson

*California's recent use has averaged nearly 5 million acre-feet annually; California has been using water not taken by Arizona.*

## Banking and Transfer of Entitlements

As this book is going to press, the Bureau of Reclamation has been seeking informal comments on certain draft regulations issued May 6, 1994. These regulations seek to inject some flexibility into the present allocation system and to meet growing demands along the river. Both intra- and interstate leasing are permitted. The water must have been previously used and made available either through conservation or land fallowing. Such water may also be "banked" in Lake Mead and later sold or used to offset excess use. The regulations specifically permit Indian reservations to sell water for use off the reservation, although they acknowledge that the authority for such use is questionable. Indeed, some experts also question the Secretary's authority to allow water banking and transfers generally without certain changes in the Law of the River. The Bureau has asked the states to meet to see if some resolution of the various issues can be worked out.

*USBR efforts to insert some flexibility into the present allocation system on the Colorado River*

## Quantification

The Bureau has also prepared a separate proposal to quantify the rights of the agricultural users. Currently, these rights are fixed only

[33] Smith and Vaughn, page 4.
[34] Brophy, page 1.
[35] Smith and Vaughn, page 2.
[36] Brophy, page 28.

in terms of the amount of water reasonably required for certain lands or acreages. As a result, total agricultural use has at times exceeded the 3.85 MAF aggregate entitlement. Clearly, the issue of such overruns and the program to bank and transfer water would be facilitated if the agricultural rights of the individual districts were quantified. However, the Bureau's initial proposal received a hostile reception from most users, and its future remains uncertain.[37]

## Endangered Species

The presence of endangered species on the Colorado River is another factor that may influence water allocation and use. The federal government currently lists four species of fish that inhabit the river as endangered: the razorback sucker, the Colorado squawfish, the humpback chub, and the bonytail chub. 58 Fed. Reg. 6578 (1993). Critical habitat has also been designated for these species. It is not yet clear how the management of the Colorado River for the protection of these species will impact the availability of water for consumptive uses.

## Other Issues

Salinity is another problem that has not been rectified. The reverse-osmosis Yarona Desalting Plant has been completed but is not in operation. The cost of operating the plant is nearly double the amount originally anticipated, and alternative methods of salinity control are under evaluation. Latent disputes on two issues between the upper and lower basin states also exist. The parties disagree as to the burden of meeting the Mexican Treaty water obligation. They also disagree on whether the upper basin must meet its Lee Ferry delivery obligations to the lower basin if doing so means that the upper basin will not realize its 7.5 million acre-feet entitlement. Finally, under surplus conditions, California is entitled to 50 percent of the surplus. However, a surplus in the lower basin has never been declared, and specific criteria for determining surplus have never been adopted. The Bureau of Reclamation is currently working on the development of such criteria.[38]

In view of the changing needs for Colorado River water, it is likely that some modification in the allocation of water will occur, achieved either by consensus or by the intervention of Congress or the courts. However, given the history of the river and the enormous interests at stake, one would not expect changes to occur easily or soon.

[37] Rieke, "Emerging Issues on the Colorado River," February 10-11, 1994, *Proceedings of the 12th Annual ABA Water Conference* (amended version), page 5.
[38] Rieke, pages 2, 4, 15.

# Principles for Agreement on Bay-Delta Standards between the State of California and the Federal Government

December 15, 1994

# Principles for Agreement on Bay-Delta Standards between the State of California and the Federal Government

## Preamble

In order to provide ecosystem protection for the Bay-Delta Estuary, representatives of the State and Federal governments and urban, agricultural and environmental interests agree to the implementation of a Bay-Delta protection plan through the California State Water Resources Control Board (SWRCB) consistent with the following principles. These Principles describe changes to the California Urban Water Agency/Agricultural Users (CUWA/AG) proposal as the base case for Bay-Delta protections, which are intended to be in force for three years, at which time they may be revised.

## Water Quality Standards and Operational Constraints

**1. February Protections:** Subject to the flexibility provisions described below, the exports during February shall be no greater than 35% of Delta inflow in years when the January Eight River Index is greater than 1.5 million acre feet (MAF). If this index is less than 1 MAF, the allowable exports will be 45% of Delta inflow. If this index is between 1 and 1.5 MAF, operational decisions will be made by the California Water Policy Council and Federal Ecosystem Directorate (CALFED) Coordination Group (Ops Group) as set forth in the Exhibit B of the Framework Agreement of June 1994. (The CALFED process is described in Attachment A.)

**2. March through June Protections:** During March through June, exports shall be no greater than 35% of Delta inflow, subject to the flexibility provisions described below.

**3. July through January:** During July through January exports shall be no greater than 65% of Delta inflow, subject to the flexibility provisions described below. Criteria for exercising this flexibility will be developed by the Ops Group.

**4. X-2 Protection Measures:** X-2 protection shall be based on the CUWA/AG proposal with the following adjustment. The Chipps Island requirement in February will be zero days when the Eight River Index in January is less than 0.8 MAF and 28 days when it is greater than 1.0 MAF with linear interpolation between 0.8 and 1.0 MAF. The requirement at the confluence shall be 150 days, except that when the May 1 90% forecast of the Sacramento River Index is less than 8.1 MAF, the maximum outflows for May and June shall be 4,000 cfs, with all other flow requirements removed. When the February index falls below 0.5 MAF, the requirement for March will be reviewed by the Ops Group. Additional refinements, which will involve no further water costs above those which are required for this paragraph may subsequently be made.

**5. San Joaquin River Protection Measures:** The protection measures will consist of the narrative standard and implementation provisions agreed to on December 12, 1994 (Attachment B). In addition, export limits during the April/May 30-day pulse flow period will be consistent with the CUWA/AG proposal. The parties agree to take immediate actions, as appropriate, to resolve the biological concerns related to the removal of the barrier and to provide adequate transport of fisheries consistent with the CALFED process identified in Attachment C. If biological problems arise before the solution(s) can be implemented, resolution of these concerns shall be made within CALFED.

**6. Additional Modifications to CUWA/AG Proposal:** Daily export limits shall be based on the average Delta inflow over the preceding three days under balanced conditions as defined in the Coordinated Operation Agreement or fourteen days under unbalanced conditions.

During the period November to January, the Delta Cross Channel will be closed a maximum of 45 days. The timing and duration of the closures will be determined by the Ops group.

During the period May 21 through June 15, the Delta Cross Channel may be rotated closed four days and open three days, including the weekend.

## ESA Flexibility

**1. No Additional Water Cost:** Compliance with the take provisions of the biological opinions under the Federal Endangered Species Act (ESA) is intended to result in no additional loss of water supply annually within the limits of the water quality and operational requirements of these Principles. To implement this principle, the Ops Group will develop operational flexibility through adjustment of export limits.

**2. Real Time Monitoring:** To the maximum extent possible, real time monitoring will be used to make decisions regarding operational flexibility. CALFED commits to aggressively develop more reliable mechanisms for real time monitoring.

**3. Additional Study Programs:** CALFED commits to aggressively pursue study programs to develop information allowing better decisions to be made about managing the Estuary and its watershed.

**4. Operational Flexibility:** Decisions to exercise operational flexibility under the Ops Group process may increase or decrease water supplies in any month and must be based on best available data to ensure biological protection and be consistent with the Federal and State Endangered Species Acts.

**5. Dispute Resolution:** Any disputes within the Ops Group will be resolved by CALFED, as set forth in Attachment A.

## Category III—Non Flow Factors

**1. Principles:** Implementation of Category III principles will be consistent with the principles set forth in Attachment C.

**2. Financial Commitment:** The water user community agrees to make available by Feb. 15, 1995, an initial financial commitment of $10 million annually for the three years of these interim standards to fund Category III Metropolitan Water District of Southern California (MWD) will guarantee this commitment. Subsequent agreements relative to Category III will credit this early commitment of funds to MWD's obligation.

## Institutional Agreements

**1. EPA Standards:** Consistent with the Framework Agreement, EPA commits to withdraw Federal standards pursuant to the Clean Water Act when the SWRCB adopts a final plan consistent with these Principles.

**2. Endangered Species Act**

a. *Limitation to Aquatic Species:* These Principles apply only to aquatic species affected in the Bay-Delta Estuary.

b. *Impacts of Additional Listings:* This Plan, in conjunction with other Federal and State efforts, is intended to provide habitat protection sufficient for currently listed threatened and endangered species and to create conditions in the Bay-Delta Estuary that avoid the need for any additional listings during the next three years. To the extent that due to unforeseen circumstances in the Estuary, or to factors not addressed in the Plan, additional listings may be required, it is understood that protection of these species shall result in no additional water cost relative to the Bay-Delta protections embodied in the Plan and will, to the maximum extent possible, use the flexibility provided within Section 4(d) of the ESA. Additional water needs will be provided by the Federal government on a willing seller basis financed by Federal funds, not through additional regulatory re-allocations of water within the Bay-Delta.

c. *Other Endangered Species Issues:* To the extent consistent with the requirements of Federal and State ESAs, all other actions related to the Plan required to implement the acts as they affect the Bay-Delta, including but not limited to future biological opinions, incidental take statements, recovery plans, listing decisions and critical habitat designations, are intended to conform to these Principles, and decision regarding ESA implementation will be made utilizing the CALFED process.

**3. Central Valley Project Credits.** All CVP water provided pursuant to these Principles shall be credited toward the CVP obligation under Section 3406(b)(2) of the Central Valley Project Improvement Act to provide 800,000 acre feet of project yield for specified purposes.

**4. Immediate Implementation**

a. *Biological Opinions:* It is agreed that there will be an immediate reconsultation on the biological opinions currently governing project operations with appropriate modifications by the end of 1994, to the extent practicable, to conform with the requirements of these Principles.

b. *State Implementation:* Consistent with the Framework Agreement, the SWRCB will finalize the Plan and immediately thereafter initiate water right proceedings to implement the adopted Plan. In implementing the Plan, the SWRCB will act in compliance with all provisions of law which may be applicable, including, but not limited to, the water rights priority system and the statutory protections for areas of origin.

**5. SWRCB Authority:** Variations in the operational criteria approved by the CALFED process in accordance with the above provisions will be communicated to the Executive Director of the SWRCB for appropriate action, if any, if accordance with the Plan.

**6. Authority under State and Federal ESA's:** Any actions or decisions of the Ops Group or CALFED which would create or alter requirements under the State or Federal ESA's shall be communicated, as appropriate, to the U.S. Fish and Wildlife Service, National Marine Fisheries Service, or California Department of Fish and Game for appropriate processing consistent with the provisions of the State and Federal ESA's.

**7. Legal Consistency.** All provisions of this agreement are intended and shall be interpreted to be consistent with all applicable provisions of State and Federal law.

**State of California**

Douglas B. Wheeler
Secretary, California Resources Agency

James M. Strock
Secretary for Environmental Protection
California Environmental Protection Agency

**United States of America**

Bruce Babbitt
Secretary of the Interior

Ronald H. Brown
Secretary of Commerce

Carol M. Browner
Administrator
Environmental Protection Agency

**Interested Parties**

Walter J. Bishop
Contra Costa Water District
By: Gret Gartrell

Stephen R. Hall
Association of California Water Agencies

Anson K. Moran
California Urban Water Agencies

David R. Schuster
Kern County Water Agency and
Tulare Lake Water Storage District

Gary Bobke
The Bay Institute

John Krautkraemer
Environmental Defense Fund

Daniel G. Nelson
San Luis–Delta Mendota Water Authority

John R. Wodraska
Metropolitan Water District
of Southern California

## Attachment A

The "CALFED process" referred to herein consists of the following steps:

■ Initial deliberations and decisions occur in the "Ops Group." "Ops Group" deliberations shall be conducted in consultation with water user, environmental and fishery representatives.

■ If the Ops Group disagrees on a particular issue, or if an Ops Group action requires additional water that it is believed cannot be made up within existing requirements, the issue will be decided by CALFED.

■ If CALFED cannot reach agreement, and if the issue involves listed species, a final decision will be made by the appropriate listing agency. Other issues not involving ESA will be decided by the appropriate regulatory or resources management agency.

## Attachment B

### Narrative Criteria for Chinook Salmon on the Sacramento and San Joaquin Rivers

Water quality conditions shall be maintained, together with other measures in the watershed, sufficient to achieve a doubling of production of chinook salmon, consistent with the mandates of State and Federal law.

#### Implementation Measures—San Joaquin River System

1. Not later than three years following adoption of this Plan, the SWRCB shall assign responsibility for the following flows, together with other measures in the watershed sufficient to meet the narrative criteria, in the San Joaquin River at Vernalis among the water right holders in the watershed. During this three-year period, the Bureau of Reclamation shall provide these flows, in accordance with the biological opinion for Delta smelt. These flows are interim flows and will be reevaluated as to timing and magnitude (up or down) within the next 3 years.

|  | *Feb–June Flows (cfs)** | *April–May pulse flows (cfs)** |
|---|---|---|
| C | 710–1140 | 3110–3540 |
| D | 1420–2280 | 4020–4880 |
| BN | 1420–2280 | 4620–5480 |
| AN | 2130–3420 | 5730–7020 |
| W | 2130–3420 | 7330–8620 |

*higher flows provided when the 2 ppt isohaline (x2) is west of Chipps Island.

2. Install a barrier at the head of Old River during the April–May pulse flows.

3. During the 3-year period, decisions by the Federal Energy Regulatory Commission (FERC) or other regulatory orders may increase the contribution from other upstream water users into the Estuary. These additional flows will benefit the Delta resources. These flows will be recognized by ClubFED in its calculation of flows available to the Delta and be considered by the SWRCB in its assignment of responsibility among the water rights holders in the watershed during its water rights proceeding.

The SWRCB will initiate a water rights proceeding to assign responsibility for meeting these flow requirements. Actions of the NMFS and FWS in the FERC proceedings will be in furtherance of their authority and responsibility under the ESA. Such actions shall not be intended to assume the responsibility of the SWRCB to assign responsibility for meeting water quality standards in the Delta.

**Sacramento River System—Additional Measures.** Close the Delta Cross Channel gates from February–May 20, and during half of the period from May 20–June 15.

## Attachment C

## Principles for Implementation of Category III

The State and Federal governments and agricultural, urban and environmental interests are committed to the implementation and financing of "Category III" measures as an essential part of a comprehensive ecosystem protection plan for the Bay-Delta Estuary.

To achieve this objective we agree to the following principles:

**1. Level of funding:** Category III activities are expected to require a financial commitment estimated to be $60 million a year.

**2. Sources of funds:** It is anticipated that new sources of funds will be required to adequately finance Category III activities. A process for evaluating existing funding and possible reprioritization will be used to finance a portion of Category III activities. Additional funds will be secured through a combination of Federal and State appropriations, user fees, and other sources as required.

**3. Monitoring:** It is further agreed that monitoring is a high priority in addition to the Category III elements, and has a high priority for separate funding.

**4. Unscreened Diversions:** It is agreed that the highest priority Category III activity for funding is the screening of currently unscreened diversion points in the Bay-Delta watershed. An evaluation of the benefits of a screening program for listed species will be conducted immediately and used to improve listed species survival no later than during the 95/96 water year.

**5. Consensus Process:** CUWA/Ag will work with CALFED and environmental interests in an open process to determine precise priorities and financial commitments for the implementation of all Category III elements. The CUWA/AG work plan currently being developed will be revised consistent with these Principles.

**6. Deadline:** This process will be under the sponsorship or CUWA/AG, which commits to an open and collaborative approach involving CALFED and the environmental community. It is agreed that detailed implementation for these Principles will be finalized before publication of the final SWRCB standards, which is currently planned by March 31, 1995.

**APPENDIX B**

# Memorandum of Understanding Regarding Urban Water Conservation in California

September 1991

# Memorandum of Understanding Regarding
# Urban Water Conservation in California

This Memorandum of Understanding Regarding Urban Water Conservation in California ("MOU") is made and entered into on the dates set forth below among the undersigned parties ("signatories"). The signatories represent urban water suppliers, public advocacy organizations and other interested groups as defined in Section 1 of this MOU.

## RECITALS

A.   The signatories to this MOU recognize that California's economy, quality of life and environment depend in large part upon the water resources of the State. The signatories also recognize the need to provide reliable urban water supplies and to protect the environment. Increasing demands for urban, agricultural and environmental water uses call for conservation and the elimination of waste as important elements in the over-all management of water resources. Many organizations and groups in California have an interest in urban water conservation, and this MOU is intended to gain much needed consensus on a complex issue.

B.   The urban water conservation practices included in this MOU (referred to as "Best Management Practices" or "BMPs") are intended to reduce long-term urban demands from what they would have been with-out implementation of these practices and are in addition to programs which may be instituted during occasional water supply shortages.

C.   The combination of BMPs and urban growth, unless properly accounted for in water management planning, could make reductions in urban demands during short-term emergencies such as droughts or earth-quakes more difficult to achieve. However, notwithstanding such difficulties, the signatory water suppliers will carry out the urban water conservation BMP process as described in this MOU.

D.   The signatories recognize that means other than urban water conservation may be needed to provide long-term reliability for urban water suppliers and long-term protection of the environment. However, the signatories may have differing views on what additional measures might be appropriate to provide for these needs. Accordingly, this MOU is not intended to address these issues.

E.    A major benefit of this MOU is to conserve water which could be used for the protection of streams, wetlands and estuaries and/or urban water supply reliability. This MOU leaves to other forums the issue of how conserved water will be used.

F.    It is the intent of this MOU that individual signatory water suppliers (1) develop comprehensive conservation BMP programs using sound economic criteria and (2) consider water conservation on an equal basis with other water management options.

G.    It is recognized that present urban water use throughout the State varies according to many factors including, but not limited to, climate, types of housing and landscaping, amounts and kinds of commercial, industrial and recreational development, and the extent to which conservation measures have already been implemented. It is further recognized that many of the BMPs identified in Exhibit 1 to this MOU have already been implemented in some areas and that even with broader employment of BMPs, future urban water use will continue to vary from area to area. Therefore, this MOU is not intended to establish uniform per capita water use allotments throughout the urban areas of the State. This MOU is also not intended to limit the amount or types of conservation a water supplier can pursue or to limit a water supplier's more rapid implementation of BMPs.

H.    It is recognized that projections of future water demand should include estimates of anticipated demand reductions due to changes in the real price of water.

## TERMS

### Section 1

#### Definitions

For purposes of this MOU, the following definitions apply:

1.1  *Best Management Practices.* A Best Management Practice ("BMP") means a policy, program, practice, rule, regulation or ordinance or the use of devices, equipment or facilities which meets either of the following criteria:

> (a) An established and generally accepted practice among water suppliers that results in more efficient use or conservation of water;

> (b) A practice for which sufficient data are available from existing water conservation projects to indicate that significant conservation or conservation related benefits can be achieved; that the practice is technically and economically reasonable and not environmentally or socially unacceptable; and that the practice is not otherwise unreasonable for most water suppliers to carry out.

Although the term "Best Management Practices" has been used in various statutes and regulations, the definitions and interpretations of that term in those statutes and regulations do not apply to this MOU. The term "Best Management Practices" or "BMPs" has an independent and special meaning in this MOU and is to be applied for purposes of this MOU only as defined above.

1.2  *Implementation.* "Implementation" means achieving and maintaining the staffing, funding, and in general, the priority levels necessary to achieve the level of activity called for in the descriptions of the various BMPs and to satisfy the commitment by the signatories to use good faith efforts to optimize savings from implementing BMPs as described in Section 4.4 of this MOU. Section B of Exhibit 1 to this MOU establishes the schedule for initial implementation of BMPs.

1.3  *Signatory Groups.* For purposes of this MOU, signatories will be divided into three groups as follows:

(a) Group 1 will consist of water suppliers. A "water supplier" is defined as any entity, including a city, which delivers or supplies water for urban use at the wholesale or retail level.

(b) Group 2 will consist of public advocacy organizations. A "public advocacy organization" is defined as a non profit organization:

    (i) whose primary function is not the representation of trade, industrial, or utility entities, and

    (ii) whose prime mission is the protection of the environment or who has a clear interest in advancing the BMP process.

(c) Group 3 will consist of other interested groups. "Other interested groups" is defined as any other group which does not fall into one of the two groups above.

1.4 *California Urban Water Conservation Council.* The California Urban Water Conservation Council or "Council" will have responsibility for monitoring the implementation of this MOU and will be comprised of signatories to this MOU grouped according to the definitions in Section 1.3 above. The duties of the Council are set forth in Section 6 and in Exhibit 2 to this MOU.

## Section 2

### Purposes

2.1 This MOU has two primary purposes: (1) to expedite implementation of reasonable water conservation measures in urban areas; and (2) pursuant to Section 5 of this MOU, to establish assumptions for use in calculating estimates of reliable future water conservation savings resulting from proven and reasonable conservation measures. Estimates of reliable savings are the water conservation savings which can be achieved with a high degree of confidence in a given service area. The signatories have agreed upon the initial assumptions to be used in calculating estimates of reliable savings. These assumptions are included in Exhibit 1 to this MOU. It is probable that average savings achieved by water suppliers will exceed the estimates of reliable savings.

## Section 3

### Limits to Applicability of MOU

3.1 *Relationship Between Water Suppliers.* No rights, obligations or authorities between wholesale suppliers, retail agencies, cities or other water suppliers are created or expanded by this MOU. Moreover, wholesale water suppliers are not obligated to implement BMPs at the retail customer level except within their own retail service area, if any.

3.2 *Agriculture.* This MOU is intended to apply only to the delivery of water for domestic, municipal and industrial uses. This MOU is not intended to apply directly or indirectly to the use of water for irrigated agriculture.

3.3 *Reclamation.* The signatory water suppliers support the reclamation and reuse of wastewater wherever technically and economically reasonable and not environmentally or socially unacceptable, and agree to prepare feasibility studies on water reclamation for their respective service areas. However, this MOU does not apply to that aspect of water management, except where the use of reclaimed water may otherwise qualify as a BMP as defined above.

3.4 *Land Use Planning.* This MOU does not deal with the question of growth management. However, each signatory water supplier will inform all relevant land planning agencies at least annually of the impacts that planning decisions involving projected growth would have upon the reliability of its water supplies for the water supplier's service area and other areas being considered for annexation.

3.5 *Use of Conserved Water.* A major benefit of this MOU is to conserve water which could be used for the protection of streams, wetlands and estuaries and/or urban water supply reliability. This MOU leaves to other forums the issue of how conserved water will be used.

## Section 4

### Implementation of Best Management Practices

4.1 *The Best Management Practices List, Schedule of Implementation and Assumptions.* Exhibit 1 to this MOU contains:

(a) In Section A: A list identifying those practices which the signatories believe presently meet the definition of a BMP as set forth in Section 1.1 of this MOU.

(b) In Section B: A schedule for implementing the BMPs to be followed by signatory water suppliers unless exempted under Section 4.5 of this MOU or an alternative schedule is prepared pursuant to Section 4.6 of this MOU.

(c) In Section C: Assumptions for use in developing estimates of reliable savings from the implementation of BMPs. Estimates of reliable savings are the water conservation savings which can be achieved with a high degree of confidence in a given service area. The estimate of reliable savings for each BMP depends upon the nature of the BMP and upon the amount of data available to evaluate potential savings. For some BMPs (e.g., public information) estimates of reliable savings may never be generated. For others, additional data may lead to significant changes in the estimate of reliable savings. It is probable that average savings achieved by water suppliers will exceed the estimates of reliable savings.

(d) In Section D: A list of "Potential Best Management Practices" ("PBMPs"). PBMPs are possible conservation practices which have not been promoted to the BMP list.

4.2 *Initial BMPs, PBMPs, Schedules, and Estimates of Reliable Savings.* The initial position of conservation practices on the BMP and PBMP lists, the initial schedule of implementation and study for the BMP list, the initial schedule of study for the PBMP list, and the initial estimates of reliable savings represent compromises by the signatories to move the process forward both for purposes of the present Bay/Delta proceedings as defined in Section 5 and to promote water conservation generally. The signatories agree that as more and better data are collected in the future, the lists, the schedules, and the estimates of reliable savings will be refined and revised based upon the most objective criteria available. However, the signatories agree that the measures included as initial BMPs in Section A of Exhibit 1 are economically justified on a statewide basis.

4.3 *Future Revision of BMPs, PBMPs, Schedules, and Estimates of Reliable Savings.* After the beginning of the initial term of the MOU as provided in Section 7.1, the California Urban Water Conservation Council ("Council") will, pursuant to Section 6 of this MOU and Exhibit 2, alter the composition of the BMP and PBMP lists, redefine individual BMPs, alter the schedules of implementation, and update the assumptions of reliable savings as more data becomes available. This dynamic BMP assessment process includes the following specific commitments:

(a) The assumptions of reliable savings will be updated at least every 3 years.

(b) The economic reasonableness of a BMP or PBMP will be assessed by the Council using the economic principles in Sections 3 and 4 of Exhibit 3.

(c) A BMP will be removed from the BMP list if, after review of data developed during implementation, the Council determines that the BMP cannot be made economically reasonable or determines that the BMP otherwise fails to conform to the definition of BMPs in Section 1.1.

(d) A PBMP will be moved to the BMP list and assigned a schedule of implementation if, after review of data developed during research, and/or demonstration projects, the Council determines that the PBMP is economically reasonable and otherwise conforms to the definition of BMPs in Section 1.1.

4.4 *Good Faith Effort.* While specific BMPs and results may differ because of varying local conditions among the areas served by the signatory water suppliers, a good faith effort to implement BMPs will be required of all signatory water suppliers. The following are included within the meaning of "good faith effort to implement BMPs":

(a) The proactive use by a signatory water supplier of legal authorities and administrative prerogatives available to the water supplier as necessary and reasonable for the implementation of BMPs.

(b) Where implementation of a particular BMP is not within the legal authority of a signatory water supplier, encouraging timely implementation of the BMP by other entities that have the legal authority to carry out the BMP within that water supplier's service area pursuant to existing legal authority. This encouragement may include, but is not limited to, financial incentives as appropriate.

(c) Cooperating with and encouraging cooperation between other water suppliers and other relevant entities whenever possible and within existing legal authority to promote the implementation of BMPS.

(d) Optimizing savings from implementing BMPs.

(e) For each signatory water supplier and all signatory public advocacy organizations, encouraging the removal of institutional barriers to the implementation of BMPs within that water supplier's service area. Examples of good faith efforts to remove institutional barriers include formal presentations and/or written requests to entities requesting approval of, or amendment to, local ordinances, administrative policies or legislation which will promote BMP implementation.

4.5 *Exemptions.* A signatory water supplier will be exempt from the implementation of specific BMPs for as long as the supplier annually substantiates that based upon then prevailing local conditions, one or more of the following findings applies:

(a) A full cost-benefit analysis, performed in accordance with the principles set forth in Exhibit 3, demonstrates that either the program (i) is not cost-effective overall when total program benefits and costs are considered; OR (ii) is not cost-effective to the individual water supplier even after the water supplier has made a good faith effort to share costs with other program beneficiaries.

(b) Adequate funds are not and cannot reasonably be made available from sources accessible to the water supplier including funds from other entities. However, this exemption cannot be used if a new, less cost-effective water management option would be implemented instead of the BMP for which the water supplier is seeking this exemption.

(c) Implementation of the BMP is (i) not within the legal authority of the water supplier; and (ii) the water supplier has made a good faith effort to work with other entities that have the legal authority to carry out the BMP; and (iii) the water supplier has made a good faith effort to work with other relevant entities to encourage the removal of institutional barriers to the implementation of BMPs within its service area.

4.6 *Schedule of Implementation.* The schedule of implementation for BMPs is set forth in Section B of Exhibit 1 to this MOU. However, it is recognized by the signatories that deviations from this schedule by water suppliers may be necessary. Therefore, a water supplier may modify, to the minimum extent necessary, the schedule for implementation of BMPs if the water supplier substantiates one or more of the following findings:

(a) That after a good faith effort to implement the BMP within the time prescribed, implementation is not feasible pursuant to the schedule. However, implementation of this BMP is still required as soon as feasible within the initial term of this MOU as defined in Section 7.1.

(b) That implementation of one or more BMPs prior to other BMPs will have a more positive effect on conservation or water supplies than will adherence to the schedule.

(c) That implementation of one or more Potential BMPs or other conservation measures prior to one or more BMPs will have a more positive effect on conservation or water supplies than will adherence to the schedule.

## Section 5

### Bay/Delta Proceedings

5.1 *Use of MOU for Bay/Delta Proceedings.* The BMPs, the estimates of reliable savings and the processes established by this MOU are agreed to by the signatories for purposes of the present proceedings on the San Francisco Bay/Sacramento-San Joaquin Delta Estuary ("Bay/Delta") and in order to move the water conservation process forward. "Present Bay/Delta proceedings" is intended to mean those Bay/Delta proceedings presently underway and those conducted until a final water rights decision is reached by the State Water Resources Control Board ("State Board"). The willingness of the signatories to enter into this MOU for purposes of the present Bay/Delta proceedings in no way limits the signatories' ability to propose different conservation practices, different estimates of savings, or different processes in a forum other than the present Bay/Delta proceedings, or for non-urban water suppliers or for other water management issues. By signing this MOU, public advocacy organization signatories are not agreeing to use the initial assumptions of reliable conservation savings in proceedings other than the present Bay/Delta proceedings. The signatories may present other assumptions of reliable conservation savings for non-signatory water suppliers in the present Bay/Delta proceedings, provided that such assumptions could not have adverse impacts upon the water supplies of any signatory water supplier. Furthermore, the signatories retain the right to advocate any particular level of protection for the Bay/Delta Estuary, including levels of freshwater flows, and do not necessarily agree on population projections for California. This MOU is not intended to address any authority or obligation of the State Board to establish freshwater flow protections or set water quality objectives for the Estuary, or to address any authority of the Environmental Protection Agency.

5.2 *Recommendations for Bay/Delta Proceedings.* The signatories will make the following recommendations to the State Board in conjunction with the present Bay/Delta proceedings and to the EPA to the extent the EPA concerns itself with the proceedings:

(a) That for purposes of the present Bay/Delta proceedings, implementation of the BMP process set forth in this MOU represents a sufficient long-term water conservation program by the signatory water suppliers, recognizing that additional programs may be required during occasional water supply shortages;

(b) That for purposes of the present Bay/Delta proceedings only, the State Board and EPA should base their estimates of future urban water conservation savings on the implementation of all of the BMPs included in Section A of Exhibit 1 to this MOU for the entire service area of the signatory water suppliers and only on those BMPs, except for (i) the conservation potential for water supplied by urban agencies for agricultural purposes, or (ii) in cases where higher levels of conservation have been mandated;

(c) That for the purposes of the present Bay/Delta proceedings, the State Board and EPA should make their estimates of future urban water conservation savings by employing the reliable savings assumptions associated with those BMPs set forth in Section C of Exhibit 1 to this MOU;

(d) That the State Board should include a policy statement in the water rights phase of the Bay/Delta proceedings supporting the BMP process described in this MOU and that the BMP process should be considered in any documents prepared by the State Board pursuant to the California Environmental Quality Act as part of the present Bay/Delta proceedings.

5.3 *Letter to State Board.* Within 30 days of signing this MOU, each signatory will jointly or individually convey the principles set forth in Sections 5.1 and 5.2 above by sending a letter to the State Board, copied to the EPA, in the form attached to this MOU as Exhibit 4.

5.4 *Withdrawal from MOU.* If during the present Bay/Delta proceedings, the State Board or EPA uses future urban water conservation savings that are inconsistent with the use of BMPs as provided in this MOU, any signatory shall have the right to withdraw from the MOU by providing written notice to the Council as described in Section 7.4(a)(i) below.

## Section 6

### California Urban Water Conservation Council

6.1 *Organization.* The California Urban Water Conservation Council ("Council") will be comprised of all signatories to this MOU grouped according to the definition in Section 1. The signatories agree to the necessary organization and duties of the Council as specified in Exhibit 2 to this MOU. Within 30 days of the effective date of this MOU, the Council will hold its first meeting.

6.2 *Annual Reports.* The signatory water suppliers will submit standardized reports annually to the Council providing sufficient information to inform the Council on the progress being made towards implementing the BMP process. The Council will also make annual reports to the State Board. An outline for the Council's annual report to the State Board is attached as Exhibit 5 to this MOU.

## Section 7

### General Provisions

7.1 *Initial* Term of MOU. The initial term of this MOU shall be for a period of 10 years. This initial term shall commence on September 1, 1991.

7.2 *Signatories.* Signatories shall consist of three groups: water suppliers, public advocacy organizations and other interested groups, arranged according to the definition in Section 1.3. Such arrangement will be made by a Council membership committee comprised of three representatives from the water suppliers' group and three representatives from the public advocacy organizations' group.

7.3  *Renewal of MOU.* The MOU shall be automatically renewed after the initial term of 10 years on an annual basis as to all signatories unless a signatory withdraws as described below in Section 7.4.

7.4  *Withdrawal from MOU.* Signatories to the MOU may withdraw from the MOU in three separate ways as described in sections (a), (b) and (c) below.

(a) Withdrawal prior to expiration of initial term. Before the expiration of the initial term of 10 years, a signatory may withdraw by providing written notice to the Council declaring its intent to withdraw. This written notice must include a substantiated finding that one of the two provisions (i) or (ii) below applies:

(i) During the present Bay/Delta proceedings, the State Board or EPA used future urban water conservation savings that are inconsistent with the use of BMPs as provided in this MOU; OR

(ii) After a period of 5 years from the commencement of the initial term of the MOU:

(A) Specific signatory water suppliers representing more than 10 percent of the population included within the combined service areas of the signatory water suppliers have failed to act in good faith pursuant to Section 4.4 of the MOU; and

(B) The signatory wishing to withdraw has attached findings to its past two annual reports to the Council beginning no earlier than the fourth annual report identifying these same signatory water suppliers and giving evidence based upon the information required to be submitted in the annual reports to the Council to support the allegations of failure to act in good faith; and

(C) The State Board has failed to require conservation efforts by the specific water suppliers adequate to satisfy the requirements of this MOU; and

(D) Discussions between the signatory wishing to withdraw and the specific signatories named have failed to satisfy the objections of the signatory wishing to withdraw.

After a signatory declares an intent to withdraw under Section 7.4(a), the MOU shall remain in effect as to that signatory for 180 days.

(b) Withdrawal after expiration of initial term. After the initial term of 10 years, any signatory may declare its intent to withdraw from the MOU unconditionally by providing written notice to the Council. After a signatory has declared its intent to withdraw as provided in this section, the MOU will remain in effect as to that signatory for 180 days.

(c) Immediate withdrawal. Any signatory who does not sign a modification to the MOU requiring a 2/3 vote as described in Exhibit 2 of this MOU may withdraw from the MOU by providing written notice to the Council. The withdrawing signatory's duties under this MOU will be terminated effective immediately upon providing such written notice.

If a signatory withdraws from the MOU under any of the above methods, the MOU shall remain in effect as to all other signatories.

7.5  *Additional Parties.* Additional parties may sign the MOU after September 1, 1991 by providing written notice to and upon approval by the Council. Additional parties will be assigned by the Council to one of the three signatory groups defined in Section 1.3 before entry into the Council. All additional signatory water suppliers shall be subject to the schedule of implementation provided in Exhibit 1.

7.6 *Legal Authority.* Nothing in this MOU is intended to give any signatory, agency, entity or organization expansion of any existing authority. No organization formed pursuant to this MOU has authority beyond that specified in this MOU.

7.7 *Non-Contractual Agreement.* This MOU is intended to embody general principles agreed upon between and among the signatories and is not intended to create contractual relationships, rights, obligations, duties or remedies in a court of law between or among the signatories.

7.8 *Modifications.* The signatories agree that this writing constitutes the entire understanding between and among the signatories. The general manager, chief executive officer or executive director of each signatory or their designee shall have the authority to vote on any modifications to this MOU and its exhibits. Any modifications to the MOU itself and to its exhibits shall be made by the Council as described in Exhibit 2.

## SIGNED BY:

Metropolitan Water District of Southern California

Los Angeles Department of Water and Power

East Bay Municipal Utility District

Southern California Water Committee, Inc.

Environmental Defense Fund

Natural Resources Defense Council

Natural Heritage Institute

Mono Lake Committee

Planning and Conservation League

City and County of San Francisco

San Diego County Water Authority

Bay Area Water Users Association

Committee for Water Policy Consensus

The Sierra Club

Save San Francisco Bay Association

League of Women Voters

Friends of the River

# Regulations Governing Water Service to Customers of the East Bay Municipal Utility District

# Water Use During Water Shortage

## A. Water Use Rates and Charges

The rates and charges for water used during the water shortage are set forth in Schedule L of the District's Schedule of Rates and Charges. The rates and charges shall take effect on May 1, 1991. Customers will receive prior individual notification of the basic allotments, applicable rates,and the opportunity to request exceptions.

### 1. Single Family Residential Customers

250 gallons per day (gpd) is allocated to each single family residential customer having up to four (4) persons in the household, at a rate set forth in Schedule L. Water used between 250 gpd and 750 gpd shall be subject to a drought surcharge as set forth in Schedule L. The customer of record may request an increase in these basic allotments as provided in subsection 3 below. Application forms and instructions will be mailed to customers in late April and will also be available at District offices.

Water consumed in excess of the basic allotments will be subject to the higher charges per unit set forth in Schedule L.

### 2. Multi-Family, Commercial, Industrial and Irrigation Customers

Consumption reduction goals by customer class for all customers other than single family residential are as follows:

| | |
|---|---|
| Irrigation | 30% |
| Commercial | 10% |
| Multi-Family Residential | 7% |
| Industrial | 5% |

For these classifications, the basic allotment for each customer will be determined by applying the applicable percentage to each customer's average use for the comparable billing period in 1986. The rate structure applicable to all water use by these classes of customers, including the basic allotment rate for multi-family residential customers and the higher charges for all of these customers for water consumed in excess of the basic allotment, is set forth in Schedule L.

### 3. Exceptions

Pursuant to the procedures set forth in Section C, exceptions to increase the amount of water which may be used without exceeding the basic allotment may be granted upon written request for the following reasons:

a. Substantiated medical requirements.

b. More than 4 residents in single family residential household—62 gpd per additional person.

c. Incorrect customer classification based on predominant use.

d. Accounts classified as single-family which provide water for livestock can be adjusted to provide an additional 30 gpd per horse, cow, or other large animal.

## B. Water Use Limitations

### 1. Restrictions on Water Use

In order to conserve the water supply for the greatest public benefit, the following uses of water have been determined to be wasteful and are hereby prohibited:

a. Using water for new filling or operation of decorative fountains or the filling of decorative lakes or ponds.

b. Washing cars, boats, trailers, aircraft, or other vehicles by hose without a shutoff nozzle. Commercial and fleet washing facilities shall post notice, provided by EBMUD, warning against wasteful use of water.

c. Washing sidewalks, walkways, driveways, patios, parking lots, or other hard-surfaced areas except where necessary for public health or safety.

d. Lawn or garden watering, or any other irrigation, in a manner which results in excessive flooding or runoff in gutter or other waterway, patio, driveway, walk, or street.

e. Flushing sewers, hydrants, or washing streets with District water except in cases of emergency and for essential operations. (Non-residential customers)

### 2. Restrictions on Water for Construction

Water for construction shall only be provided pursuant to permit issued by the District. Written applications for such a permit shall be filed with the Manager of Customer Services. When, in the opinion of the District, there is a feasible alternative source of water for construction, that source shall be utilized and the application to use water supplied by the District shall be denied.

### 3. Water Use Guidelines

In order to reduce the quantity of water used, customers are urged to adhere to the following guidelines to conserve the limited water supply available:

a. Utilize systems which recycle water where possible.

b. Serve water to restaurant customers only upon request.

c. Use water for whatever purpose in a manner which minimizes waste, and repair leaks as soon as possible.

d. Avoid use of District water for the filling of swimming pools where possible.

e. Avoid new plantings other than drought-tolerant plant materials with drip irrigation in existing landscapes.

## C. Application Procedure for Exceptions

Consideration of written applications for exceptions regarding restrictions on water use set forth in Section 28 shall be as follows:

1. Written applications for exceptions shall be accepted, and may be granted, by the Manager of Customer Services;

2. Denials of applications may be appealed in writing to the General Manager;

3. Grounds for granting such applications are:

    a. Grounds specified in Section A above; or

    b. Failure to do so would cause an unnecessary and undue hardship to the Applicant, including, but not limited to, adverse economic impacts, such as loss of production or jobs; or

    c. Failure to do so would cause an emergency condition affecting the health, sanitation, fire protection or safety of the Applicant or the public.

## D. Restrictions on New Connections

An application for a new service connection shall be granted only if the applicant agrees in writing that the use of water for outside irrigation will be limited to drought-tolerant plantings with drip irrigation systems and that not more than 25 percent of the landscaped area will be planted with sod or seeded lawn, which must be a drought-tolerant species.

## E. Surplus Water Contracts

Sale of surplus water under interruptible contracts is prohibited, except where water is used intermittently for emergency (fire fighting) or related purposes, the contracts shall not be terminated.

## F. Enforcement

1. The District may, after two warnings (one written), order that special follow-up visits be made in order to ascertain whether wasteful use of water is occurring. Charges for such follow-up visits by District staff, as fixed by the Board from time to time, shall be paid by the customer.

2. In the event the District determines that water use is still occurring at a customer's premises in violation of the restrictions on water use set forth in Section 28, the Manager of Administration may authorize installation of a flow-restricting device on the service line.

3. In the event that a further willful violation is observed by District personnel, the District may discontinue service. Charges for installation of flow-restricting devices or for restoring service, as fixed by the Board from time to time, shall be paid by the customer.

4. The District may immediately cancel a permit to use water from a hydrant when the customer is observed using water in violation of the regulations and restrictions on water use set forth in Section 28.

5. The District may immediately install a flow-restricting device on the service line or discontinue service of any customer observed to be in violation of the conditions set forth in Section 28 pertaining to new service connections.

# Prohibiting Wasteful Use of Water

## A. Regulations and Restrictions on Water Use

It is hereby declared by the Board of Directors that in order to conserve the District's water supply for the greatest public benefit, and to reduce the quantity of water used by the District's customers, that wasteful use of water should be eliminated. Customers of the District shall observe the following regulations and restrictions on water use.

1. Residential Customers shall:

   a. Use water for lawn or gardening watering, or any other irrigation, in a manner which does not result in excessive flooding or runoff in gutter or other waterway, patio, driveway, walk or street;

   b. Use water for washing sidewalks, walkways, driveways, patios, parking lots, tennis courts or other hard-surfaced areas in a manner which does not result in excessive runoff or waste;

   c. Use water for washing cars, boats, trailers or other vehicles and machinery, preferably from a hose equipped with a shutoff nozzle, in a manner which does not result in excessive runoff or waste;

   d. Reduce other interior or exterior uses of water to minimize or eliminate excessive runoff or waste; and

   e. Repair leaks wherever feasible.

2. Nonresidential Customers shall:

   a. Use systems which recycle water where feasible;

   b. Use water for lawn or garden watering, or any other irrigation, in a manner which does not result in excessive flooding or runoff in gutter or other waterway, patio, driveway, walk or street;

   c. Use water for washing sidewalks, walkways, driveways, patios, parking lots, tennis courts or other hard-surfaced areas in a manner which does not result in excessive runoff or waste;

d. Limit sewer flushing or street washing with District water as much as possible, consistent with public health and safety needs; and

e. Reduce other interior or exterior water uses to minimize or eliminate excessive runoffs or waste; and

f. Repair leaks wherever feasible.

## B. Exceptions

Consideration of written applications for exceptions regarding regulations and restrictions on water use set forth in this Section shall be as follows:

1. Written applications for exceptions shall be accepted, and may be granted, by the Manager of the Customer Service Division.

2. Denials of applications may be appealed in writing to the General Manager;

3. Grounds for granting such applications are:

   a. Failure to do so would cause an unnecessary and undue hardship to the Applicant, including, but not limited to, adverse economic impacts, such as loss of production or jobs; or

   b. Failure to do so would cause a condition affecting the health, sanitation, fire protection or safety of the Applicant or the public.

## C. Enforcement

1. The District may, after one written warning, order that a special meter reading or readings be made in order to ascertain whether wasteful use of water is occurring. Charges for such a meter reading or readings or for follow-up visits by District staff shall be fixed by the Board from time to time and shall be paid by the customer.

2. In the event that the District observes that apparently excessive water use is occurring at a customer's premises, the General Manager or the Manager of Administration may, after a written warning to the customer, authorize installation of a flow-restricting device on the service line for any customer observed by District personnel to be willfully violating any of the regulations and restrictions on water use set forth in this section.

3. In the event that a further willful violation is observed by District personnel, the District may discontinue service. Charges for installation of flow-restricting devices or for restoring service may be fixed by the Board from time to time.

## A. Charge for Water Delivered During Water Shortage

The following amounts will be charged during the period of the water shortage for billing periods beginning on or after May 1, 1991 for all water delivered.

| *Single Family Private Household Residential Accounts* | Per 100 Cubic Feet |
|---|---|
| For all water used within the basic allotments set forth under Section 28 of the District Regulations: | |
| For the first 250 gpd | $0.91 |
| For all water used outside the basic allotments set forth under Section 28 of the District Regulations: | |
| For the first 500 gpd above the allotment | 0.99 |
| For the next 450 gpd above the allotment | 1.50 |
| For all water used in excess of 1200 gpd | 3.00 |

Additional allotments of water, granted upon application to the District for additional household members, medical conditions, and livestock in accordance with Section 28 of the District Regulations, shall be charged at the same price as the first 250 gpd of water used within the basic allotment.

## B. Multiple Family Residential Accounts

For all water used within the basic allotments set forth under Section 28 of the District Regulations.0.95

## C. All Water Use Other Than Single Family Private Household Residential Accounts

| | |
|---|---|
| For all water used within the basic allotment | $0.99 |
| For the next 10% in excess of the basic allotment | 1.50 |
| For the next 10% in excess of the basic allotment | 2.00 |
| For all water used in excess of 120% of the basic allotment | 3.00 |

# Drought Management Program for 1991

## Findings

In light of the existing water shortage in the District's service area, and based upon the several reports and recommendations of the General Manager, as well as the testimony and written material received during the duly noticed public hearings on March 4, 5 and 26, 1991, and the meetings of February 26, 1991, March 12, 1991, and April 9, 1991, the Board of Directors of the East Bay Municipal Utility District hereby finds and determines that:

1. For the fifth consecutive year, precipitation and runoff have been below normal in the Mokelumne basin, which produces 95% of the District's water supply. Precipitation as of April 1, 1991 has totalled 27 inches, which is 64% of the amount normally received by this time.

2. As of April 1, 1991, total water storage in the District's Mokelumne and East Bay Reservoirs is 54% of capacity, compared to 66% of capacity for the same time last year, and 66% of the amount of water stored under average conditions.

3. If precipitation patterns for the remainder of the season are not average but instead are similar to 1985, the year with the driest April through June period, actual runoff would be 320,000 AF. If this precipitation pattern should occur, it is projected that the District's carryover storage at September 30, 1991 would be approximately 400,000 AF, compared to the District's minimum target carryover storage of 300,000 AF, assuming 15% conservation.

4. On March 22, 1988, the Board of Directors, acting pursuant to Water Code Section 350 et seq., declared a Water Shortage Emergency Condition in light of reports that runoff was projected to be 160,000 AF if conditions after April 1 remained dry. As a result of said Declaration, and in view of data presented concerning availability of water to meet demand, the Board determined that an overall 25% curtailment in total water use (32% for single family residential customers) was required and, in order to achieve this goal, adopted a Drought Management Program which placed restrictions upon the use of water, and which also included revenue-neutral inclining drought rates for all customers. The Program adopted by the Board successfully accomplished the objective it was implemented to achieve, and resulted in a greater than 25% curtailment in overall water use.

5. On May 9, 1989, in light of evidence that total system storage was only 50% of capacity, total runoff for the 1988-89 water year was projected to be 580,000 AF, and total water storage was projected to be 463,000 AF on September 30, 1989, 162,000 AF less than average, the Board determined that the District's water supply had not been fully replenished, and that the Water Shortage Emergency Condition should continue and a Drought Management Program, including inclining drought rates, be adopted to achieve an overall 15% curtailment (19% for single family residential customers) in total water use. This Program was also successful and resulted in water savings in excess of the 15% goal established by the Board.

6. On September 12, 1989, based upon information that precipitation and runoff conditions, combined with water savings from the Drought Management Program, would result in the District's water supply on September 30, 1989 being 74% of average, the Board of Directors determined that the water shortage emergency period had ended and adopted a voluntary water conservation program with the objective of reducing water consumption by 15%, which savings would provide a buffer in the event of a fourth dry year.

7. On February 26, 1991, based upon a thorough review of precipitation and runoff data, as well as projected storage conditions, the Board converted the 15% voluntary conservation program into a 15% mandatory conservation program, and after a duly noticed public hearing, amended the District's regulations regarding water use during this time of shortage.

8. Water Code Section 375 provides that "any public entity which supplies water at retail for the benefit of inhabitants therein may, by ordinance of resolution adopted by a majority of the members of the governing body thereof after holding a public hearing upon notice thereof and making appropriate findings of necessity therefor, adopt and enforce a water conservation program to reduce the quantity of water used by the inhabitants therein for the purpose of conserving the water supplies of such public entity...."

9. In light of data presented by staff concerning availability of water to meet demand, the Board hereby finds that a 15% curtailment in total water use after May 1, 1991 would help to ensure that sufficient water will be available to meet the needs of the District's consumers in the event of a sixth dry year in 1992 without extreme conservation measures.

10. The limited success in achieving significant voluntary water conservation in 1987 with a program limited to public information efforts, and demonstrated results from 1977 and 1988-89 mandatory drought management efforts described above, cause the Board to hereby find that an inclining rate structure, in combination with an effective public information program, is necessary to focus public attention on the drought situation, and achieve the desired consumption reduction.

11. District consumption records regrading water consumption by all single family residential consumers in February, 1986, a very wet month, indicated that a 200 gpd average closely approximated "interior" uses for "human needs", and use throughout the District did not vary significantly from this level.

12. In light of the evidence indicating winter water use patterns by single family residential customers, the Board of Directors, as part of the 1988 Drought Management Program, determined that 200 gpd should be set aside for human needs for households up to three occupants, and that an additional 50 gpd be granted for each additional occupant upon application to the District by the customers. In 1988,

over 60,000 exception requests were received, 90% addressed to the number of people in the household. After comparing the 1988 and 1989 situations to 1991, and in order to reduce the number of exemption requests and thereby mitigate a costly administrative burden, the Board of Directors finds that 250 gpd per customer (for single family households up to four occupants) should be set aside for human needs, and that use at or below 250 gpd should not be subject to an economic incentive to reduce water use further. The Board hereby determines that there shall be no increase in the rate paid for water use up to 250 gpd for single family residential consumers.

13. The Board hereby finds that the use of water in excess of the adjusted winter average of 250 gpd is primarily for uses outside the home, and further finds such uses to be more discretionary in character than "interior" uses. The Board further finds that the necessary reductions in water use can be achieved by reduction in the demand for water for these exterior uses.

14. The Board finds that in normal water years, 11% of single family residential customers use more than 750 gpd and account for 35% of all water sold to such customers, and that 3.5% of single family residential customers use more than 1,200 gpd and account for 17% of all water used by such customers.

15. In order to cover normal District costs, to achieve overall revenue neutrality, and to establish an economic incentive to conserve water for single family residential customers who use between 250 and 750 gpd, the Board hereby finds and determines that a drought surcharge approximately 9% higher than the rate for 250 gpd or less is appropriate and reasonable.

16. To focus public attention on the water shortage and the need to reduce water usage, and to encourage water conservation by single family residential consumers, the Board hereby finds and determines that an inclining block rate structure calling for a price of $.99 per unit for all water consumed between 250 and 750 gpd, $1.50 per unit for all water consumed between 750 and 1200 gpd, and $3.00 per unit for all water in excess of 1200 gpd is appropriate and reasonable. This rate structure, in addition to encouraging consumers to conserve water, will help to cover the extraordinary costs of programs required during the drought period, and will tend to meet the Board's goal of revenue neutrality for the entire rate structure. The Board hereby finds that this rate structure treats all single family residential customers equally, and results in customers using the same amount of water being charged the same amount. Further, the Board finds and determines that, on balance, the rate structure is the best alternative among those the Board has considered from the standpoint of attempting to equally allocate the available water, and to achieve the desired water use reduction.

17. In order to provide a system for exceptions or variances, the Board hereby finds and determines that medical requirements, presence of more than four residents in a single family household, incorrect customer classification based upon predominant use, and the provision of water for livestock by a single family residential consumer shall be grounds upon which exceptions to the basic allotment will be granted. The Board further finds and determines that the basic allotments shall be increased by 62 gpd per additional person who is resident in a single family household, and that the basic allotments shall be increased by 30 gpd per horse, cow, or other large animal. The Board further finds that all single family residential customers shall be notified as soon as possible of the existence of these categories of exceptions and of the process by which exceptions may be sought.

18. The Board hereby finds that in order to realize the 15% overall consumption reduction that is required, all classes of customers should achieve the following consumption reduction goals by customer class:

| | |
|---|---|
| Single Family Residential | 20% |
| Commercial | 10% |
| Industrial | 5% |
| Irrigation | 30% |
| Multi-Family Residential | 7% |

The Board also finds and determines that the basic allotment for each customer class shall be determined by applying the applicable percentage of each customers' average summer use for 1986 for other than single family residential customers.

19. In order to establish parity among all residential customers, and to approximate the rates adopted for the basic allotments for single family residential customers, while also providing an economic incentive to conserve water, the Board hereby finds and determines that the rate for water consumed within the basic allotment for multi-family residential customers shall be $.95.

20. In order to achieve the desired water savings, the Board hereby finds and determines that an inclining block rate structures shall be applied to the use of water above the basic allotment, and further finds that the following rate structure is reasonable and appropriate.

| | |
|---|---|
| Within basic allotment (multi-family residential) | $ .95 |
| Within basic allotment (commercial, industrial, irrigation) | .99 |
| Next 10% of base | 1.50 |
| Next 10% of base | 2.00 |
| Over 120% of base | 3.00 |

The Board also finds and determines that this rate structure is reasonably calculated to meet the Board's goal of revenue neutrality for the entire rate structure, and to assist in covering both normal and extraordinary (drought-related) District costs.

21. The rates adopted by the Board as provided for herein shall be effective May 1, 1991.

22. The Board hereby finds and determines that the restrictions on water use contained in Section 28 of the Regulations Governing Water Service to Customers adopted on April 9, 1991 will, in the sound discretion of the Board, conserve the water supply for the greatest public benefit. The Board determines that the uses prohibited by Section 28 are unreasonable and wasteful in this drought period, except to the extent that such uses may be deemed permissible and an exception granted under the provisions of Section 28.

23. The Board hereby finds and determines that a major use of water for new service connections is for the establishment of new landscaping, particularly sod or turf, and that unlimited availability of water for new service connections for this purpose would create an unreasonable demand for water during the drought. In order to permit completion of buildings and homes which have been approved by the cities and counties in the service area, and to promote long-term water conservation practices, the Board has adopted the rules concerning new connections set forth in Section 28. The Board finds and determines that for any new service connection, no more than 25% of the landscaped area may be sod

or seeded lawn, and such sod or lawn must be drought-tolerant species. The Board finds and determines that the restrictions on new connections, including planting limitations, and the drip irrigation system requirement, are appropriate and reasonable in light of the drought circumstances.

24. The Board finds and determines that the full range of enforcement measures set forth in the Regulations Governing Water Service to Customers is appropriate and may be used by the District in order to control consumption during the drought. The Board further finds and determines that the proper officers and employees of the District are fully authorized and directed to take such reasonable actions as shall be necessary and appropriate to enforce all of said Regulations.

25. The Board has considered the issues and data surrounding the question of continued sale of surplus water pursuant to interruptible supply contracts, and has determined that water supplied pursuant to said contracts may be used only for fire fighting or as an emergency supply. The Board hereby finds and determines that the actions set forth in Section 28 regarding said contracts are reasonable and appropriate.

26. The Board hereby finds and determines that use of water supplied by the District for construction projects shall be limited to the degree feasible by instituting a permit system, and by requiring applicants to utilize alternate sources of water where the District determines that it is feasible.

27. If any of the provisions of these Findings are held to be void or unenforceable by or as a result of a determination of any court of competent jurisdiction, such determination shall not result in the nullity or unenforceabiliity of the remaining portions of these Findings.

# Acronyms

**acre-foot (AF)**
A volume of water one foot deep over one acre in area; equal to 325,900 gallons

**BCPA**
Boulder Canyon Project Act

**CAP**
Central Arizona Project

**CEQA**
California Environmental Quality Act

**cfs**
cubic feet per second, a rate of flow equal to 7.48 gallons per second or 1.98 acre-feet per day

**CVP**
Federal Central Valley Project

**CVPIA**
1992 Central Valley Project Improvement Act

**DWR**
California Department of Water Resources which operates the SWP

**EBMUD**
East Bay Municipal Utility District

**EIR**
Environmental impact report required under CEQA

**EIS**
Environmental impact statement required under NEPA

**IID**
Imperial Irrigation District

**maf**
million acre-feet

**MWD**
The Metropolitan Water District of Southern California

**NEPA**
National Environmental Policy Act

**OCWD**
Orange County Water District

**SWP**
State Water Project

**SWC**
State Water Contractors who receive water from the SWP

# Index

anti-degradation policy
　Clean Water Act requirements
　　for, 124
　See also Clean Water Act; pollution;
　　water quality
APA. See Administrative Procedure Act
appropriative rights
　defined, 39-41
　development of, 31, 40-44
　dual doctrine of, 30-32, 39, 210
　due diligence requirements for, 45-47
　first-in-time, first-in-right principle
　　for, 37, 39, 40-41, 44, 45
　in groundwater, 48, 51
　"inchoate" (pending) rights, 45
　loss/severance of, 46-47, 58
　for municipal use, 44, 45, 46,
　　50, 189
　permit system authority for, 42-43,
　　46, 63, 68, 114-117, 120, 224
　pre-1914, compared to post-1914,
　　224, 226, 227, 228, 247
　in relation to
　　Article X, Section 2, 31-32
　　public trust doctrine, 87
　　riparian rights, 30-32, 37, 39,
　　　40, 47, 89-91, 97, 193-194
　　Water Commission Act, 31, 42-43
　　water transfers, 246-247
　requirements for, 27-28, 43-47
　for springs, 56
　State Board authority for, 114-117
　statutory, compared to non-statutory,
　　42, 45
　See also water rights
appropriator(s)
　inferiority of to overlying user,
　　52-53, 248
　legal access requirements for, 44
　"no-injury rule" for, 247
　resolution of shortage among, 39, 42
　rights between riparians and, 37-38
　senior vs. junior, 45, 247
　statutory, compared to non-statutory,
　　42, 45
　See also downstream user;
　　riparian(s)
aquaculture
　as beneficial use, 116
　See also agriculture; fish
aqueducts, 23, 226, 237
　failure of, 257
　See also conveyance facilities;
　　water transfers
area of origin protection, 250-252
　See also export of water; water
　　transfers
Areias Dairy Farms, 241
Arizona
　and Central Arizona Project, 233,
　　291, 298-299
　Colorado River water use in, 5,
　　133, 299
　as member of Colorado River
　　compact, 280
　opposition of to Colorado River com-
　　pact, 282, 284, 285, 286, 289-297
Arizona v. California (1963), 197, 200,
　207, 289-297
artesian wells
　as source of water supply, 3, 11,
　　16, 185

artesian wells (continued)
　in Southern California, 11, 16
　See also water quality; wells
Article X, Section 2. See California
　Constitution
Arvin-Edison Water Storage District,
　water transfer from to
　Metropolitan Water District, 229
assessment districts
　for pumping of groundwater, 56
　See also water districts
Auburn Dam and Reservoir, 104
Auburn-Folsom South Unit, 104
avulsion
　effect of on riparian rights, 35
　See also riparian rights

# B

balancing
　in relation to endangered species
　　protection, 144
　State Board procedures for, 130
　See also allocation; utilization
basin plan adoption procedures,
　122-124
　See also water management plan;
　　water quality
Bay Area
　provisions for in California Water
　　Plan, 23
　responsibility of for Bay-Delta
　　Estuary decline, 134
　State Water Project contractors
　　in, 25
　use of Central Valley Project water
　　in, 19
　See also East Bay
Bay-Delta agreement, 69-70
　See also Sacramento-San Joaquin
　　Delta
Bay-Delta hearings, 126-135
　See also Sacramento-San Joaquin
　　Delta
BCPA. See Boulder Canyon Project Act
beneficial use doctrine
　constitutional requirements for,
　　31-32, 38-39, 41-42, 47, 72,
　　201, 232-233
　in relation to
　　conservation, 257-258
　　degradation, 124, 125
　　Delta waters, 129-130
　　fish and wildlife protection, 40
　　groundwater users, 47-48, 52-53
　　overlying rights, 248
　　permit system, 115, 116, 125
　　prescriptive rights, 59-60, 62
　　reasonable use doctrine, 94-96
　　water quality, 109, 122-123,
　　　125, 130, 201
　types of beneficial uses, 28, 116
　See also reasonable use doctrine
Berrenda Mesa Water District
　(BMWD), 253-254
best management practices (BMPs)
　identified in 1992 Urban Water
　　Conservation MOU, 270-271
　See also conservation; efficient
　　water management
Beverly Hills, 14
BMP. See Best Management Practices

BMWD. See Berrenda Mesa Water
　District
Board of Tideland Commissioners, 80
bottled-water company, 59
Boulder Canyon Project Act (BCPA),
　14, 16, 197, 200, 289
　establishment of, 284-285
　objectives of, 285-287, 292
　Section 1, 285-286, 293
　Section 4(a)(2), 286
　Section 4(a), 286, 292, 294
　Section 5, 287, 293
　Section 8(b), 292, 293, 294
　Section 13(b), 287
　Section 14, 293
　Section 18, 293
　See also Colorado River
boundary dispute, "quiet title" action
　for, 82-83
Burns-Porter Act, 23
Butte County, 25

# C

Calaveras River, 252
California
　annual water supply/runoff, 2
　Colorado River withdrawals, 299
　federal agreement with for Bay-
　　Delta standards, 135-137
　freedom of for water management,
　　191
　as member of Colorado River
　　compact, 280, 292
　physical solution cases, 177-186
　public trust doctrine in, 77-81
　water system capsule view,
　　67-70
　See also state
California Aqueduct, 238
　See also aqueducts
California constitution
　Article X, Section 2, 28, 38, 43, 57,
　　59, 71, 105, 109, 116, 250
　allocations considerations,
　　95-98, 101, 119, 176-179,
　　232-233, 255
　correlative rights doctrine
　　consideration, 29
　Herminghaus case
　　considerations, 89-95
　reasonable use doctrine
　　consideration, 31-32, 89-98,
　　91n15, 120-121
　Article X, Section 5, 36
　Article X, Section, 31-32, 120-121
　Article XIIIA, 273
　Article XIV, Section 3, 31-32
　See also state law; U.S. constitution
California Endangered Species Act
　(CESA), 162-168
　consultation provisions,
　　166-168
　endangered species definition, 162
　listing procedure, 162-164
　　emergency listing, 164
　taking provisions, 164-166
　　allowance of incidental takings,
　　　167
　water management plan relation
　　to, 267
　See also Endangered Species Act

California Environmental Quality Act (CEQA)
in relation to
conservation, 273-274
consumption, 71
Endangered Species Act, 166-168
review of water transfers allowed
under, 227, 240, 241
*See also* environmental impact report
California gnatcatcher, 149, 166
*See also* endangered species
California State Water Project.
*See* State Water Project
California Urban Water Conservation Council, 270
*California v. United States*, 106, 191, 194, 195, 198-201
California Water Plan, Feather River Project as component of, 23
California Water Resources Development Bond Act (Burns-Porter Act), 23
Calleguas Municipal Water District, 15
Camanche Dam, 10
canals, 3, 194, 269
*See also* channels
CAP. *See* Central Arizona Project
Carson River, water rights priority in lands surrounding, 252
Castaic Lake Water Agency, 25, 241-242
cattle ranching, 11
*See also* agriculture
cease-and-desist order
regional board authority for issuance, 125
*See also* water rights remedies
Central Arizona Project (CAP), 233, 291, 298-299
Section 301(b), 298
*See also* Arizona
Central Basin Municipal Water District, 15
Central Coast
regional board oversight for, 122
State Water Project contractors in, 25
Central Valley
described, 19
as primary state water consumer, 7
regional board oversight for, 122
use of State Water Project water in, 26
Central Valley East Side Project Association, 128
Central Valley Project Act of 1933, 18
Central Valley Project (CVP)
contractual obligations, 5, 69
described, 3, 4, 16-21, 237
divisions, 20, 128
relation of to Endangered Species Act, 141, 211
State Board regulation of, 128, 130-131, 135, 137
state law applicability to, 202-203
water transfers within and from, 237-241
*See also* Reclamation Act of 1902; U.S. Bureau of Reclamation
Central Valley Project Improvement Act (CVPIA), 71, 137, 226, 238-241, 251

Central Valley Project Improvement Act *(continued)*
Section 3405, 239
Section 3405(a)(1), 239
Section 3405(a)(2)(A), 239
Section 3405(a)(2)(B), 239
Section 3405(a)(2)(D), 239
Section 3405(a), 239
CEQA. *See* California Environmental Quality Act
CESA. *See* California Endangered Species Act
channels
artificial
in Delta, 126
as natural watercourse, 33
for State Water Project water, 24
natural
defined, 48
for Delta water transport, 137, 138
State Board regulation of streamflow within, 42, 43, 115
subterranean
regulation of streamflow within, 42, 43
water within defined as groundwater, 48
*See also* streams
Chino Basin Municipal Water District, 15, 188
*Chino Basin Municipal Water District v. City of Chino*, 52, 64-65, 188-189
Chowchilla River, 21
cities
annual water use, 2
appropriative rights held by, 39, 50
involvement of in Colorado River project, 14
new-connection denial allowed for growth control, 263-265 riparian rights of, 35
wastewater discharge by, 274
*See also* government agencies; municipal use
citrus cultivation, 11-12
*See also* agriculture
*City of Lodi v. East Bay Municipal Utility District*, 93, 176, 177, 178-181
*City of Los Angeles v. City of San Fernando*, 54-55, 60, 174-174
civil action
in adjudication of water rights, 65
*See also* water rights remedies
Claire Engle Lake, 20
Clean Water Act, 113
in relation to
Endangered Species Act, 168-172
National Pollution Discharge Elimination System, 125
state law, 211-222
requirements of, 123
anti-degradation policy, 124
designated uses, 123
Section 101(g) (Wallop Amendment), 216-221, 222
Section 208, 212, 214, 219
Section 303, 212, 213n6
Section 402, 219, 220

Clean Water Act
requirements of *(continued)*,
Section 404, 212, 219, 220, 221
Section 510, 222
for water quality regulation, 123-124, 211-222
*See also* water quality
cleanup order, regional board authority for, 126
"Club Fed"
role of in Bay-Delta standards, 135-136
*See also* Sacramento-San Joaquin Delta
Coachella Valley, 16, 289
Coachella Valley Water District (CVWD), 25, 291
seniority of to Metropolitan Water District, 233
water transfer of to Desert Water Agency, 242
*See also* Colorado River
Coastal Municipal Water District, 15
coastal sage scrub
implementation of NCCP program in, 166
*See also* endangered species; Riverside County
Colorado, as member of Colorado River compact, 280-285
Colorado River
in relation to Central Arizona Project, 233, 291, 298-299 as source of state water, 2, 3, 5, 14, 232-233
transfers of water from, 242
*See also* Boulder Canyon Project; Colorado River Compact
Colorado River Aqueduct, 4, 12-15
Colorado River basin, 15-16
annual water use, 7
banking and transfer of entitlements within, 299
defined, 282
lower basin, defined, 280, 283
quantification of agricultural use, 299-300
regional water quality board oversight for, 122
in relation to endangered species, 300
upper basin, defined, 280, 282-283
upper basin/lower basin division, 279-280, 282, 300
Colorado River Basin Project Act, 298
Colorado River Basin Salinity Control Act, 297
Colorado River compact, 14
Article II, 282
Article II(a), 282
Article II(b), 282
Article II(f), 282
Article II(g), 283
Article III, 283
Article III(a), 283
Article III(b), 283
Article III(c), 283, 297
Article III(d), 283
Article VIII, 284
Article XI, 284
development of, 280-284
objectives of, 281

Colorado River compact *(continued)*
opposition of Arizona to, 282, 284, 285, 286, 289-297
Colorado River law, 279-300
introduction to, 279-280
*See also* federal law; state law
Colorado Ute Settlement Act, 297
commerce
relation of to public trust doctrine, 75-81, 85
*See also* economic factors; navigation
Commerce Clause, relation of to navigation, 193
common law
groundwater regulation under, 48
surface water regulation under, 193
water law regulation under, 29-30, 49, 68
*See also* federal law; state law
community
consideration of in urban water management plan, 267
effect on of water transfers, 253-254
opposition of to water transfer, 223
protection for allowed by water district, 263
protest rights of to water emergency, 257
*See also* consumers; social factors
Compton, 14
condemnation
appropriative rights loss by, 46
water rights loss by, 35, 36
*See also* eminent domain
conjunctive use
defined, 234
as element of state water ethic, 132
of surface and groundwater, 234-237
*See also* groundwater; surface water
conservation
agricultural, 268-269
application of CEQA to, 273-274
defined, 268
as element of state water ethic, 132, 225-277
planning for, 266-269
Urban Water Management Planning Act, 266-267
in relation to water transfers, 234
in relation to water use, 269-274
as authority for limiting water use, 255-265
consideration of in urban water management plan, 266-267
legal authority for, 265-266
mandatory ordinances for, 271-273
violation of ordinance for, 257, 261
Water Conservation in Landscaping Act, 271
role of in Endangered Species Act, 141-142
State Board requirements for, 120-121, 232-233
*See also* drought; shortage
conserved water, transfer of, 234, **235**
consumers
injunctive relief allowed for, 64

consumers *(continued)*
rights of to protest water emergency, 257
*See also* community
consumptive use
compared to environmental use, 71-111
consideration of in urban water management plan, 267
*EDF v. EBMUD* case study, 102-111
*Herminghaus* and Article X, Section 2, 89-95
inclining rate schedules allowed for, 273
*See also* agricultural use; domestic use; municipal use
contamination. *See* pollution
continuous and hostile use
requirements for in prescriptive rights, 61-62
*See also* prescriptive rights
Contra Costa Canal, 20
Contra Costa County, 20
conveyance facilities
use of for water transfer, 241
*See also* aqueducts; pipeline
Corning Canal, 20
Corps. *See* U.S. Army Corps of Engineers
correlative rights doctrine
defined, 29
in relation to
Article X, Section 2, 29
groundwater rights, 247-248
percolating waters, 49-50
riparian rights, 37, 247-248
Costa-Isenberg Water Transfer Act, 225
*See also* water transfers
cotton, 6
cotton mice, 161
counties
new-connection denial allowed for growth control, 263-265 *See also* cities; municipal districts
county of origin protection, 251
*See also* water transfers
county water districts, 56
authority of to limit water use, 260-261
*See also* government agencies; water districts
courts
approach of to water controversy, 174
power of to enforce physical solution, 179, 180
regulation of water use by, 67, 72
*See also* water rights remedies
Crestline-Lake Arrowhead Water Agency, **25**
critical habitat
designation procedure, 143, 145-149
destruction of by U.S. Forest Service, 160
Endangered Species Act definition, 145
occupied vs. unoccupied, 145
special protection for, 153, 154, 243, 254
wetlands, 219
*See also* endangered species; habitat

Crystal Springs Reservoir, 9
CVP. *See* Central Valley Project
CVPIA. *See* Central Valley Project Improvement Act

**D**

dams, 3, 18-19, 237
discharges from as "pollution," 214-216
failure of, 257
Fish and Game Code requirements for, 99
permit requirements for, 58
*See also* reservoirs
declaratory relief
to protect water rights, 63
*See also* water rights remedies
degradation
State Board allowances for, 124
*See also* pollution; water quality
Delta, *See also* Sacramento-San Joaquin Delta
Delta Cross-Channel, 19, 20, 135
Delta Fish Protective Facility, 26
Delta Protection Act, 129, 251-252
Delta Pumping Plant, 24-26
Delta smelt, 135, 148, 171
*See also* endangered species
Delta-Mendota Canal, 19-21
Department of Fish and Game (DFG)
agreement of with USBR, 104
authority of over appropriations, 115
Hot Creek Fish Hatchery Agreement with LADWP, 99
*See also* Fish and Game Code
Department of Water Resources (DWR)
dam approval authority of, 99
involvement of in water transfers, 225-226, 244-246
relation of with State Board, 129, 226
*See also* State Water Resources Control Board
desalination, 276-277, 297
*See also* conservation
desert areas, precipitation in, 2, 19
Desert Lands Act of 1877, 192-194, 210
desert tortoise, 143, 150, 161
*See also* endangered species
Desert Water Agency (DWA), 56
as State Water Project contractor, **25**
water transfer of with Coachella Valley Irrigation District, 242
designated uses
Clean Water Act requirements for, 123-124
*See also* Clean Water Act
development, "will serve" letter provisions for, 261-262
Devil's Den Water District, **25**, 241
Devil's Hole pupfish, 207-208
*See also* endangered species
distribution of water. *See* allocation; utilization
ditches
as source of water supply, 3, 11, 12, 17, 269
use of, as open and notorious use, 60
*See also* channels; diversion

Environmental Protection Agency
(EPA)
  interpretation of Wallop
    Amendment, 216-219
  relation of with State Board,
    125, 133
  role of in Federal Environmental
    Directorate (Club Fed), 135-137
  role of in water quality control,
    123-124
environmental use
  as beneficial use, 122
  Central Valley Project provisions
    for, 137, 238
  compared to consumptive use,
    71-111
  constitutional requirements for,
    28, 256
  effect of on state water supply, 6-7,
    27, 69, 256
  federal requirements for, 192
  *Herminghaus* case and Article X,
    Section 2, 89
  no federal allowance for, 209
  not included in Rivers and Harbors
    Act, 19
  protection for in *EDF v. EBMUD*
    case, 109, 110-111
  public trust doctrine applied to,
    81, 85
  recycled water for, 274
  transfer of water rights for, 223
  water acquisition for through
    taxes, 254
  *See also* habitat; instream use
environmentalists, 213, 243
  in litigation against State Board, 132
  water rights lawsuits brought
    by, 64
equitable apportionment
  for allocation of water, 173-176
  compared to physical solution,
    175, 176
  in relation to Colorado River
    diversions, 281-285, 292
  *See also* allocation
equity, determination of in water
    rights disputes, 178
ESA. *See* Endangered Species Act
escaped waters
  riparian rights extended to, 33
  *See also* abandoned waters
evaporation, effect of on precipitation, 2
EWMP. *See* efficient water manage-
    ment practices
export of water
  from Sacramento-San Joaquin
    Delta, 132-135
  outside of watershed, 38-39, 44,
    177-178, 185-186
  *See also* imported water; sale of
    water; water transfers


**F**

Fall-Davis Report, 284
"farming". *See* agriculture; water
    transfers
Feather River, 21-**25**, **244**
Federal Energy Regulatory
    Commission (FERC)
  relation of to state law, 204-205

Federal Energy Regulatory
    Commission *(continued)*
  and states rights, 203-206
  *See also* federal law; government
    agencies
Federal Environmental Directorate
    (Club Fed), 135-137
  *See also* government agencies
federal government
  authority of over water supply,
    5, 124
  responsibility of for Delta water
    quality, 128, 137
  role of in state water quality,
    123-124
  *See also* federal law; United States
federal law
  federal reserved rights, 206-209,
    294-297
  federal riparian rights, 209-211
  interaction of with state law,
    191-222
  *See also* common law; state law;
    United States
Federal Power Act (FPA)
  hydroelectric licensing under,
    203-204
  *See also* power project
*Federal Register*, endangered species
    listing in, 148, 149
federal storage
  in San Luis Reservoir, 21
  *See also* storage
Feigenbaum Act, 251
financing scheme
  for Boulder Canyon Project, 15-16
  for Central Valley Project, 18
  for Metropolitan Water District, 12
  for State Water Project, 24
fire protection, consideration of in
    water policy, 257
first-in-time, first-in-right principle,
    37, 39, 40-41, 44, 45, 248
  *See also* appropriative rights;
    mining
fish
  endangered
    loss of in Delta pumping, 137
    taking of for sport, 165
  no protection for, 23, 71, 209, 217
  protection of
    as beneficial use, 40, 116, 122,
      129, 131, 203, 226
    in California waters, 20, 104-105,
      106, 110-111, 226, 227, 228,
      231, 240, 241, 243, 254
    under Clean Water Act, 123,
      124, 128
    under Endangered Species Act,
      143, 165, 169
    under Fish and Game Code, 99,
      110-111, 115
    under public trust doctrine, 81,
      83, 84, 85, 100
  *See also* environmental use; Fish
    and Game Code; habitat
Fish and Game Code, Endangered
    Species Act provisions, 142
  Section 5937 and 5946, 71, 72,
    98-111
  *See also* Department of Fish and
    Game; fish

Fish and Wildlife Service. *See* U.S. Fish
    and Wildlife Service
fishing, control of in Bay-Delta
    standards, 135
flood control, 18-19, 285
Flood Control Act of 1944, 201
flooding
  effect on of hydraulic mining, 81
  effect of on San Francisco Bay, 126
flow standards
  challenges to Clean Water Act
    requirements for, 221-222
  challenges to State Board require-
    ments for, 132-134
  imposition of in water quality plan,
    133-134
  for Sacramento-San Joaquin Delta,
    6-7, 238
  for San Francisco Bay, 132-134,
    192
  state law for preempts federal law,
    205-206, 209
fluctuation in water flow. *See* variability
    of water
Folsom Reservoir and Lake, 20, 85,
    103-111
Folsom-South Canal, EBMUD diversion
    through, 103, 104, 106, 108,
    109, 119
Foothill Municipal Water District, 15
foreign water
  riparian rights not attached to, 33
  *See also* export of water; water
    transfers
forfeiture
  of appropriative rights, 47, 58
  of prescriptive rights, 58, 62
  *See also* abandonment
Fox Canyon Ground Water
    Management Agency, 56
Framework Agreement, for Bay-Delta
    protection, 137
fresh water flow standards
  for San Francisco Bay,
    132-134, 192
  *See also* flow standards;
    salinity control
Friant Dam, 20
Friant-Kern Canal, 20, 21
fringe-toed lizard, 161
  *See also* endangered species
frost protection
  as beneficial use, 116
  use of water for, 96
  *See also* agricultural use
Fullerton, 14


**G**

geology, relation of to groundwater, 48
Gila River, 280, 281, 291
  *See also* Colorado River compact
Glendale, 14
gold mining, 81
  *See also* mining
gold rush, 8
  appropriative rights development
    in, 40
  impact of on water use, 3, 17
  *See also* mining
golden-cheeked warbler, 146
  *See also* endangered species

golf courses
    recycled water for, 274
    *See also* irrigation; landscaping
*Gorsuch* opinion (*National Wildlife Federation v. Gorsuch*), 214-219
government agencies
    appropriative rights exercised by, 51, 66-67
    authority of to sell water, 230
    Endangered Species Act requirements for, 151-152
    immunity of from prescriptive rights, 46, 54-55, 58, 59, 62, 174
    public trust doctrine challenges to, 72-73
    public trust land grant limitations, 75-81
    right of to store imported water, 236
    riparian rights held by, 34
    water permit requirements for, 114-115
    water rights lawsuits brought by, 64
Grant Lake Reservoir, 99, 100
    *See also* Mono Lake
grant of land
    relation of to public trust doctrine, 75-81
    *See also* public trust doctrine
gravel
    in underflow of surface stream, 48
    *See also* mining; streams
gravel mining
    effect on of upstream appropriation, 95-98
    *See also* mining
gravel transport by water, not a reasonable use, 38
Grayrocks Dam and Reservoir, 157
graywater
    defined, 276
    use of in dual water systems, 267
    uses of, 276-277
grizzly bear, 151
    *See also* endangered species
groundwater
    conjunctive use of with surface water, 234-237
    contamination in, 57
    decreases in, within Central Valley, 17-18
    defined, 48
    groundwater banking program, 236-237
    groundwater basins, 2-3
    groundwater management districts, 57
    groundwater management plans, in relation to water transfers, 234, 250
    groundwater management statues and ordinances, 248-250
    groundwater pumping
        adjudication of, 53, 65
        annual figures for, 3
        conjunctive use of with surface water, 234-237
        in early California, 11, 17
        economic considerations for, 2-3
        effect on of federal regulations, 207-208
        mutual prescription applied to, 53-54

groundwater
    groundwater pumping *(continued)*
        overlying user's protection against, 53
        as prescriptive action, 61
        record keeping required for, 59
        *See also* pumping
    groundwater replenishment
        with agricultural water, 5-6, 268-269
        groundwater management plan consideration of, 57
        with imported water, 54
        with municipal wastewater, 274-276
        naturally occurring, 3
        sources for, 3-4
        *See also* overdraft
    groundwater rights
        acquisition of, 47-53
        as constraint on water transfers, 247-250
        limitations on, 53-57
        loss of by prescription, 59
        overlying rights, 29, 50, 247-248
        reserved rights doctrine application to, 207-208
        for springs, 44, 55-56
        for underground storage, 51-52
        of water districts, 56-57
    imported water combined with, 51-52
    overdraft of, 3
    percolation presumption for, 49
    regional board responsibility for, 125
    relation of Water Commission Act to, 31
    riparian rights not applicable to, 33
    springs, 44, 55-56
    storage rights for, 51-52
    transfer of allowed, 234
    underflow
        as classification of underground water, 27
        defined, 48
        rights to, 48, 94-95
        riparian rights extended to, 33
        in subterranean channels, 42, 43, 48
        of surface streams, 27, 34, 42, 48-49, 51
    underground water
        appropriative rights in, 51
        categories of, 48
        classification of, 27
        regulation of by State Board, 42, 43, 116
        riparian rights extended to, 33, 34
        types of, 27
    underground water rights, 47-53
        introduction to, 47-48
    water district jurisdiction for, 56-57
    *See also* percolating waters; pumping; wells
growth control
    allowed as objective of municipal water supply, 263-265
    not allowed as motive for water moratoria, 259-260, 262-265
    *See also* population

## H

habitat
    coastal sage scrub, 166
    critical habitat
        designation of, 143, 145-149
        destruction of by U.S. Forest Service, 160
        special protection for, 153, 154, 243, 254
    protection of
        in Bay-Delta Estuary standards, 135
        by (California) Endangered Species Act, 142, 143, 144, 159-160, 163
        by Habitat Maintenance Funding Act, 166
        in EBMUD case, 111
        with NCCP program, 165
        in Riverside County, 161-162, 166
    *See also* Endangered Species Act; fish; wildlife
habitat conservation plan (HCP)
    required for incidental take, 160-161, 167
    *See also* conservation; Endangered Species Act
Habitat Maintenance Funding Act, 166
Hadley, Ebenezer, 15
Hallett Creek, 209-211
Hawaiian Palila bird, 159
health risk
    associated with poor water quality, 109
    associated with wastewater reclamation, 118
    prevention of with water policy, 257
    *See also* water quality
hearing
    ESA requirements for, 148
    regional board responsibility for, 122
    required for forfeiture of appropriative rights, 47
    required for water management plan, 267
    State Board requirements for, 115
    for water emergency, 257
    *See also* Bay-Delta hearing process; public notice
heat control, as beneficial use, 116
*Herminghaus v. Southern California Edison Co.*, 31, 89-95, 96
Hetch-Hetchy reservoir, 4, **8**, **9**
    *See also* San Francisco
high quality waters
    State Board protection of, 124
    *See also* water quality
*Hillside Water Co. v. City of Los Angeles*, 184-185
Hodge, Judge Richard, 107
Homestead Act of 1862, 192
Honey Lake Groundwater Management District, 56, 249n26
Hoover Dam, 289
    update for documents of, **290**
Hoover, Herbert, 279, 281, 285
Hot Creek Fish Hatchery Agreement, 99-102
    *See also* Mono Lake

household
  water use by, 2
  *See also* domestic use
housing, regional board consideration
  of, 123
hydroelectric licensing
  as exception to state law, 203-206
  *See also* power project
hydrologic year type
  effect of on Folsom Reservoir
    releases, 110-111
  *See also* drought

I

*IID I* (*Imperial Irrigation District v.
  State Water Resources Control
  Board*, (1986), 120-121
*IID II* (*Imperial Irrigation District v.
  State Water Resources Control
  Board* (1990), 121
IID. *See* Imperial Irrigation District
*Illinois Central* case, 75-77, 80
Imperial County, special water transfer
  requirements, 236
Imperial Irrigation District (IID)
  use of Colorado River water by,
    231-233, 271, 287, 288, 289,
    291, 296
  water rights of, 298
Imperial Valley, 15-16, 284
imported water
  "imported water banking", 234
  overdraft replenishment with, 54
  in relation to safe yield determi-
    nation, 55
  riparian rights not attached to, 33
  storage and recapture of, 51-52,
    55, 236
  title maintenance for, 51
  *See also* export of water; water
    transfers
individuals
  as holder of prescriptive rights, 59
  as holder of riparian rights, 34
  *See also* private parties
industrial use
  as beneficial use, 28, 116, 122,
    128, 129
  Clean Water Act consideration of,
    123
  emergency drought water banks
    for, 243
  groundwater for, 3
  priority of use establishment
    for, 192
  recycled water for, 274, 275
  use reductions in, 269
injection wells
  for storage of imported water, 51
  *See also* wells
injunction
  physical solution in lieu of, 182,
    183-184, 186
  to enforce cleanup order, 126
  to protect water rights, 63-64, 67
  *See also* water rights remedies
injury
  from adverse and hostile use, 61
  remedies for, 63-67
inland waters, public trust doctrine
  applied to, 81

instream use
  as beneficial use, 122, 231
  Clean Water Act protection for, 124
  diversion for allowed, 44
  diversion for not allowed, 116
  *EDF v. EBMUD* case study, 102-111
  in relation to public trust doctrine, 87
  water management plan consid-
    eration of, 69
  *See also* downstream use; environ-
    mental use
inverse condemnation, 36, 46
  claims for based on water
    moratoria, 257, 259, 260
  defined, 67
  *See also* condemnation; eminent
    domain
irrigation
  acreage under, 5
  as beneficial use, 28, 116
  early efforts for, 3-5, 11, 17, 19-21
  recycled water use for, 274, 275
  regulation of under Rivers and
    Harbors Act, 19
  using stream water, 3
  *See also* agricultural use;
    landscaping
irrigation districts
  formation of, 17
  *See also* water districts

J

Jicarilla Apache Tribe Water Rights
  Settlement Act, 297
jobs. *See* economic factors; industrial
  use
jurisdiction
  exclusive vs. concurrent, 117-120
  *See also* State Water Resources
    Control Board

K

kangaroo rat. *See* Stephens' kangaroo
  rat
"Katz bill", 226
Kaweah Delta, 94-95
  *See also* Sacramento-San Joaquin
    Delta
Kern County, **25**
Kern County Water Agency, 128,
  236, 242
  opposition of to member agency
    water sales, 253-254
Kern River, 236
Kern Water Bank, 236
Kesterson Refuge, 217
Kettner bill, 284
Kings County, **25**
Kings County Water Agency, 242
Kinkaid Act, 284

L

LADWP. *See* Los Angeles Department
  of Water and Power
Lahonton region, regional board
  oversight for, 122
Lake Matthews, 15
Lake Mead, 299
  *See also* Colorado River basin

Lake Oroville, 5, 24
lakes
  littoral rights for, 33
  public trust doctrine protection for,
    87-88
  recycled water for, 274
  riparian rights extended to, 33
land
  fallowing of for water rights,
    242, 246
  non-riparian
    riparian water use allowed
      on, 39-40
    riparian water use not allowed
      on, 35, 38
  in relation to
    overlying and appropriative
      rights, 52-53, 248
    percolating waters, 49
    riparian rights, 28-30, 32-35,
      182-183
  retirement of for water rights,
    241-242
  on which appropriated water can
    be used, 44
  *See also* public domain lands; real
    property; soil
land use policy implementation, not
  allowed for water districts, 263
landowners, involvement of with NCCP
  program, 165-166
landscaping
  conservation requirements for, 270
  recycled water for, 274, 275
  Water Conservation in Landscaping
    Act, 271
  *See also* irrigation
Las Virgenes Municipal Water
  District, 15
League of the Southwest, 280, 281
leak repair, 270
  *See also* conservation
Least Bell's Vireo, 172
  *See also* endangered species
Lee Ferry, AZ., 280, 283
Lee Vining Creek, 85, 99, 100
  *See also* Mono Lake
legislature. *See* government agencies;
  state
levees, 138, 284
licensing
  Federal Power Act requirements
    for, 203-206
  *See also* permit authority
Little Tennessee River, 156, 157
Littlerock Creek Irrigation District, **25**
littoral rights
  as riparian rights, 33
  *See also* lakes;
    riparian rights
local agencies
  authority of to block water transfer,
    248-250
  authority of to sell water, 230
  *See also* government agencies
local custom
  first-in-time, first-in-right principle,
    37, 39, 40-41, 44, 45, 248
  support of by federal government,
    193
  *See also* mining
Long Beach, 14

new connections *(continued)*
    denial of in non-emergency, 262-265
    water-saving devices required
        for, 266
    *See also* domestic use;
        municipal use
New Melones Dam, 198, 201-202
New Mexico, 280
Nimbus Hatchery, 110
1992 Urban Water Conservation MOU,
    270-271
NMFS. *See* National Marine Fisheries
    Service
no-growth policy
    allowed as objective of municipal
        water supply, 263-265
    not allowed as objective for water
        moratoria, 259-260, 262-265
    *See also* population
non-essential use
    district authority for prohibiting,
        260, 261
    *See also* shortage; waste of water
North Bay Aqueduct, 24
North Coast
    precipitation in, 2
    regional board oversight for, 122
    runoff from used in State Water
        Project, 23
notice of appropriation, 41, 45, 59
    state requirements for, 59, 60, 62
    *See also* appropriative rights;
        public notice
NPDES. *See* National Pollution
    Discharge Elimination System
nuisance, prevention of, 122

# O

Oak Flat Water District, **25**
Oakland, 134
    *See also* Bay Area; San Francisco
        Bay
Ojai Ground Water Management
    Agency, 56
Oklahoma, 280
open and notorious use
    prescriptive rights requirements
        for, 60
    *See also* prescriptive rights
Orange County
    coastal sage scrub NCCP program
        in, 166
    special water transfer requirements
        for, 236
Orange County Water District, 56,
    186-188, 189
*Orange County Water District v. City of
    Chino, et al.*, 64, 186-188
oranges, 11
Oregon, 2
Oroville Dam and Reservoir, 21-23
overdraft
    in Central Valley, 17-18
    defined, 3, 47, 55
    of groundwater basins, 3, 47, 53-54
        prescriptive rights established
            by, 51
    mitigation of conditions for, 57
    in relation to water transfers, 234
    replenishment of with imported
        water, 54

overdraft *(continued)*
    *See also* groundwater; shortage;
        wells
overlying rights, 50, 65, 189
    attachment of to land, 248
    as constraint on water transfer,
        247-248
    loss of by prescription, 55
    priority determination for, 52-53,
        175
    relation of to appropriative rights,
        52-53, 94-95
    *See also* groundwater
Owens River Aqueduct, 12
Owens Valley, 3, **12**, 15, 223, 236
    *See also* Los Angeles Department
        of Water and Power
oyster beds, 73-75

# P

Pajaro Valley Water Management
    Agency, 56, 249n26
*Palila v. Hawaii Department of Land
    and Natural Resources* (Palila I
    and II), 159-160, 168
Palmdale Water District, **25**
Palo Verde Irrigation District (PVID),
    233, 242, 288, 289, 291, 296
Pardee Dam and Reservoir, 9-**10**,
    93, 178
Parker, AZ, 15
Parker Creek, 85, 99
    *See also* Mono Lake
Pasadena, 14
pasture irrigation, 6
    *See also* agriculture; irrigation
*Peabody v. City of Vallejo*, 34, 37, 48,
    67, 93, 94, 97, 176, 177, 179,
    182, 247
Peoples Water Company, 9
percolating waters
    appropriation of, 51
    appropriative rights not applicable
        to, 43, 51, 115
    correlative rights doctrine
        affecting, 49
    from agricultural runoff, 5-6,
        268-269
    physical solutions as remedy for, 65
    as real property right, 28
    riparian rights not applicable to, 33
    as underground water, 27, 48-49
    as waste, 268-269
    *See also* groundwater
peripheral canal, 26, 137-138
    *See also* Sacramento-San
        Joaquin Delta
permit authority
    for appropriative rights, 42-43, 46,
        63, 68, 114-117, 120, 224
    Endangered Species Act provisions
        for, 142, 160-162, 164-166, 167
    Federal Power Act licensing
        requirements, 203-206
    not applicable to groundwater, 47,
        50, 57
    for regulating appropriative
        rights, 42-43, 46, 63, 68,
        120, 224
    relation of to LADWP, 98-102
    requirements under, 89, 114-117

permit authority *(continued)*
    of U.S. Army Corps of Engineers,
        220-221
    *See also* moratoria; State Water
        Resources Control Board
physical solutions
    cases for in California, 177-186
        trial court cases, 186-190
    as "common sense" approach, 65,
        176-177
    compared to equitable apportion-
        ment, 176
    constitutional provisions for,
        176-177
    *See also* allocation
piers, 76
pipeline
    for appropriated water, 185
    failure of, 257
    underground, 60
planning
    basin plan adoption procedures, 122
    effect on of Porter-Cologne Act,
        114, 120-123
    for water conservation, 266-269
    water management plans, 266-267,
        268, 273
plants
    protection of, 254
        under Endangered Species
            Act, 142
    transpiration by, 2
    *See also* endangered species; habitat
Plumas County, **25**
plumbing upgrade, implementation of
    for conservation, 270
point-source surface discharge
    regulation of by National Pollution
        Discharge Elimination System,
        125
    *See also* pollution; waste discharge
police power authority
    as authority for municipal
        restrictions, 263-264
    of Department of Water Resources,
        236
Pollutant Policy Document (PPD),
    State Board formation of, 131
pollution
    affecting drinking water supply, 109
    agricultural, 138, 217
    degradation allowances by State
        Board, 124
    discharges from dam as, 214-216
    effect of on Bay-Delta water
        quality, 138
    from selenium, 217
    regulation of movements of, 57
    remedies for, 63
    *See also* Clean Water Act; water
        quality
pollution control, as element of state
    water ethic, 132
ponds
    riparian rights extended to, 33
    *See also* agriculture; lakes
pooling agreements, 238
    *See also* water transfers
population, in north coast region, 2
population growth
    effect of on water supply, 8, 10, 12,
        17, 256

vested-right uses *(continued)*
    *See also* riparian rights; water
        rights
vineyards, 96
    *See also* agriculture

# W

Walker River, water rights priority
    within lands surrounding, 252
Wallop Amendment, 216-219
    *See also* Clean Water Act
waste discharge
    Bay-Delta standards for, 135
    Porter-Cologne Act definition for,
        125
    regional board enforcement
        authority for, 122, 125-126
    *See also* pollution; water quality
waste of water
    prevention of with physical solution,
        180, 183, 186
    prohibitions against, 28, 32, 97,
        268-269
    in relation to water transfers, 231
    *See also* conservation; reasonable
        use doctrine
wastewater
    discharge of into ocean, 274-275
    reclamation of, 231
    State Board jurisdiction over,
        117-118, 218
    *See also* reclamation
water audits, implementation of for
    conservation, 270, 272
water banks
    Drought Water Bank, 236-237, 243
    emergency drought water banks,
        243-246
    groundwater banking program,
        236-237
    Kern Water Bank, 236
water brokering. *See* water transfers
*Water for California*, 251
Water Commission Act, 31, 42-43, 224
    *See also* State Water Resources
        Control Board
water connections
    moratoria on, 255-261
    *See also* municipal use; new
        connections
water conservation districts, 56
    *See also* conservation; water
        districts
Water Conservation in Landscaping
    Act, 271
water conservation programs,
    265-266
    *See also* conservation
water districts
    application to of Urban Water
        Management Planning Act,
        266-267
    appropriative rights held by, 39
    authority of to restrict service,
        262-265
    conservation districts, 56
    emergency declaration authority
        of, 255-261
    groundwater assessment districts,
        56-57
    irrigation districts, 17

water districts *(continued)*
    1992 Urban Water Conservation
        MOU among, 270-271
    as State Water Project
        contractors, **25**
    *See also* municipal districts;
        water supplier
water flow requirements.
    *See* flow standards
water law
    categories of, 27
    characteristics of, 69
    *See also* federal law; state law
water management plans, 266-267,
    268, 273
    instream use consideration in, 69
    in relation to CEQA review, 267
    *See also* planning
water marketing. *See* water transfers
Water Pollution Control Act.
    *See* Clean Water Act
water pollution. *See* pollution
water projects, modern, **4**
water quality
    Clean Water Act regulation of,
        123-124, 211-222
    consideration of in *EDF v. EBMUD*
        case, 102-111
    effect on of hydraulic mining, 81
    Porter-Cologne Act regulation of,
        113, 114, 121-123
    protection of for domestic use, 98,
        107, 109, 138
    in relation to
        beneficial use doctrine, 109,
            116, 122
        State Board decisions, 128
        water quantity, 69, 216-219,
            221-222, 269
    right of appropriator to, 44
    State Board regulation of, 53, 117,
        125-139
        regional board responsibilities
            for, 121-123
    *See also* Clean Water Act; waste
        discharge
water quality control plans
    development of under Porter-
        Cologne Act, 124
    Draft Water Quality Control Plan for
        Salinity for the San Francisco
        Bay and Sacramento-San
        Joaquin Delta, 131-135
    imposition of flow requirements
        for, 132-134
    for Sacramento-San Joaquin Delta
        and Suisun Marsh, 129
    waste discharge permit compliance
        required under, 125
    *See also* Porter-Cologne Act
water quality criteria
    Clean Water Act requirements for,
        124-125
    *See also* Clean Water Act
water quality standards, state and
    federal law interaction over,
    211-216
"water ranching". *See* water transfers
water reclamation. *See* reclamation
Water Recycling Act of 1991, 274
water requirements.
    *See* allocation; utilization

water resources
    Clean Water Act protection for, 124
    identification of in Statewide Water
        Resources Investigation, 23
water rights, 27-70
    determination of by groundwater
        management district, 57
    effect on of Porter-Cologne Act, 114
    as real property, 27-28
    relation of to Endangered Species
        Act, 171, 172
    relation of to State Water Project,
        84-85
    riparian water rights, 29-39
    State Board conditions allowed for,
        130, 131
    types of, 29-63
    as usufructuary rights, 27, 32
    waste not protected by, 28
    *See also* vested-right uses; other
        specific rights
water rights remedies, 63-67
    abatement order, 126
    cease-and-desist order, 125
    civil action, 65
    declaratory relief, 63
    injunction
        physical solution in lieu of,
            182, 183-184, 186
        to enforce cleanup order, 126
        to protect water rights,
            63-64, 67
    parties entitled to relief, 64-65
    physical solutions, 65
    reference procedure, 66, 119-120
    *See also* adjudication
"water salvage"
    as form of water transfer, 231-233
    *See also* sale of water; water
        transfers
water saving devices, implementation
    of for conservation, 270
water shortage. *See* drought; shortage
water supplier
    application to of Urban Water
        Management Planning Act,
        266-267
    authority of
        to adopt conservation
            program, 266
        to limit water use, 256-261
    defined, 234
    liability of in inverse condemnation,
        260
    "will serve" letter from, 261-262
    *See also* municipal use;
        water districts
water supply, 2-4
    Clean Water Act protection for, 123
    history of, 1-26
    impact on
        of Endangered Species Act,
            168-172
        of overdraft, 3
    regulation of under Rivers and
        Harbors Act, 19
    *See also* domestic use; municipal use
water transfers, 223-254
    "*bona fide* transferor"
        requirements, 226
    of Central Valley Project water,
        237-241

## COVER

Photograph of San Pablo Dam Reservoir copyright Armand Wright, 1990, courtesy of East Bay Municipal Utilities District, Oakland, California

## CHAPTER ONE

**4** Map from the *California Water Plan Update*, Volume 1, Bulletin 160-93, October 1994, courtesy of the California Department of Water Resources, Sacramento, California

**6, 7** Map courtesy of the San Francisco Water Department, San Francisco Public Utilities Commission

**8** Photograph courtesy of the Sierra Club, San Francisco

**9** Photograph by Carmen Magaña courtesy of the San Francisco Public Utilities Commission Photography Division

**10** Map courtesy of the East Bay Municipal Utilities District, Oakland, California; photograph courtesy of San Francisco Public Utilities Commission Photography Division

**12** Photographs courtesy of the Los Angeles Department of Water and Power

**13** Map courtesy of the Los Angeles Department of Water and Power

**14** Map courtesy of the Metropolitan Water District of Southern California, Los Angeles

**15** Photograph courtesy of the Metropolitan Water District of Southern California, Los Angeles

**20** Photograph by Tim Palmer courtesy of Friends of the River, Sacramento, California

**22** Map from the *California Water Plan Update*, Volume 1, Bulletin 160-93, October 1994, courtesy of the California Department of Water Resources, Sacramento, California

## CHAPTER TWO

**40** Courtesy of the Water Education Foundation and the California Section of the California State Library, Sacramento, California

## CHAPTER THREE

**78** Map from the *California Water Plan Update*, Volume 1, Bulletin 160-93, October 1994, courtesy of the California Department of Water Resources, Sacramento, California

**80, 86** Photographs courtesy of the Los Angeles Department of Water and Power

**87** Photograph by Athea Edwards courtesy of the Mono Lake Committee, Lee Vining, California

**88, 89** Photograph courtesy of the Mono Lake Committee, Lee Vining, California

**99** Photograph by Ilene Mendelbaum courtesy of the Mono Lake Committee, Lee Vining, California

**104** Photograph by J.C. Dahlig, U.S. Department of the Interior, Bureau of Reclamation, courtesy of the Water Education Foundation, Sacramento, California

**105** Photograph by Dr. Richard R. Whitney, published in *Inland Fishes of Washington* by Richard S. Wydoski and Richard R. Whitney, University of Washington Press, 1980

**111** Photograph by Peter Moyle, University of California, Davis

## CHAPTER FOUR

**115** Photograph by Nancy Reichard courtesy of Friends of the River, Sacramento

**127** Map from the *Delta Atlas*, courtesy of the California Department of Water Resources, Sacramento

**128** Photograph by J.C. Dahlig, U.S. Department of the Interior, Water and Power Resources, courtesy of the Water Education Foundation, Sacramento, California

**134, 135** Photographs courtesy of the East Bay Municipal Utilities District, Oakland, California

**136, 137** Photographs courtesy of the Water Education Foundation, Sacramento, California

## CHAPTER FIVE

**170, 171** Photographs by Peter Moyle, University of California, Davis

365

## CHAPTER SIX

**189** Photograph courtesy of the Orange County Water District, Fountain Valley, California

## CHAPTER SEVEN

**195** Photograph courtesy of the Sierra Club, San Francisco
**196** Photograph by U.S. Department of the Interior, Bureau of Reclamation, courtesy of the Water Education Foundation, Sacramento, California

## CHAPTER EIGHT

**232** Map courtesy of the Metropolitan Water District of Southern California, Los Angeles

## CHAPTER NINE

**268** Photograph courtesy of the Western Municipal Water District, Riverside, California
**269** Photograph courtesy of the Water Education Foundation, Sacramento, California

**270** Photograph by J.C. Dahlig, U.S. Department of the Interior, Bureau of Reclamation, courtesy of the Water Education Foundation, Sacramento, California
**271, 272** Photographs courtesy of the Western Municipal Water District, Riverside, California
**274, 275, 276** Photographs and diagram courtesy of the Orange County Water District, Fountain Valley, California

## CHAPTER TEN

**281, 283** Photographs courtesy of the Metropolitan Water District of Southern California, Los Angeles
**287** Photograph by E.E. Hertzog, U.S. Department of the Interior, Bureau of Reclamation, courtesy of the Water Education Foundation, Sacramento, California
**293, 296, 299** Photographs courtesy of the Metropolitan Water District of Southern California, Los Angeles

## Wetlands Regulation

### A Complete Guide to Federal and California Programs

By Paul D. Cylinder, Kenneth M. Bogdan, Ellyn Miller Davis, and Albert I. Herson

*Wetlands Regulation* explains how to identify and comply with laws and procedures governing California's wetlands. In clear and understandable language, the book describes how wetlands are regulated and which federal, state, regional, or local agencies have jurisdiction. Every permit applicant, public agency, environmental organization, and attorney working with wetlands issues needs this comprehensive, practical guide.

Wetlands Regulation, 1995 • Paperback, 384 pages • $40 plus California sales tax • ISBN 0-923956-20-4

## 1995 Supplement to the 1994 Edition of Guide to the California Environmental Quality Act (CEQA)

By Michael H. Remy, Tina A. Thomas, and James G. Moose

In this supplement, the authors analyze all statutory amendments approved by the California state legislature and all revisions to the CEQA Guidelines approved by the California Resources Agency in 1994. The supplement also contains the full text of the CEQA Statutes and the newest version of the CEQA Guidelines, incorporating amendments adopted in 1994.

## Guide to the California Environmental Quality Act (CEQA)

### 1994 [Eighth] Edition

By Michael H. Remy, Tina A. Thomas, James G. Moose, and J. William Yeates

*Guide to the California Environmental Quality Act* offers the reader an understandable, in-depth description of CEQA's requirements for adequate review and preparation of environmental impact reports (EIRs) and other environmental review documents. Contained in one place are the Act, the Guidelines, and 'Discussions', with expert summaries and commentary. It serves as an important resource for the most significant judicial decisions interpreting the Act.

1995 Supplement to the 1994 Edition of Guide to CEQA • Paperback, 334 pages • $30 plus California sales tax • ISBN 0-923956-36-0

Guide to CEQA, 1994 [Eighth] Edition • Paperback, 880 pages • $45 plus California sales tax • ISBN 0-923956-31-X

## 1995 Supplement to the 1994 Edition of Successful CEQA Compliance

By Ronald E. Bass and Albert I. Herson

In this supplement authors analyze legislative and administrative changes to CEQA that occurred in 1994 and the most recent case law. Their analysis includes CEQA technical advice memoranda issued by the Governor's Office of Planning and Research and revisions to the flow charts and diagrams in the 1994 Edition of the book to reflect 1995 changes.

## Successful CEQA Compliance: A Step-by-Step Approach

### 1994 [Third] Edition

By Ronald E. Bass and Albert I. Herson

*Successful CEQA Compliance: A Step-by-Step Approach* offers a practitioner's perspective on how to successfully implement the procedural and substantive requirements of the California Environmental Quality Act. Step-by-step procedures for preparing Negative Declarations and Environmental Impact Reports are presented in a clear, understandable fashion, using easy-to-follow text, diagrams, and other graphics. More than 90 figures summarize and highlight key points and important checklists

1995 Supplement to the 1994 Edition of Successful CEQA Compliance • Paper, 92 pages • $18.50 plus California sales tax • ISBN 0-923956-39-5

Successful CEQA Compliance: A Step-by-Step Approach, 1994 [Third] Edition • Paperback, 696 pages • $35 plus California sales tax • ISBN 0-923956-32-8

## Mastering NEPA: A Step-by-Step Approach

by Ronald E. Bass and Albert I. Herson

*Mastering NEPA: A Step-by-Step Approach* is the first book to present the critical steps, basic requirements, and most important decision points of the National Environmental Policy Act in a user-friendly format. It takes you step-by-step through the provisions of the Act and the environmental review process. Intended as a user's handbook, the book includes the authors' recommendations for successful compliance, with charts and illustrations clarifying key points.

Mastering NEPA: A Step-by-Step Approach, 1993 • Paperback, 250 pages, $35 plus California sales tax • ISBN 0-923956-14-X

## Understanding Development Regulations

### 205 Questions and Answers to Better Understand California's Property Development and Land Use Regulations

Edited by Robert E. Merritt and Ann R. Danforth

*Understanding Development Regulations* is the first book to address in an easy-to-follow question-and-answer format the legal requirements and political decision-making processes associated with California's complex land use regulations and environmental laws.

Developers, lenders, appraisers, title officers, property investment specialists, real estate professionals, elected officials, public agency staff, and interested citizens seeking a comprehensive understanding of land use decision making as it relates to property development should not be without this book.

Understanding Development Regulations 1994 • Paperback, 246 pages • $26 plus California sales tax • ISBN 0-923956-19-0

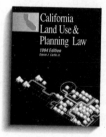

## California Land Use and Planning Law

### (Including Curtin's *Subdivision Map Act Manual*)
### 1995 [Fifteenth] Edition

By Daniel J. Curtin, Jr.

*California Land Use and Planning Law* is the well known definitive summary of the major provisions of land use and planning law that apply to California cities and counties. This book serves as—

• An easy desk reference for those interested in all aspects of California planning law and its applications

• A source for expert commentary on recent state and federal court decisions, Opinions of the California Attorney General, and the statutes themselves

• A source of practical information and guidance which features up-to-date citations, extensive references to specific California codes, a Table of Authorities, and a complete subject index

California Land Use and Planning Law, 1995 [Fifteenth] Edition • Paperback, 374 pages • $42 plus California sales tax • ISBN 0-923956-35-2

## Guide to California Planning

By William Fulton

*Guide to California Planning* by Bill Fulton, publisher and editor of the acclaimed monthly newsletter, *California Planning & Development Report*, covers all aspects of California planning requirements. In a lively and readable fashion, Fulton's book addresses land use planning issues and practices, ranging from general plans to CEQA, as well as relationships between planning, development, and municipal finance. The book has been adopted as a text at the University of California, Berkeley and at several California State University campuses.

Guide to California Planning • Paperback, 288 pages, illustrated • $30 plus California sales tax • ISBN 0-923956-05-0

## 1995 Supplement to the 1993 Edition of Public Needs and Private Dollars

By William W. Abbott and Marian E. Moe

In this supplement authors present latest information on exactions and special taxes—including the U.S. Supreme Court's decision on land dedications and "takings" in *Dolan v. City of Tigard;* post *Rider v. County of San Diego* court decisions addressing special taxes; appellate decisions reviewing the effect of vesting tentative map approvals on subsequently imposed development requirements; and school impact fees in light of California voters' rejection of constitutional amendment ACA 6.

## Public Needs and Private Dollars

### A Guide to Dedications & Development Fees

By William W. Abbott, Marian E. Moe, and Marilee Hanson

*Public Needs and Private Dollars* provides a detailed description of exactions, one of the most important contemporary means available for putting public works, facilities, and services in place. A basic source of information designed to help public officials, citizens, attorneys, planners, and developers understand exactions, *Public Needs and Private Dollars* includes case studies, special features, practice tips, drawings, and photographs to illustrate key considerations and legal principles.

1995 Supplement to the 1993 Edition of Public Needs and Private Dollars • Paper, 38 pages • $15, plus California sales tax • ISBN 0-923956-38-7

Public Needs and Private Dollars: A Guide to Dedications and Development Fees, 1993 • Paperback, 420 pages, illustrated • $38 plus California sales tax • ISBN 0-923956-26-3